T0327603

# Clusters of Innovation in the Age of Disruption

*This book is dedicated to all those who endeavor to use the power of creativity, innovation and entrepreneurship to make the world more than just the sum of its parts.*

# Clusters of Innovation in the Age of Disruption

*Edited by*

Jerome S. Engel

*University of California, Berkeley, USA*

Edward Elgar
PUBLISHING

Cheltenham, UK • Northampton, MA, USA

© Jerome S. Engel 2022

All rights reserved. No part of this publication may be reproduced, stored in a
retrieval system or transmitted in any form or by any means, electronic, mechanical or
photocopying, recording, or otherwise without the prior permission of the publisher.

Published by
Edward Elgar Publishing Limited
The Lypiatts
15 Lansdown Road
Cheltenham
Glos GL50 2JA
UK

Edward Elgar Publishing, Inc.
William Pratt House
9 Dewey Court
Northampton
Massachusetts 01060
USA

Paperback edition 2023

A catalogue record for this book
is available from the British Library

Library of Congress Control Number: 2022937583

This book is available electronically in the **Elgar**online
Business subject collection
http://dx.doi.org/10.4337/9781800885165

ISBN 978 1 80088 515 8 (cased)
ISBN 978 1 80088 516 5 (eBook)
ISBN 978 1 0353 1214 6 (paperback)

Printed and bound by CPI Group (UK) Ltd, Croydon, CR0 4YY

# Contents

# Contributors

## ABOUT THE EDITOR

**Jerome S. Engel**, *MS, CPA, Dr. HC, Adjunct Professor Emeritus, Haas School of Business; Senior Fellow and Founding Executive Director Emeritus, Lester Center for Entrepreneurship, University of California, Berkeley*

Jerome S. Engel is an internationally recognized expert on innovation, entrepreneurship and venture capital, lecturing and advising business and government leaders around the world. His research and publications explore innovation ecosystems, technology commercialization, and Lean Innovation management practices in established and emerging enterprises. Three areas where he has made major contributions are: innovation in educational methodology, leadership in the educational community's adoption of new methodologies and fostering of economic development to create a better world through collaborative communities.

Professor Engel joined the faculty of the University of California, Berkeley in 1991, after a successful business career at KPMG and Ernst & Young, to found the Lester Center for Entrepreneurship and Innovation. As its Executive Director for over 20 years, he forged a leading entrepreneurship education program, which he extended internationally to over 40 countries through Intel's Technology Entrepreneurship Education Program. Later, together with collaborator Steve Blank, he pioneered the Lean Innovation methodology and brought it to national and international prominence through the United States National Science Foundation's I-Corps, where he served as founding National Faculty Director. Recently, in his continuing efforts to support the entrepreneurship teaching community globally, he created and chairs the Lean Innovation Educators Summit Series, which regularly attracts over 400 faculty semiannually to share best practices. As an adjunct professor emeritus at the Haas School of Business, he currently instructs in both the school's MBA and Executive Education programs, specializing in entrepreneurship, corporate innovation, new venture finance and venture capital.

Professor Engel has been the founding General Partner of two successful venture capital funds, is an active Angel Investor and is a member of the investment advisory boards of several international venture funds. An author and frequent speaker, he has been cited in the *Wall Street Journal*, on National Public Radio and in other global media. His awards and recognitions include the National Collegiate Inventors and Innovators Alliance Lifetime Educational Achievement Award, and the Global Consortium of Entrepreneurship Centers Award for Outstanding Contributions to Advance the Discipline of Entrepreneurship.

## CONTRIBUTING AUTHORS

**Morten H. Abrahamsen**, *PhD, Associate Professor, BI Norwegian Business School*

Morten H. Abrahamsen is an associate professor at the Department of Marketing, BI Norwegian Business School. His research concerns how companies interact in business networks, and his research interests include buyer–seller relationships, network dynamics, managerial sensemaking and research methodology. He is presently affiliated with the Center for Connected Care at Oslo University Hospital, where he particularly investigates public procurement of innovation within the healthcare sector. He has an extensive background in executive and corporate teaching, and has wide industrial experience from various executive positions.

**Christian Bruszies**, *MSE, EMBA, PhD, Professor at the Centre of the Business Environment Observatory at the Universidad Externado de Colombia; Associate Professor, Faculty of Engineering, National University of Colombia*

Dr. Bruszies holds a Master of Industrial Engineering from the University of Karlsruhe, Germany, an Executive MBA from Henley Management College, England, and is a PhD candidate in Engineering from the National University of Colombia. He has more than 25 years of work experience in senior executive positions in large industrial companies such as Siemens, Daimler Benz and Alstom in the areas of strategic development, business planning and innovation management.

**David Charron**, *MBA, Lecturer, University of California, Berkeley*

David Charron has worked in and taught extensively about entrepreneurship and innovation. He currently teaches at the Haas School of Business, University of California, Berkeley, and is the lead faculty in the National Science Foundation and National Institutes of Health I-Corps programs, where he has worked with hundreds of startups. He is actively involved in coaching healthcare innovators at the University of California, San Francisco. Mr. Charron is also a serial entrepreneur, having started several companies, and actively advises and invests in new ventures. He has held leadership positions at Berkeley, run incubators and accelerators, and worked in technology commercialization and entrepreneurship across corporate, academic and government sectors.

**Itxaso del Palacio**, *PhD, Senior Teaching Fellow, University College London; Partner, Notion Capital*

Itxaso del Palacio is a partner at Notion, a leading European business-to-business software-as-a-service-focused venture capital firm. Prior to that, Dr. del Palacio was the Investment Partner for M12 (formerly Microsoft Ventures) in Europe. On the academic side, she is a senior teaching fellow in Entrepreneurship at University College London's School of Management. She holds a prestigious Kauffman Fellowship and is very well connected to the global network of fellow investors. By background, Dr. del Palacio is an engineer and has a PhD in Entrepreneurship and Venture Capital.

**James Demetriou**, *LLB, Master of International Business, Chair of Australian Sports Technologies Network, University of Melbourne*

James Demetriou has been one of Australia's most respected leaders in the business of sport and sports technologies for over 40 years, including being a senior professional football player and board member/player at Essendon Football Club. He is also one of the founders and first chairs of the Australian Sports Technologies Network and Sports Without Borders. He is an experienced senior executive, business transformer, innovator and educator, having worked with technology startups, middle-market companies and leading universities across sports, agriculture, education and clean energy.

**Flavio Feferman**, *MA, MBA, Lecturer and Distinguished Teaching Fellow at the Haas School of Business, University of California, Berkeley*

Flavio Feferman is a Lecturer and Distinguished Teaching Fellow at the Haas School of Business, where he teaches courses on business, entrepreneurship and innovation in developing countries, including Berkeley's Lean Startup program in Brazil. He received the Cheit Award for Excellence in Teaching in 2014. As President of Developing Markets Group, he directs international economic development projects, including regional cluster initiatives and technology projects in Brazil and other countries. He holds postgraduate degrees in Economics and Business from Stanford University and Berkeley.

**Aline Figlioli**, *MBA, MSc, Ph.D, Senior Research Fellow, Center for Change, Entrepreneurship and Innovation Management (CENTRIM), University of Brighton*

Dr. Figlioli is a researcher at CENTRIM, University of Brighton, UK. Her research focuses on innovation ecosystems and traditional and new models of innovation habitats such as science and technology parks and accelerators. She has been designing and implementing programs and tools to help startups transform their innovation potential into strong business growth. Her background includes working for universities, government and innovative businesses, which gives her a comprehensive understanding of the varied languages and unique innovation approaches to collaboration and partnerships among them.

**Shigeo Kagami**, *EDM, MBA, Professor, Graduate School of Engineering, and Deputy Director General, Division of University Corporate Relations, University of Tokyo*

Dr. Kagami has been responsible for the development of the university startup ecosystem for the University of Tokyo since 2004 as a professor of Innovation and Entrepreneurship. Before joining the University of Tokyo, he worked with three professional firms: Boston Consulting Group, Corporate Directions (a founding partner), and Hedrick and Struggles (partner). Dr. Kagami graduated from Hitotsubashi University (Tokyo), earned his MBA from IMEDE (currently IMD Lausanne, Switzerland) and completed his Executive Doctor of Management degree at Weatherhead School of Management, Case Western Reserve University (Cleveland, USA).

**Dickson Louie**, *MBA, CPA, Principal, Dickson Louie & Associates*

Dickson Louie is at the intersection of the media, strategic planning, academia and entrepreneurship. Having been in senior planning roles at both the *Los Angeles Times* and *San Francisco Chronicle*, he is now a case writer for several corporate clients and professional schools, including the Haas School of Business at the University of California, Berkeley; Anderson School of Management at the University of California, Los Angeles; and Berkeley Law. He is also a lecturer at the University of California, Davis, instructing the Business of the Media MBA elective course. Previously, he was a research associate at Harvard Business School and co-founder of a book publishing company that included a *Wall Street Journal* national bestseller.

**Per Ingvar Olsen**, *Dr. Oecon, Professor, BI Norwegian Business School*

Per Ingvar Olsen is a professor at the Department of Strategy and Entrepreneurship, BI Norwegian Business School in Oslo. His research is primarily within business network dynamics, entrepreneurship, innovation and industrial change. Most of his teaching involves executive and corporate education in business development theories and practices. He is presently also the Co-director and Head of Research at the Center for Connected Care at Oslo

University Hospital, working with the Cluster of Innovation ecosystem to research and develop innovative new healthcare services.

**Montserrat Pareja-Eastaway**, *PhD in Economics, Associate Professor, University of Barcelona*

Dr. Pareja-Eastaway is Vice-Chair of the European Network for Housing Research, Barcelona Chapter Coordinator of the Research Group on Collaborative Spaces and Director of the Cultural Management Master at the University of Barcelona. She has worked at the University of Barcelona since 1992, devoting her research to analyzing urban challenges from a comparative and interdisciplinary perspective. She has led several European Union-funded and nationally funded projects and published in national and international specialized journals.

**Chen Peng**, *Senior Economist and Deputy Director of China Road and Bridge Corporation Human Resources Department*

Chen Peng was born in Beijing, China in 1989. He received his bachelor's degree in Economics from Nankai University, an MBA from the Chinese Academy of Social Sciences and a Doctor of Management degree from ISCTE – University Institute of Lisbon. He worked in Rwanda for three years and has traveled to all seven continents.

**Josep Miquel Piqué**, *PhD, Executive President, La Salle Technova Barcelona – Ramon Llull University*

Josep Miquel Piqué is an experienced professional in university management, having led postgraduate programs, university incubators and technology transfer centers at La Salle – Ramon Llull University, where he is a member of the Innova Institute. Dr. Piqué is currently President and a member of the board of the Triple Helix Association. Previous leadership positions include being the XVII President of the International Association of Science Parks and Areas of Innovation; CEO of the Office of Economic Growth, Barcelona City Council; and CEO of 22@Barcelona. Through this experience he has promoted hybrid organizations partnering university, industry and public administration, and fostered the creation of technology-based businesses, focusing on high-growth "born global" companies. As a policy maker in government, he has developed urban and economic transformations in order to build ecologies of innovation. He holds an Engineering degree from La Salle/UPC, an MBA from ESADE School of Business and a PhD from Ramon Llull University. His research interest is Knowledge Cities.

**Danny Samson**, *PhD, Professor of Management, University of Melbourne*

Danny Samson is Professor of Management at the University of Melbourne, having previously worked as an engineer and academic in multinational companies and universities in Australia and the USA. He has published 140 articles and a dozen books on aspects of management, leadership and innovation. Professor Samson has advised senior executives in dozens of companies on matters of business strategy, operations and supply chain design and improvement, and he is one of Asia Pacific's leading executive educators. He has been a company director and advisor to numerous government agencies.

**Carlos Scheel**, *PhD, Professor Emeritus, Tecnologico de Monterrey, EGADE Business School, Mexico*

Dr. Scheel specializes in technological innovation, circular economy, systems dynamics and sustainable innovation systems. As a technological consultant for the United Nations (UN) Industrial Development Organization, United States Agency for International Development, UN Development Programme, UN Environment Programme, World Bank, IC$^2$ Institute of the University of Texas and Inter-American Development Bank, he developed Compstrac and Compstrat (1992) for assembling regional poles of innovation and technology for industrial sectors, and created a framework for incubating technology-based ventures, used by 20 projects in 11 countries.

Dr. Scheel is currently working on SWIT (Sustainable Wealth creation based on Innovation and enabling Technologies), a framework for sustainable strategies and policies based on a "disruptive, systemic and circular" innovation approach. His methodology for the "Design of Circular Economy Business Models" has trained circular economy entrepreneurs for Latin American and Caribbean countries, and several regions have used the SWIT framework to design circular businesses and communities. Dr. Scheel has been a visiting professor and research scholar at 25 institutions in 14 countries, and he is the author of 14 books and over 60 papers.

**Martin Schlegel**, *PhD, Board Member and Director, Australian Sports Technologies Network, Melbourne*

Martin Schlegel is Director at the Australian Sports Technologies Network, focusing on startup programs, global partnerships and export growth of sportstech companies. With a background in advanced materials, information technology and business, he previously worked on major sports infrastructure projects across Australasia, Europe and the USA, including for the 2008 and 2012 Olympics. In his leisure time, he actively tracks his recreational activity testing various wearables and enjoys various codes of football with his son and daughter, whom he actively coached during their junior sport.

**Helmut Schönenberger**, *PhD, Professor for Entrepreneurship Practice,*

*Vice President Entrepreneurship, Technische Universität München (TUM), Munich, Germany*

Scalable tech startups are Helmut Schönenberger's passion as Co-founder and CEO of UnternehmerTUM, the Center for Innovation and Business Creation at Technische Universität München (TUM). He also serves as TUM's Vice President Entrepreneurship and as a member of the advisory board of tech companies. With his background as a founder, aerospace engineer and venture capitalist he loves to help new ventures solve strategy, recruiting, business development and future financing challenges.

**Manav Subodh**, *MBA, Founder, One Million for One Billion (1M1B); Global Ambassador, Sutardja Center for Entrepreneurship & Technology, College of Engineering, University of California, Berkeley*

Manav Subodh has 25 years of experience working at the intersection of business, government and education. He has worked at companies such as Intel Corporation to drive corporate agendas to respond to broader agendas of social change by leveraging digital technologies. Starting in 2015, he has worked towards mentoring close to 15,000 students and 10,000 teachers through 1M1B to solve structural and systemic issues by leveraging entrepreneurial thinking and artificial intelligence. Mr. Subodh has conducted youth leadership workshops on social entrepreneurship across seven countries and holds the annual 1M1B summit at the United Nations headquarters in New York.

**Virginia Trigo**, *PhD, Professor Emerita, ISCTE – University Institute of Lisbon, Portugal*

Virginia Trigo is Director of China Programs on behalf of ISCTE. She has been working in China for more than 30 years and has lived and worked in many parts of the world. Since 2009 she has been the director of two doctoral programs in cooperation with the University of Electronic Science and Technology of China in Chengdu and Southern Medical University in Guangzhou. Her research interests are entrepreneurship and China's economic culture.

**Poh Kam Wong**, *PhD, Professor, National University of Singapore Business School; Professor (by courtesy), LKY School of Public Policy, Singapore*

A leading Asian scholar on entrepreneurship and innovation, Dr. Wong is ranked among the top 2 percent of the most highly cited researchers globally by AD Scientific Index. As Director of the National University of Singapore (NUS) Entrepreneurship Centre (2001–2019), he created several high-impact experiential entrepreneurship education programs, including the NUS Overseas Colleges program. An active Angel Investor, he founded Business

Angel Network (Southeast Asia) and is an advisor to the global venture capital fund iGlobe Partners. He received the Public Administration Medal (Silver) Award from the Singapore Government in 2013 for his contribution to entrepreneurship education in Singapore, and the Entrepreneur for the World Award (Educator Category) from the World Entrepreneurship Forum in 2015.

# Foreword
**David J. Teece**

Engel and his colleagues once again bring conceptual clarity and deep experience to a topic of great interest: Clusters of Innovation (COI). His earlier book, *Global Clusters of Innovation: Entrepreneurial Engines of Economic Growth around the World*, focused on how these clusters got started and was in a long line of research beginning with Alfred Marshall's work on industrial districts.

The 2.0 version of COI digs deeper theoretically and conceptually while at the same time updating us on recent developments in venture capital (VC) and new enterprise development. It is a prescient and timely update and elaboration of the earlier framework.

In this foreword I will not dwell upon the many observations and interpretations that will be familiar to readers with a good understanding of VC and COI. Instead, I will focus on that which is particularly new and exciting and not commonly observed or commented on in the very large academic and professional literatures in innovation which many readers will no doubt already appreciate.

## 1 AN EMERGING ECOSYSTEM PERSPECTIVE

Engel et al. are quite some way down the path of viewing COI as ecosystems. While this has been remarked on before, the treatment here adds important new dimensions. The ecosystem nature of COI is important for all participants, including governments, to understand. The authors focus not just on the structure of the system, but in particular on behaviors and cultures.

The principal participants in the ecosystem are familiar ones: entrepreneurs, VC, and major corporations. Supporting institutions are the universities, in particular the research universities, the often-overlooked professional service providers, research parks, accelerators, and, of course, government. However, it is not just the presence of these organizations that matters. It is what the authors call "behaviors," which is their synonym for (entrepreneurial) culture, and what they call "components" (tantamount to structure) and the interaction of the two that matters. I very much accept their emphasis.

The (Schumpeterian) entrepreneurs are the heroes of the COI, identifying the opportunities, developing the vision, securing the resources, and designing the business model to put ideas and plans into action along with the VCs that support them. Both the entrepreneurs and the VCs need to display humility, however, because without the rest of the ecosystems they could not succeed. Besides these key players, Engel et al. identify a large group of hybrid structures that bolster COI by bridging groups within the COI. Those include incubators, accelerators, and research parks, often sponsored by universities, governments, and sometimes corporates or philanthropists.

As with the earlier book, the authors once again stress connections amongst globally displayed COI. This drives home that innovation today is actually very much a global process, with strong ties between many COI located in disparate geographies around the world. Marshallian districts used to be isolated and national in scope. Now they are deeply connected. And with Covid-19 and the boom in online engagement, geography still remains important but less so. Virtual communities are ubiquitous and robust, so long as there are underlying bands of trust. COI 2.0 underscores that COI are now truly global; China, Korea, India, and Singapore can no longer be ignored (if they ever were), as VC is very active in such locales. Venture capital is springing into life in a spotty way in Africa, Latin America, and Australia and New Zealand.

Despite this, the authors believe, and provide some data to support the view, that existing COI are getting stronger. The authors use the distribution of unicorns as an index of connected COI strength, with China and the US ahead, followed at some distance by the UK, India, Germany, Japan, and France; many other wealthy countries are nowhere to be seen in this data. The authors hint at the reasons for this in their discussion of "behaviors" and the culture of innovation.

In China, and other authoritarian countries, how value capture is orchestrated may turn out to be quite different than in rule-of-law countries – some might say impossible. By "the rule of law" I mean court mandates based on statute and case-law-driven rule of law, not the rule of rulers. Where independent courts provide equal treatment to similarly situated companies, without attention to national origin or political influence, COI can flourish.

## 2    AN ENTREPRENEURIAL BEHAVIORAL PERSPECTIVE

As Engel and his colleagues dig deeper into the culture of well-developed COI, they focus on the entrepreneurial behavior shared by all participants. Entrepreneurial behavior is key to understanding how COI function and what distinguishes them from (Marshallian) industrial clusters.

Entrepreneurship, of course, is itself a type of behavior. It is not about getting rich quick. It is far from that. Nor is entrepreneurship about maximizing profits. While the entrepreneur must design and deploy a business model to cover all costs and leave a surplus, that is not usually the immediate goal. Building value is. Entrepreneurship is about spotting unmet needs and opportunities and garnering resources to meet those user/customer needs with a new technology or business model. Getting users to pay for this is ultimately critical, but not necessarily the initial preoccupation. When executed with a good business model and with the support of other components that share an entrepreneurial perspective, profits will eventually follow.

Entrepreneurs are "masters of speed and flexibility" and act with urgency, pivoting their newfound organization time and again in order to get the product/ service and the business model right. There is always a bias for action because action and engagement are the crucible of learning. Entrepreneurs do not love risk, but know they must embrace it as it is a necessary corollary of a voyage into the unknown, a voyage that is focused on value creation but one that must always keep value capture in mind if the new enterprise is to be viable.

Entrepreneurship is quite different from "management" or "administration" where the focus is on optimization and improvement. It is about identifying and then making the "next big thing" happen, as Steve Jobs once put it. Moreover, the entrepreneur often cannot turn to the management textbooks for help. Rather, as Elon Musk points out, they must "reason from first principles." Incremental improvement of the status quo is left to good management, who also have an important role in the economy.

## 3   VENTURE CAPITAL AND MAJOR CORPORATIONS ARE KEY PLAYERS

Expanding on their previous work, Engel et al. highlight the key role that venture capitalists and major corporations, when aligned with entrepreneurial behavior and goals, play in COI. Several new developments in VC are noted: the extraordinary growth of the amount of capital invested in VC; wider VC geographic distribution; venture-funded firms staying private longer, assisted sometimes by private equity; and VC-funded firms splashing out onto public markets via SPACs (special purpose acquisition companies).

The role of corporate R&D (research and development) was rightly emphasized in the author's earlier COI formulation. In COI 2.0, corporate development strategy is even more important, in part because what were once venture-funded firms, such as Google, Netflix, Apple, Amazon, Microsoft, Intel, Qualcomm, and Genentech, are now major firms in their own right and hold the potential to be significant alliance partners for startups. They thus provide exit opportunities for the new enterprises that emerge from the COI nursery. Not only is VC now fueling explosive growth, so too is the acquisition of newer enterprises by Big Tech and Big Pharma. Such acquisitions are one way that established companies renew themselves; it is also an important mechanism for the VC industry to recoup their investment by sale, hopefully at a substantial multiple.

COI 2.0 rightly sees major corporations as "drivers of innovation at scale." However, the authors are also correct to identify caveats, as well as ways in which the M&A (merger and acquisition) process can be a win for the economy and society, and not just the participants.

The authors' narrative on M&A flows naturally from the way they have framed innovation. By seeing innovation as being the product of "clusters" or "ecosystems," they are recognizing (implicitly and explicitly) that the health of the ecosystem is important to the innovation process. Since major corporations are key players in mature COI, they have a special responsibility to make sure they protect the health of the ecosystem. They must nurture and not cannibalize it. Engel et al. call for "constructive behavior." The authors claim that this is often "underappreciated and misunderstood" (Chapter 3), and I tend to agree. With acquisition, established enterprises inject capital into the ecosystem; but when they infringe on the IP (intellectual property) of startups, they suck capital and entrepreneurial spirit out of it.

The authors point out that in earlier days, Microsoft may have overstepped the mark a bit in this regard. The critical point that is made is that Big Tech need to see Little Tech not so much as competitors, but as complementors; and they need to add one more criteria to their M&A and IP strategies: nurturing the health of the ecosystem. Nor should they always seek control when doing acquisitions. Control is sometimes "fool's gold," as it can snuff out creativity and agility too soon. The authors remind us what is needed is a broad view of the value-creation process.

Another important thread running through the book is that major corporations can themselves become trapped serving existing customers with their standard business model à la Clay Christianson. The way out of the innovator's dilemma is of course dynamic capabilities. This requires entrepreneurial management, a subject I myself have taken a keen interest in.

## 4    A NEW VIEW OF THE ENTREPRENEUR

Finally, the authors point out that

> "a new view of the entrepreneur has gained broad cultural acceptance ... entrepreneurs may have been perceived as excellent technologists and innovators, but with limited managerial scope and experiences ... inevitably these lesser talents would have to be replaced at some point by experienced big company managers in order to grow the business. This view has greatly changed today." (Chapter 3)

The authors go on to outline what I call the entrepreneurial manager, a new hybrid executive that includes Jeff Bezos, Reed Hastings, Elon Musk, Steve Jobs (Round 2), Bob Noyce and Gordon Moore, and David Packard. These individuals all went on to successfully manage the companies they founded in later-stage growth. Gordon Moore once explained to me the terror that he felt facing managerial issues, less so for Bob Noyce,[1] in their earlier days at Intel. Larry Page and Sergey Brin at Google sought an "adult in the room" (Eric Schmidt) to ease the burden. However, the point remains: founding entrepreneurs can successfully scale companies and carry forward the (entrepreneurial) genetic structure that will keep big companies successful. That is the essence of dynamic capabilities. I am pleased to end this foreword by noting the connections between the work of Engel et al. and my own.

David J. Teece
Haas School of Business, University of California, Berkeley

## NOTE

1. Chapter 7 in *Engines of Innovation: U.S. Industrial Research at the End of an Era*, edited by Richard S. Rosenbloom and William J. Spencer (Boston, MA: Harvard Business School Press, 1996), p. 167.

# Preface: Silicon Valley – a state of mind
**Jerome S. Engel**

## WHY WRITE THIS BOOK?

In 2014 we published *Global Clusters of Innovation: Entrepreneurial Engines of Economic Growth around the World* to capture and document a framework, namely the Cluster of Innovation Framework, which describes innovation communities, based principally on my years of experience being immersed in Silicon Valley, California, as a practitioner, investor and educator. But were my observations generalizable? Did they apply elsewhere or were they unique and idiosyncratic to this remarkable innovation ecosystem? To test this hypothesis, I was joined by a wonderful group of collaborators who each applied the Framework to their own local contexts, which included 13 economic ecosystems from a diverse set of geographically dispersed economies around the world.

Our findings largely validated the broad applicability of the Framework, and its usefulness as a tool to assess the existence and robustness of the critical components and their behaviors. Beyond this we were able to discern from the data ten important "lessons learned" that could guide policy makers and others concerned with fostering healthy innovation ecosystems, and 13 questions for further investigation.

So why, only a few years later, reprise this effort? Was so much different? The simple answer is *yes*! With the rapid rise of new technologies and business models, the acceleration in venture investment, and global crises such as the 2008 banking crisis, the 2020–22 Covid-19 pandemic and the invasion of Ukraine, we have had a massive injection of stress and change into every ecosystem around the world, including every innovation ecosystem. How would these systems respond? Did they have any advantages or unforeseen challenges that would differentiate them from their surrounding environments? The Framework's operative definition of innovation states that innovation is a constructive response and adaptation to change. So this differential analysis is not simply a curious question but rather an existential one. It is this question that fueled this effort.

To pursue this question, we took several steps. First, we expanded the sample of ecosystems to include several new ones, as well as including most of the prior examples. Second, we identified trends and changes that were occurring pre-Covid to understand how Clusters of Innovation were evolving naturally, in response to changing technology, investing and entrepreneurial practices. Then, where apparent, we sought to identify the impact and response to the Covid-19 shock. This process has both affirmed some of our earlier learnings and revealed new ones.

Welcome to our journey to *Clusters of Innovation in the Age of Disruption.*

# Acknowledgments

This book is the capstone to a process that began over three decades ago when I pivoted from practitioner to educator. That transition was not planned, just a happy coincidence. So too is this book. I never planned to develop a framework for understanding innovation ecosystems. I never planned to engage in this discussion with colleagues over these many years. I never planned to create books to promulgate our thoughts and lessons learned. So I must acknowledge that this volume and all it represents is indeed the culmination of an evolving discussion with many participants and contributors, too many to mention. But I must take this opportunity to highlight key contributors to the process.

First, I must recognize the foundational and continuing contributions of my colleagues at my home institution, the University of California, Berkeley, especially David Teece, John Freeman, Henry Chesbrough, Steve Blank, David Vogel and David Charron, all of whom contributed to and challenged my thinking. My learning was further enriched by the many international educators who welcomed me to join with them in their own innovation ecosystem endeavors, most notably Josep Miquel Piqué, Helmut Schönenberger, Poh Kam Wong, Per Ingvar Olsen, Manav Subodh, Shigeo Kagami, James Demetriou and Virginia Trigo. Crafting my contributions to this volume, and its precedent academic publications, was enabled by wonderful research and writing collaborators, most notably Itxaso del Palacio, Jasmina Berbegal-Mirabent and Aline Figlioli. It is rewarding to see that so many of these key contributors to my thinking about Clusters of Innovation are contributors to this volume. And, by extension, I wish to express my sincere appreciation to all the contributing authors. This has required a considerable and sustained effort. Your dedication and persistence have been an inspiration.

I wish to thank Alan Sturmer and his team at Edward Elgar Publishing. Without his initiative and encouragement this volume would not have materialized.

And final and most sincere thanks is reserved for my wife and life partner, Shirley Fischer. Her contributions go far beyond the usual emotional and physical support a fine spouse provides. In many ways she may be the true editor of this book. Shirley made a deep and thorough review of every chapter. Her editorial guidance enhanced every contribution. For the past year she has dedicated hundreds of hours to supporting me and all our contributing authors. No expression of appreciation can fully capture my gratitude.

Jerome S. Engel
Haas School of Business, University of California, Berkeley

# 1. Introduction: *Clusters of Innovation in the Age of Disruption*

## Jerome S. Engel

## WHY READ THIS BOOK?

This book is about innovation ecosystems, Clusters of Innovation (COI) and the Global Network of Clusters of Innovation (GNCOI) they naturally form. What is innovation? Innovation is nothing less than the ability for constructive response and adaptation to change. The cause and catalyst for that change is frequently identified as technology and its unceasing pressure to improve on existing solutions and address unmet needs. The last decade has painfully demonstrated that exogenous environmental shocks are also sources of change that call for innovative responses, ranging from the obvious challenges such as global warming, regional wars and Covid-19 to the more subtle social and political perturbations of our time.

Business plays a key role in the transformation of resources into solutions. Supported by constructive societal conventions, such as governments and the laws they promulgate, the power of business is constrained and channeled. Entrepreneurship and innovation flourish at the interface between business and change. Understanding the context and the environment that enables this process is a crucial tool for both the practitioners and their enablers. In this volume we identify the principal practitioners (the Core Components of a COI) as being Entrepreneurs, who identify and pursue opportunity; Venture Capital investors, who invest in and support them; and the Major Corporations that often are the vehicles to deliver these solutions at global scale. We identify the enablers of the community of innovation (the Supporting Components of a COI) as being Universities, Government, Service Organizations, startup management executives (Management), and independent members of the service professions, such as independent lawyers and accountants (Professions). The insights and learnings in this volume are designed to contribute to the success of all these important innovation participants. Going beyond this already aggressive goal, this volume seeks to inspire leaders, educators and policy makers with a vision of the possible, and the necessary tools and pathways to enhance the innovative capacity of our communities.

## HOW SHOULD WE VIEW INNOVATION?

Innovation can be looked at in a number of different ways. It can be viewed through a technology lens, and indeed the evolution of technology is a compelling story. Much has been written about how businesses achieve success based on technology innovation. Most of the literature on business formation, creation and strategy takes a venture-centric point of view. The authors focus on the creation and growth of individual ventures and often take a competitive win–lose perspective on business development.

In this book we are also concerned with business success, but we look at innovation from an ecosystem, community-centric point of view. We apply a cultural lens, seeking to understand the dynamics of the interactions among the participants of the ecosystem.

Why is a community-centric viewpoint important? Because context matters. Whether one is an entrepreneur seeking business success, a venture investor seeking investment insights, a scientific researcher seeking to commercialize discoveries, a manager in a major corporation seeking to accelerate a company's innovative capacity, or a community leader seeking to enhance the productive capacity of a community and its institutions, one's opportunity for success is enhanced by understanding the business culture of the community within which one operates. Appropriately, therefore, in each community we investigate we go beyond identifying the key participants to expose and understand their behaviors.

There is also the personal perspective. As a transplant from the East Coast to Silicon Valley in the 1980s, I discovered in Silicon Valley a novel culture with subtly different constituents, values and behaviors. The impact was dramatic. The collective business ecosystem seemingly facilitated rapid innovation and explosive business growth. From this personal experience I learned that the context within which one operates can be a key enabler to success. Reflecting on over 40 years of in-depth immersion in this culture, first as a finance professional, then as an entrepreneur, an investor and finally as an educator, I have fully embraced the distinctive perspective of looking at innovation through the Silicon Valley COI lens. This is not a parochial or narrow view. The influence and model of Silicon Valley has become so global that it is clear that this unique ecosystem can no longer be viewed simply as a regional COI. It is a node (perhaps the principal node) in a global network of COI that share among them many like models, participants and behaviors that enable entrepreneurial success. There is a profound truth in the mantra "Silicon Valley is not a place ... It is a state of mind."[1] Its echo and resonance can be found in the vocabulary, business practices and popular culture of innovation communities around the world.

## OVERRIDING THEMES AND QUESTIONS

From the above discussion, one can see hints of the overriding themes that permeate this volume. They include:

- Understanding the ecosystem of innovation relevant to one's specific circumstance is key to gaining the ability to exploit its advantages and navigate its constraints.
- Identifying the key participants of the ecosystem is an important first step, but not sufficient.
- Less visible but more important is the culture of the ecosystem which is embodied in the values and behaviors of the participants.
- While each geography is unique, there is increasing globalization of certain behavioral norms in innovation ecosystems. This accelerates diffusion of innovation and business practices.

Looking at the innovation process from local to global perspectives, the contributing authors endeavor to answer:

- What and who are the drivers of business innovation in our local COI?
- What are our COI's strengths and constraints? Which are more conducive to change?
- Who are the key participants in the ecosystem? Are there new ones emerging or increasing in importance?
- How important is the role of geography? Are there emerging strategies for enhancing the benefits of proximity or overcoming the obstacles of remoteness?
- Are there non-geographically defined business communities that, because of their intimacy and common practices and culture, constitute a non-geographic COI?
- Is the innovation economy leading to greater well-being in general, or just for a few?
- How have our ecosystems responded to or been impacted, enhanced or impaired by the exogenous shocks of the last ten years, with a special focus on the disruption of Covid-19?
- Is our COI positioned for growth or decline? What should be our priorities and how do we mobilize the resources to utilize the power of innovation to better our respective communities?

Sometimes these themes and questions are addressed explicitly, taking them head on. Sometimes the lessons learned are more implicit, and the wisdom emerges less directly. In all instances, the COI Framework provides us with a consistent lens through which to contextualize and understand these diverse experiences.

## A BRIEF OVERVIEW OF THE BOOK'S ORGANIZATION AND INSIGHTS

This book is divided into three parts to distinguish global, regional and national perspectives on COI. Part I (chapters 2–5) brings a global perspective, updating the COI Framework, introducing new tools for the constructive engagement of major corporations and exploring the emergence of a new phenomenon: COI that are not defined by their geography, but rather by their business model. In parts II and III we then test the COI Framework against ten geographies dispersed around the world. Part II looks at the regional clusters, and Part III at national strategies. Some of these geographies are ones we looked at in our prior book, which gives us a chance to examine the temporal evolution of those COI. These include communities in Germany, Spain, China, Japan, India, Colombia, and Brazil. New geographies analyzed in this volume include Norway, Singapore and Australia.

The reader may have noticed the omission of a specific chapter on Silicon Valley itself. This is, of course, intentional. The last ten years have only seen the influence of Silicon Valley grow and its importance in the global innovation economy become even more profound. Its influence has come to be the common reference point for all other innovation ecosystems, so we have chosen not to describe its idiosyncrasies but rather its robust consistencies – those elements that have the greatest impact and longevity. These lessons are captured in the generalizable models portrayed in Part I of this volume.

The following is a brief introduction to the concepts and regions discussed in subsequent chapters.

**Part I: Clusters of Innovation – Refining and Extending the Framework**

Chapter 2, *Global Cluster of Innovation theory and practice in the 21st century: COI Components*, presents an updated and refined version of the COI Framework and looks in more detail at the ecosystem components (major actors) that comprise a mature COI. In addition to defining the distinction between the core and supporting components of a COI, it introduces a new element: Hybrid Organizations, which bridge gaps and smooth the innovation process. These include Research Parks, Accelerators, Public VC and Corporate VC, Angel Investors and Service Organizations.

Chapter 3, *Global Cluster of Innovation theory and practice in the 21st century: COI Behaviors*, examines the critical role of cultural behavior in a COI. It premises that behavior is the most difficult to document but perhaps the most important element of the ecosystem to understand. The chapter defines the characteristic behaviors that are shared by all the components, and as a major new contribution, how each individual component reflects those behaviors in its business practices. Importantly, it investigates the varying approaches of the different participants to the inherent risks and opportunities of technology-driven innovation.

Chapter 4, *Major Corporations and Open Innovation: capturing value from disruptive innovation*, addresses the potential for complementarity between major incumbents and startups. It provides strategies and tools for major corporations to achieve speed, and for startups to achieve scale through collaboration. It investigates how major corporations can gain innovation advantages from constructive engagement in their COI. Entrepreneurship and the COI that energize it are often understood as creating value via the startup. This chapter demonstrates how major corporations can exploit the entrepreneurial venture creation capability of COI to spur their own innovation capacity. It introduces the COI Fit and Location Matrix as an organizing framework for understanding how corporations can, through active engagement with the various COI components, accelerate and increase the pathways for technology commercialization, business model experimentation, speed and agility. The Matrix helps management to deploy a broad Open Innovation approach, clarifying when various transactional forms are most appropriate. The case examples investigated include the use of mergers and acquisitions, spin-outs, corporate VC, licensing and more.

Chapter 5, *Business-model-led Clusters of Innovation: the case of Product Led Growth*, presents a new concept in the COI Framework: the non-geographic COI, a network of businesses that are operating in a specific industry or a network of businesses that are targeting a specific market segment. This chapter identifies and analyzes the COI that has emerged around the business model known as Product Led Growth (PLG). Contrasting with the more traditional reliance on brand and product advertising, the PLG ecosystem is comprised of business-to-business (B2B) companies that rely principally on their own products to engage and acquire customers, exploiting the internet's easing of direct access to prospective customers, and customers' increasing willingness to experiment with internet purchases. An increasing number of businesses are using PLG strategies as a way to grow, and their scale and impact are attracting a specialized community of investors, major corporate partners, professional service providers and managers. This non-geographic community exhibits many of the characteristics of a COI, including entrepreneurial processes, mobility of resources, alignment of interests, born-global perspective and global networking. This chapter explores the unique characteristics of PLG companies and how they lead to this new non-geographic structure.

## Part II: Global Case Studies – Regional and Urban Clusters

Chapter 6, *The Munich high-tech region: development towards a leading European startup cluster*, describes the further evolution of a university-led COI in one of the leading innovation clusters in Europe. As detailed in our previous volume, after World War II Munich was a hotbed of entrepreneurship, producing large global companies such as Siemens, Allianz and BMW. The fading of large-scale entrepreneurship in subsequent decades led to a concerted effort in the beginning of the 21st century by Technische Universität München (TUM), funded by government and private sources, to build a systematic innovation and business-creation process. This chapter details how this initiative, and the COI it fostered, have evolved and expanded over the last decade, aiming to initiate more scalable high-tech startups and to position the Munich ecosystem as one of the leading startup clusters in Europe. The chapter also addresses issues of sustainability, both in the larger society and in future growth of the Munich COI ecosystem.

Chapter 7, *The Oslo case: agile and adaptive responses to Covid-19 challenges by actors in local and globally extended health technology clusters*, discusses three examples of the resilient response provided by a COI with existing ties to an international network in reaction to Covid-19. At the beginning of the pandemic, collaboration between Oslo's city government and Norway Health Tech (NHT; an organization of 250 companies and institutions hosted at the Oslo University Research Park) facilitated rapid procurement and distribution of critical protective equipment and supplies. This effort was successful due to government's quick policy adjustments and NHT's ability to rapidly pivot strategies and mobilize its existing networks. A second example was the rapid development of a digital contact tracing system, developed in a Sri Lanka node of the 79-country DHIS2 health information system developed through the University of Oslo Department of Infomatics since 1994. This pre-existing university-coordinated open-source health information system (funded by the World Health Organization and international donor organizations) allowed rapid testing and international adaptation and adoption of the contact tracing system. The third example focuses on an individual company founded by two physicians to foster digital medical and "home hospital" care that rapidly built on an existing contract with the City of Oslo to respond to increased needs for remote home care throughout Norway, and is now expanding to international applications in the UK and China. The chapter discusses the need for both agile and adaptive response capabilities.

Chapter 8, *Changing pathways, urban dynamics and governance at 22@ Barcelona*, details the progress and evolution of a government-sponsored, city-centered COI in Barcelona, incorporating city residents as a new stakeholder component in directing future sustainability and competitiveness of the ecosystem. Initiated in 1998 by the municipal government, 22@ Barcelona began as a redevelopment opportunity to transform an aging industrial district of the city into an innovation hub, focusing on five sectors: media, information and communications technology (ICT), design, medical technologies and energy. The district was designed to be a model of "the city as a laboratory," testing theories for successful urban transformation, such as the Triple, Quadruple, Quintuple Helix Model; the Knowledge-Based Urban Development (KBUD) approach; Agglomeration Theory; and the COI Framework. Over the last decade, the dynamics of governance have shifted from top-down government leadership focused on urban planning and economic revitalization to a more holistic governance process with the 2016 "Ca l'Alier Agreement" which involved resident and business associations, universities and activists in developing a framework of five pillars for future development decisions and included two new sectors (creative industries and green economy) in the district. This new "bottom up" governance model adds a new perspective to COI and other urban transformation models.

**Part III: Global Case Studies – National Strategies**

Chapter 9, *The development of Singapore's innovation and entrepreneurship ecosystem*, traces the evolution of Singapore's innovation and entrepreneurship ecosystem over four decades and the strong role of public policies in shaping that evolution. The rapid economic development of this city-state since its independence in 1965 was accomplished through public policies focused on attracting and leveraging direct foreign investments from global multinational corporations (MNCs). By encouraging MNCs to transfer increasingly advanced technologies to local subsidiaries and by investing in educating the domestic workforce, Singapore achieved rapid technological catch-up without substantial investment in public research and development. However, with the shift of innovation emerging from fast-growing startups rather than large incumbent corporations, weaknesses in Singapore's R&D performance have become more evident, and government and university efforts have focused on the development of technology entrepreneurship ecosystems. Despite significant growth, indigenous firms' innovation capabilities remain underdeveloped and have been largely focused on internet/mobile/IT services, although efforts to nurture deep-tech startups have increased since the mid-2010s. The public sector has played an important role in development of the innovation and entrepreneurship ecosystem not only on the supply side, but also on the demand side as a lead user (through government procurements), particularly in Singapore's public healthcare and smart urban infrastructure sectors. Singapore's experience provides several lessons for other newly industrialized economies.

Chapter 10, *State- and private-led Clusters of Innovation in China*, contrasts two models of the recent development of COI in China. On a national scale, the Belt and Road Initiative proposed by Chinese President Xi Jinping in 2013 is a state-led, top-down enterprise strengthening Chinese MNCs that spreads along the Eurasian continent through a heavy investment in infrastructure development, supported by diplomacy and the establishment of global networks. A contrasting model is seen in the southern city of Shenzhen and its upsurge as an innovation powerhouse, organically and bottom-up, developed by millions of immigrants from all parts of China. Its strength is threefold: talent, industry chain advantages and mobility of resources. Through secondary data, first-hand interviews and observations, this chapter examines the two contrasting models and their origins and motivations.

Chapter 11, *Strategy for economic recovery from the COVID-19 disaster: Japan aims to become a startup nation again*, examines progress in the university-led movement to foster innovation and entrepreneurship in Japan. After World War II, Japan experienced a burst of entrepreneurship which gave birth to global companies such as Sony and Honda, and rapid economic growth which continued until the 1980s. For the last 30 years, however, Japan has endured a prolonged economic depression, due in part to reliance on traditional cultural norms and bureaucratic business structures that discourage innovation and risk-taking. At the beginning of the 21st century, government policy makers looked to innovation as a driver for restarting the economy, and identified the national universities to lead in commercializing research and cultivating entrepreneurship and innovation. The University of Tokyo has been a leader in this initiative, establishing technology transfer, early-stage venture financing and entrepreneurship education programs. In the last decade all of these programs have expanded, leading to increasing numbers of new ventures. While the Covid-19 pandemic has provided opportunities for entrepreneurial startups, challenges remain in creating regulatory, organizational, policy and cultural changes to accelerate progress of the startup ecosystem in Japan.

Chapter 12, *Supporting innovation in India through a special Service Organization*, chronicles the personal journey of a manager in his evolution into an innovation enabler and catalyst, progressing through a variety of roles at the interface between MNCs and government. This chapter provides the lessons that have been gathered about bridging the gaps and aligning interests between these two important COI components. First in corporate positions at Intel Corporation in India and the Middle East, then as founder of a nonprofit focused on development in Indian rural villages, and finally as an initiative leader with IBM, the author observed major cultural and economic shifts to which government and MNCs needed to respond. Lessons learned included: the role of entrepreneurship in empowering individuals to break out of cycles of poverty, the importance of aligning MNC self-interest and social responsibility aims with government populist-driven agendas and enabling governments to take "the first big step", and the need to incorporate local educational systems in order to scale initiatives. This chapter provides a clear example of the roles of special service hybrid organizations, both within and independent of major corporations, in aligning interests and fostering positive growth within COI.

Chapter 13, *Australian Sports Technologies Network: adding value through creating synergies*, documents the development of Australia's sports technology (sports-tech) cluster and the role of a membership business organization, the Australian Sports Technology Network (ASTN), in catalyzing the creation of a COI from a disparate group of emerging sports equipment companies. The chapter also demonstrates how government policy and incentives can provide critical support, and the important role of ASTN in activating and facilitating that government involvement. Finally, this chapter explores the role of ASTN in facilitating the global extension of the national sports-tech COI into the Global Network of Sports-Tech COI. This is another example of the key role that a hybrid component, such as a professional business organization, can play in the inception and growth of an innovation cluster.

Chapter 14, *Conditions for the implementation of a biotechnology Cluster of Innovation in Colombia: a benchmark of best practices with German clusters*, compares an emerging biotechnology cluster in Valle del Cauca, Colombia with a more mature biotechnology cluster in Gatersleben, Germany using the COI Framework and the Systemic Competitiveness Model. This chapter highlights similarities and differences between these two regions and delineates factors which are necessary for the development of a successful technology cluster. One important finding is the critical and ongoing role of government in providing the enabling conditions for the development of a COI, with the most crucial enabling condition being establishing and maintaining the rule of law. There is no single roadmap or solution for COI development, since each local context is unique. However, identifying the presence and absence of key components and systemic competitive success factors can provide guidance for investment of time and resources.

Chapter 15, *The Brazilian innovation ecosystem takes off*, addresses the recent entrepreneurial boom in Brazil, focusing primarily on the São Paulo COI, which serves as the center of a regional network of innovation hubs in southeast/south Brazil. A previous surge in startup investment during the dotcom bubble (1998–2000) eventually fizzled and did not lead to sustained growth of the innovation ecosystem. In fact, despite favorable macroeconomic conditions between 2001 and 2011, Brazil endured a long "nuclear winter of tech." After a gradual restart, this fundamentally changed during 2015–2020 when Brazil experienced exceptional growth in VC funding, new deals, successful startups and other measures of progress. Surprisingly, this recent boom – much larger and likely more sustainable – happened in the midst of political turmoil, two recessions and the Covid-19 pandemic. This chapter details factors that contributed to this remarkable take-off and also how the Brazilian innovation ecosystem is helping to address the pandemic and other health, social and environmental challenges.

Chapter 16, *Clusters of Innovation: lessons learned and final thoughts*, summarizes major insights gathered in this investigation of Clusters of Innovation and questions and challenges that arise when implementing these learnings.

## WHAT WE HOPE TO LEARN

Our premise is simple:

- Innovation adds value to society.
- Innovation is often instigated by individuals and small teams that have unique capabilities or insights.
- These individuals or teams rarely have the resources they need to pursue their vision.
- Therefore, entrepreneurial behavior (the pursuit of opportunity beyond the resources one has under one's control[2]) is essential to make progress.
- The necessary resources can be derived from the various members of the ecosystem in a way that benefits all the participants.
- This exchange is enabled if an ecosystem has the proper constituents (components) and they engage in it constructively (behaviors).
- When these components and behaviors are in place, we have a mature COI.
- Emerging COI can be fostered and stimulated by any of the cluster constituents, each having their special role.
- COI tend toward a global perspective and interaction with other COI, forming networks and bonds that bring their own special characteristics.
- Building COI is a pathway for creating opportunities for individual and collective well-being.

If our simple premise is true, then engaging in the pursuit of creating COI is worthwhile and important. We wrote this volume to challenge this premise and refine our understanding of its implications and implementation. It is the collective hope of myself and all the contributing authors that this volume will prove valuable to those who practice entrepreneurship and innovation and to those who support and enable it.

## NOTES

1. Anon.
2. Paraphrased from Howard H. Stephenson, quoted in P. Cohan (2015), "Harvard's lion of entrepreneurship packs up his office," *Forbes*, www.forbes.com/sites/petercohan/2011/06/15/harvards-lion-of-entrepreneurship-packs-up-his-office/?sh=13eb950b4e89.

PART I


Clusters of Innovation: Refining and Extending
the Framework

# 2. Global Cluster of Innovation theory and practice in the 21st century: COI Components

## Jerome S. Engel and Aline Figlioli

The Cluster of Innovation (COI) Framework provides a set of tools and structures to help articulate, visualize, understand and navigate the rapidly evolving innovation economy. The Framework functions as a lens that brings the elements (components) of the COI and their behaviors into sharper focus and allows observers to track their evolution over time. This is of increased importance as the innovation economy disseminates around the world (Dutta et al., 2020).

The urgency to improve our understanding of the dynamics of the innovation economy is heightened by the stress induced by the rapid pace of change. Sources of change are both exogenous and intrinsic. Exogenous sources of change and potential disruption include incremental elements, such as environmental degradation and global warming, and sharp changes, such as economic disruption (for example, the global financial crisis of 2008), political instability or the Covid-19 pandemic. The rapid pace of technological evolution is, of course, a consistent source of change and potential disruption. When these factors collide, tipping points arise that can disrupt society, markets and day-to-day operations. Long-established embedded solutions and practices become inadequate and vulnerable. Society and customers become amenable to trying new solutions. These moments reveal the power of entrepreneurship and innovation as an adaptive capability that rapidly creates value for both the user (the customer and society) and the creator (the entrepreneur and their supporting ecosystem). COI are communities that foster such value creation.

An adaptive and creative capability is a key resource of an innovation society and is at the heart of a COI. COI are characterized by flexibility, mobility and speed based on their ability to employ entrepreneurship and innovation to exploit the opportunities stemming from technological evolution and other sources of change. Examples of how the combination of entrepreneurship and innovation can respond to such stresses include renewable energy and electric vehicles (in response to global warming), and acceleration of the adoption of digital services (as a response to Covid-19 restrictions). This robust response to stress, and its translation into economic opportunity, gives the pursuit of understanding COI strategic importance.

When we first developed the COI Framework,[1] we integrated and extended the insightful industrial and regional economic cluster theory that emerged at the end of the 20th century (Porter 1990, 2000; Saxenian, 1994). That theory focused on identifying the relative economic advantages of geographic regions. Building on that foundation, our work developed a framework to describe the particular regional economies of innovation hubs such as Silicon Valley and Tel Aviv and the global network they formed with other like communities – the Global Network of Clusters of Innovation (GNCOI). Our framework identified the participants (components) and their respective behaviors. We understood at the time that the behaviors of the participants were critical. What our observations of the last 10 years reveal is that the behaviors are in fact the key.

In our earlier work, we investigated the transportability and general applicability of the COI Framework. Were these productive structures of limited applicability, suitable only to a few regional economies like Silicon Valley or Boston, or were there generalizable principles that could be applied broadly? By looking in depth at 13 regional economies around the globe, we observed that while each community is unique, the Framework was effective at uncovering local strengths and needs, and a useful tool to identify the right combination of factors and policies to create COI that unleash the inherent entrepreneurial capacity of society, energize individual initiative, and create individual and collective benefit. Further, the Framework could similarly identify how communities could interact with other COI communities to create networks to offset deficits, leverage core competencies and realize value for their constituents.

A Cluster of Innovation combines an ecosystem and a culture. The ecosystem defines the components; the culture defines the behaviors. Since publication of the COI Framework, in addition to the critical role of behaviors becoming more apparent, we have observed the emergence of new non-geographically defined or constrained clusters. These communities go beyond the concept of linked domains (that is, the Global Network of COI). They are, in fact, single communities that span global domains. We will explore all these attributes in depth in this and the following two chapters, as we revisit, update and refine Cluster of Innovation theory and practice.

## 2.1    THE COI FRAMEWORK

COI ecosystems interact with multiple technologies contemporaneously as they evolve through their respective technology life cycles. The COI's influence and impact are greatest at the inflection point of a technology's increasing productivity where an accelerating rate of technology and product performance has the potential to produce outsized gains in value versus the level of resources required to advance it to market. This "sweet spot" can be mapped on the "S-Curve of Innovation", widely used to demonstrate the relationship between invested resources and the performance of technologies and products. The entrepreneurs and venture capitalists active in this "sweet spot" often exploit radically new technologies and use innovative and often disruptive business models. The "sweet spot" is a zone of intense interaction between technology development, business model experimentation, market segmentation and customer adoption. With success, as a technology innovation and its related business models mature, there is a shift in focus from innovation (and disruption) to efficiency and scaling. Successful scaling leads to rigidity induced by the desire to protect and exploit the assets deployed and the customer base developed. The success of a platform then can inhibit the adoption of the next emergent technology if it is disruptive to the current success. And so, a new window of opportunity arises for the ever-agile entrepreneur. This is the very essence of and distinction between incremental and disruptive innovation. Incremental innovation can be adopted without disrupting the incumbent's hold on the customer, while disruptive innovation has the ability to threaten and displace the existing solution and disrupt existing customer relationships (Christensen, 1997).

The commercialization pathway often engages various players, each with their distinct role: (a) Universities that house research labs, often government-funded, that spawn new technologies; (b) Entrepreneurs who identify opportunities; (c) Venture Capitalists who fund startup ventures organized by entrepreneurs to develop commercial products and discover entry markets and scalable business models; and ultimately (d) Major Corporations, which often engage in the process in later stages as a means of incorporating product and service innovations (Christensen, 1997; Foster, 1986; Moore 2014) (Figure 2.1).

The COI Framework represents a community that fosters a whirlpool of value creation with two central elements: the participants in the ecosystem (Components) and the nature and manner of their interaction (Behaviors). The Components, as defined by the Framework, are function-based archetypes of the main actors that operate along the Technology/Product S-Curve of Innovation, and especially in its "sweet spot". Any organization, independent of its nature or nomenclature, that performs key activities relating to an essential function of the Framework may be considered a component of the COI. The seven key components of a COI are represented in Figure 2.2.

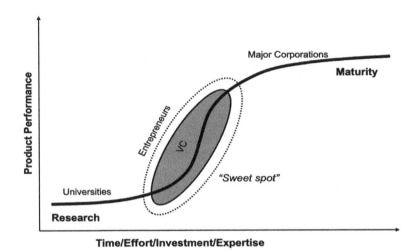

*Source:*    Developed by the author – adapted S-Curve from Christensen (1997).

*Figure 2.1*      *The Technology/Product S-Curve of Innovation, its principal
participants, and the "sweet spot" of innovation acceleration*

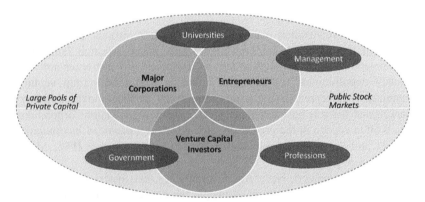

*Source:*    Developed by author. Adapted from version published in J.S. Engel (Ed.), *Global
Clusters of Innovation: Entrepreneurial Engines of Economic Growth around the World*
(Cheltenham, UK and Northampton, MA: Edward Elgar Publishing, 2014). By permission of the
publisher.

*Figure 2.2*      *Mature COI Framework: Components*

## 2.2    THE CLUSTER OF INNOVATION REVISITED

Our experience with the Framework since its original publication (Engel, 2014, 2015; Engel and del Palacio, 2009, 2011) and our desire for a more refined tool led us to explore how we might visualize and define the components of the COI at a higher level of resolution. This gave rise to some important observations.

First, we found it meaningful to differentiate between the cluster's core and supporting components. The Core Components are the Entrepreneurs, VC Investors and Major Corporate incumbents. These are the three principal engines of action in the mature COI. It all starts with the Entrepreneurs. They are the ones who identify opportunities, develop the vision and plans, secure the resources to put the plans into action and, initially at least, lead the ventures. Next are the VC Investors, who are the principal source of capital for entrepreneurs and their startups. The method by which VC Investors provide funds is just as important as the capital itself. The VC investment terms and structure, when properly designed, provide entrepreneurial incentives. Further, when taken together with constructive personal efforts by the venture capitalists, they foster a win–win non-zero-sum approach which can have ripple effects beyond the entity and diffuse throughout the cluster. Additionally, the venture capitalists' selection and vetting function helps focus the resources of the cluster on what are hopefully the superior opportunities. Securing investment from a well-regarded VC firm confers a halo of approval that assists the venture with recruiting, marketing and other benefits. The third Core Component, the Major Corporations, are often the vehicle for scaling an innovation and for providing a pathway to liquidity for investors, entrepreneurs and their teams. Without this collaboration many innovations, no matter how worthy, would never scale to have the impact they ultimately achieve, nor would the entrepreneurial skills and capital be freed up to recycle into the innovation process.

The Supporting Components include the Universities, Management, the Professions and Government. These components play essential roles, but they do not directly cause or initiate the commercial innovation process. They enable and support it.

Lastly, our analysis revealed the emerging importance of Hybrid Components that help bridge collaboration among other cluster components. Hybrid Components are organizations or programs that emerge when one or more COI components, core or supporting, engage or expand their remits to deliver activities that traditionally would be addressed by a specific COI component. These hybrids are often smaller operations with two advantages: (a) as they are often sponsored by, or have relationships with, one or more important players such as government, universities, venture capitalists and major corporations, they have the ability to leverage these relationships to create value very efficiently, and (b) as they are often relatively simple organizations that operate independently and require relatively modest capitalization, they are easy to implement. They can be relatively temporary experiments. This is important to policy makers and business leaders who often struggle against institutional inertia. We discuss them in some detail later in this chapter.

## The COI Framework Refined

How have the events of the last 10 years affected each of the COI components and their respective behaviors? In this chapter we will focus on a refined definition and description of each of the COI participants (Components). In Chapter 3 we explore the characteristic COI behaviors of each component. As a final refinement, in Chapter 4 we introduce a new tool for corporate leaders, the Fit and Location Matrix, that can help them build their company's capability to proactively participate in, and benefit from, engagement with COI. It translates the essence of Open Innovation (Chesbrough, 2003) into management practices that engage and leverage the components and behaviors of COI, especially the important interface of Major Corporations, Entrepreneurs, and Venture Capital (Engel, 2011).[2] The COI Fit and Location Matrix is represented by the small squares in Figure 2.3.

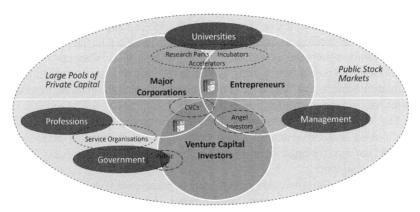

*Source:*    Developed by the authors.

*Figure 2.3    Enhanced mature COI Framework: Components*

Although the Components identified above exist in many ecosystems, in a COI they assume different characteristics and behaviors, which provide the speed and agility required to spur action, achieve traction, and focus resources on opportunities with the highest potential for strategic impact and financial return (Table 2.1).

*Table 2.1*     *Characteristics of Components in a mature COI*

| Components | | Characteristics in COI |
|---|---|---|
| Core | 1. Major Corporations | • Collaborate with other components, notably universities, startups and their investors to achieve their own innovation goals, employing mechanisms such as contractual agreements, equity investments, acquisitions and partnerships.<br>• Develop Open Innovation processes and skills. |
| | 2. Entrepreneurs | • Identify high-potential opportunities that often require raising outside equity capital.<br>• Create and grow businesses that aim to have major impact and create significant economic value.<br>• Share the investor's perspective that strives to create financial returns through a sale or IPO (initial public offering).<br>• Flexible and willing to engage in Open Innovation processes with major corporations.<br>• Recycle themselves into subsequent startups.<br>• Become advisors to, and investors in, others' ventures. |
| | 3. Venture Capital Investors | • Stable source of early-stage and growth capital.<br>• Strategy-driven.<br>• Focus on powerful high-potential opportunities.<br>• Professionally investing other people's money, often from institutions such as public pension funds and endowments.<br>• Fewer capital or geographic constraints. |
| | 4. Universities | • Achieving relevance and impact through commercialization of academic research of increasing importance.<br>• Promote the training of entrepreneurial skills.<br>• Increasingly willing to engage in collaborative industry research, and licensing.<br>• House or partner with accelerators and VC funds. |

| Components | | Characteristics in COI |
|---|---|---|
| Supporting | 5. Management | • Professional class of entrepreneurial managers with diverse experience. Stage-specialized.<br>• Motivated to engage with high-potential opportunities.<br>• Compensation arrangements provide a share in the wealth creation through ownership.<br>• Comfortable with frequent employer changes (every few years) due to volatile environment or opportunity optimization.<br>• Recycle themselves into subsequent startups. |
| | 6. Professions<br>  (a) Legal<br>  (b) Accounting<br>  (c) Recruiting<br>  (d) Consulting | • Adapt their practices to match the entrepreneurial behavior of their clients.<br>• Flexible approaches to rewards linked to the eventual success of the venture, rather than optimizing current fees. |
| | 7. Government | • Maintain a safe stable society where the rule of law is respected (legal process, adjudication, property protection, including intellectual property).<br>• Enable and sustain COI (for example, funding, tax incentives, research support). |
| Hybrid | 8. Incubators, Research Parks, Accelerators | • Support the conversion of ideas/projects into fast-paced growth companies.<br>• Often provide coaching, mentoring, engagement to relevant networks (funders, business connections, etc.) and business development support (for example, business model design, intellectual property management). May provide small investment in exchange for meaningful minority ownership. |
| | 9. Public Venture Capital initiatives | • Government-funded independent VC funds, led by VC professionals in a manner aligned with development policy strategies.<br>• Take advantage of the VC professional structure and experience. |
| | 10. Corporate Venture Capital (CVC) | • Corporate investment vehicle to gain exposure to emerging innovations and obtain minority interests in high-potential firms strategically aligned with the parent business. Has many different legal structures.<br>• Objectives include providing the parent company with strategic insights and identifying potential acquisition targets, as well as generating a financial return. |

| Components | Characteristics in COI |
|---|---|
| 11. Angel Investors | • Individuals, often previously successful entrepreneurs, investing their personal funds in the early embryonic stage of the business development.<br>• May get involved in the business as advisor or board member.<br>• Investment structures often lack the full protections or fixed valuations of professional VC investments. Sometimes pursued for a double bottom line: financial return and personal lifestyle avocation. |
| 12. Service Organizations | • Provide various public services that support the COI and its participants.<br>• May be funded by government, major corporations, charities or others. Aim is to enhance access to resources, upgrade skills and upgrade the capabilities of COI. |

*Source:*    Core Components and Supporting Components based on Engel (2014), Hybrid Components developed by the authors.

## A New Category: COI Hybrid Components

With the increasing importance of the innovation economy, we have found it meaningful to separately identify the emergence of Hybrid Components, new actors that bridge the gaps between key COI components, smoothing the innovation process. These Hybrid Components principally take three forms. First, there are those that extend the functions of the parent organization into new roles and behaviors. This enables the parent to continue to focus on its core function while dedicating resources and assigning responsibility to a subordinate entity that can function somewhat independently and focus on the task of engaging with the COI. Examples of such organizations include the following three categories:

- Startup and scale-up Incubators, Accelerators and Research Parks. These organizations are often sponsored by universities, governments, VC firms and/or major corporations. That support may or may not be obvious. Increasingly, as accelerators have proliferated, they are often providing small amounts of seed financing and facilitating investor introductions.
- Venture investors that invest for objectives other than strictly financial return or return derived directly from the venture they are investing in. This group includes elements of Corporate Venture Capital (CVC), Angel Investors (individuals) and Public VC entities, where public funds constitute the sole source or the majority of the funding.

- Service Organizations and corporate foundations, which often sponsor charitable and educational programs that provide support to the ecosystem in skill-building and economic opportunity development.

**Incubators, accelerators and research parks**

The rapid emergence and evolution of these hybrid components is demonstrated by examining the UK experience with incubators and accelerators, and their emerging variants, as the virtual and the "pre" ones (preparatory for the actual program).[3] These hybrid organizations and programs, while similar, have varying scope of services and sponsors. New venture incubators, whose origins date back decades, were often government-stimulated. More recently, commercialized models have achieved greater scale and dispersion via the co-working space business model (for example, WeWork). In the last decade, as Figure 2.4 demonstrates, these types of services have been augmented by the emergence of accelerators, which offer limited-duration immersion programs to accelerate business-model exploration and validation.

These programs take many forms. Initially many were corporate-sponsored. For example, by 2014 corporate activity already accounted for 65 percent of active programs in the UK (Bone et al., 2017). More recently the trend has shifted to private, often VC-funded, enterprises that, in addition to the development program, offer small investments in exchange for shares of founders' equity and highlight the ventures in a "demo day" where outside investors are invited (for example, Y Combinator). Many universities also offer accelerator programs, sometimes in combination with academic credit. In the US, the National Science Foundation (NSF) has established an ongoing accelerator series, the I-Corps. Since its inception in 2012 it has trained over 2,000 science-based teams. This program's impact has a broad ripple effect. It is a highly visible signal to scientists throughout the US that the NSF, which is an important source of research funding, is placing increasing emphasis on scientific translation and commercialization. The program is also being replicated by universities and governments many times over (National Science Foundation, 2021). During the Covid-19 pandemic, the trend of virtual accelerator programs, where the activities are conducted online independent of any locus with a physical location, has begun to take on scale. The emergence of such non-geography-dependent programs will likely enhance the linkages among COI and the integration of the global COI community. The UK data is representative of the pace of expansion around the world and the potential impact such hybrid organizations and programs are having and are likely to continue to have (Bone et al., 2017)[4] (Figure 2.4).

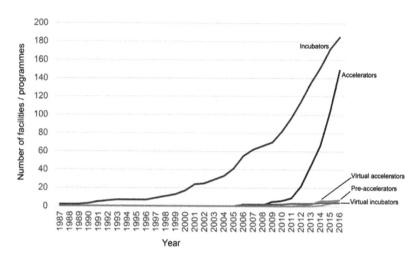

*Source:* Bone et al. (2017, p. 42).

*Figure 2.4    Evolution of incubators and accelerators in the UK*

The global importance of these support organizations will become evident as we explore the various geographic cases included in this volume, notably Barcelona, Munich, Australia, Singapore and Japan, among others.

**Double bottom line investors**

As the awareness of VC has diffused into the broader social and business communities, divergent participants have come to participate in the process for reasons that are not strictly defined by the potential of a direct return on the investment. Various parties participate in pursuit of a secondary return. We refer to that objective as pursuing a "double bottom line". This term is often used to refer to investment objectives that provide social or environmental benefits to society in addition to financial returns to the investor. We use this term wherever indirect returns are important to the investment criteria.

Examples of such investors abound. We note three major categories: Corporate Venture Capital (CVC), Angel Investors (individuals), and Public (government-funded) VC entities.

• CVC groups often invest principally for strategic return, providing benefit to the parent company, rather than strictly financial gain derived from the investment. They may operate either within the parent company investing off the balance sheet or as fully funded captive (that is, single limited partner) funds. Additionally, corporations may participate in multiple-investor funds that operate independent of supervision but provide a special set of augmented services and bespoke insights to the corporate investor.

- Angel Investors are individuals who invest their personal funds. While the VC investor category has many subcomponents, it is meaningful to separately identify Angel Investors, as their behavior often deviates in important, constructive and subtle ways from professional "institutional" venture capitalists (that is, venture capitalists that are managing other people's money). Angel Investors are individuals and invest for many diverse reasons. Some are disciplined and diligent investors, behaving similar to venture capitalists, albeit on a smaller scale. Their objective is financial return. Others, however, may invest for more qualitative or lifestyle-related motivations. Such investors may select investments for the opportunities they provide for personal involvement, or other subjective reasons. No matter their motivation, Angel Investors have accounted for an increasing share of the funding for ventures at the earliest stages and are increasingly an accepted and respected part of the venture funding process and community. Their growing influence on the venture development process merits special attention.[5] Many Angel Investors are both successful entrepreneurs and limited partner investors (passive investors) in VC funds. Some are active general partners (managers) of VC funds. In fact, more recently some VC firms have chosen to attract Angel Investors as investors in their funds to gain access to their deal flow and networks, even giving them special status and recognition. With these deep connections, Angel Investors help bridge the gap between entrepreneurs, the opportunities they are creating and VC. As such, they collectively function as a hybrid component.
- Public (government-funded) VC also exists in many forms. Some governments have experimented with creating entities where public funds constitute the sole source or the majority of the funding and the managing partners are basically chosen by the government agency involved (for example, Singapore). Others have created programs where government matches private funds (that is, the European Union) and others may limit the government's participation in the financial returns as an inducement to private participation (for example, in the US some of the Small Business Administration's support of VC in its early days). The purpose of these funds can be as a general innovation stimulus or as targeted regional or technology development.

**Service Organizations and corporate foundations**
The third category of Hybrid Components are special Service Organizations that support elements of the innovation ecosystem. Examples include government and the professional organizations that expand their traditional roles to engage actively in general support of the innovation process. These organizations tend to have a multi-sided business model, where the payer (which may be a government, a major corporate sponsor or a public charity) has no direct relationship with the beneficiary. We explore several examples of such Service Organizations later in chapters 12 (India) and 13 (Australia).

While we have described various examples of Hybrid Components, it is clear that our list is not exhaustive, nor is it intended to be. Rather it is intended to be illustrative of an organizational response to the need to enhance mobility. Some of these components arise from business strategy (for example, CVC), some from public interest (for example, government-sponsored accelerators) and some from self-interest (angel investors). What is important for us to observe is how the boundaries of the components in more mature COI are softening and converging and how sometimes this process is represented in discreet and identifiable hybrid components. This is an ongoing evolution that is likely to continue and has strategic importance and implications for all the participants in a COI, extending from corporate innovation strategy to investor deal strategy, university technology commercialization strategy, entrepreneur venture development strategy and individual career strategy.

## 2.3   THE GLOBAL NETWORK OF CLUSTERS OF INNOVATION

The Global Network of Clusters of Innovation is an extension of the Framework and places it in an international context. It demonstrates how a loose emergent network forms collaborative ties in an exchange of value. When originally produced, the COI Framework naturally built on the historical premise that innovation clusters, like the industrial clusters famously described by Michael Porter (1990, 2000),[6] were geographically grounded and located in space by fixed co-ordinates. However, the international exchanges that are intrinsic in technology and innovation demanded representation.

As already observed, because high-potential ventures in a COI pursue opportunities in new, re-segmented and/or rapidly growing markets, a win–win collaborative environment tends to evolve. Win–lose competition is displaced by co-opetition (Brandenburger and Nalebuff, 2021), where competitors may seek mutually beneficial collaborations. With opportunity-seeking entrepreneurial behavior, the investigative mindset of Lean Innovation (Ries, 2011) and the flexible attitudes of Open Innovation permeating, it is natural for a web of informal connections to emerge, especially among peer groups within a COI (Saxenian, 1994).

Furthermore, in the increasingly global business environment, with the emergence of remote work and telecommunication as the norm, the aforementioned proclivity for networking results in casual connections (which sociologists call "weak ties") between individuals in geographically divergent COI. These connections, though maybe ephemeral, over time form a mesh of connectivity that in our prior work we defined as the Global Network of COI. These connections are an extension of the COI process and create the opportunity for the emergence of formalized arrangements, such as contracts, partnerships and membership organizations, which we have labeled "durable bonds". In certain extreme instances, these interconnections become so intense between two physically remote COI that they evolve into a continual set of interactions, exchanges of ideas, information, people and opportunities, so that the two COI essentially operate in a fully integrated fashion. This integration is furthered by key individuals whose highly adaptive and mobile behavior enables them to operate natively in both connecting nodes. The COI Framework names these connections "covalent bonds" and calls the resulting linked communities a Super-COI (Figure 2.5). An example of such a Super-COI is the close working relationship of Silicon Valley and the Israeli COI. Since our original analysis over a decade ago, this process has only become stronger.

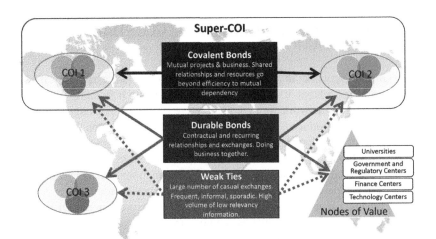

*Source:*    Adapted from Engel and del Palacio (2011); reprinted with permission from the *California Management Review.*

*Figure 2.5*    *Global Network of COI*

As we explore the structure of the Global Network of COI, one element remains: Nodes of Value. A node of value is an organization with particular knowledge or capability that provides specific contributions (for example, subject-matter expertise, financing, technology). These interactions can assume diverse formats, from informal contacts (weak ties) to more structured defined activities through contracts (durable bonds). Although there is interaction between the node of value and the component of the COI, such interaction does not reach a level of density that causes it to be integrated into the COI itself.

## 2.4 A NEW PARADIGM: NON-GEOGRAPHIC CLUSTERS OF INNOVATION

While such geographic determinism is still at work, boundaries are becoming more flexible and blurred. Networks of geographic COI have at times evolved into more fluid non-geographically defined COI. We see evidence that multi-location collaboration is at times going beyond the network structure previously described. The Covid-19 pandemic has clarified that the historical geographic definition, while continuing to be valid, is not necessarily determinative. Indeed, we premise that while proximity still is crucial, it need not be geographic proximity. Shared opportunities, business practices and business models that attract and share relationships and resources can bind a non-geographically defined COI together.

As "virtual" communities have become more robust, they have become intrinsic to business, not just as conduits of explicit information and transactions, but also as "places", as communities, as clusters. As these communities grow and specialize, they naturally aggregate and have the opportunity to share components and behaviors and thereby increase the velocity of value creation in COI. These emergent non-geographic COI are bound together by the gravitational pull of win–win relationships and behaviors. Some of this is easy to identify, such as when connections are made between geographically dispersed entrepreneurs and investors. However, much of this is tacit, subtle and not contractually defined. Without the benefit of geographic proximity, such clusters can be elusive and rapidly evolving, but their emerging importance is clear. We will explore this process in Chapter 5 when we examine the emergence of the non-geographically defined COI of companies and investors defined by their mutual pursuit of the Product Led Growth business model.

With Covid-19 as a catalyst, boundaries have become more elastic. While geographic hubs are still important, it has become apparent that geographic proximity is no longer the sole imperative to achieve the density and the efficiencies of a cluster. It is the intensity of the interaction and the shared values and behaviors that geographic proximity encouraged which yield the cluster benefits. With the increasing reliance on non-face-to-face communication and with the increasing intimacy of virtual communities, this interlocking density can become unlinked from physical proximity (Figure 2.6). As a new generation of entrepreneurs, investors and business executives emerge from the pandemic experience, and blended models of education and work take hold, we can expect the imperative of physical proximity to continue to ease and non-geographic COI to be an emerging trend.

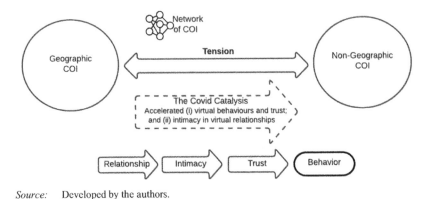

*Source:*    Developed by the authors.

*Figure 2.6*      *The emergence of non-geographic COI*

## The Old Paradigm: Existing COI are Getting Stronger

The observation of the emergence of non-geographically defined COI can be masked by a contrary set of phenomena. Even though entrepreneurship, venture capital and innovation generally have enjoyed rapid dispersion across geographies, it is also counterintuitively true that in some ways the last 10 years has seen an increasing concentration of high-growth ventures in certain localities.

The fertile soil for the emergence of world-leading innovative businesses of scale has become increasingly clustered in particular geographic pockets. The geographical concentration of "unicorns" – companies valued at over $1 billion – is a proxy for this extreme disparity. The US leads by far, chased by China, and following behind appears a pool of countries, led by the UK (Figure 2.7). This extreme geographic discrepancy can be offset somewhat by the scale of the underlying economies, but not enough to eradicate the clear demonstration of the propensity of certain regional COI to be able to generate high-potential ventures of scale.

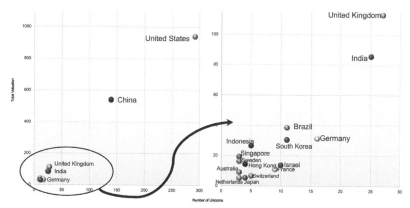

*Source:*      Based on CB Insights (2021).

*Figure 2.7      Number and total valuation of unicorns per country*

## The Tension Between Geographic Proximity and Dispersed Virtual Intimacy

How can these divergent trends be reconciled? How can we have increasing concentrations and increasing dispersion? This is simply the result of an increasing proportion of the world's economy becoming part of an interconnected innovation economy. So, while the strongest COI get stronger, the innovation economy defuses across the globe, and boundaries soften through the action of both the Global Network of COI and non-geographic COI. The strongest COI tend to have superior access to markets and capital. They are powerhouses for scaling successful high-potential firms. These firms may, due to their interconnectedness across the Global Network of COI, migrate much of their executive functions to these stronger COI to aid in capturing scaling resources while at the same time globally disseminating innovative technology, business models and commercialization pathways.

The innovation economy is fluid. As it is based primarily on knowledge assets, ventures are not physically tethered to their locales. They can migrate or simply spread their operations to co-locate them in proximity to the core assets and markets they need to scale. As knowledge becomes more and more explicit and codified, it is easier to transfer and apply it remotely (Nonaka and Takeuchi, 1995). An example of an enabler of this process is GitHub,[7] the world largest repository of source code, with more than 40 million users and 28 million public repositories. There is no contradiction between geographic COI strength and a propensity for global diffusion. They go hand in hand.

The accelerating dominance of the leading innovation geographies is high-lighted by observing the 10-year evolution of VC investment as a percentage of gross domestic product (GDP) (Figure 2.8).

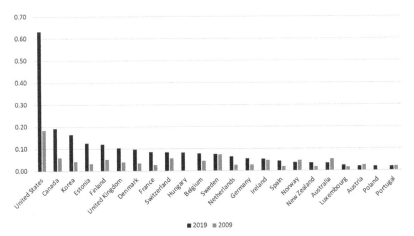

*Source:*    Developed by the authors; data from OECD (2021).

*Figure 2.8*      *Venture capital as percentage of GDP of selected countries*

## Global Innovation Dependencies: Strengths and Vulnerabilities

This new world of virtual and interconnected communities becoming more substantial elements of the business, innovation and entrepreneurial landscape comes with its strengths and vulnerabilities. For example, clusters that do not rely on geographic proximity may be more robust and less vulnerable to the waves of contagion (for example, Covid-19) that are perhaps going to be a more prominent feature of our collective future. Alternatively, their reliance on IT infrastructure calls into question their durability and vulnerability to disruption. The communications and computation networks are by their very nature evolving and imperfect. New technologies, systems and platforms emerge, scale and become obsolete faster than perhaps reliability and robust-ness can take hold.

Each revolution of computation and communication platforms, such as mainframes, PCs and smartphones, brought opportunities, risks and rewards. Now we are on the cusp of a series of multi-dimensional and likely disruptive innovations that will affect the way we interact and conduct social and business interactions. To cite a few examples:

- Mixed reality, the confluence of virtual and augmented reality, going mainstream across consumers and business, liberating screen-bound experiences into instinctual interactions integrated into real and meta-verse worlds;
- Artificial intelligence, bots and deep learning will challenge us not only technologically but also behaviorally;
- Blockchain technology, which has the potential to revolutionize network security and which has already demonstrated its impact by enabling key elements of the fintech and cryptocurrency revolution, has huge and detrimental environmental impacts; and
- Cryptocurrencies will challenge the historically reliable banking system, and perhaps even national currencies.

The pace of innovation and the urgency of commercial competition may not allow for the stress testing to ensure the security and reliability we have taken for granted in the tools of old economy. How will this instability be accommodated? Will it create its own crisis? Will it create its own opportunities? Will innovation ecosystems, such as COI, contribute to the rapid and creative responses that will be necessary?

Many of the foundational elements of the new critical infrastructure are already coming into focus: bandwidth, connectivity, cloud computing, security, etc. All these elements have their obvious vulnerabilities. The security and integrity of online communications and computational resources are vital components of our modern infrastructure. The integrity of online communications and reliable 24/7 access have emerged as vital national innovation and economic policies, as well as national security priorities.

Other risks are even more systemic and intractable. As reliance on technology to conduct business and form COI increases, the risks of the digital divide become ever more severe. Although perhaps it is too early for this hypothesis to be supported by scientific examination, it is supported by the observation of experienced eyes. Some say that the digital divide is an existential risk. Lack of access to the digital transformation that has altered much of the first world over recent decades exacerbates the already destabilizing disequilibrium in the global economy (World Economic Forum, 2021). In a world of global communication and increasing non-state actors this disadvantage can lead to political upheaval and disturbances with severe and unfortunate consequences for all.

## 2.5    LESSONS LEARNED: COMPONENTS OF CLUSTERS OF INNOVATION

In this chapter we introduced the concepts of Clusters of Innovation and the COI Framework. We examined their evolution since they were first introduced over 10 years ago, and offered revisions and updates based on our experience and the changes in the environment. In summary, we learned the following:

- Innovation economies often exhibit classic clustering tendencies, but they express themselves in unique ways. These differences from classic economic clusters warrant their own distinct analysis.
- COI are a combination of ecosystems and cultures. The ecosystems have participants. The Framework identifies seven principal participants, which the Framework calls "components". The culture of a COI is defined by its behaviors.
- The components of a COI can be meaningfully grouped into two categories: Core Components and Supporting Components:
  - Core Components include Entrepreneurs, Venture Capitalists and Major Corporations; and
  - Supporting Components include Governments, Universities, Management and the Professions.
- A COI is characterized by how these components interact and behave while engaged in a phase of rapid business discovery, often involving potentially disruptive technology and business models. This phase is portrayed as the "sweet spot" of the S-Curve of Technology/Product Innovation. These behaviors, and the agreements that emerge from them, often contribute to and reflect a business perspective that can be characterized as win–win and non-zero-sum. These behaviors are explored in depth in Chapter 3.
- The last decade has seen a greater role being played by Hybrid Components that foster mobility and bridge functions of the principal components. Examples include Incubators, Accelerators, Corporate Venture Capital (CVC), Angel Investors and specialized Service Organizations.
- The global nature of the innovation process, with broad technical and commercial deployment of innovative technology and disruptive business models, is profound.
- This global interconnectedness is represented in the Global Network of COI Framework.
- A new type of Non-Geographic COI may be emerging. These non-geographic clusters are communities bound tightly together by common business practices, such as common business models like Product Led Growth. These new ungrounded clusters may prove ephemeral, but for the moment are a significant creator of business velocity in certain sectors.

- COI have likely contributed to the capability of the modern economy to more rapidly respond to the challenges posed by the Covid-19 pandemic and other exogenous shocks.
- That capability brings its own risks and vulnerabilities, whose significance has yet to be understood.

Looking forward, in the coming chapter we will delve deeply into the behaviors of participants in a COI. It is these behaviors that are indeed the key to understanding the modern innovation economy and what distinguishes a COI from just another dense economic zone that happens to utilize advanced technology. Understanding these behaviors is essential to understanding COI.

## NOTES

1. Based on observation of business behaviors and industry dynamics in Silicon Valley (Engel and del Palacio, 2009).
2. In the COI Framework, we use the Open Innovation term broadly, as we see evidence of patterns of Open Innovation behaviors in many aspects of the cluster. We have developed a unique Open Innovation analytical tool, the COI Fit and Location Matrix, to portray this behavior. The Matrix provides unique insights into the Open Innovation processes and guidance as to how to analyze and implement them. The role of Open Innovation in the COI process will be separately described and explored in depth in Chapter 4.
3. For instance, pre-accelerators offer very-early-stage support, mainly through mentoring, to prepare the entrepreneur to join an accelerator programme in the future (Bone et al., 2017).
4. There is no further comprehensive survey available with updated numbers after Bone et al. (2017).
5. For clarity it is worth stressing the difference between programs led by the COI components – which can be found at the intersection between components – and hybrid organizations. These latter are entities that operate within the strategy of the "parent" component but take advantage of the structure, skills and/or experience of other components. For instance, public programs that invest in VC using a fund-of-funds structure – rather than investing directly in a company, investing in other funds that have their own asset portfolio – are not hybrid organizations. Likewise, Open Innovation initiatives by major corporations to identify new technologies within universities are not hybrid organizations.
6. Industrial clusters could be recognized by a geographic concentration of a critical mass of interconnected companies and institutions in a particular field, having proximity as a key factor for shared advantages through easier access to information; proximity to specialized resources, suppliers and customers; and reduced transaction costs, among others.
7. https://github.com/.

# REFERENCES

Bone, J., Allen, O., and Haley, C. (2017). *Business Incubators and Accelerators: The National Picture* (No. 2017/7). UK Department for Business, Energy and Industrial Strategy research paper.

Brandenburger, A., and Nalebuff, B. (2021). The rules of co-opetition. *Harvard Business Review*, Jan–Feb.

CB Insights (2021). Global Unicorn Club. Retrieved from www.cbinsights.com/research-unicorn-companies.

Chesbrough, H.W. (2003). *Open Innovation: The New Imperative for Creating and Profiting from Technology*. Boston, MA: Harvard Business School Press.

Christensen, C.M. (1997). *The Innovator's Dilemma: When New Technologies Cause Great Firms to Fail*. Boston, MA: Harvard University Press.

Dutta, S., Lanvin, B., and Wunsch-Vincent, S. (Eds) (2020). *The Global Innovation Index 2020: Who Will Finance Innovation?* Ithaca, NY, Fontainebleau and Geneva: Cornell University, INSEAD and WIPO.

Engel, J. (2015). Global Clusters of Innovation: Lessons from Silicon Valley. *California Management Review*, 57 (2), 36–65.

Engel, J. (Ed.) (2014). *Global Clusters of Innovation: Entrepreneurial Engines of Economic Growth around the World*, Cheltenham, UK and Northampton, MA, USA: Edward Elgar Publishing.

Engel, J. (2011). Accelerating corporate innovation: Lessons from the venture capital model. *Research-Technology Management*, 54 (3), 36–43.

Engel, J., and del Palacio, I. (2011). Global Clusters of Innovation: The case of Israel and Silicon Valley. *California Management Review*, 53 (2), 27–49.

Engel, J., and del Palacio, I. (2009). Global networks of Clusters of Innovation: Accelerating the innovation process. *Business Horizons*, 52 (5), 493–503.

Foster, R. (1986). *Innovation: The Attacker's Advantage*. New York, NY: Summit Books.

Moore, G.A. (2014). *Crossing the Chasm*, 3rd ed. New York, NY: HarperCollins.

National Science Foundation (2021). *Innovation Corps (I-Corps) Biennial Report*. Retrieved from www.nsf.gov/news/special_reports/i-corps/pdf/NSFI-Corps2021BiennialReport.pdf.

Nonaka, I., and Takeuchi, H. (1995). *The Knowledge-Creating Company: How Japanese Companies Create the Dynamics of Innovation*. New York, NY: Oxford University Press.

OECD (Organisation for Economic Co-operation and Development) (2021). Venture Capital Investments, Structural and Demographic. Business Statistics (database). Retrieved from https://doi.org/10.1787/60395228-en.

Porter, M. (2000). Location, competition, and economic development: Local clusters in a global economy. *Economic Development Quarterly*, 14 (1), 15–34.

Porter, M. (1990). *The Competitive Advantage of Nations*. New York, NY: Free Press.

Ries, E. (2011). *The Lean Startup: How Today's Entrepreneurs Use Continuous Innovation to Create Radically Successful Businesses*. New York, NY: Currency.

Saxenian, A. (1994). *Regional Advantage: Culture and Competition in Silicon Valley and Route 128*. Boston, MA: Harvard University Press.

World Economic Forum (2021). *The Global Risks Report 2021, 16th Edition: Inside Report*. Retrieved from www.weforum.org/reports/the-global-risks-report-2021.

# 3. Global Cluster of Innovation theory and practice in the 21st century: COI Behaviors

## Jerome S. Engel and Aline Figlioli

To understand people and their communities the anthropologist observes their behavior and interactions. Likewise, to understand communities that foster innovation as a fundamental characteristic, observing the behavior and interactions of its participants (components) is foundational. Behaviors are how the components within a Cluster of Innovation (COI) and the COI ecosystems create and react to stimuli. It is how they create and react to change. It is how they create or destroy value. Understanding the behaviors of the components of a COI may in fact be more important than having a precise definition of the participating components. As stated in Chapter 2, behaviors are the key to understanding the dynamic of a COI.[1] However simple and obvious this may seem, describing behaviors is a challenge. Behaviors are fluid. They are ephemeral. Behaviors are difficult to observe, quantify and understand from a distance. Despite their overriding impact, they leave scant objective evidence and must often be implied or inferred by the researcher. Yet it is fundamentally important to understand the characteristic behaviors of a COI, as they underpin the innovation process itself.

Behavior describes how the members of any community interact. It is the glue that binds people and ventures together. It can be the oil that lubricates movement or "the sand in the gears" that slows things down. These behaviors can be intentional or implicit, constructive or destructive. Often intention and behavior determine the success of relationships, be they personal or business. In business, contracts and other documents are tools expressing both the intention and range of required and permissible action of important interactions and exchanges of value. These contracts, no matter how finely crafted, often fail to capture all the elements of agreement. The complete understanding often is based in tacit cultural contexts and norms that are necessary to understand but are not explicitly documented. They are learned and understood through experience. One may adopt them without awareness, or with a keen understanding. COI have such tacit norms and tend to share many of them with like communities around the world. These norms help members of these COI to work efficiently together, allowing for standardized terms of agreement, lower friction and transaction costs, and greater speed. This subtle but foundational influence is crucial to understanding how COI function.

Behaviors not only reflect the explicit actions of the participants in a Cluster of Innovation, they are also the means by which tacit knowledge is conveyed, reinforced, disseminated and taught. From a sociological point of view (Hannan and Freeman, 1984; Cyert and March, 1992), behaviors reflect the culture of a COI and its values. They are not fixed or totally predictable in any specific case, but their violation can have long-lasting consequence for individuals and groups who operate outside the accepted norms.

## 3.1    COI BEHAVIORS

Clusters of Innovation can be seen as subcultures, with certain members (components) in predefined roles (the type of component) and with each member expected to operate in certain ways and within certain constraints (behavioral norms). We investigated these patterns of behavior and discovered some unique effects (Freeman and Engel, 2007). An initial breakthrough finding was that the business practices that evolved in Silicon Valley during the latter half of the 20th century were distinct from the usual hyper-competitive business practices. Perhaps it was the effect of operating in rapidly growing markets, as typical of technology at that time as they are today, which generated the emergence of co-opetition (a combination of simultaneous co-operation and competition) versus a pure competition (win–lose) mentality.[2] Most importantly, while these practices led to increased efficiencies, as one would expect in an industrial cluster, they also generalized across industries and formed a cluster defined by its practices, which supported the creation and flourishing of new technology-based ventures. New venture creation was itself the shared expertise and capability of this cluster. It was not limited or constrained to a specific industry. These observations later coalesced in our assertion that Silicon Valley, and like communities emerging around the world, constituted a newly defined COI (Engel and del Palacio, 2009).

In our previous publications, we provided a generalized description of these behaviors (Engel, 2014, 2015). They are summarized in Table 3.1.

*Table 3.1*        *Cluster of Innovation: description of characteristic shared behaviors*

| Behaviors | Description | Examples |
|---|---|---|
| 1. Entrepreneurial process | • Relentless pursuit of opportunity<br>• The context of resource deficit in which entrepreneurs operate leads to relentless pursuit of resources<br>• Hierarchical structures less important than team process and flexible leadership | • Staged risk-taking, experimentation and rapid iteration<br>• Short-cycle experiments that lead to rapid iteration, and pivoting if needed<br>• Failure is understood to be part (and the most probable outcome) of the process<br>• Highly developed capability for raising capital, recruiting people and other resources<br>• Continual opportunity alertness is a core skill and leads to serial entrepreneurship by entrepreneurs, and migration to a lifetime of founding and investing by many |
| 2. High mobility of resources | • Opportunity-seeking mobility is a core characteristic of COI resources, the most important being money, people and technology<br>• The potential for outsized rewards mobilizes and energizes the resources to accept risk<br>• The need to continually evaluate risk vs potential rewards helps disseminate entrepreneurial thinking and skills throughout the COI | • Intermediation of venture capital (VC) strongly influences the cycling and recycling of capital<br>• VC practices and structures (including incentives and rewards) set standards for conduct<br>• Career mobility matches and supports the dynamic nature of startups<br>• Compensation rewards the risk (for example, vesting of equity compensation)<br>• Knowledge and technology migrate with people from venture to venture<br>• Major corporations develop, or are engaged with, Open Innovation programs/processes<br>• High-value executives and key contributors place an emphasis on equity compensation |

| Behaviors | Description | Examples |
|---|---|---|
| 3. Alignment of interests | • Shared risk and shared reward<br>• Shared ownership<br>• Win–win thinking and action<br>• Alignment within the venture and throughout the COI | • Investment structures of venture capital align investors, entrepreneurs, management and employees to strive for big wins, not just individual gains<br>• Employment and compensation methodologies link rewards to the collective success of the enterprise, thus aligning employees' interests with those of the business<br>• Landlords and other resource managers as well as the professional class accept equity participation in lieu of normal terms<br>• The entrepreneurs' common struggle to displace existing incumbents and introduce new solutions creates its own cultural norms and context<br>• Mobility of people, "co-opetition" between competitors, especially emerging businesses and venture capitalists (sharing deal-flow and co-investing) reinforces a generalized win–win mentality |
| 4. Global perspective | • Born-global businesses<br>• Beachhead thinking as a springboard to global markets<br>• Exploit new technologies and business models on a global scale, as well localizing others | • Focus on large market opportunities drives global exploration for markets and resources (funds, talent and technology)<br>• Build a strong position (competitive advantage, compelling high margins) in a defined niche that allows expansion to adjacent and global markets<br>• Brazenly "borrow" and localize established innovative solutions |
| 5. Global linkages | • Linkages between COI through a web of relationships<br>• Formal and informal collaborations on an international basis | • Individuals form bridges between COI, allowing COI components to access and exploit resources (funds, talent, technology), markets and opportunities<br>• Highly mobile and multicultural executives, entrepreneurs and VC distinguish themselves by their global connections<br>• Born-global ventures view market opportunity globally and create a network of international collaborations |

*Source:*    Based on Engel (2014, 2015).

In this chapter, we take this analysis deeper and look at COI behaviors in a three-dimensional view (see Figure 3.1), examining the behaviors of each constituent component of a COI. We will pay special attention to the impact of the rapidly evolving global environment on COI components and behaviors and how this is influencing the adaptive capacity of the COI.

## Behavior of the Core Components: Agents of Speed and Scale

The innovation processes that distinguish a COI are inclined toward radical or disruptive innovation, rather than continuous or incremental innovation. Why? Because in a COI the instigators of action are the entrepreneurs. They are motivated to create high-potential firms that yield high financial returns. It is an aspiration supported by peer norms and cultural context. Real-world successes like Facebook and Google are legendary, and there are thousands of smaller but significant successes that reinforce the stereotype. They garner attention and have major cultural impact. Entrepreneurs, and the venture capitalists that back them, recognize that it is the radical or disruptive nature of the innovation that creates the opportunity for such outsized gains. They have the potential to disrupt and elude the incumbent if traction and momentum can be established quickly; therefore, the behavioral norms of a COI embrace enabling speed, scale and capital efficiency.

Each of the Core Components of the COI brings its special contribution to achieving this crucial mix: Entrepreneurs are the masters of speed and flexibility, with an appetite for exploiting opportunities to disrupt incumbents, often through new technological capabilities or business models. Venture Capitalists provide funding, with an individual and collective discipline that enforces capital efficiency. Major Corporations, when exercising constructive COI behavior, fuel scaling of effective solutions through their hunger to incorporate innovations observed, learned and acquired from the entrepreneurial high-potential ventures that populate the COI. Hybrid Components ease the transitions and interactions between and among all the elements of the COI, generating benefits for themselves and their sponsors, while the Supporting Components of the COI provide a productive and enabling context for the community. We will now examine the key behaviors of each of these components in more detail.

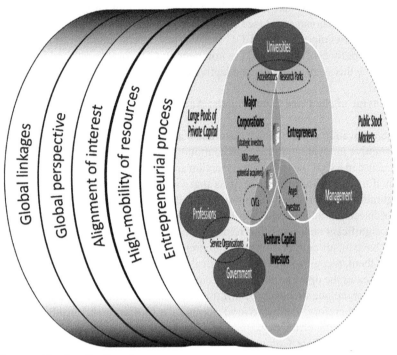

*Source:* Developed by the authors.

*Figure 3.1* *The COI Framework in three dimensions, interacting components and shared behaviors*

## 3.2 ENTREPRENEURS: MASTERS OF SPEED AND FLEXIBILITY

Entrepreneurship is a behavior. Perhaps this is best captured by the famous definition of entrepreneurship often attributed to Howard Stevenson of Harvard University: Entrepreneurship is the pursuit of opportunity beyond the resources under one's own control (Stevenson, 1983; Stevenson and Gumpert, 1985; Stevenson and Jarillo-Mossi, 1990). Entrepreneurial pursuit of opportunity is a relentless activity that involves exploration, discovery, experimentation, adjustment to changing externalities and evolving understanding of the reality as unknowns and uncertainties resolve. All this activity occurs in an environment of under-resourced uncertainty. Opportunity is the lens through which the entrepreneur makes decisions. This is quite different from an operating manager's perspective, which often focuses on optimizing the utilization of known resources. Rather, the entrepreneur utilizes the scale and quality of the opportunity to convince third parties to provide the necessary resources in exchange for economic participation in the realization of that value.

While the most obvious third party the entrepreneur needs to persuade is the VC investor, entrepreneurial resource acquisition is a much broader process. The entrepreneur will apply the same analysis, skills and ardor in recruiting the initial team, workspace, vendors and, of course, customers. All these parties, when agreeing to engage with a startup, are taking an implicit risk. In a COI, all the players – whether directly engaged in the innovation process themselves, or indirectly supporting others – share a tacit understanding of this opportunity-seeking perspective and thereby are more willing to engage, and sometimes even immerse, themselves in it.

Entrepreneurship is the engine to initiate and sustain the value-creation process, and it is well suited to stimulating and exploiting the opportunities that arise out of technological evolution. Entrepreneurial behavior requires speed. There is an urgency to get to proof points that justify the venture's initiation and continuation. Entrepreneurial behavior requires flexibility and agility to implement mid-course corrections (iterations and pivots) when evidence invalidates earlier assumptions, no matter how foundational. Entrepreneurial behavior requires endurance and courage in the face of intrinsic uncertainty and resource deficits. Because of all these, entrepreneurial behavior is inclined toward action. It engages, stimulates and motivates the embedded resources of the community. Entrepreneurial behavior is the heart and soul of a Cluster of Innovation.

**Entrepreneurship and Disruption**

High-impact entrepreneurship seeks to exploit radical or disruptive innovations (Acs, 2010). It is well understood that large incumbent organizations hold the advantage where incremental innovation is concerned. Their access to, and credibility with, existing customers is a difficult barrier to overcome. Small but valuable innovations (incremental innovations) to products or to the business models can be relatively easily introduced and absorbed, providing high marginal returns by increasing the lifetime value of these existing customers at relatively minimal cost. Accordingly, entrepreneurs and the VC investors that support them will seek new or re-segmented markets in which to introduce their new products, services and/or business models, seeking out what may be initially small markets for whom the product or service differentiation is so unique and responds to such an urgent need that the risk of dealing with a relatively unknown provider and solution is justified. From this beachhead market (Moore, 2014), the successful entrepreneur will incrementally expand to adjacent markets, adjacent services, adjacent geographies or some combination of all these. With each step, the entrepreneur will seek out the resources that best match the nature and stage of the risk being undertaken. This opportunity-seeking resource acquisition is the engine that drives the mobility of resources in a COI, be it money, technology or people.

**Entrepreneurship and Technology Disruption**

Technology evolution is an arena where entrepreneurs can often convert the opportunity for disruption and their need to operate initially on a small scale to their advantage. They can leverage their ability to run small marketplace experiments free from the constraints that hold back larger enterprises, who may be reticent to be associated with unproven offerings that can pollute their valuable brands and customer relationships. It may seem counter-intuitive, but it is significant that these small entrepreneurial experiments often exploit technology platforms that were built by some combination of government and large corporate resources. For example, two platform technology producers that have been potent disruptors and value creators and that have enabled the entrepreneurial experimental process to flourish are:

1.  Government and major telecommunications companies: Internet ubiquity and net neutrality give every startup direct access to customers worldwide, bypassing the chokehold of physical retailers, and provide everyone with the ability to create their own megaphone and personal brand; and
2.  Microsoft, Amazon, Google, and IBM: Cloud computing allows startups to scale services quickly without the fixed cost and capital intensity of building and maintaining their own server farms. This allows startups to launch on much less capital, and to scale with server costs being a variable cost funded out of operations, as opposed to inflexible infrastructure fixed costs.

Waves of innovation arise with each major new technology platform. Each new platform brings the opportunity for "creative destruction" (Schumpeter, 1942), spawning hundreds of entrepreneurial experiments as entrepreneurs journey up the Technology/Product S-Curve of Innovation (see Chapter 2, Figure 2.1), each seeking the magic resonance of resources and opportunity. Two current examples representative of that moment (identified with triangles in Figure 3.2) are the emergence of blockchain IT encryption and CRISPR gene manipulation.

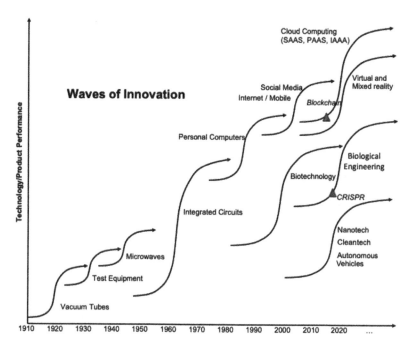

*Source:* Adapted from version published in J.S. Engel, *Global Clusters of Innovation: Entrepreneurial Engines of Economic Growth around the World* (Cheltenham, UK and Northampton, MA, USA: Edward Elgar Publishing, 2014). By permission of the publisher.

*Figure 3.2    Waves of innovation*

For decades, business thought leaders have noted this profound and recurring inter-relationship between technologically driven business disruption, entrepreneurial business innovation and value creation, and eventual major incumbent corporation participation. Major corporations still struggle to participate in early stages of technological innovation waves. This is the zone of the entrepreneur, who is able to rapidly iterate product, service and business models. According to Clayton Christensen (1992, p. 336):

> Established firms find these technologies difficult to spot because alternative architectures are often initially deployed in historically unimportant commercial applications. Typical S-curve frameworks in which a new technology S-curve rises from beneath and intersects the performance obtainable from mature technologies tend to frame architectural innovation only in technological terms. In reality, architectural technology change involves an intense degree of market innovation, in addition to technological innovation. I propose an alternative S-curve framework for assessing architectural change, one which embraces both aspects of such technologies.

## Entrepreneurship and Macro-Economic Disruption

In spite of severe economic conditions that included the global economic crisis of 2008, a series of financial market contractions around the world throughout the ensuing decade and, ultimately, the Covid-19 crisis of 2020–22, entrepreneurs' contribution to local, regional, national and international economic vitality has been incredible. While these externalities caused the failure of many entrepreneurial ventures, for others it proved a boom. It is the very diversity and agility of entrepreneurial ventures and their investors that allowed resources and efforts to be modified as situations demanded. How did this happen? A convergence of seemingly unrelated factors conjoined to make entrepreneurial behavior even more urgent and elegant, leveraging shared societal resources to generate explosive growth and value. Some of these changes have been technologically enabled (for example, cloud computing) and some have been accelerated by the emergence of new entrepreneurial business practices (for example, Product Led Growth). Often these operate in an interrelated evolution. This convergence, for example, is what allowed Zoom to explode when the Covid-19 pandemic erupted in the first quarter of 2020. A COI can be more resilient to macro shocks simply because of the large number of unrelated "experiments" underway, managed by teams who have experience of managing under stress, while under-resourced, and who have the skills and culture to respond with agility and speed.

## Entrepreneurship and Lean Innovation

Entrepreneurs in COI focus on agility and speed as a way to have the best opportunities for success while preserving cash, thereby increasing their operational freedom and preserving their equity. In the last decade this management practice has become codified in entrepreneurial practices known as "Lean Innovation". For startups, Lean Innovation has come to be understood to be a series of ongoing "experiments" to test the entrepreneurs' underlying beliefs about the venture and to respond promptly to lessons learned. When done well, it becomes a way of thinking and management rather than a static planning exercise. It generally utilizes a blend of three core tools and practices:

1. The Business Model Canvas (BMC) maps out on a single page the essence of the business. While large businesses use it to visualize their existing business, startups use the BMC to map out their hypothesis, their belief and their hope about what their business may become. A startup is operating with limited resources and data, so many of its management's core beliefs about the business may be more hopes and guesses than knowl-

edge. The BMC (Osterwalder and Pigneur, 2010) provides a visualization and a common language to define, debate and refine these guesses.

2.  Business Model Discovery is a process of inquiry and investigation and, when necessary, of making minor course adjustments (iterations) or major strategic realignments (pivots). The experiments are initially "getting out of the building" and conducting interviews that emphasize open-minded inquiry and avoid pitching one's own solution. Ultimately, products and customer solutions are presented for feedback. To keep the emphasis on learning and agility, these offerings are minimalist. They are often called Minimum Viable Products (Blank and Dorf, 2020).

3.  The Minimum Viable Product is a physical representation of the product or service whose sole purpose is to test the business hypothesis and the appropriateness of the proposed solution. This widely adopted nomenclature is misleading as the MVP need not work or be viable. It simply needs to represent the assumption being tested (Ries, 2011).

We have chosen to highlight the Lean Innovation process since it reflects elements of successful entrepreneurial practice in many COI and is a codified set of behaviors (for example, hypothesis testing and learning vs deterministic planning). Further, its adoption in this codified format has been endorsed and sponsored by a number of notables, including the National Science Foundation in the US (the I-Corps program), and is being incorporated in the curriculum of hundreds of universities and accelerators around the world.[3] While Lean Innovation is a broadly adopted process, it is certainly not the only one. Indeed, educators and consultants are continually defining and promoting explanations of the entrepreneurial process and manuals on "how to succeed". There is much to learn from many of them. However, at the current time, if one is to be conversant in the language spoken and the new venture development behaviors of a COI, one should be conversant in the vocabulary and processes of Lean Innovation.

## 3.3   VENTURE CAPITAL: DRIVER OF INNOVATION IMPACT

For much of the last 50 years, venture capital has been synonymous with COI formation and impact, and for good reason. Venture capital drives and accelerates innovation not only through the capital it provides, but also through the common set of largely constructive behaviors it promulgates. The ability to foster these behaviors is enhanced through the increasing use of standardized structures and agreements. These structures influence behavior in a profound way, creating a feedback loop that embeds the behaviors in the culture of high-potential entrepreneurship. An example of these entrepreneurial biases is a preference toward value creation and monetization, over the natural bias for control (that is, a win–win versus win–lose mentality). Further, as venture capital becomes more global, these standardized practices and the values and behaviors they engender are likewise disseminated. This enhances the global mobility of resources, as well as the international compatibility of human resources and all the elements of a COI. In the vernacular, one could say that the influence of venture capital is to foster a global entrepreneurial community that "speaks the same language".

It is beyond the intended scope of this chapter to give an exhaustive explanation of venture capital. There are many sources for this information. Rather we will here focus on the behavior of venture investors with particular attention to their contribution to their respective COI and their influence on the emerging Global Network of COI. This is especially noteworthy because we have observed that as common COI behaviors have diffused globally, it is often the VC investors who carry and help instill investment practices that have implicit behavioral influences. The very structure of venture financings influences the behavior of all the related parties. As such, these standardized investment practices have emerged as a key element of the cultural norming tools that build a common global COI culture of innovation. As an unintended consequence, they also encourage mobility of resources, entrepreneurial processes, alignment of interests and a global perspective on opportunity. This amplifies the impact of the linkages and interconnected nature of the Global Network of COI.

## Managing Risk-Seeking Capital

VC behavior drives ventures to have scale and impact with capital efficiency. VC risk and financial exposure are mitigated by deploying a stage-gated process. When faced with a strategic choice between growing exponentially through putting more money to work versus growing incrementally without further investment, the VC investor will choose to put capital to work to capture the potentially outsized opportunity. Since VC investors often sit on the boards of directors of their portfolio companies, this investment strategy influences entrepreneurs to create and implement strategies to strive for maximum scale and impact, with a sensitivity for capital efficiency. Further, the structure of venture financings and the compensation arrangements of VC-financed companies incentivize founders and managers to strive for big wins.

Successful venture capitalists do not seek to constrain worthy opportunities by undercapitalizing them. When opportunities warrant, venture capitalists actively support and seek additional capital for their portfolio companies even when this dilutes their ownership interests. Indeed, a core value proposition of venture capitalists to their entrepreneurs is being a gateway to the broader community of capital resources. The shared value and behavior are measuring success by the value created rather than by the ownership stake or control preserved.

## Why Venture Capital Likes Technology

Technological innovation is often well suited to create products and services that can prove disruptive to existing solutions and thereby ultimately create massive value. These new ventures require capital to translate technology from the lab into commercial products. When successful, the initial market uptake of these solutions provides evidence of their viability (Product Market Fit), and thereby validates the investment of more capital (at a higher valuation) to finance growth. This step function, a continuous cycle of experimentation, execution, validation and investment, is reflected in the structuring of high-potential ventures by a series of capital-raising rounds, at increasing valuations (Figure 3.3 and 3.4). This ability of technological innovation to create "big wins" is a perfect match for the strategies of venture capitalists.

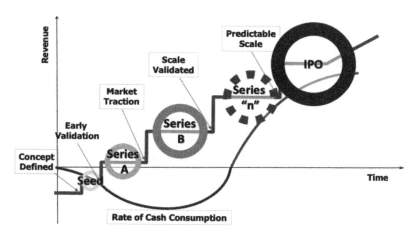

*Source:* Developed by the authors.

*Figure 3.3 New venture staged financing*

## BOX 3.1  THE FINANCING ROUNDS' EVOLVING TERMINOLOGY

| 1980 | 2000 | 2022 | Use of proceeds |
|---|---|---|---|
| • Series A | • Seed | • Pre-Seed | • Concept: V1 Product |
| • Series B | • Series A | • Seed | • Traction: Sales |
| • Series C | • Series B | • Series A | • Scaling: Domestic |
| • Series D, E, F | • Series C | • Series B | • Scaling: New Markets |
| • IPO | • Series D, E, F | • Series C | • Scaling: International |
| | | • Series D, E, F | • Scaling: Sustained Growth |
| | • Series A1 | • Series A1, B1 | • Recapitalization |
| | • IPO | • IPO | • Growth > Liquidity |

*Source:* Developed by the authors.

*Figure 3.4     VC financing rounds evolving terminology*

### Putting Capital to Work: The Screen and Scale Process

It may seem counter-intuitive that a Cluster of Innovation is strengthened by fostering the creation of new ventures that need capital. However, it is the ability of the new ventures to justify capital infusions by providing appropriate risk-adjusted financial returns to VC investors that attracts risk capital to the COI, while simultaneously affording a screening process that helps focus the energies of the members of a COI on the most promising opportunities. In a self-reinforcing spiral, it is capital availability that attracts the entrepreneurs, and this combination attracts the attention of the scientists who seek to see their discoveries have impact, and the success of the resultant ventures that ultimately attracts the attention of the major incumbent corporations, investment bankers and other sources of liquidity. It is a virtuous cycle of value creation that builds on its own success and momentum. This mobilization and deployment of resources initiates with and requires entrepreneurial behavior by many of the participants, no matter what role they are playing (Figure 3.5).

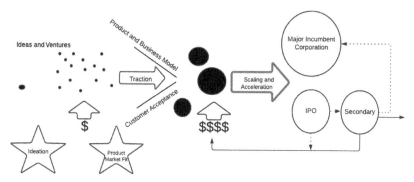

*Source:* Developed by the authors.

*Figure 3.5    The venture screen and scale process*

## Financing Structure Affects Behavior and Culture

As important as the funds provided by venture capital are the terms of such financings. While each investor and each financing is unique, a key aspect of COI is that venture financings follow a general set of norms that create a positive environment for pursuing risky ventures and an alignment of interests that foster win–win environments where investors and entrepreneurs operate as mutually supportive partners. Such norms include:

1.  Investments, no matter how structured (for example, convertible notes, SAFES,[4] preferred or common shares of stock), are never intended to be repaid – not by the company nor, even more importantly, by the individual founders, owners or managers of the company;
2.  Investors' capital is given privileges called "preferences" – common preferences include "liquidation preferences" – and other rights;
3.  Investors have a guidance and governance role through representation on the board of directors;
4.  Founders' shares may be subject to "vesting" that encourages them to stay with the company for a reasonable period post-financing; and
5.  Financings are structured in multiple rounds, at which point investors have the option but not the obligation to continue investing.

Overall, financing terms, and the general investing process, only work if both parties go at risk and work collaboratively as partners.

**Tolerance for Failure**

While failure is not desirable, it is understood that it is possible, even likely. Venture capital returns are non-linear. They are driven by the extraordinary performance of a few investments. Because of this, venture capitalists get comfortable with failure and consider it a natural element and risk of the value-creation process. Risk of failure is perhaps even exacerbated by their desire for big wins that utilize cash efficiently verses modest wins, even if they require little cash. VC investors are driven by absolute cash-on-cash returns (measured in absolute dollar amounts) more than internal rates of return (measured in annual percentage gains). Because of this, the culture of a COI where venture capital plays a big role is very tolerant of failure. The entrepreneurs that lead businesses that fail may be viewed as personally successful based on *how* they failed. Many venture investors value and invest in entrepreneurs who have endured failure and learned from it. They consider the experience an asset.

Successful venture financing is a difficult process. As we have discussed, both VC investors and entrepreneurs benefit from using a multi-step process that matches the capital invested with explicit goals to be accomplished, generally planned in amounts and time frames sufficient to accomplish objectives that will allow for the subsequent round to be done at a high round. This delicate balance can induce volatility and risk. It is difficult to measure the effect of this process unless one looks at a cohort of companies across a time frame of sufficient duration to allow for success to materialize. This is generally ten years (Figure 3.6).

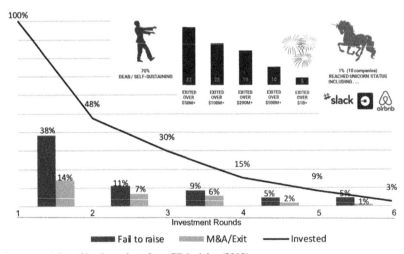

*Source:*    Adapted by the authors from CB Insights (2018).

*Figure 3.6     Success of raising follow-on rounds of VC financing 2008–2010: cohort of 1,098 companies that had successfully raised seed rounds*

## Mapping the New Venture Financing Landscape

"Venture capital" is a broad term that encompasses a complex web of capital sources with varying appetites for risk. This translates into categories of investors. While each investor is unique, they can be sorted into meaningful groups (Table 3.2). This is as much a matter of self-definition as external categorization, as communicating clearly about what types of opportunities are being sought, without being overly exclusive so as not to rule out desirable opportunities, is an important tool for managing efficiency. It is often said that time, rather than money, is a venture capitalist's most limited and precious resource. This time-based economy makes it important to know how to navigate among the great diversity of VC investors. Table 3.2 maps the venture investor community found in a mature COI.

## Rapid Growth has Affected the Venture Capital Industry Structure and Processes

Over the last ten years venture capital has undergone a quiet and under-reported revolution. In spite of the financial upheavals of the Global Financial Crisis, Covid-19 and global political uncertainty, this has been a period of unprecedented growth. This growth is due to several overlapping factors that have a profound impact on COI formation around the world. Briefly summarized, the most notable are (PitchBook and NVCA, 2021):

1. Growth in the amount of VC investment: VC in the US alone has grown almost 400 percent. Global investment has grown comparably.
2. International dispersion and regional concentration: While venture capital tends to concentrate in relatively tight geographic nodes, such as Silicon Valley, Boston and London, the decade has seen notable geographic expansion of the VC investment community to include important nodes in COI in the US, India, China and Singapore. VC is truly now a global process, but still with geographic concentrations.
3. Outsized expansion of late-stage VC investing: The expansion in funding has happened at all levels, but the disproportionate increase is in later-stage deals.[5]
4. Increase in transaction sizes and valuations: The expansion in funding has correlated to an increase in transaction sizes and valuations, especially in late-stage financings, with increasing disparity in valuation directly correlated to the size of the round.
5. New categories of investors participating in venture capital: The influx of new categories of investors, including sovereign wealth funds, corporate

*Table 3.2*      *Overview of VC typology*

| VC investor category | Characteristics | Behaviors |
|---|---|---|
| Angel investors | Individuals investing their own funds | Invest in a broad array of ventures. May be the principal source of startup funds in smaller COI. May be influenced by the opportunity for personal participation |
| Seed-stage | Institutional investors, so called because they are investing funds raised from institutions (see below). Fund size increases at later stages. Small partnerships managing multiple sequential VC funds. Incentivized by participation in investment gains | Smaller funds, often under $100 million. Invest in ideas with limited proof points |
| Early-stage | | Require some proof of concept and early customers |
| Growth-stage | | Require proven business model capable of scaling |
| Late-stage | | Invest in proven teams and business models often seeking to going global |
| Cross-over | | Invest at later private stages. Secure positions in firms they intend to hold post-IPO |
| Regional focus | | Investing in a certain geography. May have government linkages. May be stage-agnostic |
| Industry focus | | Investing strategy restricted. Definition of industry strategy may be fluid. May be stage-agnostic or have a stage preference |
| Corporate VC | Funded by a corporation with a strategic imperative | Overriding goal is creating strategic value to parent. Slower decisions. Risk of conflicts with internal projects and culture |
| Source of VC funding | Characteristics | Behaviors |
| Individuals | May invest in funds and individual deals | Relatively quick decision-making. Not solely driven be economics. May be lifestyle- and values-driven |
| Family Offices | Multi-generational wealth | Part of an asset-allocation strategy. Increasing interest in environmental, social and governance issues |
| Pension Funds | May be very large Tax-exempt (US) | Seeking return on investment to help meet funding of pension obligations |
| Endowments and Foundations | May be very large. Tax-exempt (US) | Large allocations to VC. Long-term patient investors |
| Sovereign Wealth Funds | Often natural-resource-rich countries | Increasing importance. Often strategic objectives to enhance the domestic innovation ecosystem |

*Source:*    Developed by the authors.

investors and cross-over and private equity funds, have increased the funding available, especially for growth and later-stage VC opportunities.

6. Companies staying private longer: With the growth and expansion capital available at strong valuations, companies can stay private longer. This is having an impact on the public markets, driving innovation in the going public process, most notably the rapid growth in special purpose acquisition companies (SPACs) and direct listings.[6]

These factors are of course subject to market declines and contraction. Historically such declines and contractions have been severe and lasted several years. Recent notable contractions occurred in 2000–2003 and 2008–2010. They directly correlate to activity in the public equity markets. At this writing in 2021, these markets are at all-time highs and quite vulnerable in the view of many analysts. Be that as it may, the VC market, perhaps due to the structural element of the ten-year commitments typical of fund investment terms, have proven to be a relatively resilient and stable participant in the COI ecosystem (Figure 3.7).

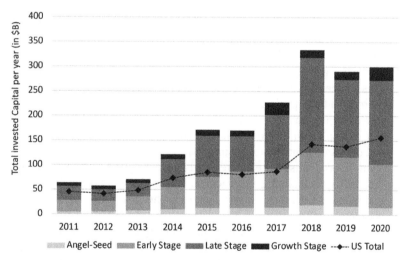

*Source:* Based on Crunchbase (2021) and PitchBook and National Venture Capital Association (NVCA) (2021).

*Figure 3.7*     *Global and US VC: a decade of growth global (per stage) and US dollar volume from 2011 to 2020*

Beyond the growth in size of the VC sector, there has been a change in structure and methods that results in increasing agility and value creation:

1.  Angel investing in startup ventures has become simplified and more efficient through standardization of investment norms. The creation and expansion of formal and informal angel investing groups, networks and clubs has aided this process. Certain investing practices (for example, the use of standard form SAFES and convertible notes) has simplified and sped up the investing process.
2.  Creation of online angel investing communities (for example, AngelList) and an increasing number of angel groups formed around affinity relationships (for example, university alumni) has eased the on-ramp for new entrants and helped the sector scale.
3.  Institutional venture investors are becoming more accepting and appreciative of the role angel investors play. Increasingly they welcome angel investors supporting entrepreneurs at the early stages. This allows the institutional venture capitalist more time to observe and reserve their investment until proof of concept and traction are achieved.
4.  Increasing specialization of VC investors (by stage, by industry, by business model) allows for quicker decision-making and the provision of more expert guidance post-investment.
5.  Adoption of management practices at the VC firm level enables quick and sharp adjustments and decisions in reactions to exogenous shocks. This can be seen in the impact of Covid-19, where many funds performed prompt and sharp triage. Selective investments were promptly curtailed (for example, travel-related), yet others were enthusiastically supported (for example, applications that support work from home, food delivery, and online content and entertainment).
6.  Venture capitalists are increasingly adopting investment strategies that focus on retaining management teams skilled at Lean Innovation, maintaining flexibility, running experiments and agile pivoting when warranted.
7.  Global dispersal of venture capital, financing and practices are increasingly facilitated through formal and informal arrangements (for example, 500 Startups, Y Combinator, funds of funds, advisory board roles).

All the above, taken together, result in venture capital being an increasingly valuable component of COI and their global networks. Beyond the capital that venture capitalists bring, their investment practices create win–win possibilities and reinforce behaviors that foster value creation at scale with speed and agility. That said, taking a long view of the financial markets, we must remain alert to their intrinsic volatility. These trends, no matter how robust, are subject to rapid disruption. That macro-uncertainty, and the vulnerability of early-stage high-potential ventures to capital starvation, are key risks in the environment that entrepreneurs and investors must navigate.

### The Increasing Global Distribution of Venture Capital

The distribution of venture capital has always been lumpy. In keeping with fundamental cluster theory, VC clustered in concentrated communities, both geographically and by industry concentration. The early notable concentrations in the US in the early 1980s were in Silicon Valley, initially focused on semiconductors, and in Boston, initially focused on computers. While industry concentrations have diversified as technology and markets evolved, these historical concentrations have had residual strength. As the entrepreneurial economy has spread its geographic footprint, venture capital has followed (but not led). Now emerging VC economies speckle the US, with notable concentrations arising in Austin, New York City, Denver, Seattle and other cities.

Similar patterns can be observed globally, with nodes of concentration emerging into self-sustaining venture economies. Notable nodes include locations in Israel, the UK, Germany, Singapore, China and elsewhere (Figure 3.8).

*Source:*     CB Insights (2021).

*Figure 3.8*     *Global distribution of VC – dollar volume of VC invested in Q4 2021*

So, while the global impact of venture capital is driving the diffusion and acceleration of the entrepreneurial technology economy throughout the world, it still functions by clustering in geographic nodes, often with market segment and technology themes.

## Reaction of Venture Capital to the Global Pandemic

In March of 2020, as the global significance of the emerging pandemic was becoming an unavoidable truth, many predicted that investment capital for risky early-stage ventures would quickly dry up. Indeed, this was the pattern in 2001 (the internet bubble) and 2008 (the global financial credit crisis). Further, much of the capital that had fueled the sustained growth of VC over the prior ten years was "new" money, from relatively inexperienced and perhaps less committed VC investors, such as the previously noted late-stage investors. Surprisingly, after just a brief period that could be measured in weeks rather than months, VC flows surged at an even greater rate than pre-pandemic levels (Figure 3.9). The causes of this quick reaction were profound – some opportunity-driven, some market-driven, and some government-induced structural shifts:

- Opportunity-driven: As people retreated to their homes for work, for recreation and for safety, the pre-existing trends of digital transformation in everything from retail to work went into hyper-drive. Emerging solutions such as Zoom rapidly displaced legacy solutions. Pre-existing market leaders such as Amazon doubled down on growth, ready to capture market share. The scale and impact of these transitions whetted the appetites of investors who fueled investment at all levels.
- Market-driven: These trends rolled right through the public equity markets, expanding opportunities for VC investor exits and reinvestment. As the public equity market valuations surged, so did opportunities for Initial Public Offerings (IPOs). Also, lax regulation in the US opened up a new avenue for accessing the public equity markets. SPACs, these "blank check" companies, raised fresh funds to acquire emerging firms. This has led to a flourishing and perhaps unsustainably robust new issues market that pours capital into the pockets of entrepreneurs and venture capitalists. These factors, and a continuing need to embrace digital transformation, has put pressure on major corporations to offer fully valued mergers to hot emerging VC-funded startups and to continue their own VC investing strategies (PitchBook, 2021).
- Government-induced structural shifts: Governments responded to the pandemic with massive capital infusions and aggressive monetary policy, driving interest rates to historic lows. This flooded many markets with capital that had few attractive low-risk investment alternatives. Some of this capital inevitably entered the public and private equity markets, accelerating, perhaps unsustainably, market valuations.

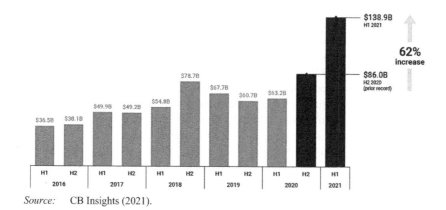

*Source:* CB Insights (2021).

*Figure 3.9    Global funding by VC: quick recovery and expansion post-pandemic*

Taken together these factors have resulted in a VC financing market that through 2021 has been operating at all-time highs in almost every dimension, including volume, velocity, valuations and liquidity. Indeed, at this moment it may be legitimate to speculate that the pandemic, rather than disrupting the VC new-venture-development market, has escalated it to new levels as global investors have focused on the imperative and opportunity of global adoption of innovation at an accelerating pace. This inevitably raises the question of whether this is a "bubble" destined to "burst". While any forecast is difficult, it is reasonable that elements of this change will have sustainable impact. That acceleration and diffusion of the VC economy will have long-term economic benefits, surviving and outlasting the inevitable market contractions that will occur when government stimulus is reduced and even reversed, should inflation control become the preeminent concern. Many of the new entrants to the later- and growth-stage investment arena may be the first to exit, as the imperatives of portfolio balancing exacerbate the gyration. We have seen this cycle before. Rather than concern us, our experience should give us confidence. The lessons from 2001, 2008 and 2020 are that while market adjustments are painful, the VC mechanism is robust. It will adjust, adapt and continue as a force to support innovation and the COI communities in which it participates.

## 3.4    MAJOR CORPORATIONS: DRIVERS OF INNOVATION AT SCALE

Major incumbent corporations are an important component of what makes a COI work, and work at scale. The natural symbiosis of the scale, operating expertise, resource wealth and global reach of the major corporation with the innovation, flexibility and speed of the emerging enterprise makes the opportunities for collaboration compelling. But no matter how apparently logical, the business landscape is strewn with examples of failed collaborations. It is a characteristic of COI that the participants are biased toward such collaborations and experienced at making them an essential element of their business strategy. Being skillful at creating synergistic combinations and collaborations between major corporations and relatively small, young, entrepreneur-driven companies is a critical competency for all COI participants.

In today's rapidly evolving world it would seem axiomatic that financial and business success depends on a productive process of continuous innovation. Yet major corporations have a history of fraught and conflicted relationships with innovation. Again, the writings of Christensen (1997), and others who have explained the innovator's dilemma, state that business success and the scale of operations and financial commitment that ensues trap the incumbent into the obvious priority of supporting its business relationship with existing customers. New ideas, new products, new business models must compete for resources with this proven business. Incremental enhancements that extend an existing franchise are welcomed. But radical or disruptive innovations are often relegated to low priority if not actively killed less they threaten the core enterprise. Examples of disruptive innovations abound in almost every industry – notable examples include:

1. Transportation: passenger train to airplane, internal combustion engine to electrical vehicle, personal automobile to personal mobility;
2. Communication: telegraph to telephone, vacuum tube to semiconductor, personal computer to smart phone; and
3. Retail and hospitality: bricks-and-mortar to online, hotels to shared facilities platforms.

The companies that have been crushed by not adapting to these changes were once household names. Many were built on century-old entrepreneurial foundations. They are now either gone or in sad decline. There is no guarantee that today's major tech incumbents will not suffer the same unkind fate, unless they master the skills needed to overcome this challenge. They may have an advantage many of their predecessors did not. They are relatively young, were founded (and often are still run) by entrepreneurs, were initially funded by VC, and have experienced and benefited from a period of rapid technological change. This history may help these companies build a culture that is more inclined to collaborate with young and aspiring ventures. However, this inclination is not enough. Unconstrained, these emerging giants can be as exploitive as the incumbents they just displaced. An example of this behavior is Microsoft in the 1990s, which earned the nickname "Darth Vader" for its aggressive win–lose approach. Many feel Amazon is likewise inclined. Yet, carefully nurtured, the entrepreneurial roots of these dominant firms can provide an avenue for these companies to build a strong collaborative culture that facilitates sourcing, assessing and incorporating innovations that emerge in the COI ecosystem. Microsoft and others have in recent years paid attention to the importance of doing this well. The Fit and Location Matrix presented in Chapter 4 is a useful tool to help with this process.

The important role of major corporations in creating and sustaining innovation ecosystems is often underappreciated and misunderstood. They bring many critical elements, notably market access, global reach, capital, technical knowledge, and an alternative pathway to liquidity for entrepreneurs and their investors. This translates into accelerating the scaling and impact of innovation and the recycling of innovation investment funds. Historically, the majority of successful technology startups rely on acquisition by major corporations to complete their entrepreneurial cycle and provide the "liquidity event" that realizes an economic return for their investors and employees. This is the incentive that creates the incredible energy of a COI. These contributions by major corporations are key ingredients in the success of Silicon Valley and COI around the world.

## Constructive Behaviors of Major Incumbent Corporations

A particular strength of high-performance Clusters of Innovation is their focus on collaboration and synergistic opportunities for all COI components to engage in behaviors that enhance the innovation capacity of the whole. Accordingly, major corporations look beyond their internal, self-centered performance-based behaviors to the cultural encouragement and rewards for pursuing their self-interested objectives in a manner that also, perhaps unintentionally, furthers the interests of the innovation community. It is this behavior that distinguishes the role of major corporations in a COI versus large companies that operate without the influence of an external innovation community.

In a high-performance COI, major corporations engage and collaborate with other components, notably universities, startups and their investors, to achieve their innovation goals. They can employ a broad array of mechanisms for this collaboration, including contractual agreements, equity investments, acquisitions and partnerships. This requires building strong Open Innovation processes, skills and supportive organizational structures. In so doing, the major corporation exhibits many of the COI characteristic behaviors:

1. Entrepreneurial process: Engaging proactively with the COI community allows the major corporation to experiment while mitigating the risk of

disturbing its core business. It can explore new technologies, new business models and markets with organizational flexibility and relatively small financial commitments. This flexibility enhances the entrepreneurial agility of the major corporation. Further, in certain transactions, the entrepreneurial culture and leadership of the smaller partner can influence the culture of the larger company in a positive way, providing entrepreneurial leadership skills that can serve as a stimulus for constructive change in the culture and practices of the major corporation. Many managers recognize the potential for this contribution and strive to enable it. In those instances, major corporate management will strive to protect the new partner, even in the case of an acquisition, from being smothered and stifled by the demands of the incumbent's bureaucratic and cumbersome processes. Sustaining the entrepreneurial behavior of the new partner is often the goal, not just a by-product of an acquisition. It cannot be accomplished without special attention, structure and managerial skill.

2.  High mobility of resources: There are two critical vectors of the major corporation's influence on mobilizing resources, namely (1) accelerating and enabling resource flows in the COI, and (2) within the corporation itself. Regarding COI resource flows, depending on the form of participation, especially in the case of equity investments and acquisitions, the major corporation is injecting capital into the COI ecosystem, often providing liquidity for entrepreneurs and venture investors. In fact, the majority of successful VC portfolio companies achieve liquidity through corporate acquisitions. Regarding enhancing the mobility of resources within the major corporation itself, the new collaboration, investment or acquisition may create avenues to access new markets with new products and services. The major corporation's array of assets and competencies can be rapidly deployed against these new opportunities.

3.  Alignment of interests: When engaging in innovation experiments that are not yet central to the core of the enterprise, major corporations have an opportunity to frame relationships with a goal of maximizing the opportunity for all parties involved. This is quite different from harvesting a mature opportunity (for example, acquiring a mature business) where a win–lose zero-sum perspective can prevail. Minority equity participation is often used as a tool to establish alignment.

4.  Global perspective and linkages: Major corporations, by their very nature, often bring a global perspective to an opportunity and the resources to exploit it. The benefit of pre-existing scale can accelerate the impact of the innovation exponentially and create financial and strategic value with relative efficiency.

## The Risk and Reality of "Bad" Behavior of Major Corporations

There are challenges for major corporations in implementing strategies to build value for themselves through constructive COI collaboration. They naturally have tremendous bargaining power relative to the other individual COI components. If they exploit that power to such an extent that it undercuts the opportunities of a win–win, non-zero-sum perspective, it reduces their attractiveness as a partner, and if done in the extreme can impair the development of the COI.

The need for constructive, win–win behaviors extends to all the other components of the COI, but perhaps are most obvious in regard to entrepreneurs, the entrepreneurial ventures they lead and the VC investors that invest in them. The causes and examples of "bad behavior" that can arise in this context include (Hannan and Freeman, 1984; Freeman and Engel, 2007):

1. Time asymmetry – Rabbit vs the Hare: Major corporations move at a slower pace. The relatively quick cycle of the entrepreneurial venture is often one of the attractions of collaborating with the entrepreneurial venture. This divergence in speed is endemic, not trivial, and cannot be overcome by simply good intentions. The slower speed of the major corporation is built into its organizational structure and multi-level decision-making. The speed and agility of the entrepreneurial venture is built on its ability to make progress despite its intrinsic lack of self-sufficiency. Entrepreneurship's "pursuit of opportunity beyond the resources under its control" (Stevenson 1983; Stevenson and Gumpert, 1985; Stevenson and Jarillo-Mossi, 1990) drives the entrepreneurial venture's culture of quick decision-making. This is a fundamental cultural misfit that can undercut and erode the enthusiasm for even the best collaborations.

2. Size asymmetry – Your pebble is my rock: Once the terms of a collaboration have been struck, major incumbent corporations can be shy to address issues they consider minor, but that to the smaller organization are urgent. In large organizations, where execution is often delegated to operating executives below the decision-making level, this can lead to rigidity and "operating by the letter" of the agreement. Rigidity and slow morbidity can follow.

3. Career asymmetry – The role of the relationship champion: In almost all situations, to move from opportunity assessment to commitment requires a deal champion, someone who personally endorses the opportunity and takes responsibility for making it happen. This is true for the major corporation, the entrepreneurial venture and the venture investor. The challenge arises in the duration asymmetry of the individual involved. For the entre-

preneurial investor, the decision is likely to be taken at the highest levels, where the individuals involved, the entrepreneurial leader and investors, are often committed to their roles for the life of the venture opportunity, or in any case, relatively long durations. This is not true for the major corporate executive, where promotions and assignment rotations may happen regularly. This loss of the deal champion for the implementation and oversight team can erode support for the collaboration, with a less than optimal result.

4.  Agility asymmetry: All the above points, coupled with the more formal decision-making cadence of larger organizations, create and exacerbate a loss of agility that can be damaging to the entrepreneurial venture.

5.  Power asymmetry: The simple resource imbalance between the parties, when put under the pressure of the risk or reality of the above issues, can lead to agreements that are win–lose. In the short term they may appear successful, but in the longer term pyrrhic. This is exacerbated when a COI is dominated by a single major corporation. Likewise, major incumbent organizations can have an immense positive impact on their respective COI. To see examples of this double-edged sword one need look no further than the impacts of Microsoft, Google, Apple, Amazon, Nokia and BlackBerry.

The first step to avoiding these bad behaviors is awareness. Knowing where the traps are is a start, but is not sufficient. Having experience framing and working in such arrangements is very helpful – but such experience is often not available or accessible. An aid to addressing these issues is having an internal advocate for the entrepreneurial venture, an ombudsman. They can help smooth the relationship and focus on making it productive for all involved parties. This internal "ombudsman" can be a formal role. It is not the same as the "deal champion" mentioned above. Sometimes, this role is played by a major corporation's Corporate Venture Capital (CVC) group. It is an ongoing role, not just at the time of the transaction. It follows the relationship for an indefinite period.

### An Example: Win–Win vs Win–Lose Behavior of Major Corporations

The distinction between constructive win–win collaboration essential to a successful Cluster of Innovation, and zero-sum win–lose behavior can be difficult for the untrained eye to distinguish. It is subtle and many times unintentional. An instructional example can help demonstrate how a major corporation might stumble when interacting with an emerging venture and its VC investors.

As we have discussed, it is increasingly common for major incumbents to seek access to innovation from external sources, and in a COI this may likely be a VC-funded startup. This process is an element of Open Innovation strategy (Chesbrough, 2003). The range of control sought by the incumbent will determine if the transaction is a corporate acquisition, a product or technology license, or a relatively passive minority-interest investment. It is natural that when an investment is made for the explicit purpose of gaining access to a new capability, corporate executives feel justified in protecting that access. And when corporate counsel draft agreements, those concerns get translated into terms of agreement that can in fact have unintended adverse strategic and economic consequences. Therefore, for our example we will look in some detail at the legal structure of the agreement. In teaching VC investing at the University of California, Berkeley (UC Berkeley), we a stress the axiom "Structure drives behavior" (Engel, 2011). This means that no matter the original intentions, over time the legal structure of an agreement has a clear impact and effect on the respective individual and organizational behavior. This is exacerbated when there is a turnover in the personnel involved and new parties look to the written agreements to understand the intent and purpose of a transaction.

In this example, the major corporation's interest is not to acquire the business but rather to observe and learn from the emerging company's exploration of a new market, new business model, or new technology, product or service. Therefore, any transaction should be carefully structured to support these objectives, and constraining the opportunities for the emerging enterprise to experiment and learn would not work in either party's interests. The potential for a win–win outcome is clear. The major corporation has scale and resource advantages, exactly what the emerging enterprise needs; that is, cash, access to manufacturing and scale-up expertise, global distribution and sales organizations, etc. Yet gaining a win–win arrangement can be difficult to achieve. If the major corporation is not skilled at COI behavior, the natural power imbalance between the large enterprise and the emerging venture can easily lead to a poorly structured agreement that works against the interests of all parties. We can explore this by looking at the potential pitfalls in just three elements of the agreement: (1) level of equity ownership, (2) participation in governance and (3) special rights (for example, right of first refusal).

1.  Equity ownership: It is natural that the major corporation will want to receive the largest stake it can for its investment. Optimizing the size of the major corporation's equity can have negative consequences for all the parties. For example:
    a.  Having a large stake can turn away other potential corporate partners or acquirers, as the venture is deemed to be already in the orbit of the major corporate investor. This can limit the potential for exploration and experimentation. Also, by limiting others' interest in the venture it can limit the potential for a profitable exit for all via acquisition.

This perception of "capping the upside" will diminish the ongoing interest of existing and new venture investors and may even erode the enthusiasm of the founders and senior management.

b.  If the valuation is perceived to be distorted (for example, too high) because of the strategic value the major corporation imputes to the investment, it can disrupt the ability of the venture to raise subsequent rounds of financing.

c.  Having a large stake or other indices of control may force consolidation of the financial results of the portfolio company (often losses) into the operating results of the major corporation for financial reporting purposes. While unlikely material to the parent, this rollup of the loss can cause negative optics and cause the venture to lose internal support, especially from the CFO (chief financial officer).

2.  Governance: Though it may seem attractive to the major corporation to have a voting board seat to protect its interests, such participation can have many of the same negative consequences as the undue equity ownership discussed above. It also carries additional fiduciary risks and can be a drain on management's time. A non-voting board observer seat may actually work to advantage of all parties.

3.  Special rights (for example, right of first refusal): Often referred to by the acronym *ROFR*, this right allows the investor, in this case a major corporation, to have the pre-emptive right to purchase the company, as long as it matches the purchase offer of a potential acquirer. In a COI, an environment characterized by a vital VC economy, the participants understand that this right destroys the ability of the emerging venture to attract its best offers. It is an unintended "poison pill" and is resisted by entrepreneurs and their VC investors. That said, it is not uncommon for an offer to invest (known as a "term sheet"), to include this and other controlling and value-destroying terms, when presented by a major corporation not attuned to the proper win–win behaviors of a COI.

These pitfalls can be avoided by keeping a broad view of the value-creation process, recognizing that what one sacrifices in control can be more than offset by the benefit gained by allowing the entrepreneurial venture to follow its own value-optimizing path. Ultimately, the opportunity exists to achieve control at a later point through a fair market value transaction when the strategic value may become a clear overriding imperative. Such behavior is counter-intuitive and foreign to many in corporate management. Successful execution requires expertise and the internal credibility to sustain it over the long duration (often measured in years) of the value-creation process.

While this example may seem full of minor details, failure to understand the impact of such matters leads to unintended damage and is corrosive to potentially valuable collaborations. It is emblematic of many other similar challenges that incumbents face in executing innovation strategies that engage actively with the COI community. The importance of this competency can be seen in the frequency that major corporations participate in the VC market, as demonstrated by Figure 3.10.

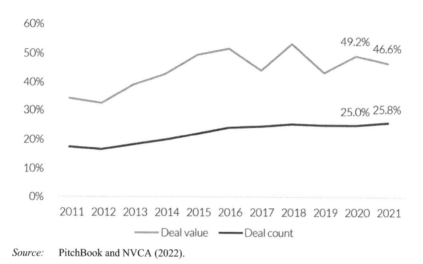

*Source:* PitchBook and NVCA (2022).

*Figure 3.10* *The percentage of US VC financings with major corporate participation*

This section focused on the critically important, and often underappreciated, role of major corporations in creating and sustaining a COI. Chapter 4 expands this discussion, including the presentation of strategies and tools that can help major corporations proactively diagnose their management structure and resource needs to help them successfully craft and implement a strategy to engage with COI and their constituents to build value for themselves, their stakeholders and their communities.

## 3.5   THE SUPPORTING COMPONENTS: ENABLING OF CLUSTERS OF INNOVATION

As stated at the beginning of this chapter, a major refinement in the COI Framework has been the grouping of the COI components into three broad categories. This is important because as the COI is observed through a finer lens, as with any subject more and more details arise. And depending on one's bias and interests, any element may seem to warrant more and more granular definition and investigation. However meritorious this perspective, it is important to remember that a prime purpose of the Framework is to provide a structure to simplify this complexity so one can see the broad patterns and elements and their interactions. So, as we identify and examine more and more detail, the question arises: Are there patterns and groupings that can simplify the complexity? Investigating this question led to noting the distinction between the core and supporting components, and to including the Hybrid Components that blur the distinctions.

The broad distinction between the core and the supporting components is that the core elements are direct principal actors in the innovation cycle. In this context the term "principal" imparts the notion that these participants directly take risk and seek to benefit directly from the value they create. The Supporting Components, as their name infers, support one or more of the core elements in their innovation activities and may support the health of the overall innovation environment and its essential preconditions (for example, government's role in maintaining the rule of law in commercial and civil society). Where these distinctions blur, there is the emergence of a growing sector of Hybrid Organizations and activities. These were discussed in Chapter 2.

The COI Framework identifies four Supporting Components: Universities, Governments, Management and Professions. Though each of these components is of crucial importance, they do not directly create specific ventures. The list is not exhaustive. Most important is to recognize the existence of the Supporting Components and the crucial role they play. With the increasing recognition of the centrality of entrepreneurship and innovation to the health of the economy and society, these Supporting Components are rapidly evolving and increasing their engagement and support for the entrepreneurship, venture capital and innovation activity in their communities.

### Universities: The Emergence of the "Entrepreneurial University"

Classically the role of the university is to generate knowledge (research), to be a repository and conveyer of that knowledge (teaching), and to help make that knowledge available for the betterment of society. It was not until recently that this latter category actually extended to encouraging the commercialization of technology. But this is changing. Over the last few decades universities have progressively undertaken commercialization as an increasingly legitimate activity.[7] In many ecosystems, government has had an active role in moving universities toward fostering commercialization efforts. For the sake of clarity, this section briefly describes this evolution as it has occurred in the US, but its general trend exists in advanced economies around the world.

## Converting research into intellectual property

Since World War II, scientific research at universities in the US has been increasingly funded by the federal government, often through competitive peer-reviewed grant-making federal agencies, such as the National Science Foundation and the National Institute of Health. Prior to the passage of the Bayh–Dole Act in 1980, the intellectual property (IP) generated by this research was owned by the federal government. At that time the US government was funding approximately $75 billion of research per year and had accumulated over 28,000 patents, but fewer than 5 percent of those patents were commercially licensed (GAO, 1998).[8]

With the passage of the Bayh–Dole Act, a subtle but crucial change was implemented: Henceforth the IP would be privately held by the university where the research was conducted. This privatization created an economic incentive for the university to proactively protect and market the IP, and enabled private enterprise to acquire licenses to the IP that would provide exclusive or other defensible advantages. This ability for private enterprise to acquire proprietary rights was crucial, as it could then justify investing in the commercialization process. These efforts are risky, often taking years, and require large financial commitments.

An early organizational step for major research universities was to build professional staffs that specialized in determining which inventions ("disclosures") merited protection and marketing the resultant IP. These "technology transfer offices" (TTOs) were responsible for filing and protecting patents. Their evolution over the decades has seen an uneven record of results, with some notably successful.[9] There have been debates as to whether the principal goal of these offices is to generate financial returns for the university or to benefit the public by easing the transfer of the technology.

It seems counter-intuitive that the privatization of IP results in the broader dissemination of public benefit, but that has been the effect. In the last 50 years, this process has emerged as a major lubricant in the mobility of, and as an accelerant in the deployment of, science and technology. As a corollary, its success has paralleled the emergence of an unrivaled VC economy of innovation and new venture creation. The law inaugurated an incremental process in which governments and universities around the world have placed an increasing emphasis on technology commercialization and, more recently, entrepreneurship. This privatization and commercialization scheme can be judged a resounding success.

## Teaching entrepreneurship

Entrepreneurship is a Core Component of the COI Framework. Today it is recognized as an honorable and even admirable professional choice. Successful businesspeople often self-identify as "serial entrepreneurs", and popular culture embraces the image of the entrepreneurial hero. This was not always the case. It was not until the late 1990s that most universities undertook to teach entrepreneurship. The field was not recognized as an academic discipline, and indeed many leading academics questioned whether entrepreneurship could be taught. In a retelling of the "nature versus nurture argument", many felt that entrepreneurs were born, not made. Since then, entrepreneurship has emerged as a vital academic discipline (Morris et al., 2013), with new courses being offered not just in business schools, but in schools of engineering, applied sciences and even the liberal arts. Acquiring an "entrepreneurial mindset" has emerged as an important life skill and core competency to be taught at all levels and many fields.[10] Prospective students value these offerings, and universities[11] compete on the merits and rankings of their programs.

Regional and national governments are often key supporters of these efforts. Some prime examples that are discussed elsewhere in this volume include the National University of Singapore (NUS), the Technical University of Munich (TUM), and the University of Tokyo (Todai). In the US, notable support has come from the US federal government through its funding and dissemination of the I-Corps program. This program, first instituted by the National Science Foundation and now supported by the National Institute of Health and other government agencies, provides hands-on experiential entrepreneurship and commercialization training to the nation's leading university-based scientists and their research teams (National Science Foundation, 2021). This highly effective immersion training, for which the main author had the honor of being the National Faculty Director, has an influence far beyond the thousands of teams it has trained. It is being replicated and the methodology disseminated at universities across the US and internationally.

**Incubating entrepreneurship: the university extends into hybrid activity**
As noted above, the last decade has seen universities increasingly extend beyond the research lab, the classroom and the library. Increasingly they see themselves as active participants in the innovation ecosystem, extending into hybrid activities including incubation of new ventures and even investing in their pursuits.

## BOX 3.2    EXAMPLES: UNIVERSITY NEW VENTURE CREATION AND INDUSTRIAL COLLABORATION

The Technical University of Munich is one of the most successful startup universities in Europe. We offer founders the best support for starting technology companies. A key to our success is the development of an entrepreneurial mindset among our researchers and students. (TUM, 2021)

The University of Arizona's mission is to improve the prospects and enrich the lives of the people of Arizona [...] Collaborating with UArizona's outstanding researchers has never been easier. Whether you are interested in partnering on novel research, connecting with Tucson's burgeoning start-ups, or locating at our award-winning research parks, our team will work collaboratively with you in an effort to identify and establish win–win partnership. (University of Arizona, 2021)

How did universities evolve into engines of innovation and proactive entrepreneurial engagement? As previously mentioned, government has played a significant role in stimulating university technology commercialization and funding-related activities. In addition, two early developments can be seen where university collaboration was principally with major corporations: industry-sponsored research and the creation of university-sponsored research parks adjacent to campus. An early notable example discussed in our previous work (Engel, 2014) is Stanford Research Park. Both these developments are now common fixtures at universities around the world.

Research parks and their entrepreneurial extension, incubators, can take many forms. For instance, research parks might be sponsored by government, as in 22@ in Barcelona (discussed in Chapter 8), or may be collaborations between university and government, as in the case of Munich (see Chapter 6). Such programs are proliferating and exist throughout the world in many different geographies and cultures, some of which are documented in this book.

It is perhaps a natural evolution that these programs have fostered an interest in providing funding. There are a diverse array of university-related venture-funding structures, including:

1.  Outright non-dilutive grants, sometimes funded by government or university donors;
2.  Equity investments, by various forms of university-affiliated venture funds, including alumni-funded funds, allocations from the university's treasury, university-related angel networks,[12] etc.; and
3.  Equity investments by independent funds that strategically align with the university to help enrich its entrepreneurial ecosystem and gain access to its deal-flow through increased familiarity.

Examples of all these and more are discussed throughout this volume. Many of our contributing authors have detailed how they arise and are deployed in the various geographies and COI. The key observation is not any one specific case – but rather the overwhelming trend of the modern research university toward engagement with the commercialization process. As articulated by Prof. Lee C. Bollinger, President of Columbia University, such efforts now rise in importance to a "Fourth Purpose", equal in stature to the original three (research, education and public service), one that "facilitates, at scale, the transfer of academic learning to real-life challenges and opportunities. Partnering university resources (ground-breaking research and innovative minds) with non-profits, corporations, government, and local organizations to create an unmatched, mutually beneficial impact" (Common Mission Project, 2020, p. 3).

## Government

In a COI the role of government is essential and profound. It is sometimes in the background, providing the precedent and enabling conditions, such as in Silicon Valley. In other economies it can be a very active participant, such as in Singapore and Barcelona. In either case, government policy and action are essential elements of creating and sustaining a COI.

The role of government is often overlooked and underappreciated, and this is especially true where establishing the preconditions for innovation and entrepreneurship are concerned. This can be clearly observed in Silicon Valley, where many entrepreneurs and investors voice libertarian political views, believing that less government is good government. However, investigation of Silicon Valley's history reveals its conversion from a quiet farming community to the heart of the global technology ecosystem was premised on decades of defense and aerospace spending by government, and policies that fostered scientific research in its foundational universities, Stanford and Berkeley.[13] These actions were not taken with the purpose of building the resultant COI. It has been a wonderful unintended consequence, which has captured the imagination of government leaders worldwide. Over the last ten years this interest has only increased globally, with direct and overt government action not being unusual. Indeed, fostering the entrepreneurship economy has become an essential element of many governments' policies.

Governments support a productive civil society through many proactive and passive means.

As it relates to creating and sustaining a COI, three categories are most important: (1) providing a safe and conducive environment, (2) providing incentives for investment and prudent risk-taking, and (3) constructive regulation.

### The rule of law: providing a safe and conducive environment
Of all the enabling conditions for creating and sustaining a COI, nothing is more essential than establishing and maintaining the rule of law. This is of course critical for many elements of civil and commercial civil society to operate and flourish. It is not pursued for the purpose of creating a COI. Nevertheless, it is

foundational and necessary. In its absence all else is futile. Short-term bursts of activity can be created with artificial incentives, but the long-term virtuous cycle of collective value creation through the legal pursuit of self-interest will not flourish without a safe stable society where the rule of law is respected (legal process, adjudication and property protection, including IP).

To understand this imperative, consider two elements: how the rule of law applies to the protection of property, tangible and intangible (for example, IP and access to timely adjudication of contracts and disputes), and to data security. These critical functions of government often fail to be appreciated, but in these times where IP practices and data security activities of nations and major corporations have become the subject of international disputes, such protections cannot be taken for granted and should not be overlooked by leaders hoping to establish productive innovation societies. IP protection and data security are important in themselves, and they serve to highlight the enabling conditions that governments must provide and protect. They have historical resonance to earlier eras of state-sponsored piracy where the safety of the seas was critical to opening global trade routes. In an increasingly resource-constrained world, where competition for natural resources (for example, rare earth minerals necessary for energy storage) may interfere with the free flow of tangible resources, it is a foreseeable consequence that competition and friction will spill over into intangible innovation assets. This will call for revisiting old assumptions and adopting new strategies and perhaps new venues for dispute resolution and enforcement.[14]

### Access to risk capital: providing incentives for investment and prudent risk-taking

Innovation inherently requires investment. In a COI, the innovation engine is the entrepreneur who, by definition, is resource-constrained. In addition to the idea, the know-how and the people to bring the solution to fruition, the key resource is the capital necessary to engage in the endeavor. If the idea and its success were obvious, of course the capital would be available. But if the idea was obvious, it would likely already be a competitive space and an entrepreneurial venture would be at a distinct disadvantage. So innovative entrepreneurial ventures are intrinsically high-risk and have uncertainties that are difficult, if not impossible, to quantify. Thus, investment in such ventures often requires government stimulus, especially in the early stages of COI formation. These incentives can and do take many forms. Examples include:

1.  Using the government as a risk-taking "first customer", as in Department of Defense spending in the US (that unintentionally laid the foundation for Silicon Valley and the emergence of the computer industry, etc.) (Blank, 2021b). Alternatively, in Barcelona the city deployed a very intentional strategy to use the "city as a laboratory" to support new ventures and new

business models, such as their deployment of personal mobility solutions (shared bicycles) that then spread quickly to other regions and countries (discussed in Chapter 8).

2.  Direct financial grants, which have the great advantage of being highly targetable and can be structured to leverage private VC investment. An example is the Small Business Investment Research (SBIR) grants in the US. These are merit-based grants to private companies doing early-stage research and commercialization. They perform a strong signaling function to venture capitalists evaluating prospective investments. In addition, the grants are non-dilutive (to entrepreneurs and their prospective venture investors). This is highly attractive and rewards targeted high-risk venturing and investing.

3.  Government investment in VC funds, usually on a matching basis with private capital raised. This allows government to endorse and accelerate VC funds that embrace desired investment objectives. Examples include the European Investment Fund (EIF, 2021), and in the US the Small Business Investment Company (SBIC) Program of the Small Business Administration (SBA, 2021a). As an added incentive, such programs sometimes limit the financial return to the government investor, thereby providing further financial upside to venture capitalists and those who invest in their funds. An alternative strategy is also being pursued by sovereign wealth funds (SWFs) who invest on straight financial terms but with arrangements to support strategies for cross-border business development or in-country venture investment (Engel et al., 2016; Engel et al., 2020).

4.  Government loan guarantees to banks increase their risk tolerance and allow them to deploy debt capital to ventures otherwise deemed not credit-worthy. Examples include the loan guarantee programs of the SBA[15] in the US, and the Brazilian Micro and Small Business Support Service (Sebrae).[16]

5.  Tax incentives are an indirect means to provide incentives to risk capital. Different governments have varying strategies, including lower tax or no tax on all capital gains. These untargeted rate differentials have little to no effect on providing early-stage risk capital. Some targeted tax incentives, such as the exclusion of certain new venture investing from taxation, have been deployed in the US and elsewhere. Their impact, while positive, has not yet proven transformative (European Commission, 2017; Denes et al., 2020).

**Constructive regulation**

Regulation is often seen as the antithesis of entrepreneurship and innovation; however, it is an important tool of the governments' role in providing the rule of law and a level playing field. Many areas are subject to government regulation, but for the purposes of fostering the creation and maintenance of COI, two areas deserve mention: antitrust regulation and capital market regulation. The first provides access to markets and the latter enhances access to capital:

1.  Antitrust regulation has traditionally been the domain of concern for major corporations who encounter it as a constraint on growth. More recently, however, it has been clear that in the new digital economy, there are viral market forces and economies of scale that create "winner take all" or "winner take most" market domination as the rule rather than the exception. Examples abound and include Amazon, Google, Facebook, etc. This market consolidation makes direct customer access an increasing barrier to new innovative enterprises attempting to break through. Truly effective regulation of this monopolistic tendency has not yet emerged, as the old guidelines were premised on a different economy where consumer protection was the priority. If entrepreneurial innovation is to be valued, then new methods will have to evolve.

2.  Capital market regulation creates a necessary tension between business access to capital and investor protection. In a COI it is important to have efficient private and public capital markets. Private markets are key at the early stages of a venture. Public markets are important at the latter stages where growth and profitability are more predictable. These two markets, private and public, differ principally in whether the shares are available to a limited set of "sophisticated" investors or to the general public. Angel investors and venture capitalists fall into the first category. Existing practices and protections vary by region and currently operate with a reasonable balance between protection and access, though they are in a state of evolution. For example, in recent years the growth in the private market volumes and valuations have been driven by new investors who have traditionally focused on public market investing becoming active in the private market. In addition, there has been a growth in the market for secondary sales (selling by shareholders rather than primary issuances by companies). The public markets are also evolving. These markets traditionally were segmented by several factors including geography and size of the company. Today's globalized digital economy has reordered these conditions. Now companies from any region can register their securities in global markets such as the NASDAC and NYSE. Regional public securities markets have traditionally been considered as important to supporting regional business ecosystems. However, they have an uneven track record, and their viability is threatened by the global platforms.[17] The situation today is fluid. The interface between private and public markets is becoming blurred by new fintech innovators. The continuous and efficient regulation of these markets is essential. They allow emerging innovative companies to access large pools of growth capital and

venture investors to access buyers for their portfolio holdings. Without these "exits" the whole system of venture investing as we know it would not exist. In that instance, the only exits for investors and entrepreneurs would be acquisitions by major corporations. Without the alternative of going public, the power imbalance would collapse the value of emerging ventures and deplete the incentive for venture capitalists and those who back them to participate in this risky sector.

As the above discussion illustrates, the role of government is sometimes overt, sometimes subtle and sometime almost invisible, but enlightened government policy and action are essential to supporting the creation, growth and maintenance of an enduring COI.

## Professional Entrepreneurial Venture Management

Over the last decade a new view of the entrepreneur has gained broad cultural acceptance. Investors' perspectives on how to build startup management teams have also evolved. In the traditional view, entrepreneurs may have been perceived as excellent technologists and innovators, but with limited managerial scope and experience. Likewise, it was the traditional view that those who chose to work in entrepreneurial ventures at the earliest stages were less experienced and qualified than those who worked in major corporations, and that inevitably these lesser talents would have to be replaced at some point by experienced big company managers in order to grow the business.

That view has greatly changed today. Managing high-potential, early-stage VC-funded (or fundable) ventures has become a highly respected specialty, with specialized curricula taught in the best business and engineering schools. These professionals are expert in the stages of business development, in addition to the traditional management specialties (operations, finance, marketing, sales, engineering, product development, etc.), and industry specialties (mobility, communications, etc.). Though comparably skilled to their colleagues in bigger enterprises, they are intrinsically different. They are willing to work in less structured, highly dynamic and higher-risk environments and are willing to function with relatively little administrative support, scaling their functions rapidly as the business scales. They are willing and able to work across disciplines while maintaining deep expertise in their own, and they bring important networks of outside resources and potential new hires. They do not seek lifetime employment. Quite to the contrary, they seek to make a high impact in a limited time, typically four to five years, and then move on to the next venture. And their compensation arrangements encourage and reward that behavior by heavy doses of equity compensation that is earned over time but whose biggest element fully vests in typically four years. Indeed, if a venture succeeds, many early employees and managers will exit with compensation worth millions of dollars. These management professionals take a portfolio approach to career development, seeking opportunities for capital gain rather than strictly level advancement. In a dense COI, this behavior and these skills predominate and seem the norm. They are a sharp contrast to the annual-raise-and-bonus culture of large company managers.

This hyper-mobility of talented managerial and technical talent is a key Supporting Component of a COI.

## Service Providers

Professional service providers such as accountants, lawyers, consulting firms and investment banks provide several important support elements to a Cluster of Innovation and the emerging ventures that it spawns. At the simplest level they provide immediate access to expertise that can be purchased on an as-needed, pay-as-you-grow basis. Fee arrangements in a COI for startups are often quite different from the traditional standard hourly rate practices of most professional service providers. Aligning themselves with the COI mentality, most providers adopt flexible fee arrangements to accommodate cash constraints and align themselves with the venture's goal of creating capital gains. Many moderate fees in exchange for equity and may even additionally invest cash in the venture. Some service firms establish formal fund structures to manage these investments.

More importantly, such professionals maintain active networks through which they can identify and introduce startups to key connections such as potential customers and investors. Their introductions are often perceived by investors and others as being value-added, since they are perceived to function as gatekeepers, screening out unwanted introductions and providing valuable matches. The best professional service providers take seriously their role as gatekeepers and screen prospective clients with care before accepting them. This creates a "halo effect" that benefits startup ventures who need to build credibility larger than their small size and lack of track record infer. Indeed, a key startup strategy is to surround oneself with professional service providers with a reputation for working with the best entrepreneurs and investors.

COI often embrace a "pay it forward" economy, where introductions and information-sharing are an element of exchange and a means of gaining stature and acceptance. Professional service providers are a trusted conduit for creating valuable connections and accelerating the virtuous cycle of value creation in a COI.

## 3.4    LESSONS LEARNED: BEHAVIOR OF THE COMPONENTS OF CLUSTERS OF INNOVATION

Understanding the behavior of the participants in an economic community is essential to understanding the extent to which that community is a COI. In this chapter we identified the shared characteristic behaviors of COI community members (the COI Components in the terminology for the COI Framework). After establishing these foundational characteristics that suffuse the entire COI, we looked at how they are manifested by each of the Core and Supporting Components. In summary, we learned the following:

1.  The behavior of the participants of a COI constitutes their culture. It reflects who they are and what they value. It reflects their aspirations and their attitudes. It embodies tacit elements of communication, co-operation and competition that may not be captured by written agreements or other media.
2.  Participants in COI have characteristic behaviors. While COI are certainly not identical, they do share certain common behaviors and values that define them and make inter- and intra-COI collaborations easier, more likely and more efficient.
3.  These shared characteristic behaviors of the components of a COI include:
    a.  Opportunity-seeking entrepreneurial processes;
    b.  A predisposition for, and mechanism to support, a high mobility of resources;
    c.  Utilizing collaborative alignment of interests as a means of amplifying impact;
    d.  Having a global perspective on opportunity; and
    e.  Utilizing networks and linkages, potentially on a global scale.
4.  Entrepreneurs are the principal initiators of action in a COI. They recognize, frame and pursue opportunities. They must excel at resource acquisition.
5.  Venture investors generally are in a support mode. They provide a key fuel to the fires that the entrepreneurs ignite. The benefit they provide goes beyond the capital they provide to the structures, values and behaviors they disseminate. Their screening provides a "halo" that amplifies the attractiveness of opportunities and attracts other resources (for example, talent, opportunities and capital).
6.  Both entrepreneurs and venture investors seek opportunities for disruption.
7.  Disruption arises from new capabilities (for example, technology), often accelerated past tipping points by exogenous shocks (for example, global warming, Covid-19).
8.  Entrepreneurs and venture investors are not risk-seekers, as is commonly thought. Risk is an intrinsic element of entrepreneurial opportunity. Great

entrepreneurs and venture investors are risk managers, and use tools to mitigate risk, such as:

    a.   Staged investment;

    b.   Vesting of ownership; and

    c.   Venture governance.

9.   COI participants have a fine-tuned tolerance for failure. They recognize occasional failures as an intrinsic risk of new venture creation. The best practitioners strive to derive value and learning from failure.

10.  Venture capital is global and segmented into strata by scale and stage (for example, individual, institutional, early, growth and expansion stages). It also has significant participation from new or "nontraditional" sources (for example, private equity, sovereign wealth, publicly traded mutual funds). These inputs are driving growth in the VC sector, increasing competition for deals and having an effect on deal terms and valuations. This may induce greater volatility in the near and longer terms.

11.  Major corporations play a key role in a COI:

    a.   They are the key to driving true scaling for many products and services; and

    b.   The COI is a major input to innovation for many major corporations.

12.  Major corporations benefit from specialized Open Innovation resources and structures designed and dedicated to COI engagement.

13.  Universities have distinct and crucial roles in COI. They have specialized resources and practices that encourage knowledge transfer and technology commercialization.

14.  Government's role is foundational and cannot be taken for granted.

15.  Service organizations, the professions and management have all adapted behaviors in a COI that enable mobility, flexibility and quick recycling of learning and talent.

The importance of understanding behavior is often overlooked in developing strategies to build effective COI and/or to constructively engage in them. Focus is often given to the sufficiency of the components – for example, the sufficiency of venture capital – rather than the way that capital behaves and how that behavior is reflected in the investments it makes, including the legal terms of investment agreements. In this chapter we have endeavored to make clear that behavior is the key to understanding, stimulating and participating in a community that thrives on creating value through entrepreneurship and innovation. In Chapter 4, we will focus on perhaps the most overlooked of the Core Components of a COI: the Major Corporation.

## NOTES

1.  Our key finding is that the shared "state of mind" of components (their behaviors) is the key attribute that differentiates regular agglomerations from COI. Previous literature about innovation in regional clusters, such as the Regional Innovation Systems (RIS), focus on their actors, networks and institutions (formal rules and informal norms embedded in socio-cultural settings) (Asheim et al., 2019). The emphasis is, by far, on the first two dimensions, relegating what we identified as the crucial element, "Institutions", to a macro/meso approach. We contribute to the literature with an in-depth granular understanding of shared behaviors expressed by each component in thriving COI.
2.  Ray Noorda, the former CEO of Novell, first coined the term "co-opetition" in 1992 to describe a common phenomenon in the computer industry: co-operation between competitors.
3.  The lead author has been very active in promulgating the Lean Innovation process, in diverse roles including National Faculty Director for the National Science Foundation I-Corps program, teaching at UC Berkeley, and conducting Lean Innovation faculty trainings at universities around the world. Currently, the author is the Chairman of the Lean Innovation Faculty Summit Series, a semi-annual gathering of the global Lean Innovation teaching community.
4.  SAFE (Simple Agreement for Future Equity) is a popular contractual structure used by startups for the seed round of financing. It functions much like a convertible note that is also used in these circumstances, both of which are intended to convert into the first structured round of financing at some future point.
5.  Three-quarters of all VC investment dollars in the US were deployed in late-stage deals, the highest portion since 2010 (PitchBook and NVCA, 2021).
6.  Compared to 2019, the number of public listings of SPAC vehicles quintupled to 250, recording a 579.6 percent jump in the value raised to $75.1 billion (PitchBook and NVCA, 2021). An interesting article that further explains SPACs and direct listings can be found at PitchBook Blogs, at https://pitchbook.com/blog/the-case-for-taking-a-company-public-without-an-ipo.
7.  For instance, in the US, the Bayh–Dole Act: Patent and Trademark Law Amendments Act (1980).
8.  Chapter 2 of the previous work, Engel (2014), provides further facts and figures.
9.  As examples, Wisconsin, Stanford, Massachusetts Institute of Technology and UC Berkeley.
10. Find in a blog written by Steve Blank (2021a) the historical view of the adoption by universities of entrepreneurship as a teaching course, and how it has dramatically changed since he created the Lean Business Model.
11. In December of 2020, the third Lean Innovation Educators Summit hosted 603 unique attendees from 65 countries (Common Mission Project, 2020).
12. Examples related to Berkeley are the House Fund (https://thehouse.fund/) and the Berkeley Angel Network (www.berkeleyangelnetwork.com).
13. For a deeper discussion of this important history, see Chapter 2 of our earlier volume (Engel, 2014).
14. For a discussion of international government actions that are likely to increase challenges to the global system, see Chapter 10's discussion of China's Belt and Road Initiative.
15. Banks and other lending institutions offer several SBA-guaranteed loan programs to assist small businesses. While the SBA itself does not make loans, it

does guarantee loans made to small businesses by private and other institutions (SBA, 2021b).

16. Sebrae is a non-profit private entity that was managed by the government until 1990. Like the SBA, Sebrae does not provide loans but offers guarantees for small and medium-sized enterprises' (SMEs') loans and an extensive variety of services to support SME development (Sebrae, 2021).

17. As examples of the fragility of these markets, let us not forget the British TechMARK (BBC, 2002), severely impacted by the bursting of the dot.com bubble in the early 2000s, and the fast rise and fall of the deceased German Neuer Markt (Carney, 2002).

## REFERENCES

Acs, Z.J. (2010). High-impact Entrepreneurship. In Acs, Z.J., and Audretsch, D.B. (eds), *Handbook of Entrepreneurship Research*. New York, NY: Springer.

Asheim, B.T., Isaksen, A., and Trippl, M. (2019). *Advanced Introduction to Regional Innovation Systems*. Cheltenham, UK and Northampton, MA, USA: Edward Elgar Publishing.

BBC (2002). London tech index hits all-time low. Retrieved from http://news.bbc.co.uk/2/hi/business/2016782.stm.

Blank, S. (2021a). Steve Blank: The class that changed how entrepreneurship is taught. Retrieved from https://poetsandquants.com/2021/07/12/steve-blank-the-class-that-changed-how-entrepreneurship-is-taught/.

Blank, S. (2021b). Secret history of Silicon Valley. Retrieved from https://steveblank.com/secret-history/.

Blank, S., and Dorf, B. (2020). *The Startup Owner's Manual: The Step-by-Step Guide for Building a Great Company*. Hoboken, NJ: John Wiley & Sons.

Carney, B.M. (2002). Teutonic tailspin: German market's rise and fall. *Wall Street Journal*. Retrieved from www.wsj.com/articles/SB103343393922429113.

CB Insights (2021). *State of Venture Report – Global: Q2 2021*. Retrieved from www.cbinsights.com/research/report/venture-trends-q2-2021/.

CB Insights (2018). Venture capital funnel shows odds of becoming a unicorn are about 1%. Retrieved from www.cbinsights.com/research/venture-capital-funnel-2/.

Chesbrough, H. (2003). *Open Innovation: The New Imperative for Creating and Profiting from Technology*. Boston, MA: Harvard Business School Press.

Christensen, C.M. (1997). *The Innovator's Dilemma: When New Technologies Cause Great Firms to Fail*. Boston, MA: Harvard University Press.

Christensen, C.M. (1992). Exploring the limits of the technology S-curve: Part I – Component technologies. *Production and Operations Management*, 1 (4), 334–357.

Common Mission Project (2020). *Lean Innovation Educators Summit*, 3rd edition. Retrieved from www.commonmission.us/thought-leadership/the-lean-innovation-educators-summit-december-2020-white-paper.

Crunchbase (2021). Global VC Report 2020: Funding and exits blow past 2019 despite pandemic headwinds. Retrieved from https://news.crunchbase.com/news/global-2020-funding-and-exit/#seed.

Cyert, R.M., and March, J.G. (1992). *A Behavioral Theory of the Firm*. Cambridge, MA: Blackwell.

Denes, M.R., Howell, S.T., Mezzanotti, F., Wang, X., and Xu, T. (2020). *Investor Tax Credits and Entrepreneurship: Evidence from US States* (No. w27751). National Bureau of Economic Research. Retrieved from www.nber.org/papers/w27751.

EIF (2021). Who we are. Retrieved from www.eif.org/who_we_are/index.htm.

Engel, J. (2015). Global Clusters of Innovation: Lessons from Silicon Valley. *California Management Review*, 57 (2), 36–65.

Engel, J. (ed.) (2014). *Global Clusters of Innovation: Entrepreneurial Engines of Economic Growth around the World*. Cheltenham, UK and Northampton, MA, USA: Edward Elgar Publishing.

Engel, J. (2011). Accelerating corporate innovation: Lessons from the venture capital model. *Research-Technology Management*, 54 (3), 36–43.

Engel, J., Barbary, V., Hamirani, H., and Saklatvala, K. (2020). Sovereign Wealth Funds and Innovation Investing in an Era of Mounting Uncertainty. In Dutta, S., Lanvin, B., and Wunsch-Vincent, S. (eds), *The Global Innovation Index 2020: Who Will Finance Innovation?* Ithaca, NY, Fontainebleau, and Geneva: Cornell University, INSEAD and WIPO.

Engel, J., and del Palacio, I. (2009). Global networks of Clusters of Innovation: Accelerating the innovation process. *Business Horizons*, 52 (5), 493–503.

Engel, J., Hamirani, H., and Saklatvala, K. (2016). *Pursuing Innovation: Sovereign Wealth Funds and Technology Investment*. Retrieved from https://ssrn.com/abstract=2864853.

European Commission (2017). *Effectiveness of Tax Incentives for Venture Capital and Business Angels to Foster the Investment of SMEs and Start-ups: Final Report*. Working Paper No 68, June. Retrieved from https://ec.europa.eu/taxation_customs/system/files/2017–06/final_report_2017_taxud_venture-capital_business-angels.pdf.

Freeman, J., and Engel, J. (2007). Models of innovation: Startups and mature corporations. *California Management Review*, 50 (1), 94–119.

GAO (US General Accounting Office) (1998). *Technology Transfer: Administration of the Bayh–Dole Act by Research Universities*. Report to Congressional Committees. Retrieved from www.gao.gov/products/rced-98-126.

Hannan, M.T., and Freeman, J. (1984). Structural inertia and organizational change. *American Sociological Review*, 49 (2), 149–164.

Moore, G.A. (2014). *Crossing the Chasm*, 3rd ed. New York, NY: HarperCollins.

Morris, M.H., Webb, J.W., Fu, J., and Singhal, S. (2013). A competency-based perspective on entrepreneurship education: Conceptual and empirical insights. *Journal of Small Business Management*, 51 (3), 352–369.

National Science Foundation (2021). *Innovation Corps (I-Corps) Biennial Report*. Retrieved from www.nsf.gov/news/special_reports/i-corps/pdf/NSFI-Corps2021Biennial Report.pdf.

Osterwalder, A., and Pigneur, Y. (2010). *Business Model Generation*. Hoboken, NJ: John Wiley & Sons.

PitchBook (2021). US VC valuations report Q2 2021. Retrieved from https://pitchbook.com/news/reports/q2–2021-us-vc-valuations-report.

PitchBook and NVCA (2021). Q2 2021 Venture Monitor (Excel data). Retrieved from https://pitchbook.com/news/reports/q2–2021-pitchbook-nvca-venture-monitor.

Ries, E. (2011). *The Lean Startup: How Today's Entrepreneurs Use Continuous Innovation to Create Radically Successful Businesses*. New York, NY: Currency.

SBA (2021a). Investment capital. Retrieved from www.sba.gov/funding-programs/investment-capital.

SBA (2021b). Resources. Retrieved from www.sba.gov/offices/headquarters/ofa/resources/11421.

Schumpeter, J.A. (1942). *Capitalism, Socialism and Democracy*. New York, NY: Harper Perennial.

Sebrae (2021). 700 service centers throughout Brazil. Retrieved from www.sebrae.com.br/sites/PortalSebrae/canais_adicionais/sebrae_english.

Stevenson, H.H. (1983). *A Perspective on Entrepreneurship*. Harvard Business School Working Paper 384-131.

Stevenson, H.H., and Gumpert, D.E. (1985). The heart of entrepreneurship. *Harvard Business Review*, March–April, 85–94.

Stevenson, H.H., and Jarillo-Mossi, J.C. (1990). A paradigm of entrepreneurship: Entrepreneurial management. *Strategic Management Journal*, 11 (Summer), 17–27.

TUM (2021). TUMentrepreneurship. Retrieved from www.tum.de/en/innovation/entrepreneurship.

University of Arizona (2021). Research, innovation and impact. Retrieved from https://corporate.arizona.edu/.

# 4. Major Corporations and Open Innovation: capturing value from disruptive innovation

**Jerome S. Engel, Dickson Louie and David Charron**

## 4.1   INTRODUCTION

As the pace of technology disruption accelerates, many CEOs know that innovation is key to their business's survival and success. However, recent surveys of senior business leaders indicate that they believe their organizations are slow to innovate (CB Insights, 2018). When they do, it is often in small incremental steps and not the radical or disruptive innovation needed to capture value from technological change or the business model reconfigurations it enables. This is a core dilemma for incumbent organizations: How to embrace radical and possibly disruptive innovation, while continuing to execute the core business and meet the quarterly performance expectations of investors? Successful innovation implementation in today's winner-take-all economy often requires operating with speed and scale (Weiblen and Chesbrough, 2015). Startups can bring speed and agility to innovation. Incumbents can bring scale, credibility, and resources. The question is: What are the right structures to align incentives among startups and incumbent organizations that encourage this robust win–win value creation? The Cluster of Innovation (COI) Fit and Location Matrix, introduced in Chapter 2 and explained in this chapter, offers a new way for leaders of incumbent organizations to develop, visualize, and communicate their innovation strategies, and determine what organizational resources they need for execution. It is also a tool for entrepreneurs leading emerging businesses, both those inside an incumbent firm and those in free-standing startups, to understand the options and strategies available for scaling through collaboration with incumbents. This framework builds on and complements concepts of COI, Open Innovation, and business model innovation.

To illustrate the use of the Matrix, this chapter examines the case of Google (Alphabet) and maps how it innovated across all the four quadrants of the

Matrix in its pursuit of geo-mapping, mobile technology, social networks, and augmented reality (AR) innovation, helping to create profound product and service innovations along the way, including Google Earth, Maps, Street View, and the mobile gaming sensation *Pokémon Go*. The COI Fit and Location Matrix is applied to illuminate the Keyhole–Google Geo–Niantic Labs value-creation pathway, where at each stage benefits and returns are generated for all stakeholders. The Matrix visualizes Open Innovation strategy in a new way, revealing a flexible innovation strategy, facilitated by a COI ecosystem, embedded in a series of transactions. It provides an integrated view that links strategy, transactions, and the tools necessary for execution and implementation: the entire flow of innovation from inside the incumbent, to a spin-out to an independent startup, the collaboration of the startup with other incumbents and venture capitalists, and finally the introduction of technical innovation embedded in a blockbuster consumer entertainment product.

### 4.1.1   The Case of Google and Niantic Labs

During the summer of 2016, *Pokémon Go*, a mobile AR game based upon the popular animated characters from Japan, found itself an unexpected worldwide hit. Within days after its July 6, 2016, U.S. release, *Pokémon Go* had an estimated 28.5 million daily unique users – equivalent to a tenth of all U.S. Internet users – and suddenly became front-page news (Frommer, 2017). Much was reported on the sudden explosion of millions of mobile phone users, many of whom had little prior experience with mobile gaming, roaming the streets trying to virtually capture one of the 721 *Pokémon* characters. Pikachu, Jigglypuff, Charizard, and their *Pokémon* buddies had never been experienced in this novel context before.

Few understood that what they were witnessing was not just a new disruptive technology but, equally important, the manifestation of one of the most cogent case examples of the Open Innovation concept. Niantic Labs, *Pokémon Go*'s publisher, was a recent spin-out from Google. Its lineage spanned a 12-year period, where it evolved from a venture-capital-funded startup, Keyhole Software, to a Google division, Google Geo, which played an important role as Google scaled from $3.2 million in revenue in 2004 to $21.5 billion in 2016. Ultimately, it re-emerged, led by many of the original management team, as an independent unit before being spun out as a standalone company. At each stage, the management team, driven by John Hanke, pursued a consistent vision that is reflected in the products and services they created. At any step along the way, this value creation could have easily been derailed by the impact of the major transactions and organizational transitions they experienced. How did they navigate this journey? At each stage, win–lose outcomes were avoided and non-zero-sum win–win strategies visualized and transactions implemented, creating value for all stakeholders: founders, employees, investors, the acquirer, and future strategic partner(s). This makes it a great case to illuminate a parallel success of entrepreneurship and corporate innovation management.

## 4.2    THE CHALLENGE OF INNOVATION

Senior executives of incumbent organizations agree that the pursuit of corporate innovation is of high strategic importance (CB Insights, 2018). Yet many have failed to prepare their organizations to take advantage of the full range of options to accelerate innovation, especially in customer-facing products, services, and business models. Too many incumbent organizations place an outdated emphasis on internal product development at the same time as investment in long-term internal research has been curtailed. As the inputs for innovation are often from existing employees and customers, innovation initiatives are often incremental (CB Insights, 2018). Incumbents are therefore at risk of being blind-sided and exposed to disruption from rapidly scaling startups fueled by venture capital and easy direct customer access through the Internet.

As we enter this century's third decade, the rate of business innovation continues to accelerate, challenging all incumbents' ability to maintain their competitive edge. The model of the enterprise that excels through internal innovation has been shattered by the reality of new ventures that achieve true scale and competitive advantage through rapid cycles of exploration, experimentation, and distribution. These patterns are perhaps most clearly demonstrated in Internet-related disruptions, such as Amazon, Google (Alphabet), Netflix, and Facebook. The current cycle of disruptive innovation is shaking every industry to its core, be it energy, manufacturing, transportation, health care, hospitality, media, consumer products, fashion, or natural resources. Managing innovation for an enterprise is no longer a simple matter of new product development, nor is it simply adapting to the new information technology realities. Instead, innovation has become an ongoing strategic imperative that engages with all aspects of the enterprise. These activities go beyond the boundaries of the legal enterprise but can engage with the entirety of the innovation ecosystem. New product, service and business model development is now only one component of a broader program that must embrace learning from and collaborating with ventures outside the enterprise (Engel, 2011). The COI Fit and Location Matrix can help managers – especially those at incumbent organizations – visualize a true Open Innovation strategy to capture these opportunities, identify the organizational capabilities necessary to exercise this strategy, and assess where action is needed to build and sustain new organizational competencies.

### 4.2.1    Innovation at Speed and Scale

Innovation in the 21st century requires speed (rapid and continuous experimentation) and scale (the ability to think and act globally) (Engel, 2011). Business models of incumbent organizations are being disrupted by new substitutes being offered by different entrants every day, or what Clayton Christensen described as "a process by which a product or service takes root initially in simple applications at the bottom of the market and eventually moves upmarket, eventually displacing established competitors" (Christensen, 2021). The challenge for these incumbent organizations is how to execute and innovate at the same time. The incumbent organization, dominant and successful in its core business, has a surprising challenge, sometimes referred to as the "success trap" (Walrave, Van Oorschot, and Romme, 2011). The very success that fuels the business traps it in execution mode, the need to continue its uninterrupted success, disabling it from the risk-taking experimentation necessary for innovation. This is especially true when such innovation involves its existing markets and customers. The solution to the success trap is the development of the ambidextrous organization, an organization that can both innovate and execute (Tushman and O'Reilly, 1996). This is often pursued through the utilization of structures that segregate new business development into specialized units, accelerators, and skunkworks (Lockheed Martin, 2021). Such structures, when properly implemented, augment an organization's dynamic capabilities and the firm's "ability to integrate, build, and reconfigure internal and external competences to address rapidly changing environments" (Teece, Pisano, and Shuen, 1997, p. 516); however, they can induce their own rigidity and self-perpetuating encumbrance on continuous innovation. So, what is the solution?

Emerging ventures have a complementary challenge. While startups have this greater flexibility, and the entrepreneurial practice of Lean Innovation enables rapid and continuous business experimentation and adaption (Blank, 2013), emerging ventures face the challenge of mounting the resources and access needed to achieve scale. These complementary factors can lead to fruitful opportunities for both the incumbent enterprise and the emerging venture if pursued by both with the necessary vision and skill.

Bringing a COI perspective can help organizations apply Open Innovation with a sustained and broad worldview. It helps incumbent organizations recognize opportunities to capture value from external innovation available from the other COI participants without distracting from the need for sustained excellence in execution of their core business. Open Innovation helps the enterprise look beyond its legal boundaries, gaining access to the agility of Lean Innovation entrepreneurship. For example, by adopting corporate venture capital practices, the enterprise can gain broad access to the startup ecosystem and selectively invest in entrepreneurial ventures without immediately encumbering them with constraints on their further evolution, or risking the enterprise's core business, customer relationships, and brand, or imposing unintended boundaries on the scope of its own future endeavors (Engel, 2011). Likewise, the incumbent can spin out valuable innovations that do not strategically align with their core business, thereby allowing the new businesses to create value on their own merit, while creating value for the "parent" enterprise through capital appreciation of the portion of ownership that is retained. Executing these strategies successfully is not simply a matter of executing transactions. Successful value creation requires adoption of the constructive win–win COI behaviors and values identified and enumerated in Chapter 3.

### 4.2.2 The 21st-Century Opportunity

Entrepreneurship and innovation have long gone hand in hand in the parlance of business lore. What is new in the 21st century is the speed and scale with which new ventures have brought forth highly successful new products and services, often at the expense of slower incumbents. Lean Innovation practices have not only accelerated product and service innovation, they have also accelerated business model experimentation, often disintermediating supply chains and disrupting customer relationships.

There are an unprecedented number of resources available to support the creation and growth of these new ventures (Weiblen and Chesbrough, 2015). On the formation front, universities, government agencies (for example, the National Science Foundation I-Corps [NSF, 2021]), and others have developed curriculum and specialized incubators and accelerators to foster technology commercialization. To scale the best of these ventures, there is an abundance of capital available to startups and emerging enterprises despite the COVID-19 pandemic (PitchBook and NVCA, 2021) – venture capital in the U.S. remains on a decade-plus long boom.[1] Combined with a continuing digital disruption, the disruptive impact of startups has never been more profound.

Startup funds are available from multiple sources, including individual (angel) investors, venture capital and private equity funds, sovereign wealth funds, and other investors who historically restricted their investments to publicly traded securities. With this surfeit of funds, firms are staying private longer, allowing them to escape or at least delay the pressure for quarterly profitability, which would otherwise constrain flexibility and investment in growth. This startup innovation capability is accelerated not just by these additional investor resources, but also by the massive reduction in the cost of business experimentation and scaling provided by the impact of the Internet, the cloud, the gig economy, and other attributes of distributed and shared technology platforms.

These emerging ventures do not need to be seen by incumbents solely as disruptors and competitors. With the lens of Open Innovation and COI, and the perspective of the COI Fit and Location Matrix, these ventures become innovation resources to the incumbent. From the emerging ventures' perspective, incumbents can provide accelerated access to markets and customers, allowing their innovations an opportunity for greater impact. So, taking a COI perspective, these competitors can become mutually beneficial collaborators.

Given this transformation of the startup ecosystem, leaders of both established incumbent and emerging enterprises are increasingly considering how collaboration can be part of their overall innovation strategy to capture value. At its simplest level this may occur through merger. More subtly, it may be through adopting corporate venture capital strategies or through lightweight governance models of engagement with larger pools of startups (Weiblen and Chesbrough, 2015). But in all cases, truly capturing the value of the innovation skills and culture requires special approaches which emphasize win–win, non-zero-sum outcomes.

## 4.3    OPEN INNOVATION

The term "Open Innovation" was originally coined by Henry W. Chesbrough at the Haas School of Business at the University of California, Berkeley, as:

> a paradigm that assumes that firms can and should use external ideas as well as internal ideas, and internal and external paths to market, as they look to advance their technology. Open Innovation processes combine internal and external ideas into architectures and systems [...] The business model utilizes both external and internal ideas to create value, while defining internal mechanisms to claim some portion of that value. Open Innovation assumes that internal ideas can also be taken to market through external channels, outside the current businesses of the firm, to generate additional value. (Chesbrough, 2006, p. 1)

The rapid pace of innovation driven by digital disruption, globalization, and shorter product life cycles has put a premium on keeping an open mind and speed. The Open Innovation concept provides a theoretical foundation for how companies can further extract the most value in bringing their products to market, using both internal and external routes, by working with startup entities.

A classic portrayal of Open Innovation is as a funnel where the portfolio of internal research and development (R&D) projects is also complemented by external projects secured through several different paths en route to market commercialization: R&D services, joint venture, in-licensing, out-licensing, external technology, spin-out, spin-in, divestiture, and merger and acquisition. The classic model is illustrated in Figure 4.1. The four key COI Fit and Location Matrix strategy categories (Internal Development, Acquisition, Investment, and New Business) are superimposed on the figure to show how they typically relate to the classic portrayal. These strategy categories, and their interrelation with the sources of innovation and the tools to implement them, are explained later in this chapter.

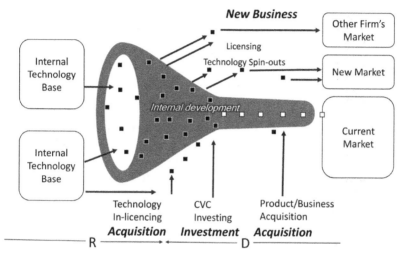

*Source:* Adapted by the authors from Chesbrough (2003).

*Figure 4.1*   *The classic Open Innovation Model and the four Fit and Location Matrix strategy categories*

The limitation of this classic visualization of Open Innovation is that it is product/service-development-centric. It does not give sufficient weighting to business model innovation. It is also silent to the need to support the elements of the ecosystem outside of the enterprise that enhance, enable, and extend core products and services. The COI Fit and Location Matrix highlights the importance of these elements, aggregating them as "non-core" but important elements. Understanding the distinction between what is core and non-core (but still important) opens up a broad array of strategy options that are discussed later in this chapter. The Matrix overcomes these deficiencies and also links the strategies, resources, and capabilities needed to identify and implement the various business relationships.

An example of a business strategy error that utilization of the COI Fit and Location Matrix might have helped avoid is the often-cited example of Xerox and the personal computer revolution. Xerox classically failed to recognize the

value of an internally developed capability and product vision that did not suc-
cinctly align with its existing product line or customer base. During the 1970s,
Xerox's scientists created an early prototype of the modern personal computer,
complete with a graphic user interface (GUI), a handheld mouse, and Ethernet
technologies, at its Palo Alto Research Center (PARC) division. Established
in 1970, PARC was Xerox's corporate research lab, whose mandate was to
"invent the technologies of the future." However, it was Apple, not Xerox, that
ultimately became the first company to commercially launch a personal computer using these technologies, with introduction of the Macintosh computer
in 1984.[2] Five years earlier, PARC had allowed Apple's co-founder Steve Jobs
to visit its lab, in exchange for the opportunity to invest $1 million for a tiny
percentage of Apple stock. Steve Jobs immediately recognized the commercial
value of PARC's work. "You're sitting on a gold mine," Jobs reportedly told
his PARC briefers. "I can't believe Xerox is not taking advantage of this"
(Isaacson, 2011, p. 97). Had Xerox not treated the technologies developed at
PARC as an afterthought to its core business of photocopying machines, and
the toner they copiously consumed, they might have supported Apple more
robustly in more of an Open Innovation mindset (Chesbrough, 2006).

## 4.4    THE CLUSTER OF INNOVATION FIT AND
LOCATION MATRIX

Chief innovation officers and managers of corporate innovation operate
across complex markets and timeframes. The COI Fit and Location Matrix
is a framework for characterizing the potential alternatives for the innovation
process. Managers use the framework to build capabilities, link to sources of
innovation, and create successful strategies that create value. The Matrix contains methodologies that exploit the broader concepts of Open Innovation and
COI, building a culture and structure around the business of innovation with
a focus on capturing value for the firm.[3]

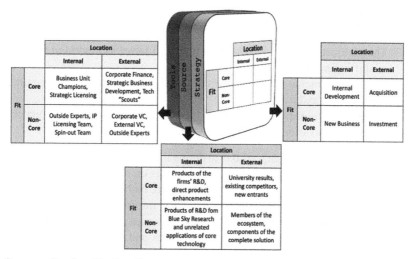

*Source:* Developed by the authors.

*Figure 4.2 The COI Fit and Location Matrix and its three layers*

The framework comprises the following elements, as illustrated in Figure 4.2:

1. Fit: The Fit is an expression of an existing business's activities. Activities that fit in the "core" are existing lines of business regardless of their growth or decline status. Non-core activities represent lines of business that are not directly related to, or not yet related to, the core businesses, but are still supportive of them and possible future business strategies.
2. Location: The Location provides an "ownership" point of view. The firm owns internal items and does not control external businesses, though it may have minority stakes in or other business connections to them.
3. Layers of activity: Innovation management requires three layers of activity. The Strategy layer sets innovation goals and matches them to methods. The Source layer represents where and how innovation arises in the ecosystem. The Tools layer provides an overview of the people, organizational units, and skills an innovation manager will utilize to implement their strategy.

The art of innovation and a firm's ability to constructively engage with its ecosystem is reflected in how it navigates the COI Fit and Location Matrix. Experienced innovators will recognize where firms fail to support the open mindset and will foresee opportunity and potential disruption. Some of the more common failure points include:

1. The embrace of status quo business lines and business models in the face of shifting markets;
2. Legal departments that are risk-averse and unfamiliar with the required transactions; and
3. Misaligned incentives and fear of failure or negative consequences (viewing innovation as a career-limiter).

The framework allows organizations to define the critical skills and competencies needed to support Open Innovation strategies on a sustained and targeted basis. Open Innovation opportunities often require mobility and flexibility that is visualized by crossing the boundaries of the framework, from external to internal and from non-core to core. The case examples presented will illustrate how opportunities move across those boundaries and how firms can capture value from those exchanges.

---

### BOX 4.1   NETFLIX'S STRATEGIC MOVES MAPPED ONTO THE FRAMEWORK

The evolution of Netflix from an entertainment distribution company into a fully vertically integrated entertainment production and distribution enterprise reflects a multitude of business model transitions and business sourcing models.

- Startup phase: Netflix started its business distributing feature films and other externally generated entertainment content through the mail on a subscription basis. The business it disrupted was location-based businesses, such as Blockbuster and Redbox, which rented DVDs on a time basis. This initial business model shift proved massively successful against these well-established incumbents. Netflix also focused on acquiring rights from content-owner studios. The combination of internal development of a disruptive distribution business model and external acquisition of proprietary content (where others had not succeeded) fueled the company's initial subscriber and revenue growth.
- Streaming phase: During the early 2000s management could see the possibility of digital distribution of content. Other companies had been experimenting with video-on-demand distribution for years, and the technology had not yet fully developed. Netflix had an advantage in its *sources* and *tools* for innovation management. That advantage stemmed

from its deep connections to its innovation ecosystem, located in Silicon Valley, where many of the relevant technologies and supporting companies were developing, and having well-connected venture capital investors.[4] While Netflix did not invest directly in the technologies (the external, non-core quadrant), its venture investors did, and were keeping tabs on the capabilities available to support the streaming. The other sources of innovation for Netflix were their content providers. Netflix did invest in building systems to enhance trust with those providers to obtain the necessary rights to stream the content.

- Shifting the definition of its core business and the spin-out of Qwikster: Video streaming started as a new business inside Netflix, and its success rapidly pushed DVD distribution out of the core business definition. Netflix attempted to spin out the DVD business (still a highly viable enterprise) in 2011 as Qwikster. Attempts to disentangle the DVD and streaming businesses caused significant customer outrage and was deemed not feasible. Netflix quickly shuttered Qwikster, and essentially terminated the business. Not all spin-outs are successful.
- Exclusive content: During the 2010s, Netflix began experimenting with exclusive content ownership and creation. In effect, it would become a second core business, a studio. This activity started with both investment in and acquisition of content created externally. That experience informed the creation of the internal studio business and the company's shift towards production. Netflix did not acquire an existing studio. It chose to build its capabilities.

Netflix is an example of a company that was willing to disrupt its business model primarily by learning from external relationships and creating new business units inside the company. As you look at the COI Fit and Location Matrix, you can see the company's activities across the quadrants and in each layer.

### 4.4.1 Defining Fit and Location

#### Core versus non-core business: defining "fit"

Fit relates to the innovation's relationship to the firm's core strategies. Core businesses are those that are owned and operated by the business, and produce significant value, whether measured by profits, expected future value, or strategic positioning. Core innovations and capabilities, whether technology, product, business model or business relationship, are by definition strategically critical to sustaining and/or growing the business.

Non-core elements are comprised of businesses or resources that might not be appropriate for the enterprise to develop itself or to acquire or control, but are appropriate for its support or investment. There are two sub-categories of non-core ventures or capabilities: (1) those that are elements of the ecosystem that support the existing enterprise (for example, apps on the iPhone at the time of its 2006 introduction that help create compelling use cases and demonstrate desirable features), and (2) those that hold the promise of potentially emerging as future core businesses for the enterprise. There are many good reasons not to acquire such ventures too early.

A common "fit" problem stems from the rigidity that arises for most large firms having a relatively fixed operational model focused on scale and scope. These relatively inflexible modes can be incompatible with new ventures, who often exploit their relative flexibility to experiment with various business models in disruptive conditions. Therefore, they are rarely steady-state. Innovation managers need to be adept at managing the challenges of the potential for pivots and iterations on product vision, business models, and dynamic movement among the quadrants.

### Dynamic movement between non-core and core

Some core businesses decline over time due to competition, market erosion, or supply chain dynamics. In such instances they may move to the non-core status before they may be phased or spun out. These are some of the most difficult and fraught decisions businesses make and often indicate the need to develop new core business lines. IBM and its transition from its core hardware-centric computer infrastructure to a software and services full-solution provider model provides an example of how substantial and challenging such transitions can be, even when successful. Innovations that are "non-core" are still important to the business taken as a whole but are not essential at the current time. They may become essential in the future or are complementary and help create a more robust capacity or dynamic user experience.

Creating new business lines that move from non-core to core happens through either internal investment like Netflix's studio business or the acquisition of new external businesses. The distinction of what is core, and therefore must, if possible, be an internal competency, versus what is important but not core is a critical, subtle, and potentially fluid distinction. For example, the chaotic emergence of crypto currencies during the early 2020s, by both fringe and mainstream providers, has many businesses across the entire business spectrum engaging in experiments to decide how to adapt to this radically new currency and payments technology. For some, like financial institutions, this is clearly an existential threat. If it succeeds at scale, as it now appears it will in some forms that may not even exist at this writing, these institutions will have to make dealing with these currencies a core competency. For others, such as retail establishments, it will undoubtedly be important, but not perhaps a necessary core competency. By analogy, one can think of credit cards. Most major retail and consumer-facing businesses offer credit cards to strengthen customer loyalty. While major retail businesses initially experimented with building their own proprietary credit card systems, today those cards are universally managed by third parties (for example, Visa and MasterCard) who have built the robust integrated systems that benefit so significantly from scale. Even banks use their services.

The distinctions and interactions between core and non-core often take years of investment (or disinvestment) and struggle. These are perhaps the most serious decisions for the highest levels of management. A clear vision and an open mind, provided superb and unbiased information and diligent non-political processes, are helpful. But these cannot guarantee success. Business leaders will need both the strategic vision and the operational capacity to execute.

### Internal versus external: defining "location"
Location identifies where an opportunity arises. Stated simply, opportunities either exist or arise inside or outside the enterprise. Some opportunities straddle the boundary with an entrepreneur internal to the firm and the technology outside, or vice versa. When considering location, first determine the locus of control for that opportunity. In the Netflix streaming example (Box 4.1), the control of the technology was outside the enterprise, but the control of the content rights was inside the enterprise (or could, through normal business practice, be acquired). The technology, however, was generally available to interested parties and not exclusively controlled. Having control (or the ability to gain control) over the more scarce high-quality entertainment content while being able to deploy it over a novel but relatively more commodified communications technology put Netflix in a powerful position.

### Exchanges between internal and external
Exchanges between the *internal* and *external* quadrants are almost always transactional. A critical distinction is the uniqueness of the element sought. If the enterprise is acquiring an opportunity through the acquisition of standard products, services, or entire firms that provide the more standard products and services, price is often at the core of the deal. When the element sought is more unique or proprietary, this distinction changes the nature of the transaction. The continuity and enthusiasm of personnel becomes more important. More of a partnership approach becomes appropriate, where win–win, non-zero-sum outcomes are essential to achieve the strategic goal. Such agreements can be complex, and negotiations extend over considerable time. Where a spin-out occurs, transactions can be equally complex. They may include transfers of

intellectual property (IP), negotiated customer access, restrictions of employee recruitment, equity ownership, and additional investment or ongoing business relationships. The details of those types of transactions are not covered here. Instead, we will focus on the strategy behind those transactions.

The goal of any of these transactions is to encourage robust value creation by the alignment of incentives among the participants (for example, startups and incumbent organizations) and to encourage robust win–win, non-zero-sum value creation. Non-zero-sum solutions are especially important when dealing with collaborations between early-stage ventures and large incumbents because often much of the value realization depends on the future evolution of the product or service, to which key personnel are essential. Further, continued innovation may depend on sustaining the entrepreneurial behavior and culture of the smaller enterprise. Therefore, while the transaction form may be identifiable, the transaction character and post-transaction environment are part of the innovation toolkit necessary to create and capture the value of the innovation. That will be made clear in the Keyhole–Google–Niantic Labs case (see Section 4.5).

### 4.4.2    The Strategy Layer

In times of constant disruption, management must listen for signals that represent potential new opportunities or the decline of existing businesses. As those signals are received and processed, mapping the opportunities on the COI Fit and Location Matrix identifies the strategies best suited for each opportunity. Before the concept of Open Innovation became popular, most firms focused on the internal development of new opportunities. Many relied on robust internal research capabilities that had fairly broad mandates (for example, Bell Labs, Xerox PARC, IBM Research). As Open Innovation began to take hold in the 1990s, firms began to experiment with the strategic acquisition of startups and technologies (for example, Roche and Genentech), the creation of new business units (for example, Xerox and its attempts at starting new units and companies), and venture capital investing (for example, Intel Capital). Knowledge management became innovation management in the 2000s, and more companies adopted Open Innovation and created innovation management groups.

In the 2020s, many are beginning to explicitly evolve a more diverse array of strategies for managing innovation, including internal development, acquisition of external companies and technologies, experimentation and development of new businesses, and investment models to develop robust ecosystems. All those efforts are focused on transitioning opportunities across the boundaries of the COI Fit and Location Matrix. The most innovative companies will have the capacity to operate in all those domains.

The Strategy layer, the initial layer of the COI Fit and Location Matrix, describes these transactions forms most likely to be appropriate in each of the four quadrants (Figure 4.3) and identifies the means of innovation value capture for each quadrant.

|  |  | **Location** | |
| --- | --- | --- | --- |
|  |  | **Internal** | **External** |
|  | **Core** | Internal Development | Acquisition |
| **Fit** |  |  |  |
|  | **Non-Core** | New Business | Investment |

*Source:*  Developed by Charron and Engel (2003).

*Figure 4.3*     *The Strategy layer*

### 4.4.3    The Source Layer

The Innovation Source layer identifies the location of the innovation within the context of the Framework's two axes: core/non-core and internal/external. This simple map is important to simplify the complex innovation ecosystem and to link it to the strategies to acquire and the tools to execute on the strategy. With innovation arising across so many domains, these core relationships can get lost in the details. The failure of firms to capture and exploit internally developed technologies and innovations is legendary (for example, Xerox and Bell Labs[5]). The increasing prominence of the universities in generating innovations that started in the 1980s and the continuous increase in venture capital investments have reshaped the R&D landscape. Innovation managers must constantly scan a broad set of sources to discover relevant ideas, technology know-how, IP, people, and other elements that can be brought to new opportunities for the enterprise.

The Source layer of the COI Fit and Location matrix describes where the opportunities reside and links them to action (strategy and tools) (Figure 4.4).

| | | Location | |
|---|---|---|---|
| | | **Internal** | **External** |
| **Fit** | **Core** | *Internal Development*<br><br>Products of the firms' R&D, direct product enhancements | *Acquisition*<br><br>University and research lab results, existing competitors, new entrants |
| | **Non-Core** | *New Business*<br><br>Products of R&D from Blue Sky Research and unrelated applications of core technology | *Investment*<br><br>Members of the ecosystem, components of the complete solution |

*Source:*   Developed by Charron and Engel (2003).

*Figure 4.4*     *The Source layer*

### 4.4.4   The Tools Layer

The tools of the innovation manager continue to develop and expand. These tools, or resources, are people who exist in the enterprise and also in the innovation ecosystems around the world. Such tools go well beyond the transactional attitudes and competencies of traditional finance and legal departments. In today's innovation ecosystem, where rapidly emerging technologies and business models rely to such an extent on the continuing engagement of the creative scientists, engineers, and business executives who created the opportunity, specialized approaches and business arrangements are important to motivate aligned behavior. Whether it is a corporate acquisition, a minority venture investment, or a spin-out, achieving the anticipated value is challenging. External relationships require active engagement, and the pace of change roils the waters continually. Innovation centers, incubators, accelerators, and venture development corporations change focus and business models seemingly on a yearly basis. Even venture capital firms evolve new investment theses on an ongoing basis. This dynamic environment is where individual incentives and corporate demands and desires play out. Innovation managers must be able to maintain clarity and flexibility to consummate the deals that will create the next innovations. The third and final layer shows the toolkit of management structures and competencies needed to implement a comprehensive Open Innovation strategy that is attuned to maximizing the benefit of engaging proactively with existing and emerging COI around the world (Figure 4.5).

| | | Location | |
|---|---|---|---|
| | | **Internal** | **External** |
| **Fit** | **Core** | *Internal Development*<br><br>Business Unit Champions, Strategic Licensing | *Acquisition*<br><br>Corporate Finance, Strategic Business Development, Tech "Scouts" |
| | **Non-Core** | *New Business*<br><br>Outside Experts, IP Licensing Team, Spin-out Team | *Investment*<br><br>Corporate VC, External VC, Outside Experts, Innovation Centres |

*Source:*    Developed by Charron and Engel (2003).

*Figure 4.5*    *The Tools layer*

## 4.5    GOOGLE, NIANTIC AND *POKÉMON GO*[6]

The story of San Francisco-based Niantic Labs provides an illustration of how the COI Fit and Location Matrix can be applied across each of the framework's quadrants (Figure 4.6) and how collaboration between major incumbents and startup ventures can achieve technology and new business model innovation as well as value creation and value capture.

A pioneer in the mobile AR gaming industry, Niantic Labs is now best known for its *Pokémon Go* game that becamse a worldwide hit immediately after its June 2016 launch. By early 2019, *Pokémon Go* was the most popular AR game globally with one billion downloads (Hanke, 2019). *Pokémon Go* helped make Niantic Labs the 24th most valuable private tech company in the U.S. by May 2019, according to a *Business Insider* survey that included the likes of WeWork, Airbnb, and Slack (Leskin, 2019).

In August 2021, with its AR games (*Pokémon Go, Ingress,* etc.) already on its Niantic Lightship platform, Niantic announced an ambitious plan to go one step further and create a highly detailed virtual map that would tie its "users and objects precisely to the physical world" (Hanke, 2021). In doing so, this map would further enhance the AR experience outdoors, encourage users to connect with others, and provide an alternative to the proliferation of indoor dystopian-like virtual reality games. According to a blog posting by the company's founder and CEO, John Hanke (2021), the map would have an "unprecedented level of detail, so that a phone or headset can recognize its location and orientation in a highly accurate way anywhere in the world" and would be similar to GPS, "but without satellites and a much higher level of accuracy ... This is one of the grand challenges of augmented reality, and it's the key to making it work the way we want to – to make the real world come alive with information and interactivity."

The roots of Niantic Labs' story and how it came about goes back over 20 years, when Hanke started Keyhole, a 30-person 3D-mapping company in Silicon Valley in 1999, using the technology licensed from Intrinsic Labs. Growing up in Cross Plains, Texas, during the 1970s, Hanke was a self-taught programmer, a gamer, and an avid reader of *National Geographic*. Hanke's story teaches an important lesson in entrepreneurship and innovation: technical innovations, and market opportunities that arise from their application, may evolve through multiple entities, and create multiple opportunities. It is the mark of a true "professional entrepreneur" that Hanke and several members of his management team were able to channel their passion for the opportunities created by the convergence of geo-location, gaming, networking, and mobility to create a sequence of successful ventures, both free-standing and as corporate divisions (Keyhole, Google Geo, and Niantic Labs) to create and capture value for customers, employees, investors, and themselves.

1.   Acquisition quadrant: Keyhole and its acquisition by Google

The Keyhole vision and opportunity were compelling: a talented technical team, an "experienced" CEO in Hanke, and the ability to configure and portray satellite imagery that previously had only been available in high-cost military and national defense applications. The main product, EarthViewer3D, transformed satellite images and aerial photography into a videogame-like experience. Later, they created a platform to add location-specific data, mapping boundaries, *Yellow Pages* listings, and address information. "Our goal is simple: to put the entire world in the hands of our customers," said Hanke in a 2001 press release.[7] Immediately after the Iraqi invasion during the Second Gulf War in 2003, a host of news organizations reported on Keyhole's newfound popularity and exposure, a result of its mapping software being used to illuminate news forecasts on CNN, ABC, CBS, and various foreign news outlets. Keyhole's equity funding had been limited at this point to a Series A financing that included funding from In-Q-Tel, the CIA's venture capital arm. In need of additional growth capital to exploit its apparently significant opportunity,

Keyhole initiated the process of raising a Series B. In October 2004, on the cusp of its completion, Google (at that time still a private pre-IPO [initial public offering] company) made a compelling offer to acquire Keyhole. Under pressure of the pending Series B, Google was able to make that decision in just one day, after a demonstration of Keyhole's product, EarthView. Importantly, after the acquisition Keyhole's entire staff was absorbed into Google, but allowed to remain intact and independent. That decision proved critical. Hanke (2009) recalled:

> We had this initial meeting with the consulting types and other aspiring business leaders on how Keyhole should be folded in Google. Then, one of their most senior and most experienced executives, Wayne Rosen, the vice president of engineering, spoke up and said, 'Leave these people alone. They know what they're doing. They're going to do great stuff. We brought them to do great stuff. Let them do that.'

2.  Internal Development quadrant: Google Geo Division, scaling up within Google

    The acquisition by Google proved a breakthrough. Able to leverage Google's world-class engineering talent and financial resources, they made tremendous progress. When Google bought Keyhole, the high-resolution imagery in EarthView was not available in some cities and other parts of the world, and the application was expensive. In 2002, the pricing of a Keyhole annual subscription was $1,200 per user. Once inside Google, Hanke and his team were no longer limited by the need to generate near-term cash flow. Google immediately lowered the price of the consumer version to under $30, and when Google Earth launched in June 2005 the software was made available for free. The acquisition was also a great strategic match for Google. The geo-products synched well with Google's simple strategic vision: organizing the world's information, improving search capabilities for that information, and making that information free. EarthView, now rebranded as Google Earth as fully manifested through Google's platform, brought a whole new dimension of information to Google's offering. Hanke (2009) noted:

> Google's all about organizing the world's information and making it useful. You can search text and you can do that great with the algorithms that Larry and Sergey originally created. That was the original core competency of the company. But [Page and Brin] were also looking at all the other domains of data, ways to organize that data, search for that data, and make that data useful to people. They had started maps, then searching for things on top of the map, and then all the data that is related to the earth and geography. [Geo] was a domain

that they felt would be [ultimately] important to Google and they wanted to be good at it.[8] So, they bought us, and poured in a lot of capital.

This quote clearly demonstrates how a capability some may have considered non-core to Google at the time (geospatial imagery) was from the CEO's strategic perspective absolutely core. So prompt acquisition and integration was the correct strategy.

The subsequent unleashing of even more vast amounts of free information, combined with the successive rise of the smart phone with its GPS capabilities and mobile location-based applications, was more than fortuitous. Application developers, large and small, were often driven by communities of users that had expectations built on exposure to Google Earth. All owed a great deal to the early Keyhole vision and the Google platform that helped build it on a global scale.

With Keyhole's technology as a base and Hanke a vice president for product development, ultimately overseeing over 2,000 "Googlers" in Google's Geo Division, Google would launch several new geo-based products over the next six years: Google Earth, Google Maps, Google Street View, Sketch-up, and Panoramio. Google Maps would eventually become one of eight Google products with one billion users or more around the world (Wodinsky, 2018).

Hanke and his team often prototyped, improvised, and tested quickly, taking a "Lean Innovation" approach to starting up new products. For example, after years of looking at overhead images of specific locations, the idea for Street View emerged when Sergey Brin asked why Google "couldn't also capture imagery the way people saw it – from the ground" (Bock, 2015). The Geo team then went out, hired contractors, and placed GPS cameras on top of cars, with the mandate to take images of every street angle possible. Another key to Google Geo's ability to scale up new products quickly was that Google followed a "crowd-sourced Open Innovation" concept where the public could help make enhancements to all its online offerings.

Today, Google's mapping products now form a platform that more than one million sites and app developers have used to build businesses, serving more than one billion users each week (Bock, 2015). These GPS-based businesses include Uber, Lyft, Airbnb, Yelp, Waze, and OpenTable.

3.    New Business quadrant: Niantic Labs within Google

In 2010, Hanke and some of the core team from Keyhole, started up a "skunkworks" project within Google called Niantic Labs. It was named after a whaling ship that was grounded and abandoned in San Francisco when its crew joined the 1849 Gold Rush (Bailey, 2012). The ship, like so many others at this time, after use as a hotel (and perhaps a brothel) settled into the San Francisco Bay mud, disappearing forever. This sense that we are surrounded by invisible traces of history and mystery was representative of the group's passion for hidden treasure and the use of AR to reveal it. The mandate for Niantic Labs and its 30-some employees was to find new opportunities for Google where mobile, geo-based maps, social, and AR gaming trends converged. At the time AR was projected to grow to a $900 million industry by 2020. This proved to be greatly understated. In 2012 Niantic Labs launched two revolutionary products. Field Trip was a demonstration of the key features of discovery of augmented information mapped onto the real world. Ingress was a collaborative global game that developed (and still sustains) a devoted user base. Both products were in tune with Niantic's values: creating products that encourage exploration, outdoor and social experiences, and social responsibility. Leveraging off Google's infrastructure and integrating with its various platforms, such as Google Maps, Google Play, Google Cloud, and YouTube, Niantic Labs was able to develop a worldwide following for Ingress.

4. Investment quadrant: Niantic Labs spun out of Google

In mid-October 2015, Niantic Labs spun out of Google as an independent company, with an initial Series A round of financing of $30 million that included three corporate investors: the Pokémon Company, Nintendo, and Google (Wingfield, 2015). Hanke (2009) explained the rationale:

> Being inside of Google we have infrastructure: offices around the world; great talents from which we could assemble the team very easily; and real estate, IT, legal, and accounting support – all those functions were available to us. We didn't have to go out and try to create those ourselves. We could focus on just the product. Obviously being part of a parent company like Google has a tremendous advantage when you're trying to introduce a new product. There were synergies with other parts of Google, the other (internal) teams that we could leverage.
> On the other hand, there were a number of cons over a longer term. We found over time that our interests and our focus were diverging from the interests of the core part of [Google], so the synergies weren't as great as maybe we initially anticipated, and it added to the luster of doing this spin out. The things that I've been wrestling with for the past several months were around the issue of IP ownership: what gets transitioned out, what licenses back are made to the company, what rights the company has, how does that trade-off against investor interests. These are very complicated things to unravel, even though we had sort of anticipated we might spin it out someday. When you start writing up those agreements, it gets very complicated very quickly.

With Niantic no longer considered core to the mission of Alphabet, Google's parent company, as an independent venture it was free to (and needed to) raise its own capital. Being free of Google's organizational constraints also meant it had to secure all the resources needed as it sought to scale up and transform itself into a leading AR gaming company. It speaks to the quality of the team that so many of them stayed together throughout the process of acquisition and divestiture. This included external partners, such as some of the early investors in Keyhole, who continued their involvement as investors in Niantic.

Being independent also allowed Niantic to enter into strategic business relationships with partners who might not have found collaborating so deeply with a giant like Google as attractive. Reflecting on Niantic's *keiretsu*[9]-like relationship with the two Japanese companies, Hanke noted:

> [The spin-out from Google allowed] us to do something like this with Nintendo and Pokémon. They can invest and be a co-owner of the company and feel like they have a very tight relationship. [The Pokémon Company and Nintendo are] putting the number two video game franchise of all time[10] in the hands of this project. It would be more difficult to do if they didn't at least own a portion of the company. They feel like there's a good alignment of interest. (Takahashi, 2015)

The spin-out benefited Google directly economically in multiple ways: through the increase in the value of the minority interest of its retained equity share in Niantic; through revenue earned on "in-app sales" of Niantic game-related virtual goods sold through Google Play; and through revenues from the licensing of its Google Maps platform. In a softer but also important benefit, it demonstrated to Google employees a positive Google management culture that valued innovation and supported its employees' ambitions, even when done independently of the direct control of the mothership.

In mid-2017, Niantic raised a Series B round of equity financing of $200 million, followed in December 2018 by a Series C round of $245 million led by VC firm Institutional Venture Partners (IVP) that included several strategic partners, including Samsung Electronics and aXiomatic Gaming (Nowak et al., 2019) which gave it a market valuation of nearly $4 billion (Roof, 2018).[11] Its fourth game, *Harry Potter: Wizards Unite*, was launched in summer 2019. In 2021 it launched the Niantic Lightship – which allows third-party game creators to seamlessly bring virtual content into the real world.

Figure 4.6 illustrates Niantic's journey throughout the strategies of the COI Fit and Location Matrix.

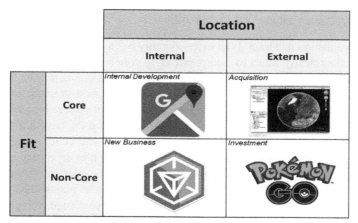

*Source:* Developed by Charron and Engel (2003).

*Figure 4.6    Niantic Labs and the COI Fit and Location Matrix*

### 4.5.1    Gaining Value by Accessing the Innovation Ecosystem

As an entrepreneur, John Hanke, and the ventures he led, benefited from their location and deep interaction with the Silicon Valley's innovation ecosystem (Engel, 2015). As importantly, his ability to create value from business collaborations and combinations exemplified entrepreneurial and Open Innovation best practice. The COI Fit and Location Matrix is a tool for those striving to engage in such management practices. It is especially helpful where it is necessary to communicate the intentionality of such practices across a large enterprise.

This is clearly demonstrated in the Niantic Labs case using the COI Fit and Location Matrix. A COI ecosystem is often analyzed by the scope and scale of certain components such as venture capital financing or research universities. But as important as these components may be, more important is how they behave. The best COI have established cultural norms that encourage win–win, non-zero-sum results and transaction forms. These value-added behaviors favor speed and lower transaction friction that is so import in quickly evolving opportunities.

While in this case both Google and Niantic Labs clearly benefited from being located in such a rich innovation ecosystem, the COI Fit and Location

Matrix identifies the need for, and the pathways towards, every enterprise creating its own unique COI around itself.

1.  Acquisition quadrant: If an external entity has a capability that an organization clearly wants to incorporate in its core business, such as Keyhole had with its unique mapping technology, then acquisition may be the best path. When dealing with early-stage ventures, a good structure and constructive post-acquisition management process can achieve broader benefits than simply business acquisition. This means going beyond financial and retention incentives, considering operational and cultural sensitivity to allow the acquired team to continue to function in an entrepreneurial manner, and when successful, to influence the broader enterprise. This was done initially by allowing the Keyhole team to pursue their vision through the development of Google Earth. Their continued entrepreneurial team practices allowed them over time to come to lead a much larger group of 2,500 individuals, leading substantially all of Google's mapping activity.

2.  Internal Development quadrant: If an internal capability already exists, which Google had, a critical factor is to overcome "not invented here" corporate antibodies, and create a collaborative organization that can accelerate scaling-up of the acquisition, as Google did with its portfolio of mapping products.

3.  New Business quadrant: If a new venture, such as Niantic Labs, is created within the organization to pursue "blue sky" innovations, but ends up not being central to the core of the enterprise, then a spin-out can be a means to capturing value. In Niantic's case this spin-out further enabled success that may not have otherwise been possible, as it allowed business relationships with Nintendo, which might have been more difficult if Niantic had stayed part of Google. The benefits to Google had many aspects. The purely financial benefits included several features, such as the growth of the value of its retained equity ownership, and substantial operating revenues from sales of in-application-purchases (IAP) through GooglePlay.

4.  Investment quadrant: By investing in Niantic (with cash and by accepting an equity position in exchange for an IP contribution) Google retained a minority equity interest post-spin-out. Through this transaction, Google enabled Niantic to have sufficient equity to motivate its founding team and to be attractive to financial and additional strategic investors. This investor- and entrepreneur-friendly capital structure is a constructive win–win element that improved the attractiveness of Niantic to others, helping to secure the financial and IP resources necessary for its initial and continued success.

*Table 4.1     COI Fit and Location Matrix: pathways for commercialization*

| Quadrant characteristics | Internal Development quadrant | Acquisition quadrant | New Business quadrant | Investment quadrant |
| --- | --- | --- | --- | --- |
| Innovation flows | Stay at the corporation<br>Some strategic out-licensing | Inbound | Outbound | Stays outside the corporation |
| Pathways for commercialization | Business units | Corporate acquisition<br>Component purchase<br>In-licensing | Spin-outs<br>Out-licensing | Corporate venture capital (strategic return) |
| Pathways for financing | Business units<br>Corporate funds | Stock, cash, debt | External venture capital<br>Corporate venturing group | Co-operative agreements |
| Requirements for success | Business unit buy-in<br>Final product success | Right technology<br>Reasonable pricing<br>Clear product integration<br>Pathways for successful human resource retention and integration | Financing<br>Freedom of operation<br>Clean exit | Value-added behavior |
| Incentives for R&D executive | Success directly influences budget | Possibility of new R&D resources: people, IP | Indirect: motivate existing personnel to innovate<br>Risk: potential loss of personnel | Intelligence<br>Relationships<br>World view |

*Source:*     Charron and Engel (2003).

## 4.6    PATHWAYS FOR COMMERCIALIZATION

Table 4.1 provides an illustration of how the COI Fit and Location Matrix can help managers identify critical success factors, benefits and challenges likely to be encountered as they pursue successful execution of each of the four strategy quadrants. They vary in obvious and subtle ways. For illustration, we show the innovation flows, pathways for commercialization, pathways for financing, requirements for success, and incentives for R&D executives for each of the COI Fit and Location Matrix quadrants. One can expand the list as suits one's respective situation. Box 4.2 presents the case example of Schibsted Classified Media and Adevinta, focusing on the mechanisms utilized in the Open Innovation journey to building a leading digital advertising platform.

---

### BOX 4.2    SCHIBSTED CLASSIFIED MEDIA AND ADEVINTA: OLD MEDIA TO DIGITAL POWERHOUSE

There are many business examples of incumbent companies using the tools and strategies of the COI Fit and Location Matrix to spur internal innovation. Similar to the Keyhole–Google–Niantic story, another example of a company mobilizing all four quadrants to leverage the speed of entrepreneurs and the scale of an incumbent company is that of Norway-based Schibsted, a media publisher more than 175 years old. At a time when many traditional media companies have lost market value due to the decline in non-digital advertising, Schibsted's market value grew eightfold between 2003 and 2018 (CompaniesMarketCap, 2021), following its 2003 acquisition of the Swedish Blocket.se classified advertising site. The Blocket model was then used as a template in different countries across Europe, then Asia, and finally Latin America. Throughout the first two decades of the 21st century, Schibsted, the eighth-largest media company in the world, was considered by its media peers to be quite forward-thinking within the digital space, especially when other media companies were slow to move or not at all, by immediately recognizing the digital disruptions that were about to take place and then capitalizing on those trends by acquiring or building its own digital ventures. In April 2019, Schibsted decided to spin off its entire standalone classified operations, now a global powerhouse in that niche, as a separate public company, Adevinta. It initially maintained a majority ownership position in the new company until Adevinta acquired eBay Classifieds a year later.

---

## Early 2000s, Prologue: Digital Disruption to an Old Business Model

Prior to digital disruptions of the 2000s, many newspapers in the Western world were locked in a business model more than a century old, with advertising revenue subsidizing most of the operating costs of a newsroom and related production and distribution expenses of news in print. Newspapers had provided audiences that advertisers wanted on an analog print platform. Over the previous 20 years, with the advent of digital technologies, dedicated apps, and increased consumer usage of smart devices, print advertising revenue, from both display and classified advertising, began to erode. Dedicated digital classified advertising sites, like eBay, Monster, and Craigslist, emerged and ate away at newspaper classified advertising revenues and offered consumers substitute ways to find a new job, purchase a house, or sell general merchandise.

## 2003, Acquisition Quadrant: Acquiring Blocket, Spinning into Schibsted

In 1994, Schibsted was one of the first media companies to have foresight of the disabling impact that digital technologies could have on their business. Schibsted only consisted then of two newspapers in Norway. The company immediately adopted a disruptive mindset by establishing Finn. no, a classified web site, in 2000 to compete against its own newspapers in Norway. After expanding into neighboring Sweden by purchasing two newspapers there in the late 1990s,[12] it also created a competing online classified advertising site. However, Schibsted could not match the growth or popularity of a pre-existing pure-play Swedish classified advertising startup site, Blocket.se, which was simpler and more user-friendly. Blocket was founded in 1996 by a Swedish entrepreneur, Hendrik Nordstrom, who had grown up in the small town of Fjakinge, Skaane, in Sweden. With Blocket, Nordstrom wanted to create a digital bulletin board for local communities to advertise things they no longer needed (Schibsted, 2020). The site became a smash hit in Sweden. "[Our classified site] grew," said Sverre Munck, then executive vice president of international, "but [Blocket] just grew faster."[13] So Schibsted decided to purchase Blocket in 2003.

## Early 2000s, Internal Development Quadrant: Expanding the Blocket Model across Europe, Scaling Up within Schibsted

Buoyed by the success of Blocket, in 2004 Schibsted decided to use it as a template and began to roll out its online classified advertising business model as part of the company's larger international expansion strategy throughout Europe. Blocket's model offered a simple interface, was custom-branded for a particular country, and employed a "freemium" model, where buyers and sellers could use the site at no cost. Sellers were charged a premium for add-ons, such as including a logo or highlighting their listings. Using Blocket as a template, over the next ten years Schibsted launched similar online classified sites in Spain, Austria, France, Italy, Mexico, Brazil, Vietnam, and other countries. Launches were managed out of the company's tech center in Stockholm, Sweden. Subsequently, launch teams were sent in to scale up each site locally.

### 2012 to 2019, New Business Quadrant: Schibsted Classified Media as a Separate Division within Schibsted

By 2012, Schibsted had decided to consolidate all of its classified sites in 45 countries into a single corporate unit, called Schibsted Classified Media, and no longer under the umbrella of its international businesses. At the time, Schibsted defined classified media as one of the two cornerstone businesses, the other being the traditional media houses. Leboncoin.fr in France, launched in 2006, was Schibsted's largest classified site outside of Scandinavia. Built on the Blocket model, by 2008 it was profitable; by 2009, it matched eBay in page views as the largest classified site in France; and by 2012, it had almost 100 million euros in revenue.[14]

### 2019, Investment Quadrant: Schibsted Classified Media Spun out of Schibsted as Adevinta

In April 2019, having expanded beyond Europe and into Asia and Latin America, Schibsted decided to spin out its Schibsted Classified Media unit as a separate company. The new company would be rebranded as Adevinta and would be led by Erik Rolv Ryssdal, a former Schibsted CEO who decided to recruit his replacement at Schibsted and then take on the CEO position at the new company. At the time of the spin-out, Schibsted retained a 59 percent ownership equity position, but the spin-out would provide the new company with the flexibility to raise capital or use equity for future acquisitions. In July 2020, eBay announced that it would sell its classified business to Adevinta in a combination of stock and cash, and it would hold an ownership equity position equal to that of Schibsted at 33 percent of the voting stock. The new company would have an estimated annual revenue of $1.8 billion US and $600 million US EBITDA (earnings before interest, taxes, depreciation, and amortization) (Adevinta, 2020).

## COI Fit and Location Matrix

### Guiding questions

*Use the questions to explore the three layers*

| Fit | Location | |
|---|---|---|
| | **Internal** | **External** |
| **Core** | Internal Development | Acquisition |
| **Non-Core** | New Business | Investment |

**Strategy**
*How to get it?*

| Fit | Location | |
|---|---|---|
| | **Internal** | **External** |
| **Core** | How should this be managed? Scaled through an existing business unit? Independent innovation group? How can we protect this asset? (IP, competitive advantage) | Should it be acquired? Should we create a partnership with the company owning it? Should we license it? |
| **Non-Core** | Are we confident it will not be critical to our future? If so, how should we monetise it? Should we sell it? Licence it? | In what way is this important and supportive of the core business? What is the likelihood it may evolve to be critical to the core. What business relationship best achieves our objectives? |

**Resource**
*What resources will it need to support it?*

| Fit | Location | |
|---|---|---|
| | **Internal** | **External** |
| **Core** | What resources are need to scale it? Are we willing to invest in it? What are the risks of doing nothing? | What resources are needed to acquire it? How much should we purchase it for? Is retention of the team critical? What are the risks of doing nothing? |
| **Non-Core** | Should we limit the resources to scale this for now? What resources are needed to keep it in maintenance mode? What are the risks of doing nothing? | How many resources should we commit? Can we put this on hold and revisit it the future? What are the risks of doing nothing? |

**Source**
*Where is it?*

| Fit | Location | |
|---|---|---|
| | **Internal** | **External** |
| **Core** | Do we have clear protectable ownership? Will it have a future material economic impact? How material is it now? | Who owns it? How can we acquire it? (Acquisition, joint venture, license) What's its future economic potential? |
| **Non-Core** | Do we own it? Will it have a material economic or strategic impact in the future? If not, should we license or sell it? | Who owns it? What's its future economic potential? How should we get involved? CVC? Blue sky R&D collaboration? Distribution? |

*Source:*    Developed by the authors.

*Figure 4.7    COI Fit and Location Matrix: guiding questions*

## 4.7 COI FIT AND LOCATION MATRIX ASSESSMENT

So where to start? Many companies are already engaged in various elements of Open Innovation strategy. The benefit of the COI Fit and Location Matrix is to assemble the components in a comprehensive framework that helps identify gaps, communicates clearly across the various constituencies in a complex organization, and amplifies the opportunities for synergy. This assessment tool is a starting point. Its goal is to help engage and structure management's thinking and to build a common understanding and innovation vocabulary, whether the concern is innovation initiation, monetization, or achieving enhanced speed and scale. By answering specific questions for each layer – Source, Strategy, and Tools – the COI Fit and Location Matrix can be put to work to assess and enhance the fitness of an organization's innovation strategy and resources, and its ability to execute (Figure 4.7).

The responses to these questions, and others that an organization will tailor to its circumstances, may help identify "blind spots" in an organization's innovation strategy and capability. It will often raise questions that must be addressed by the most senior levels of management, such as: identifying and resourcing the development of new organizational capabilities, sharpening the strategic focus of business units, and developing new external business relationships with a view to expanding the organization's engagement with its ecosystem. It may help identify internal capabilities that need higher priority, new capabilities that need to be built or acquired, non-core projects to spin out, and which to maintain with ongoing involvement and which to divest. And certainly, the process of inquiry can aid in bringing focus to monitoring and investing in external non-core projects and corporate venture capital strategies and capabilities.

## 4.8 EVALUATING SUCCESS

Open Innovation brings along with it an intrinsic ambiguity: are the strategies successful? The question raises unusual challenges because of the inevitable competition for resource allocations among internal and external stakeholders. If an acquisition generates "windfall" profits for entrepreneurs and their investors, did the enterprise overpay? If an underexploited competency is spun out to great success, should that opportunity have been retained? Success and failure are often in the eye of the beholder.

---

### BOX 4.3 SPIN-OUTS: THE CHALLENGE OF AMBIVALENCE AND AMBIGUITY

When internally developed products or technologies no longer fit the overall corporate strategy, Open Innovation would suggest spinning out the product and capturing value either through technology licensing, equity ownership, or other arrangements. In the early 1990s, Xerox was attempting to broaden its offerings from simple document reproduction to the value-added service of document management. This move was particularly insightful given the increasing importance of electronic document storage, sharing, security, and retrieval. There were, however, significant challenges. The enterprise software business was distinctly different than its core enterprise.

Xerox took multiple approaches. Internally it undertook building a document management product, and externally it provided the initial funding to a startup, Documentum. Documentum initially created bespoke solutions for major enterprise clients. Three years after founding, it acquired Xerox's internally developed and more generalizable product. Documentum went public in 1996. At the time it was generally heralded as a great success. It was later acquired by EMC and then OpenText in transactions that valued the company at over $1.5 billion.[15]

Today[16] the market capitalization of Xerox is approximately $3.7 billion, while Dropbox, a relative upstart that focused on document management, has a market capitalization of over $12 billion.[17]

This example raises questions that often plague spin-outs. Success is ambiguous. If the venture succeeds, perhaps the team and technology should have been retained and internally developed. If the spin-out fails, perhaps management "put good money after bad" and should rather have cut its "losses" earlier. Even if the spin-out generates a positive return, as in the case of Documentum, was the opportunity foregone too important to overlook? Individuals responsible for the decision between spinning out or internally developing a potentially disruptive business are often trapped in such "lose–lose" ambivalence.

## 4.9    CONCLUSION

The challenges of rapidly evolving technology, business models and business environments are placing an increasing burden on major enterprises to be nimble and responsive to opportunities. At the same time, financial markets are demanding excellence in execution and punish firms who deviate from providing predictable results. This innovation trap is exacerbated by the rise of a nimble entrepreneurial ecosystem that regularly generates startup ventures that are capable of rapid scaling and disruption of even the largest enterprises. In this environment, innovation strategy needs a broad lens, one that embraces the opportunities within the entire ecosystem, not simply capturing value from those innovations that arise from within the enterprise and its clear acquisition targets. The COI Fit and Location Matrix provides such a lens; a broad new framework for visualizing and communicating an ecosystem-centric Open Innovation strategy, providing a roadmap for the strategy and identification of the tools necessary to carry out the strategy. The power of its analytical capability is demonstrated by the innovation case studies presented, including the strategies deployed by Google in building its mapping capability and ultimately birthing the company that brought the massively successful *Pokémon Go* mobile game to market, while continuing to provide economic returns to Google.

## NOTES

1.    From less than $10 billion in 2009 to record levels in 2020 ($133 billion according to PwC and CB Insights [2021], $164 billion according to PitchBook and NVCA [2021]). The pace in the first six months was continuing on an even fast pace and sources expected another record year.
2.    The Xerox Alto, developed at Xerox PARC in 1973 by a team led by Douglas Engelbart, incorporated the use of a graphical user interface (GUI) desktop metaphor, a mouse pointer and many of the features (Thacker et al., 1979) later brought to the consumer desktop market in the Macintosh. Xerox's own belated attempt, in 1981, with the release of the Xerox Star into the business market, failed to gain traction and was discontinued.
3.    Weiblen and Chesbrough (2015) provide a complementary perspective on the engagement models between corporations and startups, based on the direction of the innovation flow (outside-in or inside-out) and the equity involvement.
4.    Early investors included well-known technology venture capital firms: In June 1998 IVP led a $6 million Series B financing, followed fairly quickly by a Series C financing in February 1999 in which TCV, Foundation Capital and Comdico Ventures participated. These firms continued to invest to support Netflix growth through multiple rounds of financing. The interconnected nature of a COI ecosystem is perhaps exemplified by the fact that IVP is also an investor in Niantic Labs, another entertainment company introducing novel technology at scale that is also discussed in this chapter.
5.    Bell Labs was perhaps, in its heyday, the leading example of a corporate R&D laboratory. It was the source of much of the technology that underlies the digital transformation of the last half-century. Many of its innovations, such as the transistor and the laser, have had huge impact but ultimately brought disappointingly little direct economic benefit to the parent company, AT&T. See Gertner, J. (2012), *The Idea Factory: Bell Labs and the Great Age of American Invention*, Penguin Books.
6.    For a thorough investigation of the evolution of Niantic Labs see *Niantic Labs and the Professional Entrepreneur: Google, Pokémon Go, and Beyond*, written by Jerome S. Engel, Haas School of Business, University of California, Berkeley, 2019, available at https://hbsp.harvard.edu/product/B5868-PDF-ENG. Portions of this section are taken from this Berkeley-Haas case series.
7.    Ibid.
8.    Over time, the work done by Google's geo-products team also helped improve the geo-targeting of Google's online advertisements.
9.    *Keiretsu* is the Japanese term for a set of companies with interlocking business relationships and shareholdings that often act as an informal business group. *Keiretsu*-type company alliances emerged during the 19th century and remain dominant in Japan's present-day economy.
10.   Nintendo's *Mario Bros.*, launched in 1983, is the best-selling video game of all-time.
11.   There was a Series B financing of $200 million in 2017, after the success of *Pokémon Go*, led by Spark Capital, which included NetEase and other co-investors and placed Niantic's valuation at about $2 billion (Nowak et al., 2019).

12. Schibsted acquired *Aftonbladet* in 1996 and *SVD* in 1998.
13. Interview with chapter co-author, August 22, 2012. Oslo, Norway.
14. Schibsted 2012 Investor Day presentation. Schibsted annual reports, 2009 (p. 19) and 2012 (p. 12).
15. "OpenText Signs Definite Agreement to Acquire Dell's EMC's Enterprise Content Division, Including Documentum," OpenText press release, September 9, 2016, www.opentext.com/about/press-releases?id=51B5E97A2C384D1DBCD941 80192DB53A.
16. As of September 2021. There are a number of document management solutions offered by large (Microsoft, IBM, Google, etc.) and emerging (Dropbox, Box, etc.) companies. Dropbox was chosen as a point of comparison as it is a document-management "pure play." The same point could be made with Box, a younger company, which has a market capitalization of $3.8 billion.
17. Box, Xerox and Dropbox market capitalizations as of September 23, 2021, https://companiesmarketcap.com.

# REFERENCES

Adevinta (2020). Adevinta Signs Agreement to Acquire eBay Classifieds Group. Retrieved from www.adevinta.com/news/adevinta-signs-agreement-to-acquire-ebay-classifieds-group/.

Bailey, B. (2012). *Mercury News* Interview: John Hanke, Vice President and Head of Google's Niantic Labs. *San Jose Mercury News*, November 4. Retrieved from www.mercurynews.com/2012/11/02/mercury-news-interview-john-hanke-vice-president-and-head-of-googles-niantic-labs/.

Blank, E. (2013). Why the Lean Start-up Changes Everything. *Harvard Business Review*, May, 63–72.

Bock, L. (2015). *Work Rules! Insights from Inside Google That Will Transform How You Live and Lead*. New York: Twelve.

CB Insights (2018). *State of Innovation: Survey of 677 Corporate Strategy Executives*. Retrieved from www.cbinsights.com/research-state-of-innovation-report.

Charron, D., and Engel, J. (2003). Building Value on Your R&D Investments: Business Models for Financing the Path to Commercialization. Industrial Research Institute. Annual Meeting, Colorado Springs, CO, May.

Chesbrough, H. (2020). *Open Innovation Results: Going Beyond the Hype and Getting Down to Business*. Oxford: Oxford University Press.

Chesbrough, H. (2006). Open Innovation: A New Paradigm for Understanding Industrial Innovation. In Chesbrough, H., Vanhaverbeke, W., and West, J. (Eds) (2006). *Open Innovation: Researching a New Paradigm*. Oxford: Oxford University Press.

Chesbrough, H. (2003). *Open Innovation: The New Imperative for Creating and Profiting from Technology*. Boston, MA: Harvard Business School Press.

Christensen, C. (2021). Key Concepts. Retrieved from https://claytonchristensen.com/key-concepts/.

CompaniesMarketCap (2021). Market Capitalization of Schibsted. Retrieved from https://companiesmarketcap.com/schibsted/marketcap/.

Engel, J. (2019). *Niantic Labs and the Professional Entrepreneur in the Silicon Valley: Google, Pokémon Go and Beyond*, Cases (A), (B) and (C), Berkeley-Haas Case Series.

Engel, J. (2015). Global Clusters of Innovation: Lessons from Silicon Valley. *California Management Review*, 57(2), 36–65.

Engel, J. (2011). Accelerating Corporate Innovation: Lessons from the Venture Capital Model. *Research-Technology Management*, 54(3), 36–43, doi: 10.5437/08953608X5403007.

Frommer, S. (2017). Millions of Americans still play Pokémon Go Every Day. *Vox*, March 23. Retrieved from www.vox.com/2017/3/23/15039626/pokemon-go-daily-users-chart.

Hanke, J. (2021). The Metaverse is a Dystopian Nightmare. Let's Build a Better Universe. Niantic blog posting, August 10. Retrieved from https://nianticlabs.com/blog/real-world -metaverse/.

Hanke, J. (2019). Keynote Speech, Mobile World Congress, February. Retrieved from www.youtube.com/watch?v=Zs-T6HNPIkc&t=808s.

Hanke, J. (2009). *Innovation at Scale: Google*. Berkeley-Haas. Presentation, August 27. Retrieved from www.youtube.com/watch?v=6NrzvMoxn2E.

Isaacson, W. (2011). *Steve Jobs*. New York: Simon & Schuster.

Leskin, P. (2019). The 26 Most Valuable Private Tech Companies in the US. *Business Insider*, May 29. Retrieved from www.businessinsider.com/most-valuable-private-us -startups-2018–10.

Lockheed Martin (2021). Corporation Skunk Works: Who We Are. Retrieved from www .lockheedmartin.com/en-us/who-we-are/business-areas/aeronautics/skunkworks.html.

Nowak, B., Cost, M., Wang, A., Chavdaroff, A., Colantuoni, J., and Redon, C. (2019). *Video Game Disruptors, Niantic, Inc.* Analyst report. Morgan Stanley, May 20.

NSF (2021). National Science Foundation I-Corps. Retrieved from www.nsf.gov/news/ special_reports/i-corps/.

PitchBook and NVCA (2021). *PitchBook-NVCA Venture Monitor Q1 2021*. Retrieved from https://pitchbook.com/news/reports/q1-2021-pitchbook-nvca-venture-monitor.

PwC and CB Insights (2021). Q1 2021 MoneyTree Funding Headline Report. Retrieved from www.cbinsights.com/research/report/venture-capital-q1–2021/.

Roof, K. (2018). Maker of Pokémon Go Refuels with $3.9 Billion Valuation. *Wall Street Journal*, December 18. Retrieved from https://www.wsj.com/articles/niantic-maker-of -hit-pokemon-go-app-refuels-with-3-9-billion-valuation-11544748877.

Schibsted (2020). Blocket: An Idea That Started a Movement. Retrieved from https:// schibsted.com/2020/09/14/an-idea-that-started-a-movement/.

Takahashi, D. (2015). How Pokémon Go Will Benefit from Niantic's Lessons from Ingress on Location-Based Game Design. *VentureBeat*, December 16. Retrieved from https:// venturebeat.com/2015/12/16/how-niantic-will-marry-animated-characters-with-mobile -location-data-in-pokemon-go/.

Teece, D. J., Pisano, G., and Shuen, A. (1997). Dynamic capabilities and strategic management. *Strategic Management Journal*, 18(7), 509–533.

Thacker, C. P., McCreight, E. M., Lampson, B. W., Sproull, R. F., and Boggs, D. R. (1979). *Alto: A Personal Computer*. Xerox Palo Alto Research Center. Retrieved from www .bitsavers.org/pdf/xerox/parc/techReports/CSL-7911_Alto_A_Personal_Computer.pdf.

Tushman, M. L., and O'Reilly III, C. A. (1996). Ambidextrous Organizations: Managing Evolutionary and Revolutionary Change. *California Management Review*, 38(4), 8–29.

Walrave, B., Van Oorschot, K. E., and Romme, A. G. L. (2011). Getting Trapped in the Suppression of Exploration: A Simulation Model. *Journal of Management Studies*, 48(8), 1727–1751.

Weiblen, T., and Chesbrough, H. W. (2015). Engaging with Startups to Enhance Corporate Innovation. *California Management Review*, 57(2), 66–90.

Wingfield, N. (2015). A Game Maker Lands Investors. *New York Times*, October 19.

Wodinsky, S. (2018). Google Drive Is About to Hit 1 Billion Users. Google, June 25. Retrieved from www.google.com/doodles/googles-20th-birthday.

# 5. Business-model-led Clusters of Innovation: the case of Product Led Growth

**Itxaso del Palacio**

## 5.1 THE IMPACT OF COVID IN BUSINESSES AND THEIR GO-TO-MARKET STRATEGIES

As a result of Covid-19, during 2020 many businesses were forced to change the way they operate. Employees moved to WFH (working from home) and businesses had to quickly adapt their operations to this new paradigm. The transition was easy for some businesses that were already operating in the cloud and had some sort of distributed workforce; for other businesses though, it was a challenging move, specifically for large enterprises that rely on legacy systems and are operating mainly on premises.

Apart from the operational changes, businesses had to adapt their go-to-market (GTM) strategies too. We refer to GTM strategy as the way a company is planning to reach new customers. Before Covid-19, many industries were heavily reliant on face-to-face sales, also known as "personal selling". Personal selling helps sales teams establish meaningful human connections with the buyers, resulting in shorter sales cycles and, in many cases, bigger contract values. However, personal sales were stopped with Covid-19 and all businesses were forced to adapt their GTM strategies to online environments. Most business-to-consumer (B2C) companies built online stores as consumers moved to shopping online. This created new challenges for businesses that wanted to capture the attention of consumers in an ever more competitive online marketplace.

Business-to-business (B2B) companies selling software in the cloud, also known as software as a service (SaaS), faced different challenges. Traditionally, SaaS companies have been selling SaaS through face-to-face meetings with customers. Enterprise sales are very complex, and in many cases prospects need education from sales reps before they feel prepared to buy. Even though they are selling an intangible asset, selling software will also require some form of testing that companies might not be able to conduct through the website (as an online store) or on the phone (with a sales rep). Additionally, many SaaS products go through long procurement processes before they are purchased, and they require the approval of several stakeholders within the enterprise to complete the transaction. Through a phone call, it is also difficult to communicate the unique value of a product and explain the way the product integrates in the workflow.

Covid-19 has set up a challenge for SaaS companies, specifically for those selling to large enterprises in highly regulated industries that have long procurement processes as well as complex security standards. However, Covid-19 has also created an opportunity for other SaaS businesses whose customers have been forced to move to the cloud and have rapidly adapted their operations to the new normal. Companies such as video conferencing firm Zoom and communication firm Slack experienced gigantic growth through 2020, and they have triggered a cultural shift in how we work as well as how we interact with our family and friends. The rapid adoption of some specific SaaS tools resulted in a large number of SaaS companies flourishing during 2020. The year 2020 was a record one for SaaS initial public offerings (IPOs), with strong companies like Snowflake, JFrog and Unity on the top of the value leaderboard.

In this chapter, we look at the GTM strategies of these SaaS companies that thrived during 2020. Specifically, we examine the characteristics that make these companies more resilient during difficult market conditions. We also analyse the positive externalities gained by Product Led Growth (PLG) companies as a result of being part of a Cluster of Innovation (COI). While these companies do not operate in a specific vertical, they follow a similar GTM strategy and belong to a specific cluster of companies that leverage their product as a way to engage with their customers and grow. PLG companies are part of a larger community, and as such they benefit from the factors that characterise a COI.

## 5.2    WHAT IS PRODUCT LED GROWTH?

Product Led Growth is a go-to-market strategy used by B2B SaaS companies to access, engage and communicate with their buyers via their products. PLG companies do not rely on marketing and sales teams to grow the business; they build their products in a way that empowers users from the bottom up, letting them discover the value of the products by themselves. Most PLG companies on-board customers through a basic free plan or a free trial, and convert them into paying customers once they have tried the product.

Companies that are based on PLG strategies also have a product-led approach and build their whole organisation around the product. Unlike in traditional SaaS organisations, PLG companies do not have sales development representatives, business development representatives or account executives. Because the product itself does much of the sales, marketing and customer success work, these companies have lower customer acquisition costs (CAC) and shorter sales cycles.

Traditionally, B2B companies have not focused their attention on building the best products and providing an outstanding user experience to their users. While companies like SAP and IBM have been trying to bring consumer-like experiences to business software, they are still lagging behind many of the upcoming software vendors that provide a superior experience to their users. These are companies such as Evernote, Zoom and Typeform that have a product-centric strategy and are obsessed with building the best products and taking their users through seamless user experiences.

There are several characteristics that PLG companies have:

- Virality: PLG companies build features that empower collaboration among people within their own company as well as externally. Products also tend to have sharing capabilities integrated in the workflow, which leads to building the referral network from within the product.
- Frictionless sign-up and on-boarding: PLG companies make it very easy for users to create an account and start using the product. In many cases, users can use the product for free for a limited period of time or with limited capabilities, letting them try the product without committing to buy it.
- Delivering value quickly: products in PLG companies are built to deliver value to the users quickly – faster than many of the traditional software solutions. Most of these products do not require any integration to get their customers started, and quickly showing customers the value of the product helps these companies retain their users. When customers discover the value of the product as they sign up, they remember the good experience and come back again to get additional value.
- Value before money: many PLG companies let the customer try their products for free before they buy. Users convert into paying customers once they experience the value of the product and they understand the benefit they can get from it. As a result, paying customers are more loyal and more inclined to tell their colleagues and friends about the product.
- End-user focus: PLG companies are obsessed with building the product that their users love. They focus on providing an extraordinary user experience for the user, rather than focusing solely on the customer (buyer persona). By focusing on the user and their experience, PLG companies benefit from the referral network that is built around their users.

## 5.3    BEING A PLG COMPANY AS PART OF A COI

In recent years, there has been an explosion of companies that have successfully grown based on PLG strategies (Figure 5.1). According to OpenView,
in early 2021 there were more than 300 PLG companies in the market and
this number is growing very fast. In 2009, LogMeIn became the first PLG
company that completed an IPO, listing its shares on NASDAQ. LogMeIn
was founded in Bulgaria in 2003 to provide cloud-based remote work tools for
collaboration and is best known for its *GoToMeeting* product. With the rise
of PLG companies, by 2020 there were more than 20 firms that were listed in
public markets, including fast-growing companies such as Slack, Zoom, cloud
monitoring company Datadog and content delivery network Cloudflare. As the
number of companies built with PLG principles is growing, these businesses
have started to work within an ecosystem or COI in which positive externalities exists. Within that ecosystem or COI, (1) resources such as people and
capital are mobile and are shared by the players in the network; (2) individuals
are specialised in building product-centric organisations that can easily adopt
PLG strategies; (3) companies are built remotely, sell globally from the start,
and do not require marketing or sales teams in a given territory to sell; and (4)
they have an internal strong alignment towards building user-centric solutions
rather than focusing on revenue and customers.

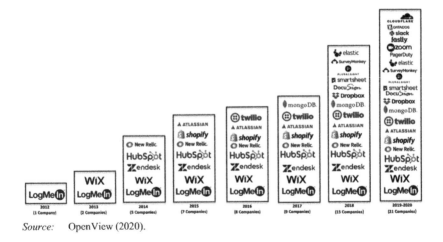

*Source:*     OpenView (2020).

*Figure 5.1*     *The rapid emergence and impact of the PLG COI*

### 5.3.1    Mobility of Resources among PLG Companies

One of the main characteristics of a COI is the mobility of resources, including people, capital and knowledge. In a COI, the mobility and rapid repurposing of resources within and among high-potential entrepreneurial firms intensifies innovation processes (Freeman and Engel, 2007). As the number of PLG companies has grown, there has been a growing number of people that have become experts in building PLG go-to-market strategies. Companies like HubSpot, Shopify and Twilio that pioneered the PLG movement have played a very important role in educating a large number of people that have become experts in building PLG businesses. These people are now leading product, product marketing and growth strategies within the new generation of PLG companies. One example of this mobility is Mickey Alon, who in 2012 founded a company called Insightera that was sold to Marketo in 2014, and is currently Chief Technology Officer at user analytics company Gainsight. All these companies (Insightera, Marketo and Gainsight) have a PLG go-to-market strategy, and Mickey is applying his previous experience to help new PLG companies grow. Another example is Kieran Flanagan, who is currently Senior Vice President of Marketing at HubSpot and was previously at Marketo, both PLG businesses. The mobility of experienced executives is facilitating the transfer of knowledge and best practices across the companies that are implementing PLG strategies to grow, and ultimately it is enabling the rapid development of the cluster of PLG companies.

Beyond the mobility of people, a growing amount of capital is also being invested in PLG companies as well as being recycled in other PLG companies after liquidity events. As an example, Alex Ferrara, a partner at Bessemer Venture Partners, invested in Shopify in 2010, and turned the $5.5 million investment into $500 million when the company went public in 2018 with a $15 billion valuation. Since then, Alex has led investments in several PLG companies, such as Pipedrive, Wix and GetAccept. As in other COI, within the PLG network, people, knowledge and capital are mobile and are accelerating the creation and growth of new PLG businesses.

### 5.3.2    PLG as a Rapid Growth Strategy

In COI, companies are specialised in a specific stage or method that results in the rapid development of the companies within the COI. In a COI of PLG companies, founders and executives are specialised in building and executing successful PLG strategies. These strategies are different from traditional enterprise GTM strategies as they are not based on marketing and sales teams. In PLG companies, customers are engaged through the product rather than through sales development representatives or account executives. Through the product, companies can qualify leads – known as product-qualified leads – and they use their own products to expand the contract values through new modules or through collaboration capacities built into the product. Kieran Flanagan at HubSpot is a good example of someone who has significant experience in building PLG companies and is using that knowledge and expertise to help other PLG companies. Apart from his position at HubSpot, Kieran is also an advisor to many other PLG companies, such as Miro and Postal.io, as well as an angel investor in some other PLG companies.

### 5.3.3    Born Global

In a COI, resources are highly mobile and frequently cross regional and national boundaries to take advantage of international opportunities. PLG companies are born global by default. As they use their products to reach out to their customers, PLG companies can sell to international customers as soon as the products are launched. Customers can discover the products on the internet through a search or advertising campaigns. Once customers discover these products, they do not need to request a demo; they can directly sign in and try the product before they buy. So anyone who has access to the internet can discover the product, regardless of their geographical location. PLG companies use localisation techniques to adapt their websites and to be able to appeal to any customer, in any language and currency around the world.

### 5.3.4    Alignment of Interest: Product-Centred Organisation

In a COI, rapid innovation and entrepreneurial processes are enhanced by the seamless interaction and strong collaboration among the players. Founders, investors, executives and employees in a COI are well aligned and committed to innovate and build fast-growing companies. In PLG companies, the alignment is stablished around the product, meaning that users' interests prevail over short-term business interests. The strategies defined and agreed upon by investors, founders, executives and employees start with user needs, then centre around problems and finally solutions. As the product is the main driver of growth, everyone within the organisation is responsible for performing according to the product-centred metrics defined. PLG companies follow user metrics instead of traditional business metrics. Metrics such as time-to-value, expansion revenue and product-qualified leads are critical, and are related to the North Star metric[1] that proves that the company is driving the best outcome for the customer. Investors that are funding PLG companies do not expect that these businesses will build traditional marketing and sales teams; they are also aligned to and supportive of investing in the product as the main channel to acquire customers. While the product team is at the heart of the organisation, the rest of the teams also have shared responsibilities and are also responsible for delivering the product-centred metrics. This product-centred strategy and alignment among founders, executives, employees and investors is a major driver of rapid growth in PLG companies.

## 5.4 THE COMPONENTS OF A PLG COI

A COI consists of a critical mass of actors whose behaviour favours innovation and new venture creation. As with other COI, a PLG COI has a set of actors that play an important role within that COI. The main actors or elements discussed in this article are the founders and CEOs of PLG companies as well as the investors investing in the space. However, there are other elements that also participate in these PLG COI, such as corporates or scale-ups, and service providers as well as education players, among others. As explained in the previous section, these actors or elements are highly mobile and born global, and are specialised in a business model that leverages their own products to grow. While the actors are not formally connected to each other, they have built a strong alignment and benefit from being somehow connected to each other.

### 5.4.1 The Founder: An Insider in an Industry, with an Outsider's View

PLG companies are started by founders that are obsessed with providing users with a superior product experience. Founders usually have an insider's view of the industry, they have experienced themselves and believe that end-users are demanding better experiences from the tools they use every day. We could probably say that the founders of PLG companies are insiders in an industry with an outsider's view, and that outsider's view is the users' view. One example of an insider founder is Eric Yuan, founder of Zoom. He founded the company in 2011 after spending over 10 years leading the engineering team at WebEx. In an interview with *Forbes* in 2019, Eric confessed his frustration with the experience that WebEx was giving to its users. He knew WebEx's product could be improved, and was embarrassed by negative customer feedback (Wingard, 2019). Similarly, the founders of Pipedrive, an inexpensive, easy-to-use Salesforce alternative, came from the sales industry. Before starting Pipedrive, Timo Rein helped build a leading sales and management training house in the Baltics. Prior to that, he was among the top 1 per cent of door-to-door salesmen with Southwestern Company. Timo and his four co-founders from Estonia started Pipedrive to build a product that people really wanted to use (Rein, 2012). They did not want to build the software for the managers, but rather for the end-users. In 2012, Timo had learnt from Gartner that 42 per cent of the licenses of customer relationship management (CRM) products were unused. He was frustrated by the idea that almost half of the software purchased in the world to support sales teams was never used, and he was determined to improve that user experience.

Designing for end-users requires the founders to understand what users really do, and to do that PLG companies collect many metrics from the start. These metrics measure the engagement that users have with the product. They measure the time it takes for the users to create an account, the number of steps they need to go through to get their product in operation, the number of customers that come back to the product after they leave and the time they spend in a day using the product. These metrics are not too different from the engagement metrics gathered in traditional, sales-led software companies. However, they are collected very early, even before anyone is buying the product, which triggers rapid experimentation and innovation. Founders of PLG companies have good visibility of the way customers are using the product, and they embrace the rapid innovation characteristic of the COI.

### 5.4.2    The Investor: The Transition from Enterprise to PLG

In the last 20 years, the number of investors focusing on B2B opportunities building software in the cloud has grown significantly. SaaS companies provide predictable, recurring revenue; they can scale by keeping fixed costs low; and they are likely to upsell to their own customers, which generates additional revenue with few or no additional acquisition costs. In terms of returns, in the last decade SaaS companies have performed well and have generated strong returns to their investors. Because of all these reasons, the investment going into SaaS companies has grown significantly and there are ever more investors hunting for the next SaaS unicorns.

However, the profile of the investors focusing on PLG companies is different from investors focusing on SaaS companies that are enterprise-first. Twenty years ago, when SaaS started to gain traction, most companies that were selling software in the cloud were focusing on enterprises. Companies like Salesforce and ServiceNow are two examples. As a result, the first generation of SaaS investors was also enterprise-focused, backing companies like Workday and Veeva. It was only around 2010 that a new generation of software companies targeting smaller and medium-sized businesses (SMBs) started to emerge. Some of these companies have been very successful and have attracted the interest of a new wave of investors that are looking to optimise sales velocity instead of contract value. Investors in PLG businesses are comfortable with pricing strategies that start with a freemium package and converting customers into premium subscriptions once they have tried the products. These investors can build conviction around businesses with contract values that are smaller than traditional enterprise contracts (below $10,000 yearly contracts); instead of contract values, these investors consider other metrics such as time-to-value, or the amount of time it takes for new users to experience the value of the product, as a central part of their investment thesis. In a PLG company, time-to-value is very short; ideally, customers should be able to experience the value of the product the first day they try it. For these investors, the expansion of the contracts and the virality coefficients which measure the times that a customer recommends a product to a colleague or a peer that also becomes a customer are critical metrics for making an investment.

Apart from the metrics mentioned, investors in PLG companies are also looking for a founder profile that is different from the traditional sales-led enterprise founder. Founders of PLG companies are product-focused rather than sales-focused, intent on providing an optimal user experience for their customers. Investors test these characteristics by looking at a product roadmap, which should include features to optimise the on-boarding of the users, accelerate the time-to-value and incentivise the users to invite their colleagues and peers to use the product.

In the same way that founders can specialise in building PLG companies, there are also investors that are specialised in evaluating, investing and helping PLG companies. An example is Alex Ferrara from Bessemer Venture Partners, who led investments in some of the most successful PLG businesses, including Shopify (a cloud-based multi-channel commerce platform designed for small and medium-sized businesses), Wix (a website builder) and Pipedrive. Another investor is Pietro Bezza, Managing Partner at Connect Ventures, who led investments in some of the fastest-growing PLG companies in Europe, including Soldo, Oyster HR and Typeform.

### 5.4.3 The New Wave of Major Corporations in PLG: The Connectors within the COI

As some of the PLG companies have become bigger, they have been consolidated as a platform for new PLG companies to emerge. Many of them have launched marketplaces so that other startups can sell their products through them. They also run conferences targeting their customers, and they invite partners who are building products on top of their platforms to showcase their products. These events foster the connections between the corporations, their customers and their partners. And all of them are part of a community that gets together over Facebook or a Slack channel to discuss topics related to their integrations with the main products, among others.

One clear example of a corporation in the PLG space which functions as a connector for the stakeholders in the PLG COI is Shopify. Shopify is a Canadian multinational ecommerce company headquartered in Ontario. The company offers online retailers a suite of services, including payment, marketing, shipping and customer-engagement tools. In May 2021, the company reported that it was powering more than 1.7 million businesses in around 175 countries. Shopify was started in 2006 by two engineers who wanted to build a snowboarding store online. As they could not find a suitable platform to do so, they built their own store from scratch using Ruby on Rails. In June 2006, they launched the first version of the Shopify store and three years later, they launched the Application Programming Interface (API) platform and the marketplace. The API allows developers to create applications for Shopify online stores and then sell them on the Shopify App Store. The company has grown bottom-up, allowing developers to build ecommerce solutions for as little as $29 per month. Shopify went public in 2015 on the New York Stock Exchange and raised over $130 million. In 2020, the company reported $2.93 billion in revenue, representing an 85 per cent year-on-year growth.

Shopify's success derives from its low entry bar as well as the community it has been able to build around its platform. As a developer or an ecommerce owner, you can try the product by yourself and do not need to be an expert to use Shopify. But more importantly, you can become an affiliate and earn an average of $58 per user you bring to the platform. This is a good way to build the community while increasing the virality effect. Similarly, as a developer or a founder, you can also promote your software through the marketplace; in 2020, the Shopify App Store had around 6,000 apps aimed at helping Shopify users maximise their sales. Shopify also has an annual conference for developers and partners that is helping it build the community around the product. In mid-2021, Shopify had a community of over 800,000 merchants and partners that have built connections with each other and benefit from supporting each another.

Shopify is only one example of a corporation in the PLG space that has grown significantly and is becoming the centre of a COI of companies that are somehow benefiting from being connected to each other. Twilio or WordPress have also built similar communities around themselves and have become the binding entity within a COI.

### 5.4.4    Management: Providing Advice to the Upcoming PLG Companies

While the number of successful PLG companies has grown significantly in the last decade, founders are still experimenting and trying to identify what the most effective strategies are to grow a PLG business efficiently. There are many reports and studies that have unbundled the GTM metrics of sales-driven companies; that is, sales cycles, customer acquisition costs and payback periods, among others. However, there is still limited data for these metrics when it comes to PLG. Founders of PLG companies are reaching out to former managers and key employees of successful companies like HubSpot, Zoom and Twilio to learn from their experiences and increase the chances of success. Managers of well-known PLG companies have quickly become experts and are now supporting the growth of other companies trying to build successful GTM strategies in the PLG space. The mobility and the knowledge-sharing that characterises COI is helping these managers to get connected to many new companies and to make a business out of it. Many of these managers are now working as advisors to the new generation of PLG companies. One example is Bill Macaitis, who was Chief Marketing Officer at Slack, Zendesk and Salesforce, and is today a growth advisor for many PLG companies. Or Andrew Capland, who led marketing at HubSpot, then growth at Wistia, and has now built his own growth consultancy focusing on helping PLG companies with lead generation and growth. All of these experts are accelerating the growth of the new generation of PLG companies.

### 5.4.5 The Community: Participating in the Global Network of COI

Community is an important aspect of COI. Due to the agile mobility of people, capital and knowledge, interactions among the participants in a COI are frequent and fluent. As in any virtuous circle, this frequent interaction enhances mobility and exchange of information, and has helped to create a strong PLG community. Within this community, participants are connected through weak ties that become stronger covalent connections as soon as they start working with each other. Organisations such as ProductLed.com or the Product-Led Growth Collective have contributed to the creation of these communities. The community is probably the most informal and still most efficient way for the upcoming PLG founders and executives to learn about the best practices in PLG.

The PLG community is global by nature. As explained earlier, PLG companies do not interact with the customers before they buy and as a result they can easily sell globally. As they do not require face-to-face interaction with customers, PLG companies tend to hire globally and leverage the connections within the community to attract the best talent regardless of their location. The Global Network of COI plays an important role facilitating the interaction among geographically distributed PLG COI. This Global Network of COI consists of a critical mass of participants that are highly mobile, enhance innovation, are born global and are not necessarily geographically collocated. Ultimately, a PLG COI is a participant of this Global Network of COI as it benefits from the existence and the behaviours of the participants in this network.

## 5.5    CONCLUSIONS: A PLG COI AS PART OF THE GLOBAL NETWORK OF COI

In this chapter, we have analysed the characteristics of a COI consisting of companies that use their own products to engage with their users and build revenue. We have described how, as in other COI, in these COI formed by PLG companies there are some Core Components (that is, the founders, the investors in PLG and the incumbent corporations), as well some Supporting Components that facilitate the interaction among the components. We have also seen that the components are somehow connected to each other and that this collaboration enhances their rapid expansion. Due to the international nature of PLG businesses that reach global markets from the start, the COI of PLG companies is also international.

But one of the most important findings of this chapter is not related to the components and the behaviours of these components within a COI. This chapter has proven that the framework of the Global Network of COI does not only apply to a city or a territory. So, it is not only locational. In this chapter we have proved that a COI can also be formed by businesses that share the same business model. In this case, we have analysed the COI network that consists of businesses whose business model is built around the product of the company and is known as Product Led Growth. We believe that this is an important contribution to the framework of the Global Network of COI which could also be used to explain the positive externalities resulting from the relationships among the components of other COI formed by companies based on different business models, such as marketplaces.

## NOTE

1.    A North Star metric is any measure that management believes is most predictive of a company's progress towards long-term success. Generally such metrics lead to revenue and reflect customers' satisfaction or perceived value. The term has been used more frequently with the emergence of online businesses, where simple measures of profitability have not been deemed satisfactory, and may include such metrics as customer engagement as measured by Monthly Average Users (MAU) or Daily Active Users (DAU), or growth efficiency as measured by the ratio of lifetime value (LTV)/customer-acquisition-cost (CAC).

## REFERENCES

Freeman, J., and Engel, J. (2007) Models of Innovation: Startups and Mature Corporations, *California Management Review*, 50 (1), 94–119.
OpenView (2020) *2020 SaaS Product Benchmarks Report*. Downloaded in September 2021. https://f.hubspotusercontent10.net/hubfs/366266/2020_SaaSProductBenchmarks .pdf.

Rein, T. (2012) *From 0 to Cash-Flow Positive*. YouTube video. Viewed in September 2021. www.youtube.com/watch?v=eisWA8WsS1s&t=405s.

Wingard, J. (2019) The Ascent Of Zoom CEO Eric Yuan: Leadership Lessons In Execution & Authenticity. *Forbes*. www.forbes.com/sites/jasonwingard/2019/05/15/the-ascent-of-zoom-ceo-eric-yuan-holds-leadership-lessons-for-all/?sh=703a3f987393.

PART II


Global Case Studies: Regional and Urban
Clusters

# 6. The Munich high-tech region: development towards a leading European startup cluster

**Helmut Schönenberger**

## 6.1 INTRODUCTION

In the late 19th century and again after World War II, Munich experienced rapid economic development, driven in part by continuing entrepreneurial initiative that developed successful local companies such as MAN, Munich Re, Allianz, Siemens and BMW into global leaders and made Munich a leading center of innovation and technology. However, despite its entrepreneurial history, ongoing economic success and strong basis of mid-sized and large corporations, in recent decades the Munich ecosystem has not continued to produce many innovative high-growth companies. This is a major challenge in the growth of the Munich Cluster of Innovation (COI).

### 6.1.1 TUM: The Entrepreneurial University

To face this challenge, at the beginning of the 21st century Technische Universität München (TUM), the alma mater of earlier famous entrepreneurs such as Carl von Linde, Rudolf Diesel, Claude Dornier and Willy Messerschmitt, developed a university-wide innovation program called TUM Entrepreneurship, whose central goal was to initiate more scalable high-tech startups. Under the brand of "TUM. The Entrepreneurial University", TUM's development process was closely connected to its former president Wolfgang A. Herrmann. The chemistry professor, who was elected in 1995, developed the vision to transform the academic institution into an entrepreneurial university not only by addressing excellence in education and research but also by building up and professionalizing the management of innovation and startup incubation. In addition to recruiting entrepreneurship professors and developing a technology-transfer office, the university established a large entrepreneurship center to build a systematic innovation and business-creation process that bridges the gap between industry and the university, and facilitates the founding of spin-off companies (see the timeline of TUM entrepreneurship development, Figure 6.1).

In 2002, the entrepreneurship center UnternehmerTUM was founded as an affiliated institute and strategic element of the TUM Entrepreneurship program. Based on the author's master's thesis, which compared the startup ecosystems of Stanford University and TUM, the concept of creating a startup center within the university was strongly supported by the TUM president and also heavily backed by German entrepreneur and investor Susanne Klatten. As a main shareholder of high-tech companies like Altana and BMW, her motivation has been to foster the next generation of entrepreneurs and innovators.

In order to generate revenue for its own sustainability and growth and to live up to its own entrepreneurial standards, UnternehmerTUM was structured as a private company owned by Susanne Klatten, who serves as chairwoman of the advisory board. To ensure its academic integration into the university, UnternehmerTUM was also set up as an affiliated institute of TUM. From the start, UnternehmerTUM has pursued supporting startup and innovation teams from a first idea to a scalable product for the mass market.

In response to corporate governance and tax law challenges, UnternehmerTUM has distributed its businesses across a number of legal entities. The first not-for-profit company, UnternehmerTUM GmbH, is the mother company and focuses on technology and entrepreneurship education, networking and startup incubation activities. Its main tasks are to inspire and educate students, academics and professionals to become entrepreneurs and innovators, to set up joint innovation projects and to support the creation of technology-based university startups.

Since 2004, UnternehmerTUM has established an extracurricular program for bachelor's, master's and PhD students called Manage & More. For this 18-month program 20 students are selected per semester from all TUM faculties and other Munich universities. Alongside their university courses, the participating students gain qualifications in entrepreneurial skills which guarantee them a better start in their professional careers, either as entrepreneurs or intrapreneurs. Corporate and startup partners provide the scholarship students with a personal mentor to offer guidance and support. The main focus is on interdisciplinary innovation and startup projects in which the students develop and market new products and services on behalf of corporate partners or with the intention of creating their own businesses.

The second company, UnternehmerTUM Projekt GmbH, manages the for-profit incubation and innovation consulting business. Together with clients from startups and established companies such as Airbus, BASF, EON, MAN and Siemens, project teams identify opportunities, develop business models and build startups and new business units for existing corporations.

The third UnternehmerTUM company is a venture capital (VC) firm called Unternehmertum Venture Capital Partners (UVC). The first fund, of 25 million euros, was structured in 2011 like most other privately held, independent VC companies. The company is financing cutting-edge technology startups with international potential originating in TUM and other German universities and research organizations.

In 2002, in addition to UnternehmerTUM, two incubator buildings were opened on the TUM campuses in Garching (GATE) and Weihenstephan (IZB). In this year TUM also officially started its School of Management. From the beginning, entrepreneurship was an important education and research field of the new faculty. One of the first appointed professors was Ann-Kristin Achleitner, who since 2001 has headed the new Chair in Entrepreneurial Finance, endowed by KfW, Germany's state-owned development bank. In May 2003 the Center for Entrepreneurial and Financial Studies (CEFS) was established as a joint institute by the Chair of Entrepreneurial Finance and the Chair of Financial Management and Capital Markets. The new center combines research on young, innovative and medium-sized companies in public and private capital markets. CEFS contributes heavily to the development of the German VC environment by training generations of VC professionals and advising the German government on entrepreneurial financing topics.

With its foundation the TUM School of Management also started the Bachelor and Master Program in Management and Technology (TUM-BWL). These modern management education programs, which include engineering and natural science courses, soon became a vital pool for entrepreneurial talents. In 2008, TUM School of Management, together with UnternehmerTUM, decided to establish the Executive MBA in Innovation and Business Creation. This executive education program helped attract many industry-experienced entrepreneurial students who were highly motivated to accelerate their startup ideas during the two-year part-time program.

In the same year, TUM also appointed a Chair for Industrial Design and introduced a master's degree program for industry designers. Within its project modules, design students supported TUM startup teams by adding product design competence into the development process. In many cases the designers also developed the corporate identity for the new companies and helped to professionalize the media channels of the startups.

In 2008, the university administration strengthened its service for TUM inventors and entrepreneurs by opening the Office for Research and Innovation (TUM ForTe). The internal university organization is the first point of contact and the central coordinating body for cooperation between the business and research sectors, research funding support and technology transfer at TUM. It also supports TUM startups with consulting services and incubation space. With TUM Patents and Licenses the office is also advising scientists on issues relating to utilizing their inventions, particularly with regard to patent and licensing matters. Additionally, TUM ForTe is in charge of managing the patent portfolio of the university.

TUM School of Management decided in 2010 to significantly expand its entrepreneurship faculty. As a first step, Holger Patzelt was appointed as Chair for Entrepreneurship. With the new chair as a nucleus, the TUM Entrepreneurship Research Institute (ERI) was founded to help develop entrepreneurship as a research field and improve the understanding of entrepreneurial individuals and organizations. One part of the research takes a psychological perspective and investigates entrepreneurial cognition and decision-making. Another research stream follows a business perspective and tries to understand the behavior of young organizations and factors that contribute to their success. Seven additional entrepreneurship professors have joined Holger Patzelt in TUM ERI.

Funding from the German government as well as the Bavarian state government has played a substantial role in facilitating the development of many programs. In the 1990s, the Bavarian government developed a central high-tech strategy to foster growth dynamics, and invested almost five billion euros in technology, education, research and infrastructure projects. Munich experienced a strong startup boom, which unfortunately ended with the collapse of the dot-com bubble in 2000–2001. Since 2006, the Bavarian government has again been promoting the development of industry and excellence clusters with funding initiatives. Federal funding, particularly through the 2006 German Excellence Initiative and the 2011 German Ministry of Economics and Technology EXIST Culture of Entrepreneurship initiative, has promoted concepts and methods to foster entrepreneurship and technology transfer within universities. On a European level, UnternehmerTUM serves as a hub for the European Union (EU)-funded Erasmus for Young Entrepreneurs cross-border exchange program, which gives aspiring entrepreneurs an opportunity to work with experienced entrepreneurs from other countries to learn how to build and run a business.

## TUM.THE ENTREPRENEURIAL UNIVERSITY.

Milestones

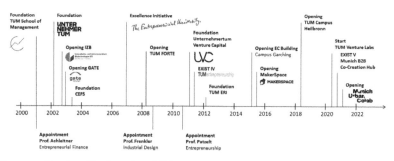

*Source:* Developed by the author, 2021.

*Figure 6.1    Timeline of TUM Entrepreneurship development*

### 6.1.2    4Entrepreneurship: Munich Universities Collaborate to Foster Entrepreneurship

In 2013, the four major universities in Munich – Ludwig-Maximilians-Universität München (LMU), TUM, Universität der Bundeswehr München and Hochschule München – joined forces to further enable students and researchers to build new companies. Each university has its own entrepreneurship center, addressing the strengths and needs of the institution and its students. Together, these four centers in Munich offer a broad spectrum of entrepreneurship courses, training and incubation programs which are open to more than 100,000 students. To further develop and coordinate entrepreneurship education, incubation and networking, the four entrepreneurship centers together found the think-tank 4Entrepreneurship, which served as a platform to develop strategies with government and local partners, create new joint entrepreneurship activities such as the Global Entrepreneurship Summer School, and bundle know-how and resources in special topic fields and share best-practice tools and methods.

## 6.2    MUNICH IN THE LAST DECADE

In the last ten years, founders in Germany have launched a larger number of rapidly growing companies such as Flixbus and Zalando and helped to develop a globally visible startup scene. In this process, Berlin and Munich have positioned themselves as leading national COI and business creation.

The German capital became the breeding ground for a high number of successful business-to-consumer internet companies in particular, with a strong focus on e-commerce and fintech. Outstanding success cases include unicorn companies such as Auto1, Delivery Hero, HelloFresh and N26. Many of Berlin's high-growth internet companies have their origin in Rocket Internet, a prominent company builder, incubator and VC fund, which was founded in 2007. Together with London and Paris, Berlin is heading most of Europe's startup city rankings.

The second largest startup ecosystem in Germany is Munich, with a strong concentration in business-to-business (B2B) tech startups. High-tech companies such as Blickfeld, Celonis, Isar Aerospace, Konux, Lilium, NavVis and Personio have originated in Munich. Most of these technology companies have been founded by students, researchers and alumni of local universities. Playing a pioneering role as an entrepreneurial university in Germany, TUM has become a particularly important incubator for these innovative, growth-oriented companies. The 2021 national ranking for startup universities, "Gründungsradar" ("Founder Radar"), puts TUM first among the big German universities for the fourth time in a row. TUM has evolved into an entrepreneurial hotspot, generating about eighty startups per year. In 2019 as well as in 2020, young companies from the ecosystem of TUM and its entrepreneurship center, UnternehmerTUM, collected more than one billion US dollars in startup and growth financing. This corresponds to about 15 percent of the national volume of VC financing in Germany.

Entrepreneurship and innovation are also addressed and encouraged by more of Munich's 20 universities with over 130,000 enrolled students. LMU and Hochschule München also provide intensive startup support to students, scientists and alumni. Both academic institutions operate large entrepreneurship centers with a focus on entrepreneurship education and startup incubation. Together with UnternehmerTUM, LMU Entrepreneurship Center and Strascheg Center for Entrepreneurship are very engaged in the strategic development and promotion of the local innovation ecosystem. In order to serve this long-term mission even better and as an evolution of the 4Entrepreneurship collaboration, the three entrepreneurship centers collectively founded a company called MUC Summit. Over the last few years, the joint company has established itself as Munich's central ecosystem builder, strategic partner and facilitator of premium networking events.

Beside these community activities, there is a long history of collaboration in the field of entrepreneurship education. A particularly successful joint program, the Center for Digital Technology and Management (CDTM), founded by LMU and TUM in 1998, has created numerous successful spin-offs. On a university level, the cooperation of the three largest Munich academic institutions has been intensified by creating the "One Munich Strategy" to further increase the cluster's international competitiveness. One specific building block is the joint Munich B2B Co-Creation Hub project (MCCH). This endeavor is financed by the Federal Ministry for Economic Affairs and Energy (BMWi) with the goal of enhancing the internationalization of the Munich startup scene and attracting even more foreign entrepreneurial students and startups.

Beside the university-related EXIST program, the federal government has also accelerated startup support by further strengthening the VC ecosystem. In 2020 a new ten billion euro Future Fund was announced, which is especially targeting the growth-financing phase of innovative startups. The new KfW-managed fund is supposed to complement existing early-stage financing instruments such as the High-Tech Gründerfonds and address the lack of sufficient growth capital in the German startup ecosystem. During the beginning of the Covid-19 crisis, the German government created an additional two billion euro package of measures to support startups and small enterprises with sustainable business models. The so-called Corona Matching Facility forms the central pillar of this initiative. Additional public funding was made available to highly innovative and forward-looking startups via established VC funds. This measure ensured that young enterprises had access to enough venture capital and could continue to grow in the difficult Covid-19 situation. Many Munich VC-backed startups benefited from these financial instruments. On top of the increased financial commitment of the federal government, the VC market is looking to expand by mobilizing more private and institutional investors such as insurance companies or foundations.

Local government has also ramped up its startup and high-tech support activities massively in recent years. In 2019, the Bavarian state government announced the Hightech Agenda Bavaria and granted special financial support for small and medium-sized enterprises (SMEs) in the form of a digital fund, a startup fund and an automotive fund. In addition, the state increased investments in artificial intelligence (AI) and "supertech" such as quantum technology, aerospace and cleantech. With this financial backing, Munich's universities and research organizations like Max-Planck-Gesellschaft and Fraunhofer-Gesellschaft have the opportunity to raise more funding for their fundamental and applied research agendas. These substantial investments will help to secure Munich's position as a leading European scientific location in the next decade.

### 6.2.1 TUM and UnternehmerTUM Ignite and Professionalize Practical Startup Support Activities

TUM is one of the top-ranked research universities in Europe, with 15 departments, about 170 degree programs and over 45,000 students, 34 percent of whom come from outside Germany. The faculty portfolio comprises engineering, natural sciences, medicine and life sciences as well as management, education and political sciences. To better foster interdisciplinary research, TUM has decided to merge its faculties into seven schools in the coming years. The university will also introduce the TUM Innovation Networks to start new research fields at the intersection of academic departments. The total annual budget of the university and its hospital exceeded 1.6 billion euros in 2019.

Over the years UnternehmerTUM has evolved into one of the leading university-based entrepreneurship centers in Europe, with hundreds of innovation and startup projects every year and with more than five thousand participants attending lectures, seminars and programs (see the structure of UnternehmerTUM, Figure 6.2). After ten years of operations the company employed over seventy people. In the 19th year of service, UnternehmerTUM now has more than 300 staff, including many experienced innovators and management consultants, venture capitalists, serial entrepreneurs and technology experts. In the last few years UnternehmerTUM has established a central incubation program called XPRENEURS. The startup program is especially designed for high-tech entrepreneurs in the fields of smart cities, urban mobility, new space, medical technology, sustainability, food and agriculture tech, and cyber security as well as B2B software and hardware. In XPRENEURS' three-month full-time incubation program, high-tech startups are supported on their way to market entry with assistance to validate the business model, win their first customers and acquire the first venture capital. These not-for-profit activities of UnternehmerTUM are mainly financed by Susanne Klatten and other donors, foundations, public grants and company sponsors. Beside these programs, UnternehmerTUM also operates other innovation and startup support offerings like the Digital Hub Mobility, the Digital Product School and the pre-incubation program XPLORE.

The second company, UnternehmerTUM Projekt GmbH, concentrates on for-profit activities. These include the management consulting business UnternehmerTUM Business Creators, the startup accelerator TechFounders and technology and industry initiatives like AppliedAI for AI and BEFIVE for innovations in the built environment. Together with clients from mid-sized *Mittelstand* companies like Festo, Hilti and Truma as well as large companies like BMW, Google, SAP and Siemens, project teams identify opportunities, apply new technology, prototype digital products, develop business models and build up startups and new business units for existing corporations. The biggest technology focus lies in the application of AI to transform existing industries. AppliedAI was formed as a neutral and trustworthy initiative that acts both as a platform and service provider. It is a driving force to strengthen the AI competence in the German startup and innovation ecosystem and helps its industry partners to accelerate the adoption of AI technology.

With its startup accelerator TechFounders, UnternehmerTUM Projekt GmbH also supports the collaboration between young and established companies. TechFounders is a 20-week international accelerator program which brings together tech startups with corporate partners by piloting joint proof-of-concept projects.

As one of the key partners of the Initiative for Industrial Innovators, UnternehmerTUM Projekt GmbH also supports technology-based founder teams and startups from its ecosystem with prototyping grants and founder-friendly convertible loans. The focus is on B2B startups with an industrial technology and enterprise software background, mainly from the fields of the Internet of Things (IoT), robotics, AI, virtual reality (VR), synthetic biology (SynBio) and medical technology (MedTech). Backed by the European Investment Fund (EIF), the initiative combines the strength of a multi-generational family office, an innovation center and a technical university. Each year, about ten Munich startup teams benefit from the prototyping grants and convertible loans.

The third UnternehmerTUM company is a VC firm called Unternehmertum Venture Capital Partners (UVC). After ten years of operation, the fund has over a quarter of a billion euros under management and is structured like most other privately held, independent VC companies in Europe. UVC is financing cutting-edge B2B technology startups with international market potential. About half of its portfolio companies are directly related to TUM or UnternehmerTUM. Most of the other startups have their origin in other German or European universities and research organizations. UVC's unique advantage is based on its close relationship with UnternehmerTUM, one of Europe's largest platforms for innovation and startups. Through this partnership, UVC provides startups with a unique network and infrastructure for accelerating their growth. The 15-person UVC team combines venture and startup experience with engineering and technology backgrounds and an understanding of how to grow and scale startups.

The fourth company of the UnternehmerTUM group is MakerSpace GmbH, operating two open, 1,500 square meter high-tech workshop facilities. Members have access to machines, software and hardware tools, as well as to a large creative community of instructors, makers and innovators. The facility serves ambitious startups, students, researchers and innovators from established companies. The do-it-yourself lab provides them with infrastructure and training to realize their ideas, build prototypes and start small serial productions. MakerSpace comprises various fabrication technologies like 3D printing, laser cutting, woodworking, metalworking, textiles and electronics. Many of Munich's most successful hardware startups, like ProGlove, Lilium and Isar Aerospace built their first prototypes in the open workshop facility.

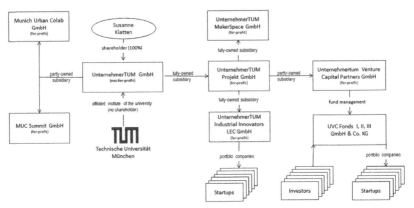

*Source*:   Developed by the author, 2021.

*Figure 6.2*    *Structure of UnternehmerTUM*

### 6.2.2    TUM: Ramping Up Entrepreneurship Education and Research as well as Technology Transfer within the University

In parallel to the build-up of practical startup support activities by UnternehmerTUM, TUM has expanded its entrepreneurship activities within its academic organization and the university administration. A central milestone in TUM's development has been the successful application for the German Excellence Initiative in 2006 and the funding of its institutional strategy "TUM. The Entrepreneurial University" by Deutsche Forschungsgemeinschaft (DFG), Germany's largest research funding organization. By its winning of the most important university funding scheme of the German government with an entrepreneurial motto, entrepreneurship became a well-accepted topic within the whole university community.

In 2011, the university decided to take the next development step of its startup activities and roll out "TUM Entrepreneurship". The new initiative was focused on generating more scalable high-tech companies. As a university-wide plan of action, its target was to encourage PhD students and faculty members in particular to commercially exploit research results and to create high-growth spin-offs. The initiative was funded by the BMWi within the national university entrepreneurship program EXIST-Culture of Entrepreneurship. Based on the existing entrepreneurship activities within TUM, the university board brought together key players from faculty and the entrepreneurship ecosystem and developed a shared vision. The university board also established a new vice president position for Entrepreneurship and Enterprise to ensure an effective and efficient implementation of the new initiative.

Within the initiative, four fields of action were addressed to generate more scalable high-tech startups. The first and central element of TUM Entrepreneurship was an efficient spin-off process. Throughout all startup development stages, from opportunity recognition until the growth phase, TUM and UnternehmerTUM wanted to support the university startup teams seamlessly. Support measures included technology scouting, opportunity assessment, team matching, consulting and coaching, customer acquisition, internationalization and fundraising. A second strategic element of TUM Entrepreneurship addressed human resources and legal topics. Within the project, TUM was optimizing administration processes for inventors and entrepreneurs, helping them to deal with intellectual property (IP), human resources and other legal concerns. This included fast and startup-friendly IP policies, working guidelines for university employees and attractive incentive systems as well as easy access to infrastructure. A third key element was networking. Startup teams benefit from a well-managed university network with partners from industry, politics and science. An entrepreneurship community was systematically built that included serial entrepreneurs, inventors, investors, potential pilot customers, industry experts and alumni. The community members were involved by offering entrepreneurship training, workshops and pitch sessions, and as guest speakers, mentors and jury members. The fourth strategic element was entrepreneurship research. With the help of TUM ERI, startup support best practices were analyzed, spin-off processes were optimized, and new modern methods and tools were developed, addressing key questions like business models, team building and development, financing, internationalization and growth management. For the successful implementation of the TUM Entrepreneurship strategy, it was very important to build up all four strategic elements in parallel, to receive constant feedback from the participants and to monitor key performance indicators like the number of scalable high-tech startups and the overall volume of VC investments in new companies.

The TUM Entrepreneurship strategy also included the plan for a new building on the university campus in Garching. The idea was to set up UnternehmerTUM, TUM ERI and the TUM startup incubator under one roof. The 6,500 square meter facility also provided the opportunity to open MakerSpace as an important high-tech infrastructure for entrepreneurs and innovators. The new entrepreneurship center was inaugurated in 2015.

A major development step for TUM School of Management came in 2018. TUM and the foundation Dieter Schwarz Stiftung signed a strategic partnership, which is one of the most important endowments in the history of German universities. The endowment is financing 20 new professorships with a focus on digital transformation, family-owned companies and entrepreneurship. As a central element of this cooperation TUM is opening a new campus in

Heilbronn, a city with about 125,000 residents in northern Baden-Württemberg (a federal state in the south-west of Germany). The Heilbronn district, one of the most innovative regions in Germany, is famous for its successful, globally oriented, family-owned companies like Lidl and Würth. The foundation also launched its own entrepreneurship center called Campus Founders. In collaboration with UnternehmerTUM, Campus Founders is offering hands-on education, incubation and startup support services in Heilbronn.

The massive ramping-up of TUM's entrepreneurship education, research and technology-transfer activities has already shown a significant increase in the startup output of the university. In 2012 twenty scalable companies were founded, and ten startups raised VC with an overall investment volume of around ten million euros. In 2019, these numbers grew to over fifty new scalable companies. More than forty TUM and UnternehmerTUM startups raised venture capital with an overall investment volume of more than one billion US dollars. TUM has evolved to become the most important source for Germans' high-tech startups. The university and its entrepreneurship center UnternehmerTUM are the cradle of around 10 percent of all new, VC-backed tech ventures in Germany.

## 6.3    THE CURRENT CHALLENGE: GAINING MOMENTUM TO GENERATE MORE EUROPEAN SCALABLE STARTUPS

This chapter discusses the strengths and weaknesses as well as opportunities and risks of TUM's entrepreneurship strategy, activities and outcomes on a university level as well as a cluster level.

With the development of TUM as an entrepreneurial university and the important contributions of the other universities and entrepreneurship support organizations, the Munich region has gained momentum as a lively European startup ecosystem in the last decade. Despite this progress in the cluster dynamics and despite its strong base of established mid-sized and large companies, the Munich ecosystem is still not producing enough new innovative, fast-growing, global companies. The Bavarian cluster has not been able to regain the momentum of the high-growth "Wirtschaftswunder" period in the 1950s and 1960s and has not kept up with the startup success in worldwide leading entrepreneurship clusters like Silicon Valley and Beijing. For example, the invested VC volume in the region is by a factor of five to ten smaller than in the leading American or Chinese startup hubs. Despite the massive growth of local startup and VC activities in the last decade, Munich is still missing value-creation dynamics with a self-reinforcing effect for generating large numbers of scalable startups. Regardless of a rising entrepreneurial culture and a corresponding startup ecosystem growth, Munich's development is still not fast enough in the global competition for producing new market and technology leaders.

With a track record of initiating over fifty high-tech startups per year, TUM and UnternehmerTUM have continuously expanded their key position in the Munich cluster and gained the reputation of being the leading tech startup foundry in Germany. However, most of the successful companies so far are founded by bachelor's and master's students or alumni. The full potential of university inventions and entrepreneurial scientists' findings has not been tapped to date. Despite all the success to date, the university still has to prove that its strategy unlocks the full commercialization potential of research results and the generation of more scalable tech startups.

The strategic entrepreneurship approach of TUM and UnternehmerTUM has turned out to be very positive for the cluster. But its implementation in practice is complex and the operation of the numerous activities is demanding for the staff. The coverage of the whole innovation and business-creation process from first idea to initial public offering (IPO) in a "one-stop agency" requires many competencies and a large organization. To address the multitude of critical issues within the new-venture-creation journey, the university and its entrepreneurship center need a large variety of experts, resources and know-how. The biggest organizational unit is UnternehmerTUM, which is run by a team of over 300 people specializing in different management and technology topics. Despite the large team, the effectiveness, innovativeness and stability of the entrepreneurship support organizations within TUM and UnternehmerTUM highly depend on key promoters like Susanne Klatten and the newly elected TUM President Thomas Hofmann, as well as a small number of executives, professors and experts. One example of the dependency on specific individuals is the withdrawal of Fritz Frenkler, the Chair of Industrial Design. With his retirement the design competence within the university decreased significantly, design education suffered and many startup projects could no longer be staffed with design students.

The sustainability of the TUM and UnternehmerTUM approach also depends heavily on long-term financial support and the backing of Susanne Klatten, the university and the government as well as generous donors and long-term-oriented corporate partners. After nearly 20 years of operations, UnternehmerTUM is generating most of its budget in its for-profit business. Nevertheless, about a third of the entrepreneurship center's funding still depends on external support in order to finance its large, not-for-profit education and startup-incubation activities.

Another big challenge is the recruitment and retention of entrepreneurship and innovation experts within the university. Without sufficient professional and experienced staff, the university and its entrepreneurship center are not able to address the needs of the different target groups and meet the demanding requirements and expectations of the top entrepreneurial scientists and startup teams. An additional challenge is to bridge cultural gaps between the university, startup community and industry, and to connect the people between these groups. Due to the broad spectrum of education, research and entrepreneurship activities and the differences between the not-for-profit operations and the for-profit businesses, the university and its entrepreneurship center have to handle cultural tensions and balance the interests and expectations of the different groups within the organization. This means that the university and its stakeholders must take extra care to integrate the different fields of activities, learn from each other, leverage synergies, and distribute resources in a fair and sustainable manner. The entrepreneurship activities at TUM are strategically managed and controlled by the TUM president, the senior vice president of research and innovation, and the vice president for entrepreneurship. The president is also a member of the advisory board of UnternehmerTUM, which is headed by Susanne Klatten.

The overall positive development of the Munich startup cluster, the good economic situation and the strong presence of attractive global tech companies like Amazon, Apple, BMW, Google, Microsoft, SAP and Siemens also create disadvantages for local startup teams. For many years Munich has been the most expensive major city in Germany, with a high salary level and a booming real estate market. Young companies compete with established companies and academic institutions for the best talent. This challenge is shared with most university cities and startup hotspots like London, Paris, Stockholm, Zurich and Berlin. The shortage of affordable living space is especially a growing challenge for students and startup teams in Munich.

On the positive side, the Munich region is firmly grounded on its concentration of mature corporations, small and medium-sized enterprises, universities, research and development centers, and various service providers. Many industries, like automotive and aerospace, were hit badly by Covid-19 and the subsequent recession, as well as by global trade conflicts and technology and market disruptions. However, the strong presence of traditional companies such as Allianz, Airbus, BMW, Burda, Infineon, Knorr-Bremse, Linde, MAN, Munich Re and Siemens continues to be an important strength of the Bavarian cluster. A positive trend for Munich in the last few years has been that leading global digital corporations such as Amazon, Apple, Google, Huawei, IBM and Microsoft have increased their strong presence in the cluster, with various research, development and sales units and plans to enlarge their local activities by hiring thousands of new employees. Learnings from the Covid-19 lockdown phases have also added momentum to the transition to a more digital economy throughout the cluster.

The community of well-educated and entrepreneurial young people in the region has been continuously growing. TUM and UnternehmerTUM alone are educating over 5,000 students per year in entrepreneurship and giving them access to the latest high-tech tools and methods. In the last decade the ecosystem has also produced a large number of successful serial entrepreneurs who remain active in a sequence of startups and act as role models, mentors and investors. The mobility of people has also improved between industry, startups and academic institutions. Many senior professionals are now interested in working for startups. With the necessary financial resources and promising exit stories, many startups are able to attract these executives and experts as co-founders and team members.

As mentioned above, the VC environment in the region has rapidly improved, and a strong and active VC community, especially for early-stage investments, has emerged. With the help of large US, Chinese and European VC, Corporate Venture Capital (CVC) and Private Equity (PE) funds like Lakestar, NEA and Tencent, even large growth-financing rounds are now possible. Examples of successful closings from 2019 and 2020 are Flixbus, with 500 million euros; Lilium, with 300 million euros; and Celonis, with 250 million euros. However, compared to Silicon Valley, Munich is still lacking large-scale local growth funds. Digital+ Partners, EMH and HV Capital and more local investment teams are filling this gap. Inspired by successful financing rounds, the local entrepreneurship community has accepted the concept of shared ownership and the alignment of incentives to reach a win–win situation between founders, investors and employees. Moreover, a growing number of entrepreneurs in the ecosystem start out with an ambitious, global perspective and want to build successful, internationally oriented companies with scalable business models.

A big opportunity for more local value creation lies in the collaboration between startups and established companies. In the last few years large corporates like Allianz, Airbus, BMW, Infineon, Knorr-Bremse, Linde, SAP and Siemens have started venturing programs and founded their own corporate venture funds. The German small and medium-sized enterprises called *Mittelstand* could also benefit tremendously from cooperation with startups. The young companies could help with digital transformation, introduce new working methods and come up with new, innovative business models. Startups could win the *Mittelstand* companies as customers, suppliers and investors and learn from them, leading to long-lasting companies. Category leaders like Brainlab, Festo, SICK and Webasto have proven that they can compete in international markets and export a large portion of their products and services. These very successful mid-sized German companies can serve as role models for the next generation of global entrepreneurs and give guidance on how to build up successful international businesses.

All in all, Munich is on a good path to become one of the leading European tech startup hotspots. The Munich COI has improved significantly on both hard and soft success factors. In the last decade the cluster was able to further grow its sound base of COI components, such as Universities, Research Centers, Government Institutions, Mature Corporations and Service Providers. The ecosystem has developed a much more active startup and VC community. Similarly, the Munich cluster has shown improvements in COI behaviors. Through educating thousands of students and closing hundreds of financing rounds, a better common understanding of the entrepreneurial process, shared ownership and scalable startups has been achieved in the ecosystem. With the growing community and an increasing number of success cases, the mobility of resources, especially people, has increased.

If the overall economic situation allows and if important stakeholders and decision makers keep entrepreneurship as a top priority, the positive trend and the rise of the Munich COI will continue. Central questions for future growth could be whether the cluster is capable of further accelerating its development speed, whether it is able to unleash its full research and industry potential, and whether it is pursuing more global strategic perspectives with strong European and worldwide connections. To reach the same cluster dynamics level as Silicon Valley or Beijing, Munich has to improve its performance in the next decade again, by a factor of five to ten.

In the following three case study sections, three priority projects of TUM and UnternehmerTUM for a high-performance startup ecosystem in Munich are described in more detail. These measures focus on a better commercialization of research results at TUM, an improved collaboration between startups and established organizations, and development of a more integrated European financial and business market.

## 6.4    CASE STUDY 1: TUM AND ITS THIRD MISSION – ENTREPRENEURSHIP

For roughly 20 years TUM has been on a development journey of becoming an entrepreneurial university which sets creativity, innovation and entrepreneurship as top priorities. To date, most universities, including TUM, have not yet reached the goal of a fully functioning and mutually reinforcing knowledge triangle consisting of (i) education, (ii) research and (iii) innovation and entrepreneurship. On a political level the importance of this knowledge triangle and its third mission, innovation and entrepreneurship, has been emphasized and supported for a long time. For example, the council and the representatives of the governments of the EU member states already agreed on this goal in November 2009.

Nevertheless, the successful implementation of the knowledge triangle concept remains to be proven, especially by a strong track record of scalable startups emerging from research. Major concerns are the missing critical mass of entrepreneurially thinking researchers within the academic departments and the underutilized entrepreneurial capabilities, processes, infrastructure and other resources in the different research and development fields. To address this unsolved challenge, TUM together with UnternehmerTUM initiated the TUM Venture Labs in 2019. It will take many years to get this strategic initiative rolled out and to achieve a reinforcing entrepreneurship culture within the whole academic institution.

In recent years, universities and other research organizations like Max-Planck-Gesellschaft and Fraunhofer-Gesellschaft have been heavily supported with new, big technology funding programs from the German and Bavarian governments, such as the Bavarian Hightech Agenda. Parallel to the massive increase of research activities, it is now critical to prioritize commercialization and transfer research results at scale into innovative products and services. Without such technology commercialization, research will not contribute to technical sovereignty, growth and the creation of new jobs as the means for achieving a prosperous, fair and environmentally sustainable future.

TUM Venture Labs are addressing this challenge. TUM and UnternehmerTUM have the common goal of leveraging their unique research power and increasing the quality and quantity of scalable technology spin-offs and ventures in the region by a factor of ten. With this output, TUM could become a driving force for the future technological sovereignty of the continent and a leading technology hub in Europe.

TUM Venture Labs are reinforcing in a unique way tech-based business creation at the interfaces of engineering; natural, life and data sciences; and medicine. They support entrepreneurial talent in technology-oriented business translation from research, offering an entire ecosystem with the necessary development environments. The labs provide a full range of development resources, from technical and social infrastructure through entrepreneurship training to hands-on support from business and investor networks. The labs are development spaces for future high-tech companies in upcoming technology fields and at their interfaces. Entrepreneurial talents, researchers and startups are free to use the training and venturing offerings. With the support of technology and market-specific expert networks, state-of-the-art development tools and infrastructure, startup teams will be able to incubate and accelerate their business ideas much more effectively and efficiently. AI, robotics and software will serve as core technologies throughout all of TUM Venture Labs. Some labs will focus on "supertech" topics like aerospace and quantum developments. The TUM Venture Lab Healthcare will focus on digital solutions as well as MedTech and biotechnology (BioTech). Environmental, nutritional, natural-resources and climate-relevant topics will be particularly addressed in the TUM Venture Labs for agrofood, energy and sustainability. Additional labs in additive manufacturing, mobility and the built environment are planned.

Each TUM Venture Lab will be operated by an experienced full-time management team and supported by academic directors for various faculties and by venture directors of the UnternehmerTUM team. The TUM Venture Labs will be coordinated by a general managing director who will directly report to the university board. All labs and their venture teams will have access to the existing entrepreneurship support activities of TUM and UnternehmerTUM.

## 6.5    CASE STUDY 2: MUNICH URBAN COLAB – A SPACE FOR COLLABORATION AND CO-CREATION BETWEEN STARTUPS AND ESTABLISHED ORGANIZATIONS

The economic strength of Bavaria, Germany and Europe is closely linked with *Mittelstand* companies. A big opportunity for the economy's innovation ecosystem lies in better collaboration and mutual exchange of knowledge between these established companies and young firms. Startups constantly produce innovative technology and disruptive business models. On the other hand, startups need established companies as strategic partners, customers, suppliers and investors to be successful. A close interaction would foster the innovation speed, accelerate the digital transformation, help to adapt to a "New Work" environment and boost sustainable solutions.

For the next development phase, UnternehmerTUM is focusing on fostering the collaboration between startups and established companies. To operationalize this approach, the entrepreneurship center is concentrating on particular technology and market segments like AI (AppliedAI), mobility (Digital Hub Mobility) and the built environment (BEFIVE). The built-environment sector – globally the biggest consumer of resources and originator of harmful emissions – in particular is in a disruption phase. This industry is characterized by high inefficiencies, a poor innovation culture and a low degree of digitization. UnternehmerTUM initiates and manages cross-company projects in impactful built-environment innovation areas. Industry networks bring experts together from established companies, research institutes, startups and authorities to jointly work in agile, hands-on projects regarding solutions for a circular economy, industrialization of construction and efficient, intelligent buildings. UnternehmerTUM's cooperation platform BEFIVE pragmatically and holistically works with companies along the entire built-environment value chain on important innovation and digitization topics. The BEFIVE objectives are to foster exchange, boost cooperation, enable cultural change in companies and thereby drive built-environment innovation. Together with its well-known industry partners, like Hilti, LafargeHolcim, Max Bögl and Peri, BEFIVE has developed a vision for the built-environment value chain in 2030 and is applying this joint picture of the future as a strategic orientation and framework to work systematically on important innovation topics.

On top of these industry initiatives, the public sector is also getting involved as an active innovation partner in the cluster. Together with UnternehmerTUM, in early 2021 the City of Munich inaugurated a new building that serves as a best-in-class innovation and business creation center: Munich Urban Colab. The Colab, located in the "Creative Quarter" in downtown Munich, has become a home to startups, innovators, scientists and creative minds to work on livable, future-proof and efficient solutions for cities of the future. The Colab aims to serve as a hotspot for collaboratively exchanging knowledge, exploring concepts and experiencing prototypes for groundbreaking city solutions together with relevant stakeholders. Using the City of Munich as a test environment, the developed solutions are improved and prepared for a global market launch, supported by an international partner network.

New technology and disruptive innovation can only be successfully developed, applied and scaled with the buy-in and support of citizens and different stakeholders from business, science and government. To facilitate the exchange of ideas and fruitful innovation processes, extraordinary spaces like Munich Urban Colab and powerful platforms like UnternehmerTUM are needed. Innovators want access to infrastructure, tools, methods, technology, co-founders, expert communities, markets and capital. They need spaces to develop, prototype, test and improve their products and services. In open locations like the Colab, civil society and interest groups, scientists and students, companies and startups, public authorities and legislators are coming together to discuss social challenges, exchange and explore new technologies and ideas, and develop, test and scale solutions.

BEFIVE and many more startup and innovation programs of UnternehmerTUM, like TechFounders, XPRENEURS and UVC, as well as academic, government and industry partners, are moving into the new, shared building to co-create and accelerate hundreds of startups and innovation teams.

## 6.6 CASE STUDY 3: MUNICH'S CONTRIBUTION TO A JOINT EUROPEAN FINANCIAL AND BUSINESS MARKET

In order to be as competitive and growth-oriented as Chinese and American startups, it is important to provide European young, scalable companies with easy access to a large single market in Europe; to reduce bureaucratic barriers; to improve public procurement of services from startups; and to build up a strong-performing, home-grown venture-financing environment. To pursue these goals, a strong network of Europe's leading entrepreneurial universities and entrepreneurship centers could become a driving force for strengthening the exchange between clusters, improving the framework conditions and jointly accelerating new European unicorn companies.

A network of these university incubators and entrepreneurship centers could support the matching of multi-national startup teams. On a European level UnternehmerTUM already serves as a hub for the EU-funded exchange program Erasmus for Young Entrepreneurs. Through this cross-border exchange program, aspiring entrepreneurs have the opportunity to work directly with experienced entrepreneurs from other European countries and get used to good business practices. The exchange also helps young entrepreneurs to think globally and get a better international market perspective. In a later stage, startups could be accompanied during the market entry in various EU member states with a "soft landing" platform in a participating entrepreneurial cluster. For young companies with B2B business models, the entrepreneurship centers could make introductions to their local industry ecosystems. This international support network could empower startups to launch their products and services quickly and efficiently on a European scale, handle local bureaucratic processes and open subsidiaries in the relevant member states. To serve this mission better, three Munich universities, together with their startup centers LMU Entrepreneurship Center, UnternehmerTUM and Strascheg Center for Entrepreneurship, have bundled their internationalization activities in the MCCH. As mentioned in the introduction, this initiative is financed by the BMWi, under the EXIST Potentiale program.

The leading European entrepreneurship universities could also help public procurement processes to open up for startups as suppliers. As users and customers, the governments on a local, state, national and European level should make much more intensive use of the expertise of startups and draw on their innovative products and services in the future. This would be an important step for Germany and Europe to remain competitive in cutting-edge technologies such as aerospace, artificial intelligence, cybersecurity, life sciences and robotics, and to maintain a country's technological sovereignty. TUM and UnternehmerTUM, with their intensive network involving government institutions, could serve as catalyzers and bridge-builders.

In the VC market public institutions and governments are already very active and supportive. Good examples are the EIF and KfW. Both financial institutions are heavily engaged as limited partners in European VC funds. UnternehmerTUM's two venture-financing vehicles – the Initiative for Industrial Innovators and UVC – are strongly supported with EIF taking a leading role as a fund investor.

UnternehmerTUM's second financing vehicle, the Initiative for Industrial Innovators, is especially pursuing a European vision. It wants to build on Europe's historic strength of supporting innovations that underpin resilient economies. The purpose of the Initiative is to systematically equip the next generation of industrial innovators to prototype, productize and deploy engineering-based, deep tech solutions. It supports young talents, teams and startups by providing translation and commercialization know-how, prototyping tools and stage-specific financial resources in the form of grants and convertible loans. The Initiative plans to connect innovation ecosystems across the continent, promoting a new generation of Europe-based companies to lead globally. It wants to facilitate the rise of the next generation of industrial entrepreneurs and strengthen innovation and entrepreneurship in Europe by combining the best of two worlds: family offices on the one side, and technical universities with strong entrepreneurship centers on the other. Industrial family businesses have been the backbone of the European economy for centuries. Family offices have historically nurtured and amplified innovations and think in generations. Leading technical universities foster young talents creating industrial inventions. Dedicated entrepreneurship centers support teams to commercialize their innovations. By partnering in one cluster, a family office can bundle its strengths with a local technical university and innovation center to support and fund startups. The Munich cluster, with TUM, UnternehmerTUM and Susanne Klatten's family office, serves as a pilot for the Initiative and a potential role model for other European local hubs.

Within the Initiative, partners can help to match cross-border teams, make cross-border investments and exchange best practices as well as opening their industrial and financial networks for startups from other hubs. Through the structuring of deal-flow and investment data and personnel exchanges, the Initiative lays the basis for creating and implementing collaborative programs to enable cross-border flows of talent, capital and know-how.

With the closing of UVC III, a fund of more than 150 million euros, UVC also plans to invest more in European startup teams and gain leading European growth funds as co-investors for its portfolio companies. UVC and UnternehmerTUM serve as a local host and partner for these large European and global VC funds in Munich and help to connect them and their own portfolio startups with the local COI.

## 6.7 LESSONS LEARNED AND CONCLUSION: MUNICH'S COI IN THE POST-COVID-19 WORLD

In the last 20 years, TUM and UnternehmerTUM have continuously set up and improved their startup support activities covering the whole entrepreneurial journey from first idea to the growth phase. The technical university is systematically pursuing the third mission, innovation and entrepreneurship, and has even given itself the central motto "TUM. The Entrepreneurial University". By enabling entrepreneurial talents, matching interdisciplinary teams and giving them access to the latest technology, methods and tools, as well as to investors and customers, a substantial number of new scalable tech companies have been built in the university ecosystem in recent years. With the hands-on acceleration of the next generation of innovators and entrepreneurs, TUM and UnternehmerTUM have become a driving force for entrepreneurship in the Munich COI and in Germany. As described above, the Munich ecosystem has positioned itself as a visible cluster worldwide but is still missing the dynamics and accumulation of resources comparable to the ones in Silicon Valley or Beijing. Measured by VC volume, Munich is still five to ten times smaller than these worldwide leading clusters. Nevertheless, with TUM as a central stakeholder and the government as a strong supporter, the ecosystem is committed to taking the next step and becoming one of the leading startup clusters in Europe.

Besides the economic perspective, it is important for the Munich cluster and its innovators and entrepreneurs to also contribute as pacemakers for new successful, sustainable solutions. Society is facing many challenges and uncertainties, such as the Covid-19 crisis and its aftermath, digitalization, climate change, limited resources and an aging population. Europe has to ensure its security, freedom, democracy and diversity, and should also take care of others and be a good partner to other nations and continents. Therefore, a strong, solution-oriented society is needed with many optimistic young leaders, innovators and entrepreneurs who are willing and able to take the responsibility for putting future visions like Europe's New Green Deal into practice.

Sustainability issues will provide great opportunities for startups in the post-Covid-19 phase. Since the definition and adoption of the international Sustainable Development Goals (SDG) in 2016, the topic has gained growing momentum. More and more founders and investors focus on this topic and want to contribute positively to reaching these goals. Also, a growing number of fund investors, such as the EIF, are committing their VC funds to examine the SDG impact of their startup portfolio and to make sure that their investments contribute in a good manner.

Entrepreneurial universities and startup centers also increasingly focus on sustainability. For example, "Shaping a sustainable living environment" is one mission of TUM. The university addresses this challenge particularly by looking at the interplay between environmental, climate, energy, nutrition and resource concerns. In research, education and entrepreneurship, TUM aims to raise the innovative potential across multiple disciplines spanning the natural sciences, life sciences, engineering, the humanities, social sciences, management and medicine.

In addition to the university activities, the BMW Foundation, together with UnternehmerTUM, launched the startup accelerator RESPOND, supporting founders in the scaling of their company and emphasizing the importance of financially, ecologically and socially relevant business models. A RESPOND startup "batch" is set up for a period of five months and is directed at teams who solve complex global issues with innovative technologies.

Additional momentum for change in the Munich ecosystem comes through Covid-19. The innovation system and especially digital transformation are in a fast-forward mode and wide open to experimentation as a result of the lockdown learnings. In this situation of crisis, the necessity and urgency of digitalization have become clear in many organizations. A number of companies and public institutions have introduced digital and innovative solutions with a new speed and keenness on experimentation. They gathered positive experiences in the time of crisis and became more open. The gained understanding and confidence could provide additional momentum for a long-term innovation and digitalization movement and its systematic implementation. In the Covid-19 crisis, startups played a major role for the digitalization and flexibilization of industry and the health sectors. One Munich example for a dynamic startup providing solutions for health services is GNA Biosolutions. The LMU spin-off developed instruments and assays for ultrafast nucleic-acid-based Covid-19 testing and was able to bring the system on the market during the pandemic.

For the post-Covid-19 time it is important to keep the positive dynamics of the recent years, learn from the experience of the lockdown phase and consistently and continuously improve the local ecosystem by implementing the strategic measures. Munich is in a good position to become a self-reinforcing COI in the future and a European and global leader.

## REFERENCES

Bayerische Staatsregierung (2019). *Hightech Agenda Bayern Regierungserklärung des Bayerischen Ministerpräsidenten am 10. Oktober 2019*. Bayerische Staatskanzlei.

Bundesministerium für Wirtschaft und Energie (2019). *Das ist EXIST 2018*. BMWi.

Bundesministerium für Wirtschaft und Energie (2019). *Wertschätzung – Stärkung – Entlastung: Eckpunkte der Mittelstandsstrategie*. BMWi.

Engel, J.S. (2014). What are Clusters of Innovation, how do they operate and why are they important? In J.S. Engel (Ed.), *Global Clusters of Innovation*. Cheltenham, UK and Northampton, MA, USA: Edward Elgar Publishing.

European Union (2009). *Conclusions of the Council and of the Representatives of the Governments of the Member States, meeting within the Council, of 26 November 2009 on developing the role of education in a fully functioning knowledge triangle, Official Journal of the European Union 12.12.2009*. https://eur-lex.europa.eu/LexUriServ/LexUriServ.do?uri=OJ:C:2009:302:0003:0005:EN:PDF.

Expertenkommission Forschung und Innovation (2019). *EFI-Gutachten 2019*. www.e-fi.de/fileadmin/Assets/Gutachten/EFI_Report_2019.pdf.

Schoenenberger, H. (2014). Germany: high-tech region Munich generating the nest wave of scalable startups. In J.S. Engel (Ed.), *Global Clusters of Innovation*. Cheltenham, UK and Northampton, MA, USA: Edward Elgar Publishing.

Stifterverband (2021, January 3). *Gründungsradar – Der Gründungsradar des Stifterverbandes vergleicht Hochschulprofile in der Gründungsförderung an deutschen Hochschulen*. www.gruendungsradar.de.

TUM (2021, January 3). *Die TUM in Zahlen – Facts and Figures*. www.tum.de/en/about-tum/our-university/facts-and-figures/.

# 7. The Oslo case: agile and adaptive responses to Covid-19 challenges by actors in local and globally extended health technology clusters

**Per Ingvar Olsen and Morten H. Abrahamsen**

## 7.1 INTRODUCTION

On March 12, 2020, the Norwegian prime minister, the minister of health, and the directors of the Norwegian Directorate of Health and the Norwegian Institute of Public Health went on national television to declare the most invasive political intervention ever during peacetime: an almost complete lockdown of society in a radical attempt to control the Covid-19 pandemic and gain time in the expected long-term battle against the virus. Schools and kindergartens closed, restrictions were imposed on home offices, shops closed, public transportation had restricted access, and so on. Norway and its population of 5.3 million has since been quite successful in controlling the pandemic – partly due to its small population scattered across a large territory and its geographical location at the northern periphery of Europe on the Scandinavian peninsula. However, agile, innovative, and adaptive responses were also important contributing factors.

Around the world, countries had to respond to the outbreak in ways that tested their abilities to be agile and adaptive under pressure. Many countries put such governance mechanisms into action within short time spans. This provides a range of learning opportunities. Agility and adaptability are not the same and may not even interact productively. Adaptability obviously depends on the characteristics of "the installed base" (Aanestad et al., 2017), and too much agility may reduce the operational ability to align existing resources and systems with the new ones (Beck et al., 2001; Boehm, 2002; Janssen and Van der Voort, 2016; Overby et al., 2006).

In this chapter, we will present and discuss a selection of three cases that demonstrates how one innovation cluster in the Oslo region responded to the crisis. These cases are not seen as broadly representative of the actors in the cluster and the activities they enacted, but they are selected to illuminate our interest in understanding more about what constitutes the ability to respond quickly and to make significant contributions to solve immediate and critical needs – what we here will denote "agile and adaptive responsiveness capability". At the same time, we will explore three different perspectives on the local Clusters of Innovation (COI) activities that extend globally in different ways – to contribute to the theory of global COI formation.

The innovation cluster formation in Norway is a particular one that results from its geography, its natural and demographic resource base, its politically orchestrated distribution of universities and industrial competence centers, its business structure, and its roles in global politics and markets. Norway is a Scandinavian country with strong historical ties across the North Sea and the Atlantic Ocean. Its main natural resource base is ocean-related, with subsea oil and gas, seafood, oceanographic sciences, and maritime industries. Norway's natural resource base is also related to its mountains and fjords at the long rainy northwestern coastline of Europe, which is the basis for its large hydropower capacity, energy-intensive industries, and industrial technology base. The main technology university, the Norwegian University for Science and Technology, is located in the middle of the country in the city of Trondheim, serving nationwide industries and local clusters of many kinds. The University of Oslo does not have a technology faculty but has a dominant role in natural sciences and information technology (IT). Jointly with the Norwegian University of Life Sciences and Oslo University Hospital, the Oslo region is dominant in IT, life sciences, and health – interacting with industries and clusters around the nation as well as global actors. The Oslo University Hospital is one of the largest hospitals in Europe, with 23,000 employees and conducts 70 percent of the nation's medical research.

Innovation-related services are primarily clustered in the capital, Oslo, such as financial institutions, venture capital firms, business law firms, international consultancy firms, subsidiaries of global companies like IBM, Siemens, Microsoft, and so on. The wider Oslo region further contains a dominant share of engineering companies and the main high-tech industry clusters that are dominated by military, maritime, subsea and space technology; and systems engineering companies. There are also several incubators, accelerators, and research and industry parks in the area, including some closely related to networked international accelerator organizations. The Oslo innovation cluster is small, and is usually seen as a node in a more extended North European networked structure that shares components and behaviors across several "innovation hubs", of which some are more dominant than others. In the following, we will focus on the part of the Oslo innovation cluster that relates to health-related technologies, products, and services, and its potential to respond to the immediate challenges caused by the Covid-19 pandemic. We will present three different perspectives on, and examples of, networked COI structures along with examples of their agile responses to immediate and critical needs for solutions and rapid transformations catalyzed by the crisis, and discuss how the existence of local as well as extended non-geographic networked clusters enabled such agile and adaptive responses.

The first concern appeared in the early phase after March 12, as it soon became clear that the healthcare system was not prepared for a major pandemic outbreak. For instance, the post-World War II emergency stockpiling of critical products had been terminated years ago, and global production and distribution took time to ramp up. The first case will present and discuss how alignment of needs and supplies in a small country emerged at the intersection of government policy adjustments and the agile responses by the health tech innovation cluster. The innovation cluster service organization for healthcare in Oslo, Norway Health Tech (NHT), is a natural focal point. Hosted at the Oslo University Research Park, it has around 250 companies and institutions as members – while also stretching out to local health tech clusters in other parts of the country. The main objective of the organization is to support the development of innovative healthcare companies and industries and to stimulate private–public collaboration. Based on this case, we will reflect on the relevance of components and behaviors that are core to the innovation cluster framework and movement in times of severe crisis.

The second case addresses the responses by the international District Health Information System (DHIS) network and its global leadership unit at the University of Oslo to the critical need for effective digital tools to manage Covid-19 disease control. In the otherwise digitally advanced Norway, registration and tracking of infected individuals and their close contacts, quarantining, testing, and so on, were done in the beginning using pen, paper, and Excel spreadsheets. On June 7, the DHIS2 global team at the University of Oslo released a standard Covid-19 application based on an early version developed in Sri Lanka. This permitted its global network of more than 70 countries in Africa, Asia, and Latin America, using the DHIS2 open-source health information system, to download the solution for free and start using it. A version in Norwegian was rapidly adopted by around 290 of the 356 municipalities in the country. This radical improvement of local Covid-19 control and management tools and capabilities made it possible for the Norwegian government to change its Covid-19 control strategy from general national regulations towards flexible policies under the responsibility of local municipalities – while still maintaining effective national overview and control. This case is an example of a globally networked COI where we want to discuss how this form of organizing enables agile responses, rapid transmission, and adoption of solutions in a variety of international and national contexts.

The third and final case will address responses to the need for information and communications technology (ICT), enabling solutions to provide treatment and care for elderly, vulnerable, and Covid-19-infected people in their homes rather than in hospitals and other healthcare institutions. This required new healthcare service models and ICT system-integration solutions between internet-based solutions and public healthcare systems to permit patients, doctors, and care providers to share and exchange data and to collaborate on shared digital platforms. Due to patient data security concerns, public healthcare ICT systems in Norway are sealed off from the internet, and efforts to develop safe ways to connect and exchange data have been slow to emerge. We will present a selected business case that illustrates how representatives of the innovation cluster ecosystem were able to respond to the crisis by providing adequate novel solutions. We will also show how these solutions expanded in response to the crisis in ways that pave the paths to more substantial healthcare transformations in Norway as well as in other countries. Based on these examples, we will elaborate on the potential of locally focused and globally extended innovation clusters to bring about institutional and market changes as well as innovative solutions by exploiting multiple opportunities in international markets that are quite different from one another.

Finally, we will pull out what we believe are core insights from the Oslo case that may be of more general interest regarding the topic of what constitutes agile and adaptive responsive capabilities.

## 7.2 PERSPECTIVES ON INNOVATION CLUSTERS AND AGILE RESPONSE CAPABILITIES IN THE FACE OF CRISIS

Agile and adaptive responsiveness to challenges catalyzed by severe crisis is a critical capacity of any society. Experiences from across the world demonstrate how the most substantial and fast contributions to crisis management often lie with those who happen to be close to the event and who have the resources and the capabilities to act, to improvise, and to mobilize whatever is available to deal with the situation. Later, organized institutions and systems may move in to take control and to deliver the support needed based on whatever has been prepared in advance for such situations, or to plan and develop what may be needed for the longer term. What has not been prepared for may require additional quick-response processes to reach a sufficient level of effectiveness and control.

Agile methods have been popular in the software industry in relation to technical innovation and have become essential to design thinking and entrepreneurship practices in COI more broadly. These methods contain the insight that fast, iterative, and creative interactions between conceptual and practical explorations to create and establish a solution to a problem or a need are more effective and efficient than the alternative approach of diagnosing, analyzing, planning, developing, and implementing in sequential steps. In the face of immediate crisis, no one has the time to follow a slow strategy, and agile, high-intensity interactional processing naturally bypasses any attempt at sticking to such established procedures.

Entrepreneurs and innovators typically have substantial agile competencies, and broadly also represent truly diverse resources and capabilities. It is also clear that in times of crisis, one critically depends on what is already in existence. These are not situations calling for creative startups to contribute the most. One must be able to deliver and scale on short notice, to adjust and change based on resources, business models, networks, and clusters that are already in place. Hence, the ability to deliver to a considerable extent depends on the agility that is built into existing systems, practice, and cultures. Therefore, to understand the basis for the observed agile responsiveness to the Covid-19 pandemic, we should also look at the historical origins, the ways of thinking and the agile capacities that have been built by founders and developers over time to make them adaptable to external changes (Janssen and Van der Voort, 2020).

Agile response capabilities may also be analyzed in terms of how actors and COI are interacting across the globe. The waves of innovative technologies that may be used anywhere, and the collaborative networks that exist, provide networked systems of interaction between people engaged in parallel and sequential interactional creative responses in different countries. Solutions may develop in a variety of places, and the networks may quickly share and distribute solutions and learning. Hence, the ability to provide agile responses by providing significant contributions also depends on the extendedness and reach of innovation clusters and their ecosystems in globally networked structures.

During these extremely critical days, as researchers we were able to access a range of government, healthcare, and industry actors due to ongoing research on innovative public procurement procedures and to digitally enabled transformations in the Norwegian healthcare system. The insights reported in this chapter are primarily based on interviews with key actors and on secondary data such as publicly available documents.

In the following, we will present and discuss each of the three cases, before summarizing what we may learn from the Oslo case in the final discussion and conclusion sections.

### 7.2.1 Agile and Adaptive Responses in the Early Phase: The Role of Innovation Cluster Service Organizations in the Orchestration of Markets

Facing the unprecedented pandemic, Norway went into lockdown on March 12, 2020. The closing of national borders and disruption of international supply chains meant a limited or non-existent availability of critical hospital equipment and medical supplies, such as face masks, face shields, protective body gear, disinfection products, and remote care solutions for non-hospitalized Covid-19-infected individuals. Adding to the urgency of the situation, the lack of knowledge about the duration and impact of the pandemic, along with dramatic reports from countries already severely affected, required swift action by the government in the form of adaptive measures and agile responses from public administration and industry actors.

One of the first measures introduced by the Norwegian government concerned public procurement regulations. Public purchases are subject to strict regulations and procedures to ensure fair competition, equal treatment, and transparency. Even though there have been recent moves towards procedures and formats permitting closer interactions between buyers and sellers in public sector markets, public purchasing is still subjected to tight competitive tender regulations. However, existing public purchasing regulations also include *force majeure* situations, national crises, and emergencies, where the regulations can be adjusted or even bypassed. The Ministry of Industry interpreted the pandemic to indeed fall within these criteria, and as a result gave permission to simplify and shorten purchasing processes and to award contracts directly to suppliers without prior tendering. This adaptive response, regulation interpretation, and introduction of emergency procurement regulations happened within days.

To organize the purchasing of medical supplies in response to the pandemic, another adaptive measure was undertaken, as the national Hospital Procurement Agency (Sykehusinnkjøp) was put on red alert. This agency normally handles major purchases by the national healthcare system at a national level, whereas the hospital regions and the municipalities handle purchases of medical and healthcare supplies at the local level. In this emergency, the agency received wide authorization – from the Ministry of Health – to reorganize its operations and resources. In response, the agency established itself as a centralized, single channel for procurements done under the emergency regulations on the national as well as regional and local levels of purchasing. One of the four state hospital regions of Norway, the South East Health Region, was authorized as the formal buyer in each new contract awarded under this emergency procedure.

With the buyer side now organized by adapting legislative and organizational measures, attention turned to the supply side. The Hospital Procurement
Agency was of course interested in mobilizing potential suppliers who could
satisfy critical needs, either by supplying from a range of existing products and
services or by setting up new manufacturing and supply chains in cooperation
with public purchasers and medical expertise at the hospitals. The agency was
also aligned with the services of Innovation Norway, a funding body under the
Ministry of Industry. Innovation Norway provides government funding des-
ignated to aid the development of innovative solutions by private companies.

To mobilize potential suppliers, the agency reached out to several organizations, including the NHT innovation cluster organization. Representing
250 member companies, hospitals, universities and research institutions,
international consultancy firms, startups, venture capital, and other financing
institutions, NHT was keen to help connect needs with the resources and
competence held by its member organizations. In the beginning, NHT's focus
was on responding to the considerable number of calls from suppliers eager to
help, and on guiding their initiatives to the appropriate procurement channels.
This soon proved to be difficult to track, and with the emergency procurement
regulations in place, the Hospital Procurement Agency and NHT therefore
decided to arrange an online seminar for potential suppliers to provide direct
information on immediate needs, priorities, procedures, and so on.

The online seminar took place on March 16. Three hundred fifty suppliers
were present, and public healthcare sector leaders presented their immediate
needs within four prioritized categories: protective gear, disposable equipment for intensive care, remote care solutions, and other medical equipment.
In addition, Innovation Norway and other government agencies presented
funding opportunities and public support opportunities to help develop and
test new products in response to the call. Finally, the Hospital Procurement
Agency explained how the purchases would be organized in the centralized
model directly through the Agency's procurement office.

To channel all calls and inquiries from potential suppliers, the Agency set
up a single e-mail address. The result was overwhelming: over 5,000 suppliers
made contact within days. Responses ranged from people finding a plastic bag
of facemasks in their basement to large firms with state-of-the-art technology
that could be applied to produce substantial volumes. Chaos erupted as the
Agency could not handle the considerable number of calls and tenders, even
after having reorganized and ramped up its internal operations for the task.
Suppliers became increasingly frustrated with the lack of response to their
calls and made multiple contacts also to NHT in the hope of finding ways to
speed up the process. Adding to this frustration were the ongoing news reports
describing a pandemic escalating day by day and repeatedly-published invita-
tions by the government urging businesses to help in a state of national crisis.

The NHT managers soon realized that such a centralized system had become a complete bottleneck in the matching of supply and demand, and quickly took the initiative to reorganize – thereby setting in motion several adaptive measures to decentralize responsibilities and distribute demand and supply interactions to regional and local levels. Hence, the centralized emergency procurement model immediately failed. The NHT approached institutions and authorities at regional and municipal levels to direct the attention of frustrated suppliers to appropriate recipients. The Norwegian Association of Local and Regional Authorities (Kommunenes Sentralforbund), representing all of Norway's 356 municipalities, set up a task force to bypass the Hospital Procurement Agency's system. This could be done based on established legislation giving responsibility for local healthcare and local health emergency measures to the municipalities, not the state. NHT also made direct contact with the larger Norwegian municipalities such as Oslo, which needed substantial volumes of medical supplies. In the days following the lockdown, Oslo Municipality alone was contacted by 1,000 suppliers. Additionally, NHT contacted the Norwegian Association of Medical Doctors, which faced a similar need for new supplies as well as for technical support as the lockdown also meant that patients needed to be consulted and treated using online technology. As a result, for instance, two of NHT's members supplying video technology for general practitioners rapidly increased their sales. In the following weeks NHT organized additional webinars where companies pitched their products, technologies, and services to representatives of municipalities and hospitals – effectively connecting buyers with innovative suppliers.

More wide-ranging examples of agile responses may also be mentioned, such as the producer of sails for sailboats who was encouraged to start producing protective body gear. Another example of substantial technological adaptation was a producer of machines for disinfecting surgery wards who quickly developed a mobile solution that could be moved from room to room for automatic disinfection, which was utilized from the early days of the pandemic. One of the more curious examples was a call from the American Embassy, requesting assistance to supply facemasks and protective gear to American hospitals, that received the attention of 30 Norwegian suppliers before lunch the following day!

To accelerate the matchmaking, NHT contacted another of its members: Schibsted. This company is Norway's largest media group, with branches in countries such as Denmark, Finland, Poland, and Sweden. Being an owner of traditional print media, it also has a focus on innovation and digitalization in the media landscape. Of particular interest are its digital marketplaces, connecting millions of individual buyers and sellers every day. Schibsted had long toyed with the idea of setting up a digital marketplace for business-to-business markets, and the pandemic provided a good opportunity to accelerate this initiative. NHT therefore asked Schibsted to develop and present a solution where hospitals and municipalities could post their needs for supplies, and where suppliers could post their offerings. Schibsted presented their initial idea to potential contributors during an online seminar hosted by NHT, but received lukewarm responses. Schibsted nevertheless has continued developing this technology for other uses.

The re-direction of suppliers away from the Hospital Partner Agency made it possible for the Agency to direct efforts to developing a structured system to manage the screening, selection, and control of suppliers to orchestrate major procurement procedures in compliance with the emergency regulations. This gradually provided opportunities to a range of NHT members. To handle the many calls from suppliers, the Agency adapted the new structured purchasing procedure to speed up the supplier selection process. Now suppliers were screened by evaluating their financial situation and production capacities, their product specifications and technical competencies, their cost estimates, and finally their compliance with various regulatory standards. Selected solutions were produced in small quantities to be tested in use before supplies were ramped up to larger volumes. This screening and iterative procedure enabled sound screening, selection, and testing of the most promising supplier initiatives, as well as the development of several interesting and innovative solutions.

A good example is Checkware, a supplier of remote patient treatment solutions within the area of mental health. This supplier had for some time been in contact with relevant authorities to develop and test its technology on a larger scale. At the start of the pandemic, Checkware contacted a municipality, a regional health authority, and the Hospital Procurement Agency to tailor its solution to the immediate need for organizing remote treatment of mental care patients. Within two days the supplier had tested and verified its solution with a hospital and could start scaling and distributing its solution – a process which normally takes months.

At the other end of the technological spectrum, we find an example highlighting the major challenges suppliers faced resulting from the agile responses to needs catalyzed by crisis. The company ASAP is a manufacturer of disposable hospital bed linen, primarily supplying maternity wards. Having sewing technology and in-depth knowledge of materials and resources needed for production of such products, ASAP was challenged to start producing disposable protective body wear. Through a rapid response, the manufacturer was able to produce a prototype in two days which was tested at a hospital the day after. Having passed the technical requirements and standards testing, ASAP was quoted an order of 400,000 pieces, with an option of an additional 200,000 pieces. This meant that the company needed to hire and train many more people (an increase from 12 to 120 employees in four months), invest in new machinery, rent larger premises, and raise additional funding. In three weeks, ASAP managed to get the production up and running. However, the company is uncertain about the future. As the pandemic came under control, the need for protective body wear diminished, whereas the supplier had invested heavily in people, facilities, and machinery. A year into the pandemic, the company was laying off some of its workforce. Other suppliers gave similar stories, suggesting that after the initial mobilization of suppliers, there was no directed effort to maintain their supplies, as public procurement would revert to low-cost and large-scale global suppliers.

### 7.2.2    Discussion of Oslo Healthcare Innovation Cluster Case

The local healthcare innovation cluster in Oslo is a semi-organized entity in a regional economy with several similar cluster entities. These can be seen as "mini-COI" shaped through policies in a small country at the periphery of dominant global markets. These mini-clusters share many of the same major components and are accordingly parts of a regional COI that at the micro level appears to be separated into distinct industrially focused mini-clusters, and at the meso level has the characteristics of a geographically distinct regional COI. If we zoom out to observe it from a macro perspective, it represents a regional node in several internationally extended COI, sharing major components with others. Because COI have expanded and transformed innovation policies, innovation systems, and behaviors across the world, people more easily interact across regional and national boundaries.

A mini-cluster, such as the healthcare cluster in Oslo, is not a complete COI of its own. It only works because it is part of these other more extended networks of COI. The entrepreneurs move around and exploit any available resource. Companies set up accelerators and incubators across regional COI, and entrepreneurs move to where they believe they will find the ecosystem they need. The relevant VC component is international, with regional venture capitalists having a limited role. Local universities are critical but not sufficient. Corporate VCs, angel investors, Public VCs, and fund in fund operators also operate across geographical boundaries.

Because COI have emerged with a constrained set of standard components, systems, procedures, and behaviors, these also become core to what we observe in mini-COI such as the healthcare innovation cluster in Oslo. The simplified core of COI makes it easy to interact across regional entities even though the contexts and the industrial focuses may be extremely different.

When observing the responses of the Oslo region innovation cluster and its service organization to the immediate challenges catalyzed by the Covid-19 crisis in March 2020, there is an interesting interplay and dynamic between the adaptive policies and capabilities of the government and public healthcare systems on the one hand, and the agile responses of the innovation cluster as well as the wider business ecosystem on the other. We observe that the agile responses were quick and massive in terms of number of actors engaging to contribute.

Neither the government nor the healthcare system were really prepared to deal with a fast-accelerating pandemic. However, there was a level of adaptive capacity established in the legislative and institutional structure that permitted the government to take adequate actions to mobilize local suppliers when global markets were unable to supply critical products. However, the response strategy partly had to be improvised and went through major pivots as unexpected responses overwhelmed heavily centralized government strategies to manage and control the operations. A clear learning point is that adaptive capacity in response to large-scale crisis critically depends on the ability to orchestrate decentralized and distributed market structures rather than centralized ones in the early phase. Development of higher-quality procedures and systems in a centralized managed structure requires time and resources. These will gradually take over as the dominant structure in ways that also improve quality and control and thereby also sustain public trust in the market and the government. While the decentralized and ad hoc organizing of the market at the early stage permits smaller and less professional suppliers to contribute, suppliers with a larger and more competent installed base of resources and capabilities will increase their dominance in the subsequent stages.

The membership-based organization of the health tech innovation cluster turned out to play a significant role in the rapid transformation and orchestration of demand and supply for immediate supplies of important products, through its established nationwide network and its representation of a large base of actors with a broad range of capabilities, roles, and relations to the healthcare system. This obviously supported the collective action capability of the cluster.

The case highlights the interplay between adaptive and agile responses. Facing the pandemic, the government adapted the legislative procedures already in place and reorganized the public procurement process. In return, industry responded quickly and massively. NHT responded both as a representative of the cluster, and by mobilizing its members to respond to the needs. The early adaptive responses by the government were not sufficient to match supply and demand, and NHT responded by finding new and decentralized ways of organizing procurement and mobilizing suppliers through collaboration with other parts of the government system. These initiatives are examples of iterative learning and pivoting loops in situations that require rapid, agile, adaptive, and coordinated responses at national, regional, and local levels. As such, the case illustrates the valuable role of basic civil society organizing of clusters in various forms of associations and service organizations that have the legitimacy and authority to act on behalf of their members and associates. In combination with the internal cultural behaviors learned and shared through numerous entrepreneurial processes among the diverse components of the cluster, an organized and focused cluster may respond quickly, coordinate effectively, mobilize flexibly, and align resources to deliver quick results when faced with dramatic societal challenges.

The case also illustrates risks and problems facing suppliers that engage in agile responses to such crises. For instance, NHT mobilized the Schibsted Corporation to develop a new digital platform to match supply and demand. However, the proposed solution did not fit the immediate needs of buyers and sellers who had already found other ways to find one another. Thus, the window of opportunity was limited for more radical approaches not already in use. The ASAP story illustrates another challenge with agile responses. This supplier was successful in responding to the immediate situation, but the limited commitment of the public buyers over time represented substantial downside risks on the supplier side.

## 7.3    NON-GEOGRAPHIC CLUSTERS IN GLOBAL HEALTHCARE: THE SRI LANKA DISTRICT HEALTH INFORMATION SYSTEM CASE

We will now present and discuss a different example of agile and adaptive responses to the Covid-19 pandemic: early responses in Sri Lanka, which was among the first countries in the world to develop and implement a digital solution to manage Covid-19 disease tracking and control, just a few days after the first suspicious incident occurred on the island on January 26, 2020. In comparison, during the first months of the outbreak in Norway, healthcare employees relied on pen, paper, and Excel spreadsheets to register infected and suspected individuals and to track close contacts. Registrations were time-consuming and cumbersome, and authorities did not have sufficient local, regional, and national data, overview, and control – resulting in a centralized, inflexible lockdown strategy at an extremely high cost to society.

This case can be seen as describing a global network of multiple collaborating local COI that have emerged in the context of health information systems in "the Global South". As such it is a case of the interacting of the information technologies and typical practices of COI with components that are distinct to the domain of international development help.

In early April, the DHIS team at the Department of Informatics of the University of Oslo, in collaboration with the Norwegian Institute of Public Health, started working on the idea to use an app solution developed in Sri Lanka to Norwegian municipalities. At the time of the global release of the first global standard application based on the early Sri Lanka solution, on

June 7, a Norwegian version became available and could be downloaded by municipalities on the home web page of the Norwegian Association of Local and Regional Authorities (KS) and from the private supplier ReMin.

In the following we will look at why and how this rapid development of an electronic Covid-19 management package first happened in Sri Lanka, and why and how Norway, as well as many countries in the Global South, were able to acquire the solution and distribute it so quickly to those who needed it.

Sri Lanka is one of 79 countries that use the DHIS2 health information system.[1] University of Oslo researchers have, since DHIS2's origins in post-apartheid South Africa in 1994, been the central coordinating hub for what has become the most extended health information system in the world, covering around 2.3 billion people. Acting as the global leadership node, the University of Oslo collaborates with 15 DHIS2 teams around the world – including one in Sri Lanka – to further develop the system and to support the development of new applications fitted to the contexts and needs in each country. The core of these many teams is the more than 60 former PhD students from across Africa, Asia, and Latin America who have been part of the doctoral Digital Health Information System Program (DHISP) at the University of Oslo and who have returned to their home countries to continue developing the system.

In Sri Lanka, the Ministry of Health provides funding for medical officers pursuing medical specialist postgraduate education, including health informatics, and, from 2009, a master's program in Biomedical Informatics was established at the Postgraduate Institute of Medicine at the University of Colombo with financial and academic support from the University of Oslo. The aim of the program was to produce medical specialists that could strengthen the national health information system in Sri Lanka and reduce dependence on foreign experts. The collaboration with the University of Oslo enabled the use of the open-source-based DHIS2 as a training tool for the students. Through their studies, and later as employees in various parts of government health institutions, they developed what gradually became a complete DHIS platform in different units of the public healthcare system in 2013. These graduates, with extensive medical and informatics skills, became core technical and administrative experts in the work to further develop the national health information systems in the following years.

The first discussion between Ministry of Health and the local DHIS2 unit HISP Sri Lanka on the possibility of developing a Covid-19 tracking application occurred in late January 2020 – following the observed increase in Covid-19 cases in South Asia and the high expectancy for cases entering Sri Lanka through incoming tourists. A first application to track passengers entering at the airport was created and tested by the end of the month, just before the country registered its first Covid-19 incident on January 27. The new DHIS2 platform-based app was used immediately along with scaled-up training on Zoom (Amarakoon et al., 2020).

The first domestic case was reported in mid-March, and the app solution was quickly expanded to include clinical management information of cases, including symptoms, daily updates, test results, and outcomes, using a tracker component in the DHIS2 platform. Various adjustments of the DHIS platform were also done to shape the system to a range of specific needs. To rapidly deal with all of this, the ministry gathered representatives from core government institutions, including the Information and Communication Technology (ICT) Agency of Sri Lanka, and the DHIS2-related entities. The DHIS2 platform was then installed on the ICT Agency's cloud hosting service, which permitted rapid nationwide scaling. Next, the ICT Agency organized a hackathon with global reach to entrepreneurs and experts in various fields to work on solutions to several listed needs. The participants included the University of Oslo team and the global DHIS network – providing support, mentors, and necessary changes in the core of the DHIS2 software platform. Crucial elements of this work were to develop direct and automatic data exchange with other systems, such as with the customs agency's data systems.

With a surge of migrant workers returning home in late March from Covid-19-infected countries like Italy, focus changed to quarantine management and facilities, and the system was rapidly expanded to follow up on cases by adding a second tracker program. The system was further developed as a tool to manage Covid-related needs at all the hospitals under the responsibility of the Ministry. A particular solution for intensive care unit (ICU) care was also added, including the ability to track ICU beds nationwide. By early April, all these functions had been put in place.

The first tracking application developed by HISP Sri Lanka in January was shared in the DHIS2 community, who started making the solution generic. Further developments in Sri Lanka were also guided from Oslo and other nodes in the network to ensure that the solutions developed had generic properties. With this collaboration, the first version of a generic application in English was released in the second week of May, permitting the network to test it and to generate feedback from early users (Amarakoon et al., 2020). A component which provided full oversight of Covid-19 laboratory tests across all laboratories in a nation was also developed and included, along with a component that allowed citizens to self-report and monitor their own health via a mobile application.

With the final release of the upgraded global Covid-19 DHIS2 package by the global leadership unit in Oslo on June 7, an international version of the package developed in Sri Lanka could be downloaded, translated into local languages, and used across the world on the non-proprietary open-source DHIS2 platform.

The role of the University of Oslo in this development process made it possible for Norway to quickly start using the DHIS2 Covid-19 solution: 290 out of 356 municipalities now use this solution as their digital management system for local tracking, quarantining, and so on. This has radically improved the speed and effectiveness of local tracking of Covid-19-infected individuals and their social contacts. Based on these improved capabilities as well as other complementary IT solutions, the government policy to control the pandemic gradually shifted towards a decentralized and flexible approach to battle the outbreaks in the local communities where they occurred while permitting other regions to remain more open, keeping effective national overview as well as distributed agile response capabilities.

### 7.3.1    The Roots of and Development Paths of DHIS2 and its International Developmental Network

To understand why and how these developments in Sri Lanka could emerge and have such an impact, we need to see this in the context of the historical development of the networked innovative platform system.

In November 2020, Professor Kristin Braa and Professor Jørn Braa at the University of Oslo's Department of Informatics received the prestigious Roux Prize for their work on the development of the DHIS2 system to improve health across the world. The system is used to collect, validate, analyze, and present health information data. It is based on free open code, is freely available to any country, and can be implemented on almost any level of technical infrastructure. According to a report published by Johns Hopkins University's Global mHealth Initiative in July 2020, DHIS2 is one of the two globally leading digital platforms with a presence in low- and medium-income countries that could easily be reconfigured for Covid-19 tracking and management needs and that stands out for its maturity, flexibility, and large-scale deployment (Agarwal et al., 2020).

The University of Oslo's Department of Informatics is internationally known from its role in the first development of an object-oriented programming system and language called Simula in the 1960s. The DHIS network has emerged in the tradition of the early Simula pioneers through the work of some of their students. It is also closely related to the tradition of Scandinavian action research and the work–life democracy movement in the 1970s, emphasizing user involvement, social development, evolutionary approaches, and iterative stepwise prototyping.

The early DHIS development was done in post-apartheid South Africa in 1994. During the apartheid period the healthcare system was highly fragmented and racially segregated, and the aim of the project was to develop a unifying health information system as well as a system to support local healthcare development and management in poor districts. DHIS began as a small development project between a Norwegian PhD student at the University of Oslo and colleagues at the University of Cape Town and the University of the Western Cape. Several other projects emerged in South Africa at the time to address the fragmented-system problem, and gradually the DHIS solution emerged as the integrative system in the Western Cape province. Through this period, most of the funding came from the Norwegian development aid agency NORAD (Norwegian Agency for Development Cooperation). By defining the technical standards and gateways in an open-source platform, DHIS became the system that could easily integrate with other parallel development projects, eventually forming the core of the national health information system in the country (Adu-Gyamfi et al., 2019; Braa et al., 2007; Sahay et al., 2013).

DHIS expanded to Mozambique in 1998, and then to two states in India and further to countries such as Vietnam, Botswana, and Ethiopia. A critical part of this expansion was the doctoral program in Oslo for PhD students from these countries. Through this development process, DHIS was adapted to stand-alone solutions in vastly different contexts and healthcare domains. This lack of systemic integration made it difficult to share solutions across the network. The solution to this problem was to radically transform DHIS to a software platform denoted "DHIS2", with a limited, stable core; standard gateways; and a software platform "app store" which permitted flexible developments of apps adapted to local contexts and needs.

The further development of the system took place in Sierra Leone after the country's civil war, when DHIS, in collaboration with the World Health Organization (WHO) and funding organizations like the Gates Foundation; PEPFAR (the US President's Emergency Plan for AIDS Relief); the Global Fund to Fight AIDS, Tuberculosis and Malaria; UNICEF (the United Nation International Children's Emergency Fund); GAVI (the Global Alliance for Vaccine Alliance); the CDC (US Centers for Disease Control and Prevention); and NORAD, developed DHIS2 into a regional system for the East African region to fight the Ebola epidemic. Several international development aid and medical support organizations also started integrating their systems with DHIS2 to build a unified information system.

Step by step, the DHIS network grew to include 15 international HISP units in different African and Asian countries and regions, and funding partners, to further develop the system in line with the WHO's global standards for health information systems. The department in Oslo is still the core hub providing technical competence, control of the technical core, and global leadership. The Covid-19 pandemic has put substantial pressures on the capacity of the university to deliver these services, and other universities, such as Johns Hopkins in the US, have stepped in to do more of the work – thereby expanding the cluster-to-cluster network collaboration on core research and development and global leadership.

### 7.3.2    Discussion of DHIS2 and the Sri Lanka Case

Unlike our first case, which focused on responses by the local ecosystem in the Oslo region, this case illustrates the value of being globally connected. It is not a given that rapid, agile, and effective responses in one region easily translate to other parts of the world. This example illustrates how such translations depend on the characteristics of the ecosystem, the already installed base and its networks of actors and technologies. The DHIS2 case illustrates a system designed to be extremely adaptive to different contexts, technical infrastructures, and sudden outbreaks of diseases in parts of the world that are the most vulnerable. Its ability to respond obviously depends on more than 25 years of history in developing and using systems to control a variety of deadly diseases such as AIDS, Ebola, and tuberculosis in countries with limited infrastructures and extreme obstacles to making a digital system and a healthcare system work. The network is aligned in a system with clear hierarchical structures around the core roles of the University of Oslo, the WHO, and global financial partners (donor organizations) focused on global health issues. On the other hand, it is an extremely decentralized, flat, flexible, and locally adaptable system. Through these core organizations, there are multiple links to major COI around the globe. Hence, eventually, we need to see these networks as assemblages of loosely coupled networks that share many of the same components and behaviors.

The DHIS2 network can be seen as a form of non-geographic innovation cluster. It is globally extended and has many of the components and behaviors found in geographic COI as local COI are nodes of the network. Given the extendedness across continents and countries, it deals with extreme diversity of contexts. To be able to do this and at the same time provide integrated data-sharing and structured services, it maintains a quite simple and stable technical core under tight control that permits extreme adaptability to local needs and circumstances, and which requires a shared, evolutionary development process over time to integrate and align actors, resources, and activities. As such, it has similarities to how the internet is organized as a generalized non-geographic COI infrastructure at the large and globally extended scale. These kinds of infrastructures are critical to how these extended COI function.

The ability to act as quickly as one did in Sri Lanka depended on a local network of individuals with combined medical and IT expertise and familiarity with a shared platform that could easily be re-formatted to track Covid-19 and add more functionality. These people had positions in a variety of government health institutions that could coordinate initiatives based on shared knowledge and familiarity with the global DHIS2 network. This made the "Sri Lanka DHIS2 node" an effective local DHIS2 actor-network with strong agile and adaptive capabilities.

The shared values and understanding underlying these behaviors had in part been developed through shared learning processes and socializing in the DHISP doctoral educational program in Oslo. This was further supported by a shared commitment and culture to support the establishing of nodes/hubs in the global network – to start engaging with the local ecosystem, to provide funding for the regional hubs in collaboration with committed funding partners. The gradual translations of local clusters that shared the same insights, cluster components, and behaviors were also actively supported, such as through the master's program in Sri Lanka educating healthcare system leaders.

The funding partners played similar roles to those of venture capital investors in other typical COI. They provided funding for new startup nodes, supported the processes of standardization of the system across national borders, supported the early technological shift to a platform for app-store infrastructure, and integrated DHIS2 into their own global operations, thereby powerfully contributing to technological development and market expansion as well as standardization of systems across national borders.

Based on the early Sri Lankan version, the hierarchical structure of the DHIS2 ecosystem made it possible to quickly adapt the solution to a global standard in English, which could then be translated and adapted to local contexts by the 15 different DHIS2 units around the world. In Norway, DHIS2 was not in use in the existing healthcare system, but was easily installed as an internet-based solution. Because the work with the global standard was done in Oslo, the Norwegian version could quickly be launched. The Norwegian government's financial backing of DHIS was Norway's largest funding of any global healthcare project. Despite not being used in Norway, the project was well known both within the government healthcare administration and in the IT expert community. By connecting DHIS2 to two different software platforms already in use by the municipalities, the new DHIS2 application was easily and quickly distributed across the country.

As such, the case illustrates the importance of relatedness for the ability to respond quickly and to adopt novel solutions. A globally extended innovation cluster represents an incredible capacity to mobilize brains and resources, to share insights and innovations, and to exploit them via those who are connected.

## 7.4    TRANSFORMING HEALTHCARE IN THE COVID-19 ERA: THE DIGNIO REMOTE CARE CASE

We shall now turn to our third example of an agile and adaptive response that may illustrate how entrepreneurial companies contribute to the transformation of healthcare in the aftermath of the outbreak of the pandemic: the case of Dignio and its remote healthcare technology. Apart from the immediate responses to the crisis, this case examines how the pandemic experience may accelerate further transformation of healthcare systems, in this case by strengthening trends towards moving medical treatment and care from hospitals and institutions to where people live. There is presently a surge in companies providing such solutions across the world, so this case is representative of a current broader trend. Digitally enabled healthcare solutions are recognized as high-potential opportunities by governments and developers worldwide. The pandemic has accelerated the existing trends and expanded them to an international arena. We will illustrate these processes by discussing Dignio's engagement with the city of Oslo and its activities in China.

The municipal Emergency Medical Agency in the city of Oslo (Oslo Legevakt) has capacity to receive 750 phone calls per day. At the beginning of the Covid-19 crisis, the number of calls peaked at 40,000 in one day. Government authorities advised people not to go to doctors and medical centers but to remain in their homes. Hence, a first response by many was to seek help by phone. The need for alternative ways to connect people with healthcare providers exploded.

General practitioners, medical emergency centers, and hospitals quickly turned to video consultations on the internet. Video consultations and other forms of remote healthcare services had gradually evolved over time, and general agreements and governance systems regulating practice, payments, data security, and so on, had mostly been put in place before the crisis emerged. Government policies to stimulate a gradual transformation of the healthcare system to include more of these new practices were also in place. Internet-based solutions such as video consultations easily scaled to widespread use, both in Norway and globally.

The innovation clusters in Norway had limited roles in this early transformation to remote health communications. However, the immediate needs of the healthcare sector catalyzed by the crisis extended far beyond the ability to do video consultations. In Norway, the public healthcare information systems are not connected to the internet, due primarily to very tight patient data security requirements. This means that patient data cannot be shared unless the strict data safety requirements are met and there is a safe gateway to connect the external database to the internal healthcare information system. Hence, the capacity of the existing IT systems to rapidly adapt is a seriously constraining factor.

In this situation, the key role of local health tech companies is to create solutions that fit the contextual circumstances. To develop such solutions requires an ecosystem of specialized companies with distinct roles in the innovation and implementation of projects and processes. Some are developers of ICT-enabled healthcare services; others are system integrators, legal experts, system architects, or suppliers of technical devices. Furthermore, public sector acquisition of a new solution must be done in accordance with ordinary public tender regulations and procedures, and bidding for such projects most often requires actors to form consortia of companies with complementary roles, competencies, and contributions. Sometimes these consortia are purely local firms, but more often they involve large international companies such as Siemens and Microsoft, and large international system integrators like Accenture, CGI, and Sopra Steria. Hence, the local innovation cluster extends globally through actors that engage in similar clusters around the globe.

When the pandemic emerged, companies with already established, proven solutions or with a relevant position within some part of the healthcare system were able to respond quickly to the immediate needs. The Dignio case serves as is good illustration here. Dignio offered solutions and tools extending what could be done with the DHIS2 platform – such as integrating two-way communication between patients and healthcare systems with structured patient self-reporting and self-monitoring of symptoms.

Previously, Oslo Municipality and Dignio signed a contract in January 2020 to implement Dignio's ICT-enabled solution for remote medical care in all of Oslo's city districts to improve the quality and effectiveness of home care for the elderly and for others in need of medical home care. Dignio started up in 2010 in the city of Fredrikstad, 100 km southeast of Oslo, led by medical doctors who saw the opportunity to develop advanced systems to monitor elderly or chronically ill patients in their homes. The technology was developed in collaboration with several municipalities, including Oslo, and was previously tested in four of Oslo's 15 districts.

Dignio's solution uses a cloud-based data storage system with tight data security functionality in accordance with government regulations of Norwegian patient data. Data are gathered from patients' daily self-registrations and from sensors and devices used by the patients. These are automatically analyzed by Dignio before results and warning notices are forwarded to patient surveillance centers in the municipal healthcare system. The patients also receive the results and can follow the development of their medical condition from day to day through the Dignio App on an iPad, while the medical staff receive the data in a structured way that fits their needs. The system uses an ordinary green/

yellow/red-light system to indicate which patients need attention and intervention. When there is a red-light warning, a nurse will immediately contact the patient for consultation by phone or video. In this way, the home care medical staff can monitor the medical conditions of many vulnerable patients simultaneously, concentrate their efforts on those in most need, and reduce the amount of time used to travel from patient to patient to check their conditions. The patients also get a tool to better understand their own medical conditions and to see the results of whatever they do to take better care of themselves. They can also bring their iPad with the data if they go to the hospital, to immediately update the doctors on the status and the history of their condition.

When the pandemic erupted in March 2020, the "COVID-19 tracking teams" in each of the 15 city districts had nothing but a telephone, a pen, paper, and Excel to update information and communicate effectively. This manual work overloaded the staff and resulted in a loss of control in contacting infected people. In response to this situation, Dignio quickly developed a clinically approved Covid-19 format for self-registration of symptoms, which was offered to all its municipal customers, including Oslo Municipality. Due to an already signed contract in place, Oslo could quickly move to test how the solution could be used as a tool for the local Covid-19 teams to track all coronavirus-infected patients based on people self-reporting their symptoms. After testing the solution in one of its districts, the city quickly expanded it to all 15 districts during the early fall, when there was a window of opportunity between the first and second wave of the disease to train the Covid-19 tracking teams on how to use the Dignio system. Throughout this process, healthcare experts, Dignio's team and additional complementary specialists worked closely to coordinate a swift process to build the capacity, connecting Dignio's solution to other sources such as test data and medical record data. Ultimately, super-users were trained who could then educate their colleagues. The introduction of Dignio's solution dramatically reduced the workload of the teams and improved the ability to manage tracking, testing and quarantining, and health supervision of infected vulnerable individuals.

As a result, Oslo had a digital system in place that worked locally when the second wave of the disease emerged in October 2020. Dignio's Covid-19 solution has subsequently been implemented in other municipalities across the country, to complement the DHIS2 solution and other information systems. Dignio recently also won a tender in the UK and is presently implementing its first project there.

### 7.4.1 The Development of Remote Care and Home Hospitals in Response to the Crisis

Social distancing has been the most important strategy to reduce the spread of the coronavirus, and in multiple ways the crisis has spurred the acceleration of healthcare services treating people in their homes, rather than in hospitals and care institutions. Regions with a highly developed primary care system and a first principle of keeping infected patients in their homes or in local facilities, rather than moving them to hospitals, such as the Verona region in Italy, performed much better than other Italian regions with less developed primary care and more dependency on hospitals, such as the Lombardy region.

The swift transformation to video consultations by both general practitioners and hospitals demonstrated the radical opportunities that new information technologies represent for how healthcare may be transformed in the years to come. Similarly, the agile responses of the DHIS2 network and companies like Dignio, in terms of rapid development and implementation of effective digital solutions, also contributed to policy shifts to transform healthcare towards much more use of remote care and "home hospital" solutions. In Norway, home hospitals are defined as solutions for treatment of patients in their homes while the patient is formally registered as a patient in the ordinary hospital. For instance, Oslo University Hospital recently launched a new policy to change 30 percent of the treatments it presently does in the hospital into ICT-enabled home-based hospital treatment solutions for its inscribed patients.

This change occurred in the wake of the general trend of a gradual transformation and improvements in IT and internet-based services in healthcare in Norway as well as other European countries (Aanestad et al., 2017). It also emerged as a response by governments to address the demographic changes and escalating healthcare costs in society.

In 2012, the European Commission presented its *eHealth Strategies Report*, pointing out that eHealth strategies and attempts at implementing them had almost universally proven much more complicated and time-consuming than anticipated (Stroetmann et al., 2011). This is still the case a decade later, although there has been some progress. A critical element of the strategy has been the development of "Government Patient-Oriented eHealth Infrastructures", on which novel solutions can be integrated with internet-based solutions and scaled in ways that comply with strict regulations to ensure patient data and infrastructure security. In Norway, the national eHealth platform was launched in 2011 and gradually developed into a complex platform enabling a broad range of services gradually linking existing systems that were previously separated silos. The strategy is one of gradual transformation, of complementing, partially substituting, and expanding the information infrastructure as a system (Aanestad et al., 2017).

Dignio developed its range of solutions in response to the needs of municipal home care providers and patients. In the hospitals, several clinics had started using internet-based services as stand-alone solutions that can only handle insensitive patient data. Many research units had also developed research-based healthcare services such as apps to support treatment of patients remotely. However, in most cases these were not implemented as the information infrastructure was not in place with appropriate software platforms and standardized gateways, leaving both researchers and doctors frustrated by the limited adaptability of the system.

The crisis also had the consequence that either patients in need of treatment and care did not show up for their appointments, or treatments were postponed as hospital beds and healthcare providers had to attend to Covid-19 patients. The government quickly supplied additional funds to projects with a potential to respond to these challenges. Among the projects that received funding was an initiative by Dignio to develop digital out-patient clinical care solutions with a selection of medical clinics at Oslo University Hospital and with the University Hospital of Northern Norway. With the already approved cloud-based patient data storage system and the service system already being used by the municipalities, this gave the clinics opportunities to tailor-make app solutions using Dignio's platform. Different healthcare service designs and clinical studies were organized in integration and agile developing, testing, and verification processes in parallel with efforts to create a safe gateway for connecting the Dignio platform to the hospital information infrastructure. Eventually, this may permit a scalable solution in the regional hospital information architecture that can be used by all the hospitals in the region and their different medical clinics.

The connection of an internet-based solution through safe gateways to both the municipal healthcare system and the regional hospital system, as well as to patients, general practitioners, and municipal care providers, may eventually lead to a more people-centric rather than hospital-centric healthcare system based on the ability to share data and tailor services to needs. The Covid-19 pandemic has substantially accelerated the processes needed to reach these targets, thereby also increasing opportunities for many actors in the innovation cluster ecosystem to contribute.

In response to the experiences with the pandemic, the government has ramped up its policy to develop the IT infrastructure to transform the healthcare system in the direction of distributed digitally enabled home care and home hospitals. None of these initiatives are new. What is new is the force by which policies are being expressed and the speed by which government agencies are being instructed to prioritize such policies.

## 7.4.2 Expanding to International Markets

The pandemic has caused considerable problems for many companies in the Oslo innovation cluster who aimed to expand to international markets. In most cases, interactions with customers, operational testing abroad, product demonstrations, and so on, became impossible as lockdowns, restrictions on international travel, and social distancing policies tightened. However, companies with technologies and solutions relevant to solving immediate problems caused by the pandemic faced escalating demand from across the world and were striving to ramp up production and distribution. Other companies had to close activities – relying on receiving government support to maintain critical resources and prevent bankruptcy until international activities picked up. The pandemic hit the innovation cluster in ways that had extremely different consequences.

Funded by venture capital investors, Dignio had also started expanding its operations internationally before the pandemic hit – for instance, by participating in public tenders in the UK. With the new Covid-19 feature and the evidence from its successful use in Oslo, the company won a contract with a major home care and nursing home operator in England, which is presently in the process of being implemented. This permitted Dignio to establish an office in the UK and to start its first international operations.

In 2018, Dignio signed a collaboration agreement with two university hospitals in Shanghai to test the use of Dignio's technology in out-patient clinical use. The parties applied for and received research grants from both Chinese and Norwegian government research programs and are presently developing healthcare service design for post-operative heart and lung patients, conducting clinical research, and developing and testing collaborative models to deliver and expand activities if the results are encouraging. The plan is to expand the testing and exploration of the use of the solution to ten more university hospitals in different cities in a second step.

Dignio has also signed a collaboration agreement with the National Development and Reform Commission (NDRC) in China, which is the Chinese government institution responsible for carrying out and coordinating major reform and development policies under the current five-year plan. China is facing dramatic demographic changes during the coming decade, as the number of elderly citizens will dramatically increase while the young generations entering the labor force are declining. The collaboration with NDRC is focused on China's efforts to develop and scale effective primary care for the elderly and for people with chronic diseases to increase their ability to take care of themselves while also improving the efficiency, quality, and effectiveness of public healthcare providers. The first collaborative testing is with nursing homes and home care organizations in Shanghai, with more than 40,000 beds in operation and extended home care services. NDRC has also shown keen interest in testing Dignio's platform and Covid-19 solution in China as part of its efforts to develop more effective ways to manage future outbreaks of disease.

The context of healthcare in China is vastly different from that of Norway, and the translation of solutions adapted to the Norwegian context to solutions that fits to the Chinese is a challenging one. On the other hand, China is highly active in searching for technologies and solutions from across the world that may be tested and potentially acquired and scaled to millions of users in China. The expansion to China challenges our understanding of what it takes to develop future-oriented systems that are adaptive to vastly different contexts as well as to new waves of technological change and possible unpredictable pandemics that most certainly will erupt in the future.

### 7.4.3    Discussion of the Dignio Case

There are several suppliers of solutions like Dignio's. These emerge at the intersection between new waves of technological innovations and the opportunities entrepreneurs see for using these innovations to create new and better solutions in healthcare. As more entrepreneurs engage at the frontiers of technological change, they also become the change agents that drive the processes. In many ways COI become agglomerates of actors, resources, and activities that do the work that moves the waves further – in this case towards moving non-acute treatment and care out of hospitals. As such, the Dignio case is illustrative of how long-term global technology trends evolve in a particular domain.

While DHIS2 is a health information system for the collection and management of health data, Dignio is a two-way communication platform to permit people to register their own health data and to do much more themselves to manage their health issues in interaction with professional health personnel. The development of such solutions is presently obstructed by public sector healthcare ICT infrastructure architectures that prevent sharing of data between public healthcare systems and between these systems and internet-based systems.

The successful resolution to these problems will transform healthcare. The use of international standards for software platforms and gateways and the use of open APIs (application programming interfaces) to connect to existing internal data systems can create opportunities for healthcare providers to develop and implement solutions that are scalable in domestic contexts as well as in other countries.

Single-payer public healthcare systems like those in Norway, the UK and essentially also China are adapting to these long-term technological and service delivery trends in gradual steps. Companies like Dignio open gates that are usually closed, by collecting and securing their own patient data, analyzing them, and offering them as data services in combination with operational care systems to public healthcare providers. This requires data integration and data-sharing with the previously closed data systems. Healthcare needs are extremely diverse, and the IT enabling the moving of non-acute care out of hospitals to people's homes requires development of a large number of IT applications of a similar kind as those of Dignio. Many of those will only use the internet, but for doctors and nurses to use them effectively, data need to be integrated and shared. In this way, the growing number of companies like Dignio will also gradually transform the organizing of public healthcare as private firms become necessary co-suppliers of the IT-enabled healthcare services.

Similar to Dignio, many of these companies expand to international markets where they also need healthcare systems to provide access to data-sharing. These interconnections need to be standardized for companies to be able to "plug and play" their solutions across local markets. Hence, the wave of change moves towards standardization of system interfaces that further opens the markets for additional entrepreneurs and global competition. Over time, this will lead to the developing of local clusters of companies specializing in IT-enabled healthcare services that will also contribute to the further growth of non-geographic COI in terms of representing the components and behaviors typical of COI, and of collaborating global networks of innovation in the domain of healthcare.

In this case, we have focused on the ability to respond to a severe crisis in agile and adaptive ways – to exemplify and discuss what it takes to not only have a trained entrepreneurial culture to respond in such a way, but also what it takes to be able to deliver. The case is illustrative of behaviors that are typical for entrepreneurs in small national markets at the periphery of larger markets: they need to move out of their local markets early to seek opportunities in the markets where development and scaling opportunities are larger – thereby contributing to the building of networked innovation structures internationally.

What made Dignio stand out as an interesting case of agile response capability is that it was able to immediately respond in ways that had significant impact. The ability to deliver a solution to the city of Oslo rested on previously established conditions: Dignio had already won a public tender and signed a supplier contract to scale its digital platform to all city districts, Oslo had a clear policy to integrate the cloud-based data and machine learning system with the municipal healthcare infrastructure, and super-users had already implemented Dignio's solution in home care activities when the crisis occurred. Hence, the Covid-19 solution could easily be developed and added to the system, and employees were quickly able to implement it. Once again, this exemplifies how agile and adaptive responses depend on the agile and adaptive capabilities already installed at the time of the crisis.

Dignio evolved from a startup and a venture-capital-backed company over a period of ten years before the pandemic hit. It is part of an ecosystem with multiple assemblages of networks representing a local innovation cluster as well as nodes in extended global networks. In this case, the ability to deliver in times of crisis critically depended on the positions and the networks already in place.

## 7.5  SUMMARY AND CONCLUSIONS

In our presentation and discussion of the responses of the innovation cluster in the Oslo region to the Covid-19 crisis, we have used three different cases to illustrate and discuss selected aspects of COI with Oslo as a starting point. The first case is about a local mini-cluster in the area of health technology focusing its responses to the Covid-19 epidemic. We have then exemplified how a regional COI can be viewed as an assembly of such mini-clusters, sharing components at the regional level, and how they can be understood as nodes in various extended global COI networks.

Our discussion helps us reflect upon what it takes to be able to respond effectively in such situations, and how these capabilities are reflected in major characteristics of COI such as entrepreneurial behaviors. It seems clear that effective responses must include both agile developmental and adaptive user capabilities. It is, furthermore, obvious that adequate responses are those that can solve the problem at the relevant scale, rapidly and in ways that improve the situation in significant ways.

Agile and adaptive capabilities must, therefore, be part of the existing governance systems and of the innovation cluster ecosystem, to be able to deliver effective responses. At the same time, the Oslo case also illustrates that the ability to immediately respond in novel situations is more effective if the systemic response supports a decentralized market system rather than one of tight hierarchical coordination and control. Centralized approaches are quickly overloaded. On the other hand, a distributed response that permits many to respond quickly will have to accept variation in the quality of these responses. However, the alternative of not providing an immediate response is worse.

The broad, decentralized response will also take immediate stress away from central coordination and planning, which will permit the mobilization of higher-quality responses that will gradually take control and take over the work and the supplies. The role of Norway Health Tech in our first case illustrates how a collective action capacity already in place, representing relevant parts of the innovation cluster, may be particularly useful in the orchestration of both the first and the second wave of responses, in taking the role of a collective counterpart to the government, in helping pivot crisis management strategies when needed, and in contributing to the effective orchestration of markets.

The second (DHIS2 and Sri Lanka) case exemplifies how a collaborative global COI network may act in very agile and adaptive ways to develop, standardize, distribute, and scale solutions. In this case, the networked innovation cluster had been developed over time to deal with international diseases in a multinational context with hugely different healthcare systems. Hence, the DHIS2 case and the Sri Lanka agile development process is particularly illustrative of what constitutes the built-in response capability of entrepreneurs in times of severe crisis. The global COI network is a network of local mini-clusters that interacts with their regional COI in very diverse international contexts. This particular network is held together by a few core resources such as a shared technical platform-infrastructure, global financial supporters and system integrators, and a shared doctoral program educating core people and shaping and building the knowledge base and culture of the extended network. Collaborative global COI seem to depend on such stabilizing and integrative resources and mechanisms in forms that are partly similar to those of global corporations.

Finally, the Dignio case, apart from exemplifying similar observations of agile and adaptive response capabilities, points to longer-term impacts of the experiences and responses catalyzed by the Covid-19 pandemic. There will be many long-term effects, such as the acceleration of the trend towards moving non-acute treatment and care out of hospitals, and the integration and standardization of healthcare information infrastructures that will open markets and opportunities to extend networked COI to develop solutions and undertake the building of engaged actor-networks to make us better prepared for the next unpredictable pandemic. As such, the Dignio case is illustrative of entrepreneurial companies that emerge out of local COI that are at the forefront of both regional and international processes that gradually transform public healthcare systems towards becoming more like hybrid private–public interacted care systems.

## NOTE

1.   DHIS2 is a modern, open platform infrastructure for multiple applications, whereas the original DHIS was a system of standalone solutions in each country.

## REFERENCES

Aanestad, M., Grisot, M., and Hanseth, O. (2017), *Information Infrastructures within European Health Care: Working with the Installed Base*. Springer International, Cham.

Adu-Gyamfi, E., Nielsen, P., and Sæbø, J. I. (2019), The Dynamics of a Global Health Information System Research and Implementation Project, *Proceedings of the 17th Scandinavian Conference on Health Informatics*, 12–13 November, Oslo, Norway.

Agarwal, S., Jalan, M., Pandaya, S., Ferguson, R., Mustafa, D., Ng, C., and Labrique, A. (2020), *Digital Solutions for COVID-19 Response: An Assessment of Digital Tools for Rapid Scale-Up for Case Management and Contact Tracing.* Johns Hopkins University Global mHealth Initiative (JHU-Gml) – Johns Hopkins Bloomberg School of Public Health, Baltimore, MD.

Amarakoon, P., Braa J., Sahay S., Siribaddana P., and Hewapathirana R. (2020), Building Agility in Health Information Systems to Respond to the COVID-19 Pandemic: The Sri Lankan Experience. In: Bandi, R. K., Ranjini, C. R., Klein, S., Madon, S., and Monteiro E. (eds), *The Future of Digital Work: The Challenge of Inequality.* IFIPJWC 2020. *IFIP Advances in Information and Communication Technology*, Vol. 601. Springer, Cham. https://doi.org/10.1007/978-3-030-64697-4_17.

Beck, K., Beedle, M., Van Bennekum, A., Cockburn, A., Fowler, M., and Jeffries, R. (2001), Manifesto for Agile Development. www.agilemanifesto.com.

Beohm, B. (2002), Get Ready for Agile Methods, with Care, *Computer*, 35 (1), pp. 64–69.

Braa, J., Hanseth, O., Heywood, A., Mohammed, W., and Shaw, V. (2007), Developing Health Information Systems in Developing Countries: The Flexible Standards Strategy, *MIS Quarterly*, 31 (2), pp. 381–402.

Janssen, M., and Van der Voort, H. (2016), Adaptive Governance: Towards a Stable Accountable and Responsive Government, *Government Information Quarterly*, 33 (1), pp. 1–5.

Janssen, M., and Van der Voort, H. (2020), Agile and Adaptive Governance in Crisis Response: Lessons from the COVID-19 Pandemic, *International Journal of Information Management*, December. https://doi.org/10.1016/j.ijinfomgt.2020.102180.

Overby, E., Bharadwaj, A., and Sambamurthy, V. (2006), Enterprise Agility and the Enabling Role of Information Technology, *European Journal of Information Systems*, 15 (2), pp. 120–131.

Sahay, S., Sæbø, J., and Braa, J. (2013), Scaling of HIS in a Global Context: Same, Same, but Different, *Information and Organization*, 23, pp. 294–322.

Stroetmann, K. A., Artmann, J., and Stroetmann, V. N. (2011), *European Countries on Their Journey towards National eHealth Infrastructures: Evidence on Progress and Recommendations for Cooperative Actions – Final European Progress Report.* European Commission, DG Information Society and Media ICT for Health Unit, Bonn and Brussels.

# 8. Changing pathways: urban dynamics and governance at 22@Barcelona

## Montserrat Pareja-Eastaway and Josep Miquel Piqué

## 8.1 INTRODUCTION

A profound change is taking place in the arguments underlying the competitive positioning of the city. While historically cities sought their competitiveness based on the creation of a critical business mass capable of producing and exporting with reasonable costs and quality, cities currently diversify the search for competitiveness, including not only economic but also social, cultural and environmental objectives. Urban competitiveness becomes much more complex, given the confluence of these different dimensions which do not always agree on their goals. Thus, cities are not only a set of economic or cultural resources but also spaces for the generation and absorption of benefits (Healey, 2002). Frequently, the distribution of those benefits generates tension and conflict between the different appropriations of the space by the city actors.

The integrated regeneration of an area presents some specific challenges when dealing with previously occupied areas that already belong to the existing urban fabric. The physical, economic and social characteristics inherent to these areas present particularly complex challenges for those exercising political and technical leadership of the process. For these reasons, the planning of districts like 22@Barcelona, which combines economic vitality with social and environmental sustainability, requires sophisticated leadership and a proactive approach (Barber and Pareja-Eastaway, 2010).

In its conception, the 22@Barcelona project was more than a planning intervention. It reflected a new way of understanding the city (Oliva, 2003). The project's main purpose was to transform the old paradigm of industrial society in Barcelona into a knowledge society, focused on next-generation activities related to education, creativity and innovation. The development of the 22@ project over the first 15 years and the achievement of the progressive regeneration of the district relied on the indisputable leadership of the City Council of Barcelona.

The 22@Barcelona project used the Urban Clusters of Innovation (COI) strategy for developing economic activities linked to the urban district promoting the location and interaction of the components like Entrepreneurs, Major Corporations, Universities and Research Centers, Venture Capital firms and Government, among others. The policy of clusters started in 2007 with the strategic plans of the ICT (Information and Communication Technologies), Media, Energy and Health clusters, and in 2008 with the Design cluster (Pareja-Eastaway and Piqué 2011). All of them promoted the connection of talent, technology and capital, and included entrepreneurship programs that encouraged new firms' creation and growth. In a unique innovation, they used the city itself as a lab; a starting point on the path to grow globally, augmented by relationships facilitated by global associations like the 22@Network.

As urban competitiveness takes on a much more polyhedral meaning, collective effort in making a diagnosis, setting priorities and determining the type of interventions required to address these priorities becomes a key element for success, without downplaying the difficulties inherent in this negotiated type of progress. Nevertheless, from 2016 a turning point in the governance process took place. The definition of the district's future pathways was debated and defined involving compromise and commitment from the different actors that were involved in the district, from urban planners to neighbors. As a result of this debate, 22@Barcelona included two new urban clusters in the strategy to develop the north of the District: a new cluster of heritage, culture and creativity at Pere IV street, and a new Green cluster at Cristobal de Moura street, following the pattern of COI.

The purpose of this chapter is to analyze the case of 22@Barcelona's innovation district in the framework of COI (Engel and del Palacio, 2009), considering the drivers of that governance change in approaching the future of the city, moving from a classic top-down approach to the use of a collective process as an endorser of a shared future path. The so-called 'Ca l'Alier Agreement' (Ajuntament de Barcelona, 2018; see below) could be a tangible example of a collective effort. However, only the coming years and the actions that will be taken during them can legitimize the agreements and priorities embodied in the document. This is not a clean slate. It is an expression of the commitment of the area's various stakeholders. In short, it is a way of basing the area's new competitiveness on more social and sustainable factors.

Today, 22@Barcelona is a benchmark for many cities that share a desire to transform old underused industrial zones, and their decisive backing for new sectors that generate jobs and wealth. The model applied to Barcelona has been a source of inspiration for other cities around the world, granting the added value of transferability. The change in the governance approach may also enlighten future developments in other areas.

## 8.2 CLUSTERING TO SUCCEED: THEORIES AND FRAMEWORKS TO PROMOTE COMPETITIVENESS AND SYNERGIES BETWEEN ORGANIZATIONS AND ACTORS

The theoretical foundations of this section come from different sources. First, the Triple Helix model (Etzkowitz and Leydesdorff, 2000), which focuses on the relationships between universities, government and industry. This model is used as a framework that helps to better understand how ecosystems of innovation develop in cities. Second, to understand how cities are transformed with respect to different dimensions—urban, economic, social and governance— the Knowledge-Based Urban Development (KBUD) approach (Yigitcanlar et al., 2008a, 2008b) is considered. And finally, the Agglomeration and Cluster theories (Marshall, 1920; Porter, 1998) provide the framework of the economies of scale and network effects while the Clusters of Innovation theory (Engel and del Palacio, 2009) is used to understand the components of ecosystems of innovation, paying attention to the interaction between startups, venture funds and corporations, contributing to the creation and development of high-potential entrepreneurial ventures.

### 8.2.1 The Triple, Quadruple and Quintuple Helix Model

The Triple Helix model is one of the most referenced models used to characterize an innovation ecosystem. The Triple Helix thesis postulates that the interaction among universities, industry and government is the key to improving the conditions for innovation in a knowledge-based society: (a) industry operates as the center of production, (b) government as the source of contractual relations that guarantee stable interaction and exchange, and (c) the university as a source of new knowledge and technology.

The university has traditionally been viewed as a support structure for innovation, providing trained people, research results and knowledge to industry. Recently the university has increasingly become involved in the formation of firms, often based on new technologies originated thanks to academic research. The Triple Helix raised the university to an equivalent status in a knowledge-based society, unlike previous institutional configurations where it had a secondary status. Rather than being subordinated to either industry or government, the university is emerging as an influential actor and equal partner in a Triple Helix of university–industry–government relations (Etzkowitz, 2008).

Triple Helix agents play different roles in urban, economic and social transformation. The role of each agent of the Triple Helix model (Government, Universities and Industry) is different depending on the dimension of the transformation (Piqué et al., 2019a; Piqué et al., 2019b). Although each of the three helices continues with its traditional functions—teaching and basic research at universities, market operation and experimental development in the industry sphere, and multilevel decision-making and rule-setting in government—in the most developed forms of the Triple Helix model the helices interact and transform each other, thereby moving from single functions to multiple shared functions, and promoting the active circulation of people, ideas and policies among and within the three core spheres (Dzisah and Etzkowitz, 2008; Etzkowitz, 2008; Carayannis and Campbell, 2011). The three agents can act separately or can coordinate by developing new knowledge, economic sectors, regions or cities. In promoting an ecosystem of innovation, players can assume the roles of the others, and permanent hybrid structures that articulate joint actions may also be created (Kim et al., 2012).

The Quadruple Helix can add a fourth sphere; that is, the public and larger society (Carayannis and Campbell, 2009). By acknowledging the role of the public in using, applying and also generating knowledge, this formulation explicitly introduces the democratization of knowledge production and innovation, as well as the impact of culture and creativity. Culture encompasses diversity in terms of values, lifestyles and multiculturalism, and in terms of multilevel regional, national, global and *local* approaches. This diversity promotes creativity, a key component for new innovations and knowledge to spur (Nikina and Piqué, 2016).

The Quintuple Helix adds the natural environment as a fifth sphere for knowledge and innovation models, thereby positioning sustainable development and social ecology as a component equivalent to the other four helices for knowledge production and innovation (Carayannis et al., 2012). Since socioecological concerns are incorporated as a key driver of innovation, this model is positioned to support the development of innovations simultaneously oriented towards problem-solving and sustainable development, and informed by multilateral interactions with the four other helices (Nikina and Piqué, 2016).

To summarize, the Triple Helix model of university–industry–government relations (Etzkowitz, 1993, 1996; Etzkowitz and Leydesdorff, 1995, 2000) serves as both an illustration of and a roadmap for moving from linear knowledge flows to non-linear and interactive modes of innovation. The Quadruple Helix incorporates the viewpoints of civil society and media and culture-based publics, while the ecologically sensitive Quintuple Helix adds the perspective of the natural environment (Carayannis and Campbell, 2009, 2010, 2011; Carayannis et al., 2012).

## 8.2.2 The Knowledge-Based Urban Development Approach

Cities have always been centers for economic and social development, and knowledge has become a key factor driving urban development (Knight, 2008). In the rapidly growing knowledge economy, talent and communities are crucial for economic and urban spatial transformation (Powell and Snellman, 2004). Cities have become the localities of 'knowledge community precincts' (Carrillo, 2006; Yigitcanlar et al., 2008b); that is, spaces for knowledge generation and places for knowledge communities (Yigitcanlar and Dur, 2013). More specifically, such precincts are initiated with the lead of government, but also with support from either industry or/and academia following the Triple Helix model. Central urban locations are the home for such precincts in order to benefit from the socio-cultural environment of the city in this place. Knowledge community precincts have also been analyzed in eight asset bases (Yigitcanlar and Dur, 2013): (1) symbolic assets, (2) social assets, (3) human assets, (4) heritage and cultural assets, (5) natural environmental and infrastructural assets, (6) financial assets, (7) knowledge assets and (8) relational assets.

Cities play an important role in the new economy where personal networking is of paramount importance (Landry, 2000). The tendency of urban planners is to transform old urban industrial zones into knowledge cities, which emerge as a balance between working and living (Yigitcanlar et al., 2008c). Cities that stimulate forms of knowledge serve as knowledge centers (Knight, 1995) and attract creative and highly skilled talent (Florida, 2008). In recent years some scholars have also included the artistic, cultural and social approach into this research field and have focused on analyzing creative cities and creative industries for local development (Scott, 2000, 2006; Lazzeretti, 2007; Cabrita et al., 2013; Pratt and Hutton, 2013; Daubeuf et al., 2020).

The association of the terms 'knowledge' and 'city' (as in 'knowledge city') combines the clustering of activities related with science, technology and innovation in urban areas, operating as engines of economic development (Carrillo et al., 2014). Universities, industry and government are promoting knowledge-based activities for urban development as innovation districts (Pareja-Eastaway and Piqué, 2011).

During the last decade, scholarly articles dealing with urban development issues have notably grown. However, there have been very limited investigations combining the topics of knowledge creation/diffusion and innovation spaces (Yigitcanlar et al., 2016). According to Bontje et al. (2011, p. 1), 'the economic future of cities and city-regions increasingly depends on the capacity to attract, generate, retain and foster creativity, knowledge and innovation'. This paradigm, namely Knowledge-Based Urban Development, was introduced during the last years of the 20th century as a result of the impact of the global knowledge economy on urban localities and societies (Yigitcanlar et al., 2008a, 2008b). In 1995, Richard Knight argued the need for a new approach to explain the development of cities given the knowledge-based development (Knight, 1995). He defined KBUD as 'the transformation of knowledge resources into local development' (Knight, 1995, pp. 225–226).

Several models have been proposed for the conceptualization of KBUD (Sarimin and Yigitcanlar, 2012), yet they all include: (1) social and cultural development (for example, housing, community facilities, education, social capital and knowledge workers), (2) economic development (for example, R&D [research and development] centers, knowledge-based companies and startups), (3) environmental and urban development (for example, green areas, green infrastructures—mobility, energy, waste, water—and green building) and (4) governance development (for example, public and/or private bodies that manage the urban transformation and the process of participation of the citizens).

### 8.2.3    Agglomeration and Cluster Theories

Under the principles of Agglomeration Theory, these concentrations consist of producers of a particular industry who have strong incentives (known as positive externalities) to be located next to each other (Marshall, 1920) as (1) they increase their access to specialized inputs, (2) they share knowledge among producers and (3) they attract skilled human resources and facilitate the search for workers possessing specialized skills. Companies operating in these specialized agglomerations benefit from what is known as 'external economies of scale', a concept developed initially by Marshall and further analyzed by Arrow and Romer (Henderson, 2003). Also, building on Marshall's theories, Becattini rediscovered the phenomenon of industrial districts linked to local development (Becattini et al., 2003).

Porter (1998) defined these agglomeration structures as clusters or geographic concentrations of interconnected companies and institutions in a particular field. In a Porterian cluster, companies do not necessarily operate in the same industry; however, they do operate in complementary industries and optimize their collective productivity by having easy access to related customers (downwards); suppliers, universities, trade associations, government institutions and others (upwards); and even to complementary and competitive companies (lateral extensions). The mass allocation and networking of industries and other organizations affect competition in three broad ways (Porter, 1998): (1) by increasing the productivity of companies based in the area; (2) by driving the direction and pace of innovation, which underpins future productivity growth; and (3) by stimulating the formation of new businesses, which expands and strengthens the cluster itself.

Clusters of Innovation are global economic 'hot spots' where new technologies germinate at an astounding rate and where pools of capital, expertise and talent foster the development of new industries and new ways of doing business. A COI is similar to, but somewhat different from, the well-established understanding of a business cluster (Freeman and Engel, 2007). In a COI, the entrepreneurial process is a mechanism for continuous and rapid innovation, technology commercialization, business model experimentation and new market development, and the process is encouraged by a dense venture capital cluster and the related facility for the creation of well-structured, well-funded and well-connected startups. In these environments, startups benefit from being co-located with other providers, including lawyers, bankers, venture capitalists and a myriad of consultants who are well versed in the needs of startups and small technology companies (Saxenian, 2007).

The emergence of clusters in new industries that do not benefit from agglomeration externalities indicates the presence of several factors that characterize a COI, namely: (1) new firm creation as a rapid and frequent mechanism for innovation, technology commercialization, business model experimentation and new market development; (2) staged risk-taking and commitment of resources; (3) rapid market testing and validation or failure; (4) tolerance of failure; (5) continuous recycling of people, money, ideas and business models; (6) intra- and inter-firm mobility of resources; (7) shared identities and values; (8) alignment of incentives and goals; and (9) a global perspective (del Palacio, 2009).

In 2009, Engel and del Palacio extended Porter's definition of industrial agglomeration to delineate a global COI framework that describes business clusters defined primarily not by industry specialization but by the stage of development and innovation of the cluster's constituents. While industry concentrations do exist, they are not definitive. Rather, it is the nature and behavior of the components that is distinctive—the rapid emergence of new firms commercializing new technologies, creating new markets and addressing global markets (Engel, 2015).

## 8.3 GOVERNING THE CITY: FROM GOVERNMENT TO GOVERNANCE IN DISTRICTS OF INNOVATION

Cities and regions have experienced a shift in the way they define policies: from traditional top-down approaches, where the discussion about procedures and tools has been limited to stakeholders and politicians, to a more bottom-up-oriented intervention where the wishes and preferences of people are considered.

The reasons for these dynamics are manyfold. Urban planning has been strongly affected by the new approaches in urban regeneration projects where integrated approaches have become the rule rather than the exception. The diminishing role of the public sector due to budget constraints or deficit commitments with supranational bodies is opening the scene to other actors and other sensitivities in the way policy is delivered. These processes require involvement and commitment through the process, avoiding opportunism or changes in priorities during its development.

This phenomenon can be seen in innovation districts as well. While traditionally innovation districts targeted competitiveness and efficiency of the business landing in the territory, the range of goals has broadened, as well as the means to achieve them. Other understandings are currently considered to jointly define a pathway for action. The rationale of business ecosystems transformed into innovation ecosystems unfolding new approaches to innovation where a varied range of actors deploy new avenues to knowledge production and innovation (Cohendet et al., 2020) is deeply affected by the change in the management and organization of governance procedures.

In terms of governance, the power relations within organizations often determine their competences to make flexible arrangements with partners and workers to adapt to new situations. A similar situation can be seen in territorial modes of governance, where changes in the macro scenario at policy or economic level can determine strategies of adaptation. Adaptative governance is considered to be adequate to deal with problems or projects that are complex in essence, with several actors involved with a varied range of interests and where uncertainty is generalized (Nelson et al., 2008). The conceptualization of adaptative governance responds to the organic evolution of monocentric and multilevel governance as a response to managing multiscale problems and conflicts between divergent interests (Termer et al., 2010). The complexity and uncertain scenarios of socioecological systems require agile methods to address change and disruption, balancing stability and adaptability. In the case of regeneration processes, governance represents a key factor for successful policy delivery.

Many authors have explored the relevance of governance models in regeneration interventions (Davies, 2002; Degen and García, 2012; Atkinson et al., 2019; Seo, 2020) as the power relationship between actors is essential in the articulation of a successful intervention with respect to the goals previously defined and eventually agreed upon. Other authors have focused on innovation districts and governance (Griffith, 2016; Gianoli and Palazzolo Henkes, 2020). Innovation districts that drive urban regeneration and promotion of growth and employment and that emphasize the use of knowledge and creativity as a source for innovation agglutinate a wide diversity of actors, public and private. Governance dwells on the relationship between these actors and their involvement in the policy delivery of the innovation district. To do that, institutional and organizational factors are key in the choice of policy intervention (Palazzolo Henkes, 2016).

Traditionally, innovation districts are initiated, funded and managed by the local government. However, a flourishing district encompasses multiple relations in the physical space of the district, including civil society, companies and universities (Acuto et al., 2019). The strong dependence on the public initiative may or may not last during the shaping and building of the district. Whatever the case, alliances may vary, and new leaderships can emerge in the governance of the process.

## 8.4 CREATING OPPORTUNITIES: THE 22@ BARCELONA DISTRICT AS A POLICY INTERVENTION TO INCREASE LOCAL COMPETITIVENESS

The 22@Barcelona district was driven by public initiative with a long-term vision (20 years). It became a real laboratory of experimentation of the above-mentioned theories (Triple Helix, KBUD and COI). Different initiatives were developed involving investors, companies, universities, civil society and public authorities.

### 8.4.1 Path Dependency

Since the end of the 19th century, Barcelona has taken advantage of the celebration of large international events to redevelop or regenerate certain areas in need of attention (Pareja-Eastaway and Piqué, 2011). The two International Exhibitions held in 1888 and 1929 were the first local celebrations which involved the regeneration of certain parts of the city (the Ciutadella area and the redevelopment of the Montjuic district).

In 1992, the Olympic Games were a turning point in the city's trajectory; the leap to fame allowed the city to benefit from the momentum gained. The improved connectivity (construction of two ring roads surrounding Barcelona) and the creation of two residential areas on the periphery of the city are two examples of the regeneration promoted during this period. In addition, and thanks to the huge success during the development of the Games, the popularity of Barcelona noticeably increased, and it became attractive not only for tourism, but also for talented people and business (Pareja-Eastaway and Piqué, 2011).

The 22@Barcelona project began as a unique opportunity to partially transform Poblenou, a neighborhood containing the old textile industrial district of Barcelona, into a platform for an innovation and knowledge economy at an international level (Pareja-Eastaway and Piqué, 2014). In 1998, after a considerable political debate about how to regenerate the 200 hectares of obsolete industrial areas, Barcelona bet decisively and unequivocally to preserve the production profile of this territory while also aiming at combining residential uses in it. The 22@Barcelona District looked for a long-term urban transformation that progressively regenerated industrial areas, both through the revaluation of its architectonic environment as well as through improving the quality of its public space. Instead of the conventional practice of completely changing the urban space, this process was developed to establish a balance between maintaining and renewing, which allowed the definition of new urban images in a context of continuity with earlier forms.

### 8.4.2    The Process

The process started in 2000 with an initial phase of urban renovation and the provision of high-quality infrastructures. In 2004, 22@Barcelona approached a new era of intense economic and social renewal. Several strategies were developed, aiming to create urban COI focusing on various emergent sectors which Barcelona considered important to be represented in the city's economy. These sectors were media, information and communication technologies, medical technologies and energy. In some cases, the sectors were clearly rooted in the territory, like the media or information and communication technologies; in other cases, they were good targets for attracting and promoting in the city. At a later date, in 2008, design was added to the first four (Pareja-Eastaway and Piqué, 2014). The process aspired to concentrate on the territory's businesses, public administration agencies and scientific and technological centers of reference in these strategic sectors.

The society 22 ARROBA was created to manage the district from the very beginning. Its goals were economic promotion and the international projection of business and academia (research, education and knowledge transfer) and creation of a diverse and balanced environment where the most innovative companies coexist with research centers, with training and technology-transfer operations, and with shops, housing and green zones, promoting social and entrepreneurial dynamism (Piqué et al., 2019a).

### 8.4.3    Results

According to the last available data (Institut Cerdà, 2018), the 22@ district had 113,526 inhabitants and 19,358 companies are located in the area. The 22@Barcelona urban planning transformation had reached approximately 77 percent of the Poblenou industrial areas (Ajuntament de Barcelona, 2020). The total approved plans account for 1,018,682.72 square meters of floor space

(Ajuntament de Barcelona, 2019). The regeneration of the district has led to the establishment of 10 universities with a total of more than 25,000 students, and 12 R&D and technology-transfer centers. The current census of businesses in the 22@Barcelona area shows continued growth.

## Infrastructures and urban development at 22@Barcelona

The stated objectives of the 22@Barcelona Plan were to renew the urban and economic Poblenou (Pareja-Eastaway and Piqué, 2011), envisioning a compact and diverse city with a balanced and sustainable focus, instead of a model specialized on industrial land. Therefore, the new economic activities coexist with research, training and technology transfer, housing, equipment and trade, in one high-quality environment, whose density makes it compatible with a balanced allocation of open space and equipment.

On the one hand, through a system of incentives for real estate, urban renewal processes contribute to the redevelopment of all streets with the renewal of infrastructure, improved quality and capacity of the urban services, and new organization of urban mobility. In addition, free land was generated for the community through the transformation. From an initial status of 100 percent private land ownership, 30 percent of the land will now become public land to create new green zones, facilities and social housing. On the other hand, the so-called '@' activities are favored. These activities are those that use talent as a main productive resource.

Thus, the progressive transformation of the industrial land solves historical deficits and restores the social and business dynamism that has historically characterized Poblenou. From the project's inception in 2000 until now, the urban renewal project has involved the creation of a diverse and balanced environment that promotes social and entrepreneurial dynamism.

## Companies and economic development at 22@Barcelona

A cluster strategy was developed in the district in order to promote the Knowledge-based Economy. In 2004, adding value to the physical transformation (urban and infrastructure), 22@Barcelona developed policies centered on emerging sectors with local assets and international opportunities to grow: media, information and communication technologies, medical technologies and energy. In 2008, the design cluster began as a new strategic sector of Barcelona.

Promoting urban clusters in the territory of 22@Barcelona, the district improved the innovative capacity of the ecosystem of innovation. Each of the five clusters of 22@Barcelona was located in the district in different levels of maturity. The methodology followed in all cases was on establishing a cluster program: 22@Barcelona promoted the creation of sectorial centers of technology transfer as tools for better connection between research (universities) and companies. It worked on consolidating these with Barcelona Media Foundation in the audio-visual sector and Barcelona Digital Foundation in the information and communication technologies sector. Later, support was given to BCD (Barcelona Center of Design) and the consolidation of IREC (Institute for Energy Research Catalonia), which together with b_TEC led the Energy cluster.

Since 2000, 4,342 companies have landed in the 22@ area. Of those, 1,379 are knowledge-intensive services and 132 represent sectors with medium and high technology. These companies have created 47,408 jobs and an added value of 2,684 million euros. The distribution of this development is not homogeneous, as nearly 84 percent of the companies, 85 percent of workers and 86 percent of the added value created are concentrated in the southern part of the district. With respect to the original objectives (high occupation density, creation of knowledge and production of added value), data confirms that the 22@ district doubled the amount of companies per hectare (22/Ha) compared to the rest of the city of Barcelona (11/Ha). The district has nearly three times the amount of employees per hectare (238/Ha) with respect to the rest of the city (86/Ha), as well more than double the direct creation of Gross Added Value (13 M€/Ha versus 5 M€/Ha, respectively) (Institut Cerdà, 2018).

**Talent and social development at 22@Barcelona**
To develop a talent management strategy that supplied the raw material for the knowledge economy, 22@Barcelona managed the implementation of university centers in the district with the objectives of locating talent in the sector, installing a critical mass of talent and developing new generations of talent.

Primary and secondary schools promoted scientific and technological vocations, entrepreneurship and understanding of global citizenship. These actions connected schools with cluster businesses developed in the district (the CreaTalent Program), promoting career guidance (Porta 22), workplace internships (Staying in Company) and employability (Talent 22@ Marketplace). Likewise, with the aim of developing a community of professionals in the district, 22@Barcelona promoted events such as the 22@Breakfast which served to create cross-sector relationships and develop a sense of belonging.

Universities and companies acted as true international magnets for talent. Landing programs and benefits were promoted for the international community, ensuring a comprehensive welcome. Publications such as *Welcome to Barcelona*, which describes international schools or practical processes of life in Barcelona, facilitated the implementation and integration of newcomers. In parallel, 22@Barcelona developed social programs in order to involve the neighborhood. For example, Digital District has included grandparents and parents in the activities of the district through digital training programs.

**The need for a holistic approach at 22@Barcelona**

The 22@Barcelona renovation plan theoretically included three dimensions: (1) urban planning, (2) economic revitalization and (3) a social dimension orchestrated by a particular governance strategy based on the leadership of the municipality. The sequence of development at the origin of the project focused first on the urban and infrastructure transformation followed by the landing of companies guided by the urban clusters strategy, which also involved universities. The social dimension was included in the initial planning; however, it mainly targeted foreign talent without keeping track of the impact of the urban revitalization model in the existing social fabric. Bottero et al. (2020) used community impact evaluation (CIE) for assessing 22@Barcelona, and concluded that 'the impacts of the operation were positive, especially according to the economic dimension (relaunching of the labor market and attraction of new enterprises) and the environmental sphere (reuse of brownfields). Conversely, the effects in terms of social integration were negligible' (p. 11).

The new governance process launched in 2016 aimed to close the previous social dimension gaps in terms of actors' involvement. The decision to involve all the stakeholders in the collective process of the co-creation of the 'Agreement' for 22@Barcelona, including not only universities, government and associations of companies, but also neighborhood and cultural associations, assured the inclusion of all interests and the commitment to a long-term view, sharing the vision and the strategy of development.

## 8.5 RETHINKING 22@BARCELONA: DRIVERS OF CHANGE

In 2016, in an effort to evaluate the tangible results of the district after 15 years, several challenges for the 22@Barcelona district were identified. Among others, the need to increase the involvement of all the interested actors in the decision-making process about the future of the district was of paramount importance.

The district of innovation, 22@Barcelona, had experienced two different governance approaches since its conception. While the start of the intervention was managed and led by the municipality, the follow-up since 2011 has been led by different organizations. Three periods can be distinguished in the articulation of governance in the district.

- Stage 1, 1998–2011: 22@ emerged under the direct leadership of the local government and the advice of scholars at the Autonomous University. The 22 ARROBA S.A. agency was created in 2000 to promote and manage the different stages that had been foreseen in the urban development of the district. In addition, the five economic clusters, aimed at concentrating the economic activity in the district (Media, ICT, Design, Energy and Bio-med), were managed by different bodies, all of them non-profit organizations with different levels of maturity (Pareja-Eastaway and Piqué, 2014).

- Stage 2, 2011–2016: The society 22 ARROBA was dismantled in according with the decision of the local government, and public responsibilities were divided between Barcelona Activa, the local agency for economic development, and the Urban Department of the city council. Simultaneously, the leadership of the project shifted towards the business association 22@ Network. The relevance and commitment with the district of this network has increased over time. Nowadays, the 22@Network (n.d.) 'gathers the innovative, technological, and creative sector of the city of Barcelona. With more than 205 associates, [it is] responsible for the consolidation of the 22@District as a dynamic, [a] transformative, and an advanced technological space: the innovation district'.

- Stage 3, 2016 to now: In 2015, the newly elected local government radically changed the approach to the 22@ district. After a period of hesitation, a new pathway with respect to the district was elaborated. The local government, through the BIT (Barcelona Institute of Technology) Habitat Foundation, started a conversation with all the actors involved in the district:[1] institutional (local government, provincial government, regional government), residents' associations, business associations, activists and universities. '*Repensem el 22@*' ('Let's rethink the 22@') was a shared endeavor by the different institutions, associations, professionals and individuals to redefine the priorities and future challenges of the district. Three discussion groups were created (social, urban planning and economic), facilitated by scholars from three universities (Pompeu Fabra University, Polytechnic University and the University of Barcelona) with the goal of drawing up a shared roadmap to guide the future transformation of Poblenou.

### 8.5.1   The Ca l'Alier Agreement

In 2018, an agreement was signed by the partners that had been participating in several discussions of the three groups. The discussion took place over a year and a half and worked as a non-compulsory but advisory 'think tank'. In the history of 22@, no other discussion group like this had happened. The so-called 'Ca l'Alier Agreement: Towards a More Inclusive and Sustainable 22@ within Poblenou' (Martínez Garcia and Planelles Oliva, 2018) was the result of a negotiation and adaptation to the demands and commitments of the different partners representing government, neighbors, businesses, universities and other institutions.[2] Since then, the municipality has elaborated a new roadmap to develop and expand the commitments assumed at that time. The implementation of this agreement started with the publication of the 'Criteria Document' in 2019, where the new direction in urban planning is stated, and the publication of the municipality directive '*Impulsem el 22@*' in July 2020.

With this shared strategic planning, the roadmap of 22@Barcelona was agreed upon, diminishing possible tensions between actors in the future. In addition, if any of the actors were going to be replaced (for example, a change in government), the written commitment guaranteed the continued authority of the existing planning.

The agreement defined five pillars for development (see Figure 8.1) with different actions and interventions related to each of them. They all represented the result of the discussions among universities, companies, governments and citizens, prior to the signing of the 'Ca l'Alier Agreement'. Unsurprisingly, these axes embraced economic targets where creative and cultural industries were of paramount importance, but also aimed to solve pending challenges such as affordable housing or environmental sustainability. As a permanent axis, governance and participation was meant to be responsive and resilient to all possible developments of the district.

*Source:*     Ajuntament de Barcelona, 2018.

*Figure 8.1     The axes for future development of 22@Barcelona*

Two new avenues of growth were defined from this public debate: Creative Industries and the Green Economy. The previous five clusters (ICT, Media, Design, Bio-med and Energy) around which 22@ welcomed new or existing companies were already related to creative industries but in a more focused way; that is, targeting media and design companies with an existing tradition in the city and information and communication technology businesses where videogames, for instance, played a key role. The cluster theories were readapted here, providing a territorial dimension in the form of two main roads of the district, Pere IV and Cristobal de Moure, which will accommodate creative and cultural industries and the green economy respectively.

### Creative industries
Under the 'creative industries' label, two targets were considered. On the one hand are the promotion and knowledge of existing cultural tangible and intangible heritage. As an underlying principle, the renewed 22@ contemplated

social and cultural facilities as central elements for providing social interaction, contributing to preserving Poblenou's identity and collective memory. On the other hand is the transformation of Pere IV, a road that existed before the Cerdà grid, that concentrates industrial heritage elements such as Can Ricart into a hub of heritage, culture and creativity. Urban planning will be used to redirect cars and promote pedestrianized areas and the use of alternative mobility solutions, like bicycles. The Special Plan of the Industrial Heritage will be revisited, involving citizens' participation to reconsider the degree of protection of some heritage elements or the addition of new ones. The former factory Can Ricart, together with Central Park of Poblenou, will become a central point of reference for the neighborhood.

The challenge for implementing the creative and cultural industries at the Pere IV Avenue involves not only the urban and economic transformation as in the previous clusters, but also the social dimension, since the citizens are an active part as users of the cultural industries and could be part of co-creation activities. The 'Ca l'Alier Agreement' included different anchors of creative and cultural industries, such as Can Ricart and La Escocesa along the Avenue, in order to (1) transform old factories into new cultural industries, (2) regenerate the streets with new infrastructures, (3) locate cultural clusters with key magnet tenants as epicenters of the ecosystem, (4) involve academic agents for providing creative talent and (5) promote the street as a boulevard of cultural activities.

**Green economy**
Green and sustainability principles facilitate the renewed 22@ functioning as a laboratory for the rest of the city of Barcelona to become an inclusive, healthy and sustainable city. Since residents have claimed more green areas and open public spaces in the district, the road Cristobal de Moura will be urbanized with a large presence of urban greenery and will become an axis with the ability to connect the Poblenou Central Park with the Besòs and Maresme districts and beyond to the river Besòs. Urban planning actions become essential to identify equal access to public spaces and overcome previous problems, such as the ground water in the service galleries, the lack of proper infrastructure to accommodate cars, and the lack of public lighting. The 22@ district was built by means of a PEI (Special Infrastructure Plan) launched at the very start of the project. A new PEI is envisaged to update the existing one. The general mobility and road hierarchization schemes must be updated in accordance with the latest needs and criteria. Alternative modes of transport (bicycles, electric and shared vehicles, pedestrian walkways, and so on) will be prioritized.

The green economy involves the Sustainability dimension of the Quintuple Helixes and also the role of the city and the citizens as active actors for working and living in a green dimension. The challenge is for the implementation of the strategy of the cluster in order to create and grow a green economy. The city is a magnet for entrepreneurs that can use it as a lab. With regulation and public procurement, the city council could develop from the demand side the best ecosystem for creating products and services that do not exist anywhere else. In that moment the COI is the platform of the first mile of the global innovation, learning locally in order to scale globally. On the other hand, the citizens, as users and buyers of products and services, can decide and inspire innovation in their daily lives, stimulating a circular economy to avoid non-recyclable waste by: (1) reusing products, (2) regenerating materials, (3) sharing resources or (4) virtualizing solutions (MacArthur, 2013).

## 8.6 THE NEW NORMAL AND COVID-19'S IMPACT IN THE 22@BARCELONA ECOSYSTEM

The society of the 21st century has had to respond, react and adapt to a huge external shock with the Covid-19 pandemic. The global situation has required responses articulated between government and society. While in many cases governments have provided strategic direction, the emergency has forced the creation of daily innovative solutions by non-governmental bodies. Surviving households, organizations and institutions have shown their resilient capacity in the face of this crisis. And they have also exhibited their capabilities for joint action. Agile governance that senses events and responds quickly, and adaptative governance that—without losing stability—keeps track and redirects divergent interests (Janssen and Van Der Voort, 2020), have both been essential in the response of the 22@ innovation district of Barcelona to the emergency created by the pandemic.

In response to Covid-19, Triple Helix agents reacted during the crisis in different ways around the world. Other crises have already hit local innovation ecosystems in the past 50 years (such as the 2008 financial crisis and other recent health crises; for example, Ebola, SARS) but not with the depth and systemic impact brought by Covid-19, such as the interruption in global supply chains and mandatory policies of social distancing (for example, quarantine, lockdown, partial release).

Understanding the context and the agile and innovative responses (actions) by the COI to the crisis became critical to the elaboration of policies that are able to generate the rapid recovery of the economy, while considering the impacts on the health system and level of contamination.

Evaluating secondary data regarding 48 actions of the agents of 22@ Barcelona during the Covid-19 pandemic in the year 2020 (22@Network, n.d.), we analyzed how the COI responded to the rapid digital transformation prompted by Covid-19 as an accelerator. We examined both the hard factors (the key components of Universities, Government, Entrepreneurs, Venture Capital, Major Corporations, Research Centers and Service Organizations) and the soft factors (behaviors and structures such as mobility of resources, entrepreneurial process, global strategic perspective, alignment of interests and global connections).

We found that Universities, Government, Entrepreneurs, Major Corporations, and Research and Technology Centers were working together to solve challenges. The funding was provided by donors. The agents were sharing common challenges, providing key resources and creating new ventures. Some of them were shared with other international ecosystems.

We concluded that the way of responding to Covid-19 could be classified in different categories:

- Providing solutions in a very fast way against Covid-19: The agents of 22@ reacted in a very agile way, designing and producing key solutions in a very short period of time in order to provide critical supplies such as masks, protectors, cleaning robots and ventilators.
- Changing the way of producing: Using previous capabilities of production, some mature companies changed their lines or production in order to produce new solutions for Covid-19. For example, car companies produced ventilators and clothes fashion companies produced health-related clothes and masks.
- Providing connectivity and technology for sick people: In order to avoid the personal isolation of sick people in hospitals and residential care facilities for elderly people, corporations and entrepreneurs provided tablets, videoconferencing tools and connectivity in order to connect them with their families.
- Providing digital tools for information during Covid-19: New ventures like health and food apps were created by entrepreneurs in conjunction with corporations to provide key information about Covid-19, or to connect donors of food with people in need. Health and food apps were created from scratch, leveraging the pre-Covid-19 capabilities for new needs, organized by common focus.
- Reacting with solidarity: In order to collect funding for projects and people with needs, the ecosystem reacted rapidly in fundraising. Companies and workers could make contributions for different requests, providing money for specific projects or simply giving money to persons in critical situations (for food or rent payments, among other needs).
- Creating a new normal: Government, universities and companies reacted in a very diligent way, creating new forms of organizing e-working and e-learning and developing telematic services in order to avoid the need for people to be mobile. In this case, public and private organizations were

flexible and agile in allowing e-working as a way to continue working and still prevent the health impacts of personal contact. Similarly, the universities put their campuses in the cloud in order to teach lessons.

In summary, key components such as Universities, Government, Entrepreneurs and Major Corporations of the COI of 22@Barcelona developed agile behaviors in order to reuse resources in different ways, sharing a common vision and alignment for solving the Covid-19 challenges, using the entrepreneurial way of doing things as the more effective way of reacting, resolving the problems, developing the resilience of the organizations and the ecosystem, returning to the new normality and reimagining the post-Covid-19 times.

## 8.7    CONCLUSION

The 20 years of evolution of the COI of 22@Barcelona have provided valuable lessons in several areas.

### 8.7.1    The Governance Model in Urban Clusters of Innovation

Since its inception, 22@Barcelona has become an international reference point as a prosperous ecosystem of innovation where theoretical models of different sorts have been put into practice. From cluster theories to new modes of public transportation, the district has been often used as an urban laboratory to test innovative products and processes.

In the last two decades and under different political mandates, the 22@ district has organically evolved towards more sustainable governance models where participation, commitment and involvement have been pursued. As in many other economic development models, sustainability is nowadays considered as essential as any other criteria for a company landing in the territory.

After two years of consultations, the new governance model of the 22@ district was put into practice in 2018 with the involvement and commitment of several actors, public and private, under the signature of the 'Ca l'Alier Agreement'. Governance in the district has shifted from a 'top-down' approach to a 'bottom-up' strategy where civil society is involved in co-creating the vision, the strategy and some of the actions in the district. This process adds a new perspective on COI theories where, besides the urban, economic and social dimensions, governance becomes essential in delivering a holistic approach and enhances the resilient capacity of the district in front of external shocks.

### 8.7.2 The City as a Lab of Clusters of Innovation

The COI Framework has proved to be a useful tool for city transformation. The dynamics and experience of implementation in the transformation of the territory enrich and sharpen the theories that back many of the processes of intervention. This bilateral relationship between theory and reality needs to be acknowledged and reinforced. The 22@ district in Barcelona is currently acting as a laboratory, adding the demand side to COI models. Health issues, culture consumption and sustainable mobility, to name a few, are demand aspects that can stimulate and prioritize the focus of entrepreneurs, companies and investors. Likewise, universities and government need to be aligned with the new holistic strategies that draw the new direction of the district.

### 8.7.3 Clusters of Innovation as a Tool of Resilience in Front of Crises

The case of 22@Barcelona during Covid-19 demonstrates that the components of a COI, including Universities, Government, Entrepreneurs, Major Corporations and Research and Technology Centers, can provide key resources and innovative entrepreneurial solutions when confronted by a common challenge. This innovative response is strengthened by the COI behaviors, notably alignment of interests, mobility of resources and entrepreneurial behavior. These shared behaviors fostered resilience in the face of crisis.

The project 22@Barcelona has reached 20 years of life. The attractiveness of the project has gone hand in hand with the attractiveness of the city of Barcelona, and the project has been dynamic and sensitive to the macro variables affecting the city, such as the global financial crisis in 2008 and the Covid-19 pandemic from 2020. Despite the difficulties, the project is alive and has been renewed according to the new societal demands. One of the main challenges ahead for the 22@ district is to reconcile citizens' demands and needs with the 2030 Sustainable Development Goals. The district is key to demonstrating the economic vitality of the city's innovation capacity, and portraying the renewed image of Barcelona, well aligned with global endeavors to be achieved at the local level.

## NOTES

1. The participatory process extended across different departments of the municipality: the budget, flagship projects like the 'superblock', sewage planning, and so on. See www.decidim.barcelona.
2. Partners signing the agreement were: the Municipality of Barcelona, Federació d'Associacions de Veïns de Barcelona, Taula Eix Pere IV, Associació d'Empreses i Institucions 22@ Network, Poblenou Urban District, Universitat de Barcelona, Universitat Politècnica de Catalunya, Universitat Pompeu Fabra,

Pla Estratègic Metropolità de Barcelona, Consorci del Besòs and Consorci b_TEC-Campus Diagonal Besòs.

# REFERENCES

Acuto, M., Steenmans, K., Iwaszuk, E., and Ortega-Garza, L. (2019) Informing urban governance? Boundary-spanning organisations and the ecosystem of urban data. *Area*, *51*(1), 94–103. https://doi.org/10.1111/area.12430.

Ajuntament de Barcelona (2018) *Ca l'Alier Agreement: Towards a Poblenou with a 22@ More Inclusive and Sustainable.* Barcelona: Fundació Barcelona Institute of Technology for the Habitat.

Ajuntament de Barcelona (2019) *Document de Criteris*. Unpublished.

Ajuntament de Barcelona (2020) *Mesura de Govern. Impulsem el 22@. Cap a un Poblenou amb un 22@ més productiu, més inclusiu i més sostenible.* Barcelona: Ajuntament de Barcelona.

Atkinson, R., Tallon, A., and Williams, D. (2019) Governing urban regeneration in the UK: A case of 'variegated neoliberalism' in action? *European Planning Studies*, *27*(6), 1083–1106. https://doi.org/10.1080/09654313.2019.1598020.

Barber, A., and Pareja-Eastaway, M. (2010) Leadership challenges in the inner city: Planning for sustainable regeneration in Birmingham and Barcelona. *Policy Studies*, *31*(4), 393–411. https://doi.org/10.1080/01442871003723309.

Becattini, G., Bellandi, M., Del Ottati, G., and Sforzi, F. (2003) *From Industrial Districts to Local Development.* Cheltenham, UK and Northampton, MA, USA: Edward Elgar Publishing.

Bontje, M., Musterd, S., and Pelzer, P. (2011) *Inventive City-Regions: Path Dependence and Creative Knowledge Strategies.* Farnham: Ashgate.

Bottero, M., Bragaglia, F., Caruso, N., Datola, G., and Dell'Anna, F. (2020) Experimenting community impact evaluation (CIE) for assessing urban regeneration programmes: The case study of the area 22@ Barcelona. *Cities*, *99*, 102464. https://doi.org/10.1016/j.cities.2019.102464.

Cabrita, M. do R., Machado, V.C., and Cabrita, C. (2013) Managing creative industries in the context of knowledge-based urban development. *International Journal of Knowledge-Based Development*, *4*(4), 318–337.

Carayannis, E.G., Barth, T.D., and Campbell, D.F. (2012) The Quintuple Helix innovation model: Global warming as a challenge and driver for innovation. *Journal of Innovation and Entrepreneurship*, *1*(1), 1–12.

Carayannis, E.G., and Campbell, D.F. (2009) 'Mode 3' and 'Quadruple Helix': Toward a 21st century fractal innovation ecosystem. *International Journal of Technology Management*, *46*(3–4), 201–234.

Carayannis, E.G., and Campbell, D.F. (2010) Triple Helix, Quadruple Helix and Quintuple Helix and how do knowledge, innovation, and environment relate to each other? *International Journal of Social Ecology and Sustainable Development*, *1*(1), 41–69.

Carayannis, E.G., and Campbell, D.F. (2011) Open innovation diplomacy and a 21st century fractal research, education and innovation (FREIE) ecosystem: Building on the Quadruple and Quintuple Helix innovation concepts and the 'Mode 3' knowledge production system. *Journal of the Knowledge Economy*, *2*(3), 327–372.

Carrillo, F.J. (Ed.) (2006) *Knowledge Cities: Approaches, Experiences and Perspectives.* New York, NY: Routledge.

Carrillo, J., Yigitcanlar, T., Garcia, B., and Lonnqvist, A. (2014) *Knowledge and the City: Concepts, Applications and Trends of Knowledge-Based Urban Development.* New York, NY: Routledge.

Cohendet, P., Simon, L., and Mehouachi, C. (2020) From business ecosystems to ecosystems of innovation: The case of the video game industry in Montréal. *Industry and Innovation, 28*(8), 1046–1076. https://doi.org/10.1080/13662716.2020 .1793737.

Daubeuf, C., Pratt, A., Airaghi, E., and Pletosu, T. (2020) Enumerating the role of incentives in CCI production chains. CICERONE. https://cicerone-project.eu/ wp-content/uploads/2020/05/D3.2-Enumeratingthe-role-of-incentives-in-CCI -production-chains.pdf.

Davies, J.S. (2002) The governance of urban regeneration: A critique of the 'governing without government' thesis. *Public Administration, 80*(2), 301–322.

Degen, M., and García, M. (2012) The transformation of the 'Barcelona model': An analysis of culture, urban regeneration and governance. *International Journal of Urban and Regional Research, 36*(5), 1022–1038. https://doi.org/10.1111/j.1468 -2427.2012.01152.x.

Del Palacio, I. (2009) *The Capital Gap for Small Technology Companies in Spain: Public Venture Capital to the Rescue?* PhD thesis, Universitat Politècnica de Catalunya.

Dzisah, J., and Etzkowitz, H. (2008) Triple helix circulation: The heart of innovation and development. *International Journal of Technology Management & Sustainable Development, 7*(2), 101–115.

Engel, J.S. (2015) Global clusters of innovation: Lessons from Silicon Valley. *California Management Review, 57*(2), 36–65.

Engel, J.S., and del Palacio, I. (2009) Global networks of clusters of innovation: Accelerating the innovation process. *Business Horizons, 52*(5), 493–503.

Etzkowitz, H. (1993) Technology transfer: The second academic revolution. *Technology Access Report, 6*(1), 7–9.

Etzkowitz, H. (1996) From knowledge flows to the Triple Helix: The transformation of academic industry relations in the USA. *Industry & Higher Education, 10*(6), 337–342.

Etzkowitz, H. (2008) *The Triple Helix: University–Industry–Government Innovation in Action.* New York, NY: Routledge.

Etzkowitz, H., and Leydesdorff, L. (1995) The Triple Helix: University–industry–government relations – A laboratory for knowledge-based economic development. *EASST Review, 14,* 14–19.

Etzkowitz, H., and Leydesdorff, L. (2000) The dynamics of innovation: From National Systems and "Mode 2" to a Triple Helix of university–industry–government relations. *Research Policy, 29*(2), 109–123.

Florida, R. (2008) *Who's Your City? How the Creative Economy Is Making Where to Live the Most Important Decision of Your Life.* New York, NY: Basic Books.

Freeman, J., and Engel, J.S. (2007) Models of innovation: Start-ups and mature corporations. *California Management Review, 50*(1), 94–119.

GAPS (2015) *Cens empresarial i Activitat Econòmica al 22@.*

Gianoli, A., and Palazzolo Henkes, R. (2020) The evolution and adaptive governance of the 22@ innovation district in Barcelona. *Urban Science, 4*(2), 16. https://doi.org/ 10.3390/urbansci4020016.

Griffith, J.C. (2016) Metropolitan-wide governance and an innovation district: Smart growth reforms to increase economic competitiveness in Warsaw, Poland. *Studia Iuridica, 63*, 15–46.

Healey, P. (2002) On creating the 'city' as a collective resource. *Urban Studies, 39*(10), 1777–1792.

Henderson, J.V. (2003) Marshall's scale economies. *Journal of Urban Economics, 53*(1), 1–28.

Institut Cerdà (2018) *Avaluació del impacte i funció socioeconòmica del 22@ per a la Ciutat de Barcelona*. Internal document.

Janssen, M., and Van Der Voort, H. (2020) Agile and adaptive governance in crisis response: Lessons from the COVID-19 pandemic. *International Journal of Information Management, 55*, 102180. https://doi.org/10.1016/j.ijinfomgt.2020.102180.

Kim, Y., Kim, W., and Yang, T. (2012) The effect of the triple helix system and habitat on regional entrepreneurship: Empirical evidence from the US. *Research Policy, 41*(1), 154–166.

Knight, R. (1995) Knowledge-based development: Policy and planning implications for cities. *Urban Studies, 32*(2), 225–260.

Knight, R. (2008) Knowledge-based development: The challenge for cities. In Yigitcanlar, T., Velibeyoglu, K., and Baum, S. (Eds), *Knowledge-Based Urban Development: Planning and Applications in the Information Era*. Hershey, PA: IGI Global.

Landry, C. (2000) *The Creative City: A Toolkit for Urban Innovators*. London: Earthscan.

Lazzeretti, L. (2007) Culture, creativity and local economic development: Evidence from creative industries in Florence. In Cooke, P., and Schwartz, D. (Eds), *Creative Regions: Technology, Culture and Knowledge Entrepreneurship*. London: Routledge.

MacArthur, E. (2013) Towards the circular economy. *Journal of Industrial Ecology, 2*, 23–44.

Marshall, A. (1890/1920) *Principles of Economics*. London: Macmillan [1920 Edn].

Martínez Garcia, D., and Planelles Oliva, P. (2018) *Towards a More Inclusive and Sustainable 22@ within Poblenou* [*Pacte: 22@ Cap a un Poblenou amb un 22@ més inclusiu i sostenible*].

Nelson, R., Howden, M., and Smith, M.S. (2008) Using adaptive governance to rethink the way science supports Australian drought policy. *Environmental Science & Policy, 11*(7), 588–601. https://doi.org/10.1016/j.envsci.2008.06.005.

Nikina, A., and Piqué, J.M. (2016) *Areas of Innovation in a Global World: Concept and Practice*. Malaga: IASP – International Association of Science Parks and Areas of Innovation.

Oliva, A. (2003) *El districte d'activitats 22@bcn*. Barcelona: Aula Barcelona.

Palazzolo Henkes, R. (2016) *External Forces and Adaptative Governance: The Evolution of the 22@ Barcelona between Regeneration and Innovation*. Master's thesis, Urban Management and Development, HIS-Erasmus University. https://thesis.eur.nl/pub/42257.

Pareja-Eastaway, M., and Piqué, J.M. (2011) Urban regeneration and the creative knowledge economy: The case of 22@ in Barcelona. *Journal of Urban Regeneration and Renewal, 4*(4), 319–327.

Pareja-Eastaway, M., and Piqué, J.M. (2014) Spain: Creating ecologies of innovation in cities – The case of 22@Barcelona. In Engel, J.S. (Ed.), *Global Clusters of Innovation: Entrepreneurial Engines of Economic Growth around the World.* Cheltenham, UK and Northampton, MA, USA: Edward Elgar Publishing.

Piqué, J.M., Miralles, F., and Berbegal-Mirabent, J. (2019a) Areas of innovation in cities: The evolution of 22@Barcelona. *International Journal of Knowledge-Based Development, 10*(1), 43–74.

Piqué, J.M., Miralles, F., Teixeira, C.S., Gaspar, J.V., and Ramos Filho, J.R.B. (2019b) Application of the Triple Helix model in the revitalization of cities: The case of Brazil. *International Journal of Knowledge-Based Development, 10*(1), 3–25.

Porter, M.E. (1998) Clusters and the new economics of competition. *Harvard Business Review, 76*(6), 77–90.

Powell, W.W., and Snellman, K. (2004) The knowledge economy. *Annual Review of Sociology, 30*, 199–220.

Pratt, A.C., and Hutton, T.A. (2013) Reconceptualising the relationship between the creative economy and the city: Learning from the financial crisis. *Cities, 33*, 86–95. https://doi.org/10.1016/j.cities.2012.05.008.

Sarimin, M., and Yigitcanlar, T. (2012) Towards a comprehensive and integrated knowledge-based urban development model: Status quo and directions. *International Journal of Knowledge-Based Development, 3*(2), 175–192.

Saxenian, A. (2007) *The New Argonauts: Regional Advantage in a Global Economy.* Cambridge, MA: Harvard University Press.

Scott, A.J. (2000) *The Cultural Economy of Cities: Essays on the Geography of Image-Producing Industries.* London: SAGE.

Scott, A.J. (2006) Creative cities: Conceptual issues and policy questions. *Journal of Urban Affairs, 28*(1), 1–17.

Seo, U.S. (2020) Urban regeneration governance, community organizing, and artists' commitment: A case study of Seongbuk-dong in Seoul. *City, Culture and Society, 21*, 100328. https://doi.org/10.1016/j.ccs.2019.100328.

Termer, C., Dewulf, A., and Van Lieshout, M. (2010) Disentangling scale approaches in governance: Comparing monocentric, multilevel and adaptive governance. *Ecology and Society, 15*(4), 29.

22@Network website (n.d.) Home page. www.22network.net.

Yigitcanlar, T. (2011) Position paper: Redefining knowledge-based urban development. *International Journal of Knowledge-Based Development, 2*(4), 340–356.

Yigitcanlar, T., and Dur, F. (2013) Making space and place for knowledge communities: Lessons for Australian practice. *Australasian Journal of Regional Studies, 19*(1), 36–63.

Yigitcanlar, T., Guaralda, M., Taboada, M., and Pancholi, S. (2016) Place making for knowledge generation and innovation: Planning and branding Brisbane's knowledge community precincts. *Journal of Urban Technology, 23*(1), 115–146.

Yigitcanlar, T., Velibeyoglu, K., and Baum, S. (Eds) (2008a) *Knowledge-Based Urban Development: Planning and Applications in the Information Era.* Hershey, PA: IGI Global.

Yigitcanlar, T., Velibeyoglu, K., and Baum, S. (Eds) (2008b) *Creative Urban Regions: Harnessing Urban Technologies to Support Knowledge City Initiatives.* Hershey, PA: IGI Global.

Yigitcanlar, T., Velibeyoglu, K., and Martinez-Fernandez, C. (2008c) Rising knowledge cities: The role of knowledge precincts. *Journal of Knowledge Management, 12*(5), 8–20.

# PART III

# Global Case Studies: National Strategies

# 9. The development of Singapore's innovation and entrepreneurship ecosystem

**Poh Kam Wong**

## 9.1 INTRODUCTION

Since its political independence in 1965, the small island state of Singapore has achieved rapid economic growth and transformed itself into a major global financial, business and transport/information technology (IT) hub. In terms of gross domestic product (GDP) per capita, Singapore surpassed Japan in 2010 and caught up with the United States in the mid-2010s (World Bank 2018). Despite decelerating growth in recent years, Singapore's GDP (purchasing power parity) per capita in 2021 still ranked as the second highest in the world (IMF 2021).

The rapid economic development of Singapore from developing to developed country in less than four decades was achieved through a consistent public policy focus on attracting and leveraging direct foreign investments from global multinational corporations (MNCs) to achieve continuous technological-capability-upgrading and productivity growth (Wong 2003). By encouraging global MNCs to transfer increasingly more advanced technologies and know-how to their subsidiary operations in the city-state, and by investing heavily in education and on-the-job training to enable the domestic workforce to rapidly absorb and diffuse new technologies, Singapore has been able to achieve rapid technological catch-up, industrial upgrading and productivity improvement. This is despite not having substantially invested in public research and development (R&D) to develop indigenous technological innovation capabilities until late in its economic development, compared with Japan, Taiwan and South Korea; indeed, even today, Singapore lacks a science and technology ministry. Moreover, much of the public R&D spending has been directed at the innovation needs of the global MNCs and some of the large government-linked corporations (GLCs) in strategic sectors, with relatively less going to local small and medium-sized enterprises (SMEs) – in contrast to, for example, the priorities followed in Taiwan (Wong 2019).

While this unique economic development model – an open economy framework combined with strong state intervention – has been the basis for Singapore's remarkable economic success, concerns have been growing among the city-state's intelligentsia and political leadership that this development model needs to be significantly changed for the city-state to continue to prosper in the new millennium. With its high developed-country costs, Singapore now needs to compete close to the technological frontier of the global knowledge economy, as opposed to the earlier, easier task of technological catch-up. Moreover, economic growth and innovations in the global marketplace are increasingly coming from young but fast-growing entrepreneurial firms ("scale-ups"), rather than large, incumbent corporations. While the Schumpeterian destruction of large incumbents by new disruptive innovators has been a constant in economic history, the speed at which such disruptions are occurring appears to have increased in recent years as digital transformation intensifies and the so-called Fourth Industrial Revolution begins to take shape. As highlighted by Schwab (2016), while digital technologies have enabled revolutionary advances in internet/mobile applications and e-commerce, it is when they are applied to rapid advances in technologies that are physical (autonomous vehicles, new materials, 3D printing, advanced robotics, and so on) or biological (genetic engineering, neurotechnology, bioprinting, and so on) that major transformational impacts occur. I use the term "deep technologies" (deep tech) as a short-hand for these advanced physical and biological technologies underlying Industry 4.0.

Public policymakers' growing concern with promoting technology entrepreneurship has become a worldwide phenomenon, with many countries and regions announcing their intentions to grow their own versions of Silicon Valley (Lerner 2009). In a number of earlier works (Wong 2001, 2003, 2006 and 2019; Wong and Singh 2008), I examined the emerging shift of Singapore's economy from the late 1990s to the mid-2010s toward a more "balanced" development model that reduces its high degree of reliance on large enterprises (both local GLCs and foreign MNCs) by growing the technology entrepreneurship sector. In this chapter, I will use the lens of the Cluster of Innovation (COI) Framework for this book to re-examine this emerging shift, and to update the progress of this shift up to early 2021, one year after the start of the Covid-19 global pandemic. In particular, I show that while there has indeed been significant growth of the technology entrepreneurship sector within Singapore's COI, driven in part by various new supply-side public policies, this growth has been primarily in internet/mobile/e-commerce services, with relatively few indigenous deep-tech-based "scale-ups" emerging. However, I show that, in a number of innovation clusters where the public sector can play a critical demand-generation role, such as urban infrastructure and healthcare services, Singapore has made significant progress in terms of innovation deployment, which in turn has stimulated the growth of indigenous innovative start-ups. In addition, I observe that the Covid-19 pandemic appears to have accelerated the development of these innovation clusters. I argue that the experience of Singapore suggests a much greater public sector role in stimulating innovation through demand-side policies, and that this needs to be reflected more prominently in the COI Framework.

The chapter is organized as follows. In the next section, I provide a stylized institutional analysis of Singapore's public policy approach to developing its innovation and entrepreneurship ecosystem. In the third section, using the COI Framework, I provide some salient empirical evidence on how the ecosystem has evolved, and how public policies may have contributed. In the fourth section, I provide a closer look at a number of innovation clusters where the public sectors have played a particularly significant role: smart cities and healthcare. Finally, I make some concluding observations and highlight a number of relevant implications for other economies, as well as for the COI Framework.

## 9.2    SINGAPORE'S INSTITUTIONAL FRAMEWORK FOR INNOVATION AND ENTREPRENEURSHIP POLICYMAKING AND IMPLEMENTATION

A national institutional framework for innovation and entrepreneurship policymaking tends to be complex and is often path-dependent on historical contexts and political legacies, even as it evolves over time in response to changing global and domestic environments (OECD 2012). As such, the institutional framework of every nation tends to have its own idiosyncratic elements, and Singapore is no exception.

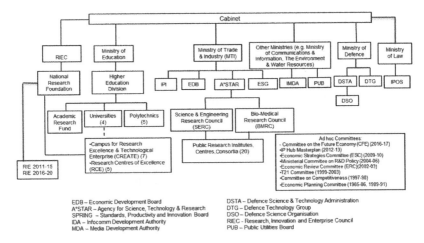

*Figure 9.1      Singapore's institutional framework for innovation and entrepreneurship policy as of early 2021*

Lacking an official version of how the Singapore government organizes its innovation and entrepreneurship policy functions, I have created a stylized overview of the institutional framework for innovation and entrepreneurship policymaking and implementation in Singapore that has emerged since the early 2000s, or about two decades ago (see Figure 9.1). Policymaking related to innovation and entrepreneurship in Singapore falls within four basic groupings of state institutions:

1. The National Research Foundation (NRF), under the prime minister's office, which provides overall funding and broad policy guidance through five-year research, innovation and enterprise (RIE) plans, the first three being RIE2011–15, RIE2016–20 and RIE2021–25.
2. The Ministry of Education (MOE), which oversees the education and research activities of the various institutions of higher learning.
3. The Ministry of Trade and Industry (MTI), which oversees the key economic implementation agencies: the Economic Development Board (EDB, responsible for attracting inward foreign investments); Enterprise Singapore[1] (ESG, responsible for promotion of local enterprises, particularly SMEs and start-ups); and the Agency for Science, Technology and Research (A*STAR, responsible for implementing mission-oriented public R&D).
4. Agencies within other ministries that have significant innovation-promotion mandates within their specific industry verticals. Figure 9.1 highlights the most important ones: (a) the Infocomm Media Development Authority (IMDA) under the Ministry of Communications and Information (MCI), for the information and communications technology (ICT) and media industries; (b) the Public Utilities Board (PUB) under the Ministry of the Environment and Water Resources, for the water industry; (c) the Ministry of Health (MOH), for the healthcare industry; and (d) the Defence Science and Technology Agency (DSTA) under the Ministry of Defence, for the defense industry. I also separately highlighted the Intellectual Property Office of Singapore (IPOS), under the Ministry of Law, which is not industry-specific but promotes innovation broadly through enabling legal frameworks for intellectual property (IP) protection and transactions.

Collectively, these four groupings of state institutions have been responsible for policies and programs that have had significant direct or indirect impacts on innovation and entrepreneurship activities in Singapore. I highlight the main roles of the key agencies identified in Figure 9.1 under the four key policy roles (see Table 9.1).

*Table 9.1*    Key innovation policy roles of public institutions in Singapore

| State institutions | Creating indigenous sources of technological capability | Leveraging foreign sources of technological capabilities | Facilitating diffusion and adoption of new technologies by existing firms | Promoting the formation and growth of tech start-up firms |
|---|---|---|---|---|
| National Research Foundation | Fund public R&D | Fund foreign universities to establish R&D in Singapore (through the CREATE program) | Fund university–industry collaboration and entrepreneurship education activities | Co-fund venture capital (VC) funds (the Early Stage Venture Funding scheme; ESVF) and incubators (Technology Information Scheme; TIS) |
| | | | Co-fund VC funds (ESVF) and incubators (TIS) Co-fund corporate venture funds | Incubate and invest in tech start-ups through SGInnovate |
| *Ministry of Education (MOE)* | | | | |
| – Universities | Develop technical talents | Attract foreign students to Singapore through scholarships, and so on | | Develop entrepreneurial talents |
| | Conduct basic R&D | Recruit foreign scientists through professorships and postdoctoral positions | Transfer R&D results to industry through licensing | Promote R&D commercialization through spin-offs |
| – Polytechnics and vocational schools | Conduct applied research | | Assist enterprises to absorb new technologies and innovations | Develop entrepreneurial talents |
| | | | Train workforce in relevant skills to absorb new technologies | |
| *Ministry of Trade and Industry (MTI)* | | | | |

| State institutions | Creating indigenous sources of technological capability | Leveraging foreign sources of technological capabilities | Facilitating diffusion and adoption of new technologies by existing firms | Promoting the formation and growth of tech start-up firms |
|---|---|---|---|---|
| – Agency for Science, Technology and Research (A*STAR) | Conduct public R&D | Develop local STEM (science, technology, engineering and mathematics) talent through PhD scholarships in prestigious overseas universities | Transfer R&D results to industry through licensing | Promote R&D commercialization through spin-offs |
| | | | Transfer R&D personnel to local SMEs | |
| – Economic Development Board (EDB) | Attract foreign MNC R&D and innovation activities to Singapore through tax incentives, and so on | Fund MNCs and large local enterprises to help local SMEs to upgrade (through the Local Industry Upgrading Programme; LIUP) | Invest in tech start-ups (through the VC fund EDBI) | |
| – Enterprise Singapore (ESG) | | | Promote adoption of new technologies and innovation by local SMEs through grants, subsidies and technical services | Co-fund angel investments and incubators |
| | | | Promote industry networking | Promote tech start-ups through various grant schemes |
| Industry-Specific | | | | |
| *Ministry of Communications and Information (MCI)* | | | | |

| State institutions | Creating indigenous sources of technological capability | Leveraging foreign sources of technological capabilities | Facilitating diffusion and adoption of new technologies by existing firms | Promoting the formation and growth of tech start-up firms |
|---|---|---|---|---|
| – Infocomm Media Development Authority (IMDA) | | Attract foreign MNCs and talent in ICT and media to Singapore | Promote adoption and diffusion of ICT and digital media innovation | Invest in start-ups in ICT and digital media (through VC fund Infocomm Investments) and procure from start-ups |
| *Ministry of Defence* | | | | |
| – Defence Science and Technology Agency (DSTA) | Fund defence-related R&D | Procure critical defence technologies from overseas | Diffuse defence technologies to local defence industry | Invest in start-ups in defence technologies (through VC fund CapVista) |

*Source:*    Compiled by the author.

Unlike many other countries, Singapore does not regularly create five-year economic development plans. Instead, the government convenes ad hoc, inter-ministerial committees to formulate national economic development strategies as and when deemed necessary, often in response to significant external changes. For example, the Economic Planning Committee 1985, the Committee on Competitiveness 1997 and the Economic Strategies Committee 2009 were convened in response to the severe recession in 1985, the Asian financial crisis in 1997 and the global financial meltdown in 2008, respectively. The Future Economy Council (FEC) was formed in early 2017 to chart new strategies in response to Industry 4.0 disruptions (FEC 2017). The FEC in turn established an Emerging Stronger Taskforce in response to the Covid-19 pandemic.

Through these strategic plans, new strategic directions related to innovation and entrepreneurship were announced, which then led to the subsequent introduction of policy and program changes. In some cases, changes are made to the institutional framework as well. For example, the 1999–2003 Technopreneurship 21 Committee for the first time identified the promotion of technology entrepreneurship as a key policy goal, which led to a slew of new programs, including the establishment of a $1 billion Technopreneurship Investment Fund (TIF) under A*STAR (then called the National Science and Technology Board) to invest in VC funds and to jump-start the VC industry, and the creation of the Start-up Enterprise Development Scheme (SEEDS) under the EDB to match investment in start-ups by angel investors. The 2002–03 Economic Review Committee further expanded the promotion of tech start-ups by making it a new function for the Standards, Productivity and Innovation Board (SPRING), which also took over the SEEDS scheme from the EDB, while the 2004 Ministerial Committee on R&D Policy led to the establishment of NRF in 2006 (Wong and Ho 2008). The 2017 FEC Report led to the merger of SPRING with International Enterprise (IE) Singapore in 2018 to become Enterprise Singapore (ESG), addressing a concern that IE Singapore had in the past focused only on helping the larger, more established local enterprises to go overseas, not early-stage tech start-ups.

## 9.3 SINGAPORE'S INNOVATION AND ENTREPRENEURSHIP ECOSYSTEM DEVELOPMENT

As highlighted in Figure 9.2, the COI Framework emphasizes the symbiotic role of two key actors – large innovative enterprises and start-up/scale-up Entrepreneurs – and one key enabling resource supplier: the Venture Capital investors that fund them. The Framework also acknowledges the important contributing roles of two major institutions – Government and Universities –

and two specialized human resources: Management that have the experience to scale up start-ups, and Professional Services that reduce the transaction costs of the start-up to scale up to the exit process (IP and venture lawyers, mergers and acquisitions and initial public offering [IPO] investment bankers, and so on). A number of sub-categories of the above seven key actors are also identified: Research Parks, Accelerators and Incubators that facilitate the interactions of universities with the three key actors; Corporate Venture Capitalists (CVCs) and Angel Investors that emerged from the large corporations and (previously successful) entrepreneurs; and professional Service Organizations and venture investment programs that have significant public sector involvement, either directly or indirectly.

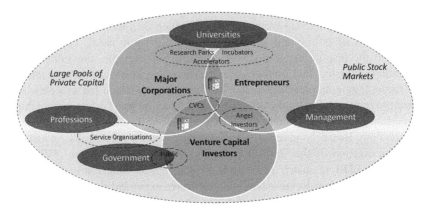

*Figure 9.2        Cluster of Innovation Framework*

Using the COI Framework, I attempt in this section to collate relevant empirical evidence from various sources, including my own research, to provide a picture of how Singapore's innovation and entrepreneurship ecosystem has developed over three time periods: before 2000, early 2000–2010 and after 2010. While there are unfortunately information gaps, I believe a number of clear and salient patterns can be discerned, which I will seek to highlight below.

### 9.3.1    Overview of the R&D Performers in Singapore

The size and composition of Singapore's R&D performers can be measured through a number of well-established indicators: R&D intensities, scientific publications and patenting.

## Investment in R&D

After two decades of rapid growth from 1990–2010, gross R&D spending (GERD) in Singapore appears to have entered a period of more moderate growth over the last 10 years, with the GERD-to-GDP ratio stabilizing around 2 percent in the mid-2010s and actually showing a slight decline since (see Figure 9.3). While this puts Singapore comfortably within the lower half of the middle band of Organisation for Economic Co-operation and Development (OECD) countries, it is notably behind South Korea, Japan, Taiwan and China in Asia, and small advanced economies like Switzerland, Denmark, Finland and Israel.

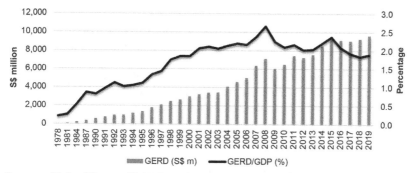

*Source:*    National Survey of R&D Expenditure and Manpower (various years), Science Council of Singapore (prior to 1990); National Survey of R&D in Singapore (various years), National Science and Technology Board (for 1990–2000) and Agency for Science, Technology and Research (2001–2019).

*Figure 9.3*    *Growth in Singapore R&D spending, 1978–2019*

The share of Singaporean R&D by private sector has also been relatively stable at around 60 percent over the last decade (Figure 9.4). However, the share of local firms in this private R&D spending has actually steadily decreased from around one-third in 2005 to just above one-quarter since mid-2015, suggesting continuing low engagement in innovation activities by indigenous firms. In particular, the share of local firms in private R&D spending has declined the most in manufacturing, falling to less than 20 percent since the early 2010s.

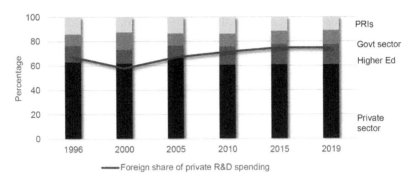

*Source:*     National Science and Technology Board (for 1996–2000) and Agency for Science, Technology and Research (2005–2019).

*Figure 9.4       Share of R&D expenditure, by origin, 1996–2019*

The sectoral composition of private R&D has also changed rapidly over the years, with the share of manufacturing dropping steadily to less than 50 percent by 2019 (Figure 9.5). Over the last decade, there was a moderate rise in the share of R&D in the deep-tech-related sector (defined more narrowly to comprise only biomedical, clean-tech/energy, and advanced engineering) to over one-third, while that of ICT and internet/mobile-related services increased from around 15 percent over 2005–2015 to almost one-quarter by 2019.

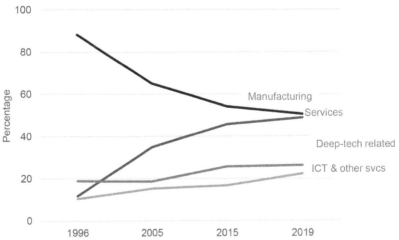

*Notes:*     Deep-tech-related comprises: biomedical sciences; chemicals; R&D services. ICT and other services comprises: ICT + logistics + wholesale/retail + others
*Source:*     National Science and Technology Board (for 1996–2000) and Agency for Science, Technology and Research (2005–2019).

*Figure 9.5       Private sector R&D expenditure, by industry, 1996–2019 (%)*

## Scientific publications

The number of scientific publications has also continued to grow steadily over the last decade compared to earlier periods. Measured in terms of the number of publications per million population, Singapore was already ranked among the highest in the world by 2013 (NSF 2016). This quantitative growth has continued since, and is also accompanied by a moderate increase in quality, as measured by Web of Science citation impacts (Wong 2021).

Further analysis of the sources of this steady improvement in scientific publication outputs suggests that the public sector research organizations, particularly the two universities – the National University of Singapore (NUS) and Nanyang Technological University (NTU) – along with A*STAR, have contributed disproportionately to the growth in both quantity and quality. Various annual global rankings of universities in the world have shown a steady rise in the ranking of NUS and NTU over the last 20 years, with NUS ranked 24th and 15th in the world (and second and first in Asia) by Times Higher Education and Quacquarelli Symonds respectively in 2019–20. If we remove publications by public research organizations, Singapore's scientific publication outputs by private firms appear to be much less impressive (Wong 2021).

## Patenting intensities

In contrast to scientific publication output and R&D spending, Singapore's patenting outputs (as measured by patents granted by the United States Patent and Trademark Office to inventors based in Singapore) have increased much more sharply, from 943 over the period 1996–2000 to 5,350 over 2001–2010 and 7,823 over 2011–2020 (Wong 2021). However, the growth in patenting outputs is faster among foreign versus local organizations; indeed, if we remove public sector organizations, including public research institutes and universities, growth of patenting by local private sector firms has been significantly slower than for foreign firms, confirming the substantially lower technological innovation intensities of local firms. As of the end of 2020, only four among the top 20 U.S. patent owners in Singapore are Singaporean entities, with three being public sector organizations (A*STAR, NUS and NTU). With one exception (Creative Technology), none of the indigenous firms in Singapore owned more than 100 patents. In particular, none of the large GLCs, including the three large telecommunications firms and those in advanced engineering (ST Engineering) and offshore engineering (Keppel, Sembawang), had more than 50 patents (Wong 2021).

Taken together, the above indicators strongly suggest that Singapore's R&D performers continued to be highly dominated by foreign firms and public sector research organizations. This skewness underscores the slow progress made by Singapore toward developing the R&D capability of its indigenous firms.

### 9.3.2    Contribution of R&D Investments to Singapore's Economic Development

To further examine the implications of the above empirical observations, I conducted an econometric analysis of the contribution of R&D investment to Singapore's economic growth over the period 1978–2012 (Ho and Wong 2017). The analysis results, summarized in Table 9.2, show that Singapore's short-run productivity impact of R&D (as measured by the elasticity of total factor productivity [TFP] changes to R&D changes) over this period was comparable to those of smaller advanced economies among the OECD countries. However, in terms of long-run R&D productivity, Singapore lagged behind these smaller OECD countries and far behind the large G7 countries. I further tested for possible changes in R&D productivity in the 2003–2012 period versus the earlier period but found no evidence of significant structural breaks. Lastly, my analysis found weaker direct productivity effects of public versus private sector R&D, although additional Granger causality analysis reveals that public R&D did stimulate private sector R&D in later years.

*Table 9.2      Estimates of R&D–TFP elasticities in Singapore versus OECD countries*

|  | Singapore (Ho and Wong 2017) | Singapore (Ho et al. 2009) | Greece (Voutsinas and Tsamadias 2014) | 16 OECD Countries (Guellec and van Pottelsberghe de la Potterie 2001) | 22 OECD countries + Israel (Coe and Helpman 1995) |
|---|---|---|---|---|---|
| Dependent variable | TFP (based on GDP) | TFP (based on GDP) | TFP (based on GDP) | Private sector TFP | Private sector TFP |
| Period of estimation | 1978–2012 | 1978–2001 | 1987–2007 | 1980–1998 | 1971–1990 |
| Short-term elasticity with respect to R&D | 0.025 | 0.013 | Non-significant | 0.024 (private R&D) 0.028 (public R&D) | N/A |
| Long-run elasticity with respect to R&D | 0.091 | 0.081 | 0.038 (total R&D) 0.075 (public R&D) | 0.13 (private R&D) 0.17 (public R&D) | 0.078 (non-G7) 0.234 (G7) |

*Source:*    Ho and Wong (2017).

In view of the high share of Singapore's R&D by foreign firms and public R&D institutions, the above findings suggest (1) leakage of value capture from R&D, possibly made worse by the greater propensity of foreign firms to commercialize their R&D knowledge outside Singapore; and (2) frictions in transferring public R&D knowledge to private firms, possibly made worse by the low absorptive capacity of local firms. The finding that overall R&D productivity had not improved much up to the early 2010s also suggests that there had been no significant structural changes in Singapore's innovation system, despite various public policy changes, up to the early 2010s. To the extent that these interpretations of our econometric findings are valid, they highlight the urgency of more significant policy changes to address this fundamental weakness of Singapore's innovation ecosystem – the under-development of R&D capability of indigenous firms.

### 9.3.3 Development of the Technology Entrepreneurship Ecosystem

To complement the above analysis on R&D activities, I now turn to examine the development of technology entrepreneurship, based on data from two research projects I have conducted. The first (Wong et al. 2017) involves a compilation of unpublished census data from the Singapore Department of Statistics (DOS) on new firm formation in Singapore over the period 2004–15, as well as primary data on 530 tech start-ups collected through a questionnaire survey in 2016. The sectoral composition of the survey respondents was found to be representative of the DOS census data. The second study (Wong and Ho 2018) draws on an ongoing online database of start-ups called TechSG that I initiated in 2015 to identify Singapore-based tech start-up entities and their founders/investors by periodically trawling the most popular websites of business news and start-up social media (for example, e27, TechinAsia), and the homepages of VC funds, incubators and government agencies, as well as through crowdsourcing of inputs from the start-up community. Further information about these start-ups is gathered from their websites and in some cases their company registration records, to remove start-ups that have de-registered and other non-relevant cases and to provide more fine-grain classification. Despite possible biases in coverage (for example, start-ups that did not have their own websites were usually excluded), TechSG has been widely acknowledged as the most comprehensive publicly available information on Singapore's tech start-up ecosystem; as of early 2018, it contained information on over 2,600 start-ups and their founders, over 230 venture investors, 42 incubators and 50 other professional services firms/organizations.

I start with an overview of the aggregate growth trend of start-ups and their share of total employment in the economy (Wong et al. 2017). For the purpose of this analysis, start-ups are defined as firms five years old or younger, with at least 50 percent of capital individually owned (to remove young firms that are subsidiaries of other firms). As can be seen from Figure 9.6, the number of start-ups in Singapore more than doubled, from about 22,800 in 2004 to over 48,000 in 2015, while total employment likewise more than doubled from 156,500 to 345,300. Start-ups' share of total employment also increased from 7.1 percent in 2004 to 9.4 percent in 2015 (note that the temporary peak of around 10 percent over 2008–10 was due to slower employment growth in existing firms, especially large firms, caused by the global financial crisis in 2008).

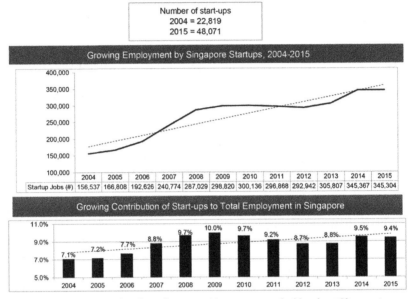

*Note:*     Start-ups defined as firms five years old or younger and with at least 50 percent individually owned capital.
*Source:*   DOS unpublished data compiled by author.

*Figure 9.6*     *Growth in start-up employment, 2004–2015*

The above trend pertains to all start-ups, not just tech start-ups. Following other scholars, I define tech start-ups as those in industries that have above-average R&D intensities (using three-digit ISIC [International Standard Industrial Classification] levels where available). As shown in Figure 9.7, the total number of tech start-ups increased at a lower rate than total start-ups, from around 2,760 in 2004 to over 5,100 in 2015. This is due to a decline of tech start-ups in the manufacturing sector since 2007, while tech start-ups in services more than doubled from around 1,540 in 2004 to over 3,900 in 2015.

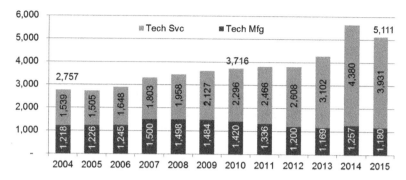

Annual growth in number of startups (%)

|  | Tech Mfg | Tech Svc | All Tech Startups |
|---|---|---|---|
| 2004-2010 | 2.59% | 6.89% | 5.10% |
| 2010-2015 | -3.64% | 11.35% | 6.58% |

*Source:*   DOS and Accounting and Corporate Regulatory Authority (ACRA), unpublished data compiled by the author.

*Figure 9.7*      *Growth in number of tech start-ups in Singapore, 2004–2015*

A more detailed breakdown of the sectoral composition of tech start-ups suggests that the biggest growth has been in ICT-related sectors, with the share of deep-tech sectors (defined more narrowly as biomedical, clean-tech/energy, and advanced engineering) largely stagnating at around 6 percent (see Figure 9.8).

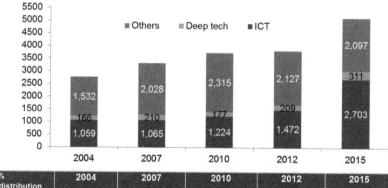

| %<br>distribution | 2004 | 2007 | 2010 | 2012 | 2015 |
|---|---|---|---|---|---|
| ICT | 38.4% | 32.2% | 32.9% | 38.7% | 52.9% |
| Deep tech | 6.0% | 6.4% | 4.8% | 5.5% | 6.1% |
| Others | 55.6% | 61.4% | 62.3% | 55.9% | 41.0% |
| n | 2,757 | 3,303 | 3,716 | 3,808 | 5,111 |

*Source:*   DOS and ACRA, unpublished data compiled by author.

*Figure 9.8*      *Sectoral composition of tech start-ups in Singapore,*
                  *2004–2015 (census data)*

The above data from DOS did not provide a meaningful breakdown of the ICT sector into more specific sub-sectors, especially the mobile/internet app subsector. To obtain more insights on this subsector, I utilized data from the TechSG database (Wong and Ho 2018). Based on data on the year of founding extracted as of March 2016 covering 1,300 verified tech start-ups on TechSG, I found a similar trend of significant increase in the share of tech start-ups in the ICT sector; in particular, I found the increasing share of ICT to have been due to the growth in internet/mobile (see Figure 9.9a). The shares of start-ups in "deep technology" and other high-tech sectors have either stagnated or declined.

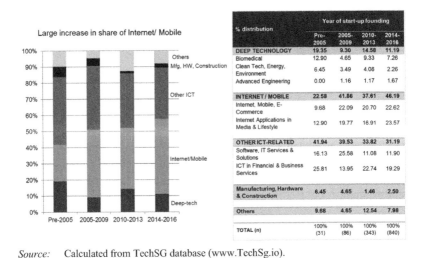

| % distribution | Year of start-up founding | | | |
| --- | --- | --- | --- | --- |
| | Pre-2005 | 2005-2009 | 2010-2013 | 2014-2016 |
| **DEEP TECHNOLOGY** | **19.35** | **9.30** | **14.58** | **11.19** |
| Biomedical | 12.90 | 4.65 | 9.33 | 7.26 |
| Clean Tech, Energy, Environment | 6.45 | 3.49 | 4.08 | 2.26 |
| Advanced Engineering | 0.00 | 1.16 | 1.17 | 1.67 |
| **INTERNET / MOBILE** | **22.58** | **41.86** | **37.61** | **46.19** |
| Internet, Mobile, E-Commerce | 9.68 | 22.09 | 20.70 | 22.62 |
| Internet Applications in Media & Lifestyle | 12.90 | 19.77 | 16.91 | 23.57 |
| **OTHER ICT-RELATED** | **41.94** | **39.53** | **33.82** | **31.19** |
| Software, IT Services & Solutions | 16.13 | 25.58 | 11.08 | 11.90 |
| ICT in Financial & Business Services | 25.81 | 13.95 | 22.74 | 19.29 |
| **Manufacturing, Hardware & Construction** | **6.45** | **4.65** | **1.46** | **2.50** |
| **Others** | **9.68** | **4.65** | **12.54** | **7.98** |
| TOTAL (n) | 100% (31) | 100% (86) | 100% (343) | 100% (840) |

*Source:*   Calculated from TechSG database (www.TechSg.io).

*Figure 9.9a      Change in business activities of tech start-ups in Singapore*

Data from the 2016 survey of 530 tech start-ups in Singapore (Wong et al. 2017) further indicate that the majority of Singaporean ICT start-ups in general and internet/mobile start-ups in particular were mostly founded by relatively young university graduates, in contrast to founders of deep-tech start-ups where a higher proportion had master's degrees or doctorates. In addition, founders of tech start-ups outside the ICT sector tended to be older and a higher proportion had significant prior professional/managerial work experience in industry.

Figure 9.9b provides further insights on the sectoral composition of tech start-ups in Singapore by comparing our TechSG data with those of

London and New York, which were compiled using a similar methodology. Interestingly, the share of start-ups in ICT in Singapore was comparable with those of London and New York (76 versus 79 versus 73 percent), and likewise for internet/mobile only (43 versus 50 versus 42 percent). The share of deep-tech sectors in Singapore was also comparable to that of New York City (12 versus 10 percent), with London lower (6 percent).

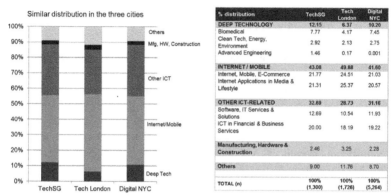

| % distribution | TechSG | Tech London | Digital NYC |
|---|---|---|---|
| DEEP TECHNOLOGY | 12.15 | 6.37 | 10.20 |
| Biomedical | 7.77 | 4.17 | 7.45 |
| Clean Tech, Energy, Environment | 2.92 | 2.13 | 2.75 |
| Advanced Engineering | 1.46 | 0.17 | 0.001 |
| INTERNET / MOBILE | 43.08 | 49.88 | 41.60 |
| Internet, Mobile, E-Commerce | 21.77 | 24.51 | 21.03 |
| Internet Applications in Media & Lifestyle | 21.31 | 25.37 | 20.57 |
| OTHER ICT-RELATED | 32.69 | 28.73 | 31.16 |
| Software, IT Services & Solutions | 12.69 | 10.54 | 11.93 |
| ICT in Financial & Business Services | 20.00 | 18.19 | 19.22 |
| Manufacturing, Hardware & Construction | 2.46 | 3.25 | 2.28 |
| Others | 9.00 | 11.76 | 8.70 |
| TOTAL (n) | 100% (1,300) | 100% (1,726) | 100% (5,264) |

*Source:*     Calculated from TechSG database (www.TechSg.io).

*Figure 9.9b*     *Business activities of tech start-ups in Singapore versus London and New York*

The above comparative analysis suggests that Singapore's tech start-up pattern as of the mid-2010s reflected other global financial, business and information services hubs such as London and New York City, with a significant focus on internet/mobile services that leverage off their digital information hub role. Despite significant R&D investment in various deep-tech fields, Singapore still lacked the depth and specialization of other high-tech start-up hubs, such as Boston and San Diego in life sciences; Silicon Valley in semiconductor/ digital devices, big data, clean-tech and energy; and Munich in advanced engineering and manufacturing. Indeed, while several internet/mobile e-commerce start-ups from Singapore have successfully scaled up regionally and achieved valuations of more than S$500 million in recent years (for example, SEA, Grab, PropertyGuru, Carousell), there has so far been only a couple of deep-tech scale-ups (Nanofilm in nanotechnology and PatSnap in IP big data/ machine learning analytics).

### 9.3.4    Summary Assessment using the COI Framework

Further expanding on the above analysis of the growth trend and salient characteristics of R&D performers and entrepreneurial start-ups in recent years,
I have also analyzed the development trends of the key specialized resources
identified in the COI Framework (Venture Capital Investors, Incubators/
Accelerators and Service Organizations) over the same periods. Table 9.3
summarizes the key changes in the size and composition of the key COI actors
in Singapore's innovation and entrepreneurship ecosystem over three periods:
before 2000, 2000–2009 and 2010 onwards.

### 9.3.5    Role of Public Policy in Singapore's COI Development

Corresponding to each major COI actor/specialized resource development
trend identified in the first column of Table 9.3, I have also provided in the
second column salient information on the possible public policy interventions/
programs that may have been an important contributing factor. For example,
the significant growth of VC funding in the second development phase
(2000–2009) had been driven largely by the launching of a number of government funds, some as fund-of-funds (for example, the $1 billion TIF) to attract
overseas VC to establish operation in Singapore, and some as co-investment
(for example, ESG's Business Angel Co-Investment Scheme and NRF's
ESVF).

In the absence of detailed research to assess the actual impacts of many
of the policy interventions/programs listed in Table 9.3, it is not possible to
ascertain the effectiveness of many of these specific government interventions.
A detailed study on one such program, A*STAR's GET-UP program, by me
and others (see Ho et al. 2016) has found the program to have significant
positive impact. However, the effectiveness of some programs (for example,
NRF's TIS, intended to be modelled after Israel's technology incubator
program) have been questioned (Wong 2019), and concerns have been raised
that generous public funding has resulted in too many internet/mobile start-ups
being funded (Wong et al. 2017). Nevertheless, there is little doubt that government agencies in Singapore have played a very significant role in driving
most of the COI development trends observed in Table 9.3. As highlighted by
a recent World Bank review of Singapore's start-up ecosystem, the significant
role of the public sector is among its most prominent characteristics (World
Bank 2021).

*Table 9.3* Key changes in Singapore's innovation ecosystem based on the COI Framework

| Salient COI characteristics | Possible role of public policies |
| --- | --- |
| **1985–late 1990s** | |
| *Key performers* | |
| Mainly subsidiaries of global manufacturing MNCs doing in-house process innovation or software/IT services, a small number of MNCs doing software development and IT services | EDB played a key role in attracting global MNCs to establish operations in Singapore, and in providing R&D tax incentives to encourage them to raise productivity through applied R&D activities and software/IT services |
| | The first Science Park was established by Jurong Town Council (JTC; a state-owned property developer) in the mid-1980s to facilitate the location of these MNCs doing applied R&D activities and software/IT services |
| Some spin-outs from these MNCs in manufacturing, mainly in precision engineering and contract manufacturing | The LIUP program contributed to developing the technological capabilities of the suppliers to these MNCs |
| Very few tech start-ups (Creative Tech is the rare exception) | EDBI was established by EDB to provide VC and Private Equity (PE) investment, but its investment targets are primarily global, late-stage and with the view of attracting them to establish operation in Singapore later |
| *Supporting institutions* | |
| Local universities, mainly teaching institutions with limited R&D budgets and capabilities | There were few patenting and licensing outputs from NUS and NTU during this period, and although the first Science Park was located next to NUS, there was little interaction between NUS and the tenant companies in the Science Park |
| A*STAR was formed in 1991, but its mandate was mainly to do applied R&D to support the MNCs operating in Singapore | A*STAR's patenting and licensing outputs were low during its first 10 years of operation |
| *Specialized resources* | Several R&D institutes under A*STAR and other ministries (for example, the Defence Science Organization; DSO) were co-located in the first Science Park |

| Salient COI characteristics | Possible role of public policies |
|---|---|
| The VC industry was nascent and focused primarily in later-stage, overseas investment deals | An early VC fund was established by the government (EDBI), but it focused primarily on investing in growth-stage ventures |
| Specialized professional services firms in the nascent stage | |
| The pool of scale-up professionals was very limited | |
| Late 1990s–early 2010s | |
| *Key performers* | |
| Subsidiaries of global MNCs continue to dominate in R&D spending, some emerging shifts to product innovation; growth of technology-intensive services MNCs, especially IT/software, and pharmaceutical MNCs | EDB significantly expanded its inward investment attraction focus to cover tech-intensive services MNCs in addition to manufacturing MNCs, as well as diversifying the latter to cover pharmaceutical MNCs |
| Limited growth of local SMEs with innovation capabilities; some of the large local firms, including GLCs, began limited R&D and innovation programs, as well as acquisition of start-ups | SPRING introduced innovation support grant schemes for SMEs; A*STAR began the GET-UP program of seconding R&D personnel to local SMEs at subsidized salaries, with the option to return to A*STAR |
| Emergence of a critical mass of tech start-ups, primarily in the internet/mobile sector | SPRING and IMDA introduced tech start-up co-investments and grants |
| *Supporting institutions* | |
| Local universities, particularly NUS, significantly expanded their entrepreneurship education and incubation support program, particularly targeted at undergraduates | NUS established NUS Enterprise and NUS Overseas Colleges (NOC) programs in 2001; NTU established Intuitive in 2003 and an MSc program in Technopreneurship |
| Local universities also significantly expanded their R&D capabilities and budgets, and their technology licensing offices | NRF was established in 2006 and began providing funding to the local universities for innovation-related activities |
| A*STAR significantly expanded its R&D scope, especially in life science/biotech, and established Exploit Tech to commercialize its invention | A*STAR expanded the number of R&D institutes under its umbrella, with the majority of the new institutes in the life science/biotech sector and located in the Biopolis |
| One-North, a new tech park by JTC, began construction in 2006, and opened its first phase, the Biopolis, in 2011 | |

| Salient COI characteristics | Possible role of public policies |
| --- | --- |
| *Specialized resources* | |
| Emergence and growth of angel investor and VC industry | A US$1 billion fund of funds, TIF, was launched by the government in 2000, primarily to invest in overseas VC funds to attract them to establish operations in Singapore, although a number of indigenous VC funds were spawned (for example, TDF, iGlobe); the first angel network (BANSEA) was established in 2002; SPRING introduced an angel co-investment scheme in 2003; NRF launched the ESVF in 2008 to jump-start early-stage venture capitalists (VCs) |
| Emergence of specialized professional services firms | A number of overseas incubators and accelerators (for example, Plug and Play, StartUp 500) and IP advisory services (for example, Transpacific IP) established a presence in Singapore; some local law firms began start-up practices |
| The pool of scale-up professionals remained limited | A small number of experienced scale-up professionals from overseas, especially Silicon Valley, returned or moved to Singapore to join the first wave of scale-ups funded by overseas VCs |
| Early 2010s–early 2020s | |
| *Key performers* | |
| Increasing establishment of regional R&D centres/innovation hubs/ corporate accelerators by global tech MNCs | EDB's inward investment attraction strategy increasingly focused on innovation-driven global MNCs (for example, Facebook, Google, Dyson), and broadened to include Chinese (for example, Huawei, Tencent, TikTok) and regional tech companies (for example, Gojek from Indonesia) |
| A small number of large local enterprises began investing more in R&D, corporate accelerators and corporate venture funds | NRF provided co-investment into several local CVCs |
| More local SMEs began investing in digitalization and automation, spurred by government subsidies and the adverse impacts of Covid-19 (reduction of foreign workers, work-from-home requirements) | ESG provided generous digitalization and supply chain automation grants; industry-specific technology development centres were established to support innovation projects of local SMEs; A*STAR expanded the GET-UP program |

| Salient COI characteristics | Possible role of public policies |
| --- | --- |
| Rapid expansion of tech start-ups in the internet/mobile sector and emergence of a cluster of regional scale-ups and even a small number of unicorns | EDB broadened its inward attraction strategy to include the attraction of experienced entrepreneurs (the Entrepass program) |
| Emergence of a critical mass of deep-tech start-ups, but only a small number reached scale-up stage | An emerging trend of experienced technical and managerial professionals leaving their MNC jobs to become internet/mobile/fintech start-up founders |
| | Most of the deep-tech start-ups were spin-offs from the local universities and A*STAR, with a small number started by experienced technical professionals leaving their MNC jobs, or foreign entrepreneurs starting up in Singapore to tap VC funding and public innovation funding |
| *Supporting institutions* | |
| Increasing shift of local university entrepreneurship education and incubation support activities toward graduate students and deep-tech spin-offs | NUS launched the Lean Launchpad@Singapore in 2013 and the GRIPS program in 2019 |
| SGInnovate was established in 2016 by the government to offer accelerator programs and co-investment of deep-tech start-ups | SGInnovate invested over S$50 million in more than 80 tech start-ups by mid-2021 |
| One-North became fully developed by the end of 2020, comprising Biopolis, Fusionopolis, Mediapolis, Vista and Launchpad@One North | NUS established Block 71 in One-North, which later expanded to become Launchpad@One -North; a new Launchpad@Jurong is being developed next to NTU |
| *Specialized resources* | |
| More experienced entrepreneurs and investors are attracted to operate VC funds and family offices in Singapore | EDB broadened its inward attraction programs to attract family offices by high-net-worth individuals and experienced scale-up professionals |
| VC funds began to look into investment in deep-tech start-ups through co-funding support from the government | SGInnovate introduced the Startup SG Equity scheme in 2017 to co-fund 22 VC funds over the next three years to invest in deep-tech start-ups; Xora Capital was established in 2020 with funding from Temasek and NRF to invest in seed- and Series A-stage deep-tech start-ups that have global growth potential |

| Salient COI characteristics | Possible role of public policies |
|---|---|
| A pool of experienced professionals from the first wave of scale-ups has emerged, and some of them have begun to join the second wave of scale-ups | First-wave mobile/internet scale-ups spawning scale-up professionals to staff second-wave scale-ups include Grab, Zopim/Zendesk, Lazada and PropertyGuru |
| A pool of experienced deep-tech start-up mentors has emerged | Lean Launchpad@Singapore helped build a national network of mentors (many were senior executives with global MNC experience); some entrepreneurs who exited in the first wave of scale-ups (for example, Zopim/Zendesk) have become angel investors and mentors to the second wave of start-ups |

## 9.4     THE ROLE OF GOVERNMENT ON THE DEMAND SIDE

While the above analysis using the COI Framework appears to capture the salient characteristics of Singapore's innovation and entrepreneurship ecosystem at different development stages, there appears to be an implicit bias of the framework in terms of looking at the performers and the enabling institutions, resources and services; that is, the supply side of the ecosystem. In the context of Singapore, I realize that the above narrative has missed out, or downplayed, an additional set of actors driving Singapore's COI development – changes in actors on the demand side, and the potential role of government in influencing those changes.

As prior research literature on innovation clusters has highlighted (see, for example, Karlsson 2010), central to all analysis of innovation and entrepreneurship ecosystem is the role of users and customers who adopt and pay for new innovative products and services that the ecosystem actors supply. The changing behaviors of these demand-side actors – the changing mix of enterprises, consumers and public sector organizations that constitute the markets for innovation – are arguably important in influencing the level and kind of innovations coming out of any innovation and entrepreneurship ecosystem over time. Globalization of markets notwithstanding, the characteristics and behavior of local and regional market users toward new, unproven products and services often have a significant impact on any local COI, especially in the early stage of development of those clusters. In particular, the innovation literature has highlighted the important role of lead users in catalyzing technological innovation for enterprises (Von Hippel 1986). Likewise, sophisticated, tech-savvy end-consumers have also been recognized as important in driving demand for consumer-oriented technological innovation in China (Dychtwald 2019). By not explicitly incorporating these demand-side actors and how they vary across locations and change over time, the COI Framework appears to be incomplete.

In the case of Singapore, while most of the government's facilitating roles that have been identified in Table 9.3 are on the supply side, we can discern significant demand-side public policy roles as well, especially in the wake of the global Covid-19 pandemic. In particular, the following key public policy roles in influencing market demand for innovation can be identified:

- The public sector itself as a lead user/customer
- Public subsidies for usage/adoption by private market users (enterprises or consumers)
- Public provision of infrastructure support for the deployment of the innovation

- Government testing/certification to increase public trust in the safety and efficacy of new, unproven innovation
- Public education and marketing communication to promote awareness, acceptance and adoption of the innovation

A great example to illustrate these demand-side government roles is that of Covid-19 vaccination. While the large pharmaceutical companies like Pfizer and AstraZeneca and biotech therapeutics companies like Moderna are the key actors on the supply side for the Covid-19 mRNA vaccine innovation, the U.S. government – and governments of many other nations – played a critical market-demand-generation role by:

- Underwriting the purchase of these vaccines (even while they were still under development and in early trials) on behalf of their citizens, and distributing them for free
- Establishing (and paying for) the scientific infrastructure to test and certify the safety and efficacy of the vaccines
- Establishing (and paying for) the public health outreach infrastructure to distribute, train and administer the vaccination injections
- Carrying out the massive public education and marketing communication campaign to convince the public to take the vaccination

The Singapore government has certainly played a proactive intervention role in the deployment of Covid-19 vaccinations. Besides signing early procurement contracts and options for three major vaccines (Pfizer, Moderna and Sinovac) while all three were still under development, the government had established a well-administered vaccination program and public education/ outreach campaign to achieve a high vaccination rate by international standards as of mid-September 2021 (81 percent fully vaccinated).

While the scale and urgency of the public intervention in the market for Covid-19 vaccination is extraordinary, and entirely justified due to the enormous public interest at stake and the inability of purely private market mechanisms to achieve fast and near-universal adoption, the same considerations may also be applicable in varying degrees to other innovations that have some elements of public interest and private market failures justifying government interventions.

In the context of Singapore, two clusters that appear to have emerged with the strong support of government on the demand side are worth examining in greater depth: public healthcare and "smart urban infrastructures".

### 9.4.1    Public Healthcare

Like other advanced economies, Singapore has invested heavily in public funding of R&D in life sciences and biomedical technology (Wong 2007; Pearson & Partners 2019). What I want to highlight here, however, are some of the demand-side policy interventions that have made tangible impacts in terms of innovation adoption in Singapore's public healthcare system.

**Contact tracing**
To track the movement of prisoners under a home detention scheme, Singapore's prison authority had, since the early 2010s, deployed an electronic tracking device, developed by a local wireless technology start-up called iWow. When Covid-19 struck, iWow was able to quickly innovate a tracking device for home quarantine, and subsequently a contact tracing device (TraceTogether Token) for large-scale deployment among Singapore's resident population. The widespread adoption of contact-tracing technology has enabled Singapore to react rapidly to contain the spread of Covid-19.

**Rapid Covid-19 diagnostic test**
Since the 2003 SARS outbreak, A*STAR had established a Diagnostic Development Hub (DxD) to coordinate national research programs to develop a rapid SARS test kit as well as diagnostic technologies for various diseases. When Covid-19 cases emerged at the end of 2019, a DxD research team was able to work with a local hospital (TTSH) to quickly adapt the technology to detect Covid-19. With certification by the National Public Health Laboratory at the National Centre for Infectious Diseases, the test kit was approved by Singapore's Health Sciences Authority (HSA) in February 2020 for rapid deployment in 13 hospitals and labs in Singapore. With the validated use in Singapore, the test kit has since been deployed to more than 20 countries globally, including New Zealand and the United States (A*STAR 2021).

More recently, in December 2020, HSA approved a new diagnostic test kit jointly developed by DxD and the DSO that shortened testing time from more than two hours to one hour, by using saliva instead of a conventional PCR test using a nasal swab (A*STAR 2021). In May 2021, the HSA gave provisional approval to a breath-testing technology developed by a spin-off from NUS, Breathonix, that can be administered on-site and provide results in 30 minutes (NUS News 2021). The government is expected to scale the deployment of either of these in land immigration checkpoints as well as airports and seaports, once their use in selected hospitals and labs is validated.

**Preventive care**

Only about 3 percent of the total health expenditure among OECD countries is spent on preventive care. In Singapore, about 5 percent of the MOH's non-Covid-19-related budget in recent years has been on preventive care. These preventive healthcare efforts include public education campaigns; healthy lifestyle activities in schools, workplaces and community settings; engaging industry to spur reformulation of staple food products; subsidies for health screening and recommended vaccinations; regulations to protect our health; and subsidized digital health technology adoption (MOH 2021).

As an example of public policy to encourage adoption of digital health technology, the Health Promotion Board (HPB) provides all Singaporean citizens and permanent residents 17 years old and above with a free fitness tracker if they sign up for a regular National Steps Challenge that offers reward points for shopping vouchers on achieving Total Physical Activity (TPA) targets, defined as at least 150 minutes of moderate-intensity or equivalent activities per week. This "nudging policy" has contributed to an increase in TPA among adult Singaporeans (aged 18 to 74) from 73.1 percent in 2013 to 80.1 percent in 2019 (HPB 2021).

The significant investment by the government in adopting healthcare innovations has contributed to making Singapore's public healthcare system a key innovation cluster in Asia. In 2020, the Bloomberg Health-Efficiency Index, which tracks life expectancy and medical spending, ranked Singapore second in the world for the most efficient healthcare system (Bloomberg 2020). As of 2019, Singaporeans have the world's longest life expectancy, 84.8 years at birth. Females can expect to live an average of 87.6 years with 75.8 years in good health, and men have a life expectancy of 81.9 years with 72.5 years in good health.

## 9.4.2 Smart Urban Infrastructures

The concept of "smart cities" has been popularized in recent years, but its definition tends to be rather broad and typically encompasses both technological dimensions as well as socioeconomic and cultural ones. For example, the Smart City Index project of the International Institute for Management Development (IMD) broadly divides the various dimensions into two main pillars: a Structures pillar (referring to the existing infrastructure of the cities) and a Technology pillar (describing the technological provisions and services available to the inhabitants), with each pillar covering five key areas: health and safety, mobility, activities, opportunities, and governance (IMD 2020).

In the context of Singapore, I identify several key components of its urban infrastructure – urban mobility, built-environment energy management, and urban water and sewerage management – that have experienced significant improvement through adoption of technological innovations.

### Smart mobility

Being a small city-state, Singapore's government has paid significant policy attention on achieving global transport connectivity on the one hand, and smooth intra-city urban traffic flow on the other, since the early 1980s. To maintain its status as a global air and sea transport hub, Singapore has also built among the most efficient airports and seaports in the world, consistently ranking first in the world in the last two decades.

To achieve efficient intra-city transport, Singapore was among the first to deploy electronic area road pricing technology to reduce vehicular traffic congestions in peak hours. Singapore was also among the first in the world to implement a policy of high vehicular ownership tax (a "certificate of entitlement") to complement its high investment in public transport (LTA 2021).

With the growth of the ride-hailing platform innovation around the world in the early 2010s, Singapore was able to attract Grab, a start-up originating from Malaysia, to establish its headquarters in Singapore quite early on, followed by Gojek from Indonesia several years later. Grab's rapid growth to become the leading player in Southeast Asia (including its acquisition of Uber's operations in the region) was enabled by VC funding from VCs based in Singapore, including Vertex Ventures, owned by Temasek, the sovereign fund of the Singaporean government.

Singapore has also been among the earliest cities in test-bedding commercial deployment of driverless vehicles. Singapore's first trial of self-driving buses was in 2015, while a trial of driverless road sweepers was launched in early 2021. Both were developed by a consortium of a local university and local engineering firms. The 2020 Autonomous Vehicles Readiness Index by KPMG ranked Singapore first among 30 countries covered, up from second in 2019 (KPMG 2020).

Singapore's seaport and airport have been consistently ranked among the best in the world over the last two decades. Besides investing heavily in innovation to enhance their operational effectiveness and global connectivity, both have also been lead users of innovations that improve their multi-modal integration with on-land transport. For example, the Port of Singapore Authority (PSA) has innovated a highly automated flow-through gate process that enables more than 10 container truck flows per minute between the port terminal and land. Through its corporate accelerator, Unboxed, and its Container Port 4.0 vision for its new port at Tuas, PSA has provided funding and test-bedding of not only sea-side and within-port innovations, but also innovations in third-party logistics partners that improve port–land interface (PSA 2021).

While some of the large local enterprises (for example, ST Engineering and YCH Logistics) have benefited from these public sector lead users, several innovative local tech scale-ups have been spawned as well in recent years, with the Singapore public sector as their first validating customers before expanding to overseas markets. These include Swat Mobility (employee transport optimization software, validated in trials with LTA in Singapore before expanding deployment to Japan, Australia and the Philippines); VersaFleet (transport management software targeting the "last mile" of urban delivery, which has expanded to four countries in Southeast Asia); and Haulio (a platform connecting hauliers and shippers to improve container movement on land, which has gained traction in Singapore with the support of PSA before expanding to Thailand).

An Overall Urban Mobility ranking of 24 global cities by McKinsey in 2018 (covering Availability, Affordability, Efficiency, Convenience and Sustainability) ranked Singapore first, ahead of Paris and Hong Kong (McKinsey 2018).

### Smart built-environment energy management

Technological innovations, particularly the use of digitalization, data/artificial intelligence (AI) and the Internet of Things (IoT) to improve energy management and environmental sustainability, have figured centrally in all policy discussion about smart cities. In the case of Singapore, the public sector played a major role in deploying such innovations, coordinated through an inter-ministerial Smart Nation and Digital Government Office (SNDGO).

A key initiative of SNDGO is the roll-out of a Smart Nation Sensor Platform (SNSP), a nationwide wireless IoT network to improve municipal services, city-level operations, planning and security. As part of the network roll-out, trials with smart wireless electricity, water and gas meters were conducted from 2018, with large-scale deployment commencing in 2022. As part of the SNSP project, the first of a series of public tenders was awarded in 2018 to turn the 100,000 lamp-posts on Singapore streets into "smart" lamp-posts. Besides replacing the existing lighting with energy-saving LEDs, the lamp-post-as-a-platform project will outfit all lamp-posts with digital cameras and other wireless sensors and connect them into a wireless IoT network with a remote control and monitoring system that can sense external weather conditions (temperature, humidity, environmental pollutants, and so on) and foot traffic, enabling the street lights to be dimmed or brightened automatically, as well as providing faster incidence responses for public safety. Navigational beacons are also being added onto the lamp-posts to guide autonomous vehicles as they get rolled out onto Singapore's streets (SNDGG 2021).

Major public sector organizations were also lead users in deploying built-environment energy management innovations. The Housing &

Development Board (HDB), the government agency responsible for developing affordable public housing and community facilities in Singapore, had built more than 1 million flat units in 26 townships across the island, providing homes to over 80 percent of Singapore's resident population. Through the Green Towns Programme, HDB had been a major demand driver for the adoption of various energy management/sustainability innovations in Singapore, including solar panel installations (50 percent of all HDB blocks were already covered by 2020), conversion of the top decks of multi-storey carparks into urban farms and community gardens, pneumatic waste conveyance systems and "cool" paints that reflect more sunlight. In 2020, HDB awarded a contract for the development of a Smart Estate Management System (SEMS) for managing HDB's complex and diverse portfolio of properties, digitalizing all workflows onto a singular platform as well as creating applications and tools to enhance service offerings to the public.

Incorporating cutting-edge technologies such as 3D digital twinning and machine learning, SEMS seeks to innovate energy management and redefine the shopping experience in all HDB commercial complexes and precinct shops, and is the largest and most technologically advanced project of its kind in Southeast Asia (HDB 2021).

The Energy Market Authority (EMA) operates the critical delivery infrastructure used in the supply of electricity, and develops and regulates Singapore's electricity and gas industries as well as district cooling services. Initiatives by EMA that spurred innovation adoption include the launching of an Open Electricity Market program in 2018 to fully liberalize the electricity retail distribution markets for all households and business premises, a national program in 2019 to replace all household electricity meters with advanced meters that can be read via mobile apps, and numerous research/innovation grants to rest/pilot new energy technologies, including Singapore's first floating Energy Storage System in 2020 (EMA 2021).

Public sector innovation deployment projects such as those above had contributed to the growth of several local technology scale-ups. A good example is Anacle Systems, which had leveraged public sector customers such as HDB, JTC and Changi Airport to dominate the private commercial property management in Singapore as well, beating out global competitors like IBM and SAP. For example, the Jewel Complex in Singapore's Changi Airport had implemented advanced IoT solutions, enterprise asset management and an energy management system developed by Anacle Systems. The company had emerged as the largest real estate management software provider in Southeast Asia and went through an IPO on Hong Kong's Growth Enterprise Market in 2017. The company had also developed the world's smartest power meter, leapfrogging ahead of established global leaders like Schneider and GE, with Singapore's public sector agencies among its first customers (Anacle 2021).

Crucially, during the pandemic period, when the private commercial property sector had substantially cut back its investment in new technologies, demands created by these public sector agencies had been critical in sustaining the growth of Anacle and other innovative start-ups in the built-environment energy management industry.

**Urban water and sewage treatment**

As a small island state with no natural water resources beyond rainfall, Singapore has always regarded water as a vital strategic resource ever since it became politically independent in 1965. Initially relying wholly on two water supply agreements with Malaysia's Johore State (the first was signed in 1961 and expired in 2011, and the second was signed in 1962 and will expire in 2061), Singapore has invested heavily in research and technology to treat and recycle water so as to grow and diversify its sources of water as its water consumption requirements grew in tandem with rapid urbanization and industrialization.

Spearheaded by the PUB, the national water agency, an integrated water and sewage management strategy was implemented, in close coordination with the National Environment Agency (NEA). Besides expanding the number of reservoirs and innovating the efficiency of collecting rain water from local catchments, PUB has invested heavily in water treatment technologies, from advanced membrane technologies to ultra-violet disinfection and a deep-tunnel sewage system, to purify and recycle sewage water. By 2020, 40 percent of Singapore's water needs were supplied through this "NEWater" approach, and this is expected to increase to 55 percent by 2060. Singapore has also built four desalination plants, with a fifth due by the end of 2022, each time deploying the latest available innovations in desalination technologies. PUB also invested heavily into digital technologies, AI/big data and the IoT to improve water management (PUB 2021).

Generous public funding for R&D and innovation test-bedding were provided by PUB and NRF to promote both local R&D and pilot scale and demo plant studies as well as R&D collaborations with leading global research institutes. In 2013, Lux Research ranked two universities in Singapore, NUS and NTU, as the top two water research institutes in the world in the field of membranes, desalination and re-use (Lux Research 2013). In addition, to ensure that PUB is able to tap the best technological innovations in water technology globally, EDB has made the attraction of global water technology corporations to establish R&D operations in Singapore one of its priorities.

By the early 2020s, Singapore had emerged as one of the leading global "hydrohubs" and home to a vibrant and thriving ecosystem of 180 water companies with more than 20 water research centres spanning the entire water value chain. While foreign firms remain dominant in this innovation cluster,

PUB as an innovation lead user has certainly played an important anchoring role for the cluster. Moreover, leveraging from the capability in membrane technology initially developed for water treatment, Singapore's universities and membrane-tech companies are expanding into other areas of membrane separation applications such as gas separation and purification, purification of pharmaceutical ingredients and controlled drug delivery. With funding support from NRF, EDB and ESG, the Singapore Membrane Consortium was formed in 2021 to diversify this innovative cluster beyond water treatment (NRF 2021).

### 9.4.3    Summary Observations

As the examples above illustrate, even though Singapore is not the originator/ creator of many of the technological inventions being adopted or deployed, it has often been among the first to test-bed and subsequently fully deploy at scale these technological inventions in the public sector; that is, the Singapore government has been a lead user in testing, validating and adapting these new technologies, often enabling them to become viable commercial innovations that can be more broadly diffused to private sector users. Thus, although Singapore ranked only 28th among the top 99 city-regions of the world in 2020 in terms of science and technology (S&T) innovation outputs as measured by patents (supply-side measures) according to the Global Innovation Index (Cornell University et al. 2020), Singapore's ranking is substantially higher when innovation adoption measures (demand-side) are taken into account. The Smart City Index by IMD also ranked Singapore first out of 109 cities in the world for 2019 and 2020, in large part because of its high score in innovation adoption under the Technology pillar (IMD 2020).

In terms of the COI Framework, while Singapore may not have created many successful actors yet on the supply side of innovations in these two innovation clusters, they have nonetheless become highly vibrant innovative clusters due to the advanced stage of innovation adoption, and the sophistications in usage among the lead-user organizations, which in turn arguably make these organizations (seaport, airport, public housing, public healthcare systems) highly efficient and globally competitive. As such, Singapore's innovation cluster development experience suggests the need for the COI Framework to be augmented with the explicit incorporation of an actor category called "Innovation Lead Users" as indicated in Figure 9.10. While lead-user government organizations is the most important subset in the case of Singapore, in other nations or regions the dominant lead users could be private firms (for example, the German *Mittelstand* have been characterized as lead users of manufacturing innovations), or tech-savvy consumers (for example, China's young consumers have been recognized as sophisticated lead users of mobile social media [TikTok], mobile fintech [WeChat] and mobile e-commerce [live-streaming]).

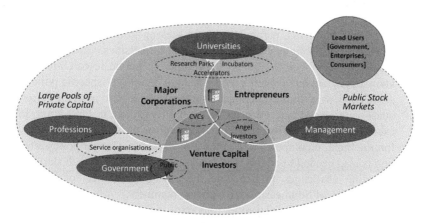

*Figure 9.10    (Augmented) Cluster of Innovation Framework*

## 9.5    CONCLUDING OBSERVATIONS

While the COI Framework has been developed primarily based on the experience of advanced market economies and regions, especially Silicon Valley in the United States, it can be usefully applied to late-comer economies and regions seeking to catch up rapidly, provided we contextualize the framework to the key drivers for market demand of these economies/regions that may differ from those of the advanced economies, especially in terms of the role of the public sector. Based on the above analysis using such an augmented COI Framework, the following conclusions can be made about Singapore's innovation and entrepreneurship ecosystem development:

1.  Despite significant quantitative growth, a fundamental weakness remains in Singapore's innovation ecosystem: the under-development of indigenous firms' innovation capability. This under-development is particularly manifest among the local SME sector, although some of the large GLCs have also been slow to invest in innovation capability development.
2.  While tech start-up activities have increased substantially over the last decade, these are still predominantly in the internet/mobile/IT services sector. A critical mass of deep-tech start-ups appears to be finally emerging in the early 2020s, but few have become "scaled-ups" with potential to be globally leading high-tech firms.

3.  Public policy changes to support technology entrepreneurship until the mid-2010s largely focused on enabling start-ups in the digital innovation space, particularly internet/mobile/IT services, where start-up capital requirements and gestation time for product development are relatively low. Efforts to nurture deep-tech start-ups have increased significantly since the mid-2010s, particularly those seeking to commercialize R&D outputs from public research institutes and universities. Going forward, greater policy focus to address the hurdles in public research-industry knowledge transfer, as well as more technology-cluster-specific policies, are needed. In addition, a deliberate strategy is needed to push the various quasi-state-owned enterprises or GLCs to invest more in innovation; for example, by reducing their traditional reliance on the domestic market and forcing them to compete more in the global market. Greater policy attention is also needed to address the "scale-up" challenges of tech start-ups, including challenges to penetrate the emerging markets of ASEAN (Association of Southeast Asian Nations) members.

4.  The public sector has played an important innovation and entrepreneurship ecosystem development role not only on the supply side, but on the demand side as well for certain key innovation clusters where the public sector lead-user role can be catalytic, or where it is actually necessary and critical due to private market failure and social network externalities.

## 9.6    IMPLICATIONS FOR OTHER NEWLY INDUSTRIALIZING ECONOMIES

My findings on Singapore's experience in developing its innovation and entrepreneurship ecosystem hold a number of implications for other newly industrialized economies. First, policies to promote innovation system development need to be better integrated with policies to promote the growth of technology entrepreneurship. In the case of Singapore, the two sets of policies appear to be poorly integrated initially: much of the investment in public R&D has not been translated into technology commercialization, because the absorptive capacities of the existing local enterprises have not been sufficiently developed; at the same time, the many new start-ups being supported by the technology entrepreneurship promotion policies were mainly in the internet/mobile sector, which did not draw much on the public R&D investment.

Second, as late-industrializing Asian economies intensify their efforts to catch up with advanced economies through the development of more indigenous firms with capabilities in the advanced technology sector, Singapore's mixed experience in this regard suggests the need for policymakers to take a holistic approach toward nurturing indigenous capability building. As highlighted earlier, commercializing advanced technologies can be achieved through new start-ups or existing enterprises, so public policy needs to be framed broadly to encompass the facilitation of both pathways. Singapore's experience suggests that policymakers in recent years have paid much attention to the entrepreneurial start-up pathway, but perhaps not enough to increasing the innovative capability of existing firms, especially the large incumbent local enterprises, particularly the GLCs. In contrast, economies like South Korea may have over-emphasized the second pathway to the detriment of the first.

Third, for late-comer economies with small domestic markets and limited supplies of indigenous talent, Singapore's experience in innovation and entrepreneurship ecosystem development highlights the critical importance of building strong international connectivity to attract talents as well as to access markets and VC. Policy-wise, Singapore has done relatively well in attracting both overseas R&D and entrepreneurial talents (and to a certain degree, overseas VC funding), although it has not done as well in terms of helping indigenous start-ups to scale up internationally.

Fourth, Singapore's I&E ecosystem development experience over the last decade suggests that the university can play a potentially important role in fostering technology entrepreneurship. While improving venture funding facilitated by public grants and co-funding has clearly contributed, the proactive role of local universities in providing start-up incubation support appears to have been important as well. It is also likely that the significant increase in emphasis on entrepreneurship education over the last 20 years by local universities, particularly NUS, may have also increased the supply of young university graduates pre-disposed to pursue start-ups versus working in large companies and the public sector (Wong et al. 2019).

Last, but not least, Singapore's relatively good performance in developing a number of vibrant innovation clusters with significant public good characteristics, like healthcare and smart urban infrastructure, highlights the importance of integrating demand-side policies with supply-side policies. As good public governance and high public trust appear to be important, if not a pre-requisite foundation, for both supply- and demand-side public policy in sectors with significant public good characteristics, Singapore's experience suggests the need to integrate analysis of public governance and public trust in any discourse on such innovation cluster development (Yusuf 2020).

## NOTE

1. Enterprise Singapore was created on April 1, 2018, through the merger of SPRING and International Enterprise Singapore, which cover the domestic and international development of local enterprises respectively.

# REFERENCES

Agency for Science, Technology and Research (A*STAR). Various years. "National Survey of R&D in Singapore". Singapore: A*STAR.

Agency for Science, Technology and Research (A*STAR). 2021. "Translating R&D into Covid-19 Kits: DxD Hub and Local Medtech Firms Ramp Up Singapore's Testing Capability", www.a-star.edu.sg/News-and-Events/a-star-innovate/ innovates/innovate/translating-r-d-into-covid-19-kits-dxd-hub-and-local-medtech -firms-ramp-up-singapore-s-testing-capability.

Anacle. 2021. Website anacle.com (various pages).

Bloomberg. 2020. "Asia Trounces U.S. in Health-Efficiency Index Amid Pandemic", www.bloomberg.com/news/articles/2020-12-18/asia-trounces-u-s-in-health -efficiency-index-amid-pandemic.

Coe, D.T., and E. Helpman. 1995. "International R&D Spillovers". *European Economic Review* 39, no. 5: 859–887.

Cornell University, INSEAD and WIPO (World Intellectual Property Organization). 2020. *The Global Innovation Index 2020: Who Will Finance Innovation?* Ithaca, Fontainebleau, and Geneva: Cornell University, INSEAD and WIPO.

Dychtwald, Z. 2021. "China's New Innovation Advantage". *Harvard Business Review* May–June. https://hbr.org/2021/05/chinas-new-innovation-advantage.

EMA (Energy Market Authority). 2021. Website NEA.gov.sg (various pages).

FEC (Future Economy Council). 2017. *Report of the Committee on the Future Economy*. Singapore: FEC.

Guellec, D., and B. van Pottelsberghe de la Potterie. 2001. "R&D and Productivity Growth: Panel Data Analysis of 16 OECD Countries". *OECD Economic Studies* 2001, no. 2: 103–126.

HDB (Housing and Development Board). 2021. Website HDB.gov.sg (various pages).

Ho, Y.P., Y. Ruan, C.-C. Hang and P.K. Wong. 2016. "Technology Upgrading of Small-and-Medium-sized Enterprises (SMEs) through a Manpower Secondment Strategy: A Mixed-Methods Study of Singapore's T-Up Program". *Technovation* 11, no. 1: 21–29.

Ho, Y.P., and P.K. Wong. 2017. "The Impact of R&D on the Singaporean Economy". *STI Policy Review* 8, no. 1: 1–22.

Ho, Y.P., P.K. Wong, and M.H. Toh. 2009. "The Impact of R&D on the Singapore Economy: An Empirical Evaluation". *Singapore Economic Review* 54, no. 1: 1–20.

HPB (Health Promotion Board). 2021. Website HPB.gov.sg (various pages).

IMD (International Institute for Management Development). 2020. *Smart City Index 2020*. N.p.: IMD World Competitiveness Centre.

IMF (International Monetary Fund). 2021. *World Economic Outlook April 2021 Database*. www.imf.org/en/Publications/WEO/Issues/2021/03/23/world-economic -outlook-april-2021.

IPOS (Intellectual Property Office of Singapore). 2021. *Singapore IP Strategy 2030 Report*. Singapore: IPOS.

Karlsson, C. (ed.). 2010. *Handbook of Research on Innovation and Clusters*. Cheltenham, UK and Northampton, MA, USA: Edward Elgar Publishing.

KPMG. 2020. "2020 Autonomous Vehicle Readiness Index". https://home.kpmg/xx/ en/home/insights/2020/06/autonomous-vehicles-readiness-index.html.

Lerner, J. 2009. *The Boulevard of Broken Dreams: Why Public Efforts to Boost Entrepreneurship and Venture Capital Have Failed – and What to Do about It.* Princeton, NJ: Princeton University Press.

LTA (Land Transport Authority of Singapore). 2021. Website LTA.gov.sg (various pages).

Lux Research. 2013. "Singapore Universities Top Ranking of Water Research Institutes". www.luxresearchinc.com/press-releases/singapore-universities-top-ranking-of-water-research-institutes.

McKinsey and Co. 2018. *Elements of Success: Urban Transportation Systems of 24 Global Cities.* www.mckinsey.com/~/media/McKinsey/Business%20Functions/Sustainability/Our%20Insights/Elements%20of%20success%20Urban%20transportation%20systems%20of%2024%20global%20cities/Urban-transportation-systems_e-versions.ashx.

MOH (Ministry of Health). 2021. "Preventive Care Spending and Impact (Parliament QA No. 1132, May 11 2021)". www.moh.gov.sg/news-highlights/details/preventive-care-spending-and-impact.

National Science and Technology Board. Various years. *National Survey of R&D in Singapore.* Singapore: National Science and Technology Board.

NRF (National Research Foundation). 2021. "Singapore Membrane Consortium". www.nrf.gov.sg/programmes/technology-consortia/singapore-membrane-consortium.

NSF (National Science Foundation). 2016. "Science & Engineering Indicators 2016". www.nsf.gov/statistics/2016/nsb20161/#/.

NUS (National University of Singapore) News. 2021. "60-Second Breath Test to Detect COVID-19". https://news.nus.edu.sg/60-second-breath-test-to-detect-covid-19_20201026094346785/.

OECD (Organisation for Economic Co-operation and Development). 2012. *Innovation for Development.* Paris: OECD.

Pearson & Partners. 2019. "Relentless Rise of the Biomedical Sector in Singapore". *Medium.* https://medium.com/@noah_69287/relentless-rise-of-the-biomedical-sector-in-singapore-b5b983d61395.

PSA (Port of Singapore Authority). 2021. Website SingaporePSA.com (various pages).

PUB (Public Utilities Board). 2021. Website PUB.gov.sg (various pages).

Schwab, K. 2016. *The Fourth Industrial Revolution.* Geneva: World Economic Forum.

Science Council of Singapore. Various years. *National Survey of R&D Expenditure and Manpower.* Singapore: Science Council of Singapore.

SNDGG (Smart Nation and Digital Government Group). 2021. Website www.smartnation.gov.sg/why-Smart-Nation/sndgg.

Von Hippel, E. 1986. "Lead Users: A Source of Novel Product Concepts". *Management Science* 32, no. 7 (July): 791–805.

Voutsinas, I., and C. Tsamadias. 2014. "Does Research and Development Capital Affect Total Factor Productivity? Evidence From Greece". *Economics of Innovation and New Technology* 23, no.7: 631–651.

Wang, J. 2018. " Innovation and Government Intervention: A Comparison of Singapore and Hong Kong". *Research Policy* 47: 399–412.

Wong, P.K. 2001. "Leveraging Multinational Corporations, Fostering Technopreneurship: The Changing Role of S&T Policy in Singapore". *International Journal of Technology Management* 22, no. 5/6: 539–67.

Wong, P.K. 2003. "From Using to Creating Technology: The Evolution of Singapore's National Innovation System and the Changing Role of Public Policy." In

*Competitiveness, FDI and Technological Activity in East Asia*, edited by S. Lall and S. Urata. Cheltenham, UK and Northampton, MA, USA: Edward Elgar Publishing.

Wong, P.K. 2006. "The Re-making of Singapore's High Tech Enterprise Ecosystem". In *Making IT: The Rise of Asia in High Tech*, edited by H. Rowen, W. Miller and M. Hancock. Stanford, CA: Stanford University Press.

Wong, P.K. 2007. "Commercializing Biomedical Science in a Rapidly Changing 'Triple-Helix' Nexus: The Experience of the National University of Singapore". *Journal of Technology Transfer* 32: 367–395.

Wong, P.K. 2011. *OECD Review of Innovation in Southeast Asia: Country Profile of Singapore*. Research report commissioned by the Organisation for Economic Co-operation and Development.

Wong, P.K. 2015. "Angel Investing: Singapore". In *Angels Without Borders: Trends and Policies Shaping Angel Investment Worldwide*, edited by J. May and M.M. Liu. Singapore: World Scientific.

Wong, P.K. 2019. "Developing Singapore's Innovation and Entrepreneurship Ecosystem: From Internet/Mobile Services to Deep Technology Commercialization?" In *Shifting Gears in Innovation Policy: Strategies from Asia*, edited by Y.S. Lee, T. Hoshi and G.W. Shin. Washington DC: Brookings Institute Press.

Wong, P.K. 2021. *The Changing Structure of Singapore's National Innovation System: Evidence from Patenting Data*. Draft research report commissioned by the World Intellectual Property Organization and Intellectual Property Office of Singapore.

Wong, P.K., and Y.P. Ho. 2018. *The Changing Structure of Singapore's Technology StartUp Ecosystem: Evidence from the TechSG Project*. NUS Enterprise working paper. Singapore: National University of Singapore.

Wong, P.K., Y.P. Ho, and C.S.J. Ng. 2017. *Growth Dynamics of High-Tech Start-Ups in Singapore: A Longitudinal Study*. Research report prepared for the National Research Foundation.

Wong, P.K., Y.P. Ho, and C.S.J. Ng. 2019. *Nurturing Entrepreneurial Talent: The NUS Overseas Colleges Program: Findings from the Inaugural Survey of NOC Alumni*. NUS Entrepreneurship Centre Research Report. Singapore: National University of Singapore.

Wong, P.K., Y.P. Ho, and A. Singh. 2011. *Study on High-Tech Start-Ups in Singapore. Final Report*. Prepared for the National Research Foundation.

Wong, P.K., Y.P. Ho, and A. Singh. 2014. "Toward a 'Global Knowledge Enterprise': The Entrepreneurial University Model of the National University of Singapore". In *Building Technology Transfer within Research Universities: An Entrepreneurial Approach*, edited by T.J. Allen and R.P. O'Shea. Cambridge: Cambridge University Press.

Wong, P.K., and A. Singh. 2008. "From Technology Adopter to Innovator: The Dynamics of Change in the National System of Innovation in Singapore". In *Small Economy Innovation Systems: Comparing Globalization, Change and Policy in Asia and Europe*, edited by C. Edquist and L. Hommen. Cheltenham, UK and Northampton, MA, USA: Edward Elgar Publishing.

World Bank. 2018. "World Development Indicators: Size of the Economy". http://wdi.worldbank.org/table/WV.1.

World Bank. 2021. *The Evolution and State of Singapore's Start-Up Ecosystem: Lessons for Emerging Market Economies*. Washington D.C.: World Bank.

Yusuf, S. 2020. *Building Human Capital: Lessons from Country Experiences – How Singapore Does It*. Washington D.C.: World Bank.

# 10. State- and private-led Clusters of Innovation in China

## Virginia Trigo and Chen Peng

## 10.1 INTRODUCTION

One of the most intriguing and disrupting phenomena of the past decades has been the economic development of China, its ascent to being the world's second largest economy and a technological powerhouse where, in the very short span of less than a decade, entrepreneurship and innovation are a mantra in government directives, opinions, educational programs, speeches, and conferences across the country. Adding to the previous description of the emergence of an entrepreneurial economy in China (Trigo and Qin, 2014), in this chapter we look at specific aspects of China's approach to entrepreneurship and innovation. Unlike what was speculated in 2014, the state-owned sector has been strengthened, although streamlined, and has taken the lead in many entrepreneurial ventures, especially in the establishment of global networks, of which the Belt and Road Initiative (BRI) proposed by Chinese President Xi Jinping in the fall of 2013 is a prime example. Spurred on by a nationwide shared spirit of "country mission above personal interests", government officials act as entrepreneurs pursuing opportunities, aligning interests, and moving forward with speed.

Through secondary data, observations, and first-hand interviews we examine the motivations behind the BRI as it swiftly and stealthily develops along the vast Eurasian continent, and we refer to a special case of a state-owned enterprise to analyze this entrepreneurial behavior. We argue that this government-led, top-down initiative is establishing covalent and durable bonds that lead to mutual dependence and to the emergence of Super-Clusters of Innovation (Engel and del Palacio, 2009). We then examine a contrasting model – if anything, China is a country of paradoxes – represented by Shenzhen, a bottom-up creation by millions of immigrants who flock into the city and, arguably, the most successful city-centric economic circle that China has built so far. In a country where the state is so intimately involved in economic processes, a distant observer may wonder how Shenzhen came to be a technological hub and indeed a Cluster of Innovation (COI).

## 10.2    CHINA'S INTERNATIONALIZATION AND THE BRI AT THE ONSET

After more than 40 years of reform and opening up, China has accumulated a large amount of technology, capacity, experience, and funds, and a whole industrial chain featuring complete and advanced infrastructure construction and achievements in communications, ports, bridges, roads, railways, and tunnels. On the downside, it has also generated a severe excess capacity and a huge demand for resources. Both these factors have prompted a strong need for internationalization and led not only to the rise of China's emerging multinational enterprises (of which Huawei and China Communications Construction Company are only two examples), but also to the construction of the ambitious project that is the BRI.

The BRI, pictured in Figure 10.1, represents the Silk Road Economic Belt and the 21st Century Maritime Silk Road. The Silk Road Economic Belt lies on the Eurasian continent and includes the following important routes: from China to Southeast Asia, South Asia, and the Indian Ocean; from the Commonwealth of Independent States to Europe; and from China to Central and West Asia, and then all the way to the Persian Gulf and the Mediterranean Sea. The 21st Century Maritime Silk Road extends from ports in Southern and Eastern China to the South China Sea and the South Pacific, and from ports in Southern and Eastern China to the Indian Ocean and the Mediterranean Sea.

There are 4.4 billion persons, over 70 economic and trade cooperation zones and more than 60 countries in Asia, Europe, and Africa along the BRI. Most are developing countries and emerging economies, with a total economic volume exceeding 21 trillion US dollars, nearly 30 percent of the world's total economic output, and nearly 60 percent of the global population (Wang et al., 2016). Most of these countries and regions are in a period of economic growth, feature broad opportunities for reciprocity and cooperation and, due to limited funds, have local infrastructure conditions which are in urgent need of development.

For Chinese enterprises, the BRI is a hard-won and huge historical opportunity to go global and further develop networks to expand "made in China" innovation. It is also an opportunity to consolidate mutual projects and recurring relationships, and for "doing business together" along the routes. Such a vast spatial agglomeration of economic activities is generally assumed to incite innovation and improve productivity but, in China's case, it has also addressed the problem of overcapacity that has plagued economic development and seriously hindered economic benefits, sustainability, and the healthy

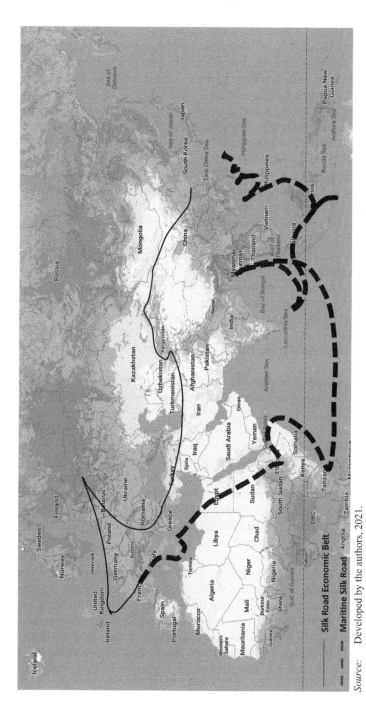

*Source:* Developed by the authors, 2021.

*Figure 10.1* *A map portraying the Belt and Road Initiative*

growth of enterprises. In 2012, the Chinese government launched a 4 trillion yuan (about 618 billion US dollars) stimulus package which brought huge consumer demand for infrastructure construction industries including iron and steel, thus helping to solve problems in the economic crisis but also creating overcapacity due to redundant construction (SWUFE, 2018). According to the *Guiding Opinions of the State Council on Resolving Serious Overcapacity Contradictions* issued in October 2013, the capacity utilization rate of China's iron and steel, cement, electrolytic lead, and other industries did not exceed 75 percent. The BRI provides a way out for China's overcapacity since the urbanization rate of the countries and regions along the routes is only 10 to 20 percent when compared to China's and they have a strong desire to promote their own industrialization (China International Contractors Association, 2018).

With 3.5 trillion US dollars in foreign exchange reserves, China can ensure sufficient funds to invest in the infrastructures required while transferring labor-intensive industries to countries along the route and stimulating international cooperation for rapid development. The Belt and Road can solve domestic overcapacity, improve industries' prosperity index, and promote the development of services and more added-value industries to assist China's ascent in the value chain (Wang et al., 2016).

### 10.2.1   How Important is the BRI for China?

From an economic point of view, the BRI is a demand to open new markets and adjust the opening-up mode. It is also a platform for generating innovative activity in complementary industries sharing a common technological base. The 2008 financial crisis broke the model of "Consumed in the West, made in the East", and led to the reorganization and division of international labor while the consumption power in Europe and Japan is declining. From the perspective of China's own economic development, its opening-up strategy has mainly focused on "bringing in", but now wages of Chinese labor have been rising along with economic development, and labor-intensive industries have gradually been transferred to neighboring lower-cost countries, challenging the traditional opening-up strategy.

On the other hand, China's relationship with the world has undergone fundamental changes. China has become the world's second largest economy, the largest trader in goods, the largest exporter, the third largest investor, and the largest foreign exchange reserve holder (China's State Council Information Office, 2019). China's ability to actively lead global economic cooperation and promote changes in global economic governance has gradually been formed, not only attracting commodities from developed countries with its vast domestic market, but also providing important sources of funds to emerging countries. Extensive consultation, joint contribution, and shared benefits – durable bonds and win–win cooperation – are principles advocated by the BRI.

Guided by such principles, efforts are being made to develop and improve the infrastructure construction of countries along the routes to form a safer, faster, and more unified transportation network that can lead to a significant increase in the ease of investment and trade, and to the establishment of high-level and high-standard free-trade local area networks. Over the past six years many landmark projects with extensive influence have been carried out one by one, from infrastructure construction to initiatives in such areas as trade, industry, education, and humanitarian assistance.

The indispensable and crucial bridge for the connectivity of people, trade, infrastructures, and exchanges is transportation. In 2017 its value along the BRI routes amounted to 232.15 billion US dollars, an increase of 1.69 billion US dollars and representing a year-on-year growth rate of 7.9 percent. Another key element is the power infrastructure, which in 2017 had a total value of 217.78 billion US dollars, an increase of 2.53 billion US dollars compared to the previous year with a growth rate of 13.1 percent, significantly higher than that of construction (China International Contractors Association, 2018).

Under the BRI, a new development model of international infrastructure construction is surfacing. New technologies, new financing models, and new policies are gradually injecting a new impetus into the infrastructure development of countries and regions along the routes.

Guided by the Baltic Railway Project Agreement, Estonia, Latvia, and Lithuania have sought to promote regional economic transformation, develop, and deepen the transnational infrastructure construction of the BRI, while Russia has facilitated the integration of the Initiative via the Polar Silk Road, closing an important loop. Central and Eastern European countries are also cooperating with China through the 16+1 Cooperation Platform, which specifies the development direction of interconnection and infrastructure construction increasing mutual dependency.

Since 2017, commercial banks, central banks of various countries, and international multilateral financial institutions have improved the financial infrastructure and channels for investment. The Asian Infrastructure Investment Bank, for example, has provided financial support to the BRI projects via both non-sovereign and sovereign secured financing. Central banks, such as those of Russia and Switzerland, signed a bilateral currency swap agreement with the People's Bank of China, effectively reducing exchange rate risk, thereby further ensuring the security of international infrastructure construction and investment along the routes.

Economic exchanges among countries are essentially embodied in exchanges among enterprises, and such has been the case during the integration of the Chinese economy into the world system. In 2018, Chinese enterprises invested

15.64 billion US dollars in non-financial direct investment in 56 countries along the BRI, accounting for 13 percent of the total amount, a year-on-year increase of 8.9 percent, mainly in Pakistan, Cambodia, Serbia, Belarus, Kenya, and Angola. They signed 7,721 contracts for new projects in the countries along the routes, with an amount of 125.78 billion US dollars, representing 52 percent of China's foreign contracted projects, a drop of 12.8 percent if compared with the previous year, but still with a completed turnover of 89.33 billion US dollars, a year-on-year increase of 4.4 percent, accounting for 52.8 percent of the total amount in the same period (Ministry of Commerce of China, 2018). Concurrently, China maintains good political and economic relations with most countries along the BRI, which were originally China's main choices for foreign trade and foreign investment. In 2013, when the BRI was implemented, half of the top 20 countries and regions in China's foreign direct investment were already located there (Cao and Liu, 2016).

Since the BRI is promoted at government level, Chinese state-owned enterprises, as the major market players and carriers, can access more foreign markets at a lower cost and establish cooperative relations with foreign governments or enterprises more easily. The costs of going global, such as those associated with market expansion or trade barriers, have been reduced. In addition, they have benefited from special domestic policies and financing support and can obtain higher benefits at a lower cost.

## 10.3    THE CASE OF CHINA ROAD AND BRIDGE CORPORATION

One case in point is China Road and Bridge Corporation (CRBC). The history of CRBC starts with its predecessor, the Foreign Aid Office of the Ministry of Communications of China, which in 1958, in the aftermath of the 1955 Bandung Conference, undertook China's foreign aid construction tasks in some developing countries. In 1979, CRBC was formally established and began to compete in the international engineering contracting market. It is currently a wholly owned subsidiary of China Communications Construction Co., one of the top 500 companies in the world. CRBC is not only one of the first four large state-owned enterprises in China in this market, but also the first Chinese enterprise to be listed among the top 100 of the 225 largest contracting companies in the world. It also ranked tenth and eleventh respectively among the top 50 enterprises with the largest completed turnover and most signed contracts of China's foreign contracting projects announced by the Ministry of Commerce in 2012 (Chen, 2019).

The business scope of CRBC has expanded from the early low-volume highways and bridges to high-volume highways, extra-large bridges, ports, railways, airports, tunnels, hydraulic engineering, municipal works, dredging, investment, and other fields. It has completed many domestic and international influential projects in different periods, including China's earliest expressway (Liaoning–Shenyang–Dalian Expressway); China's earliest inter-provincial expressway, Jinjiang Expressway; the "First National Road", Beijing Capital Airport Expressway; the first super-large bridge with a diameter of more than one thousand meters, in Jiangsu (Jiangyin Yangtze River Bridge); the world's longest sea bridge (Qingdao Bay Bridge); the first bridge built by a Chinese enterprise in Europe (Serbia's Zemun-Borca Bridge); the longest road tunnel in Central Asia (the Shahristan Tunnel of the Tajik Highway in Tajikistan); the Karakoram Highway in Pakistan, known as the "Eighth Wonder of the World"; the Friendship Port of Mauritania, known as the "Model of South–South Cooperation"; and Kenya's Mombasa–Nairobi Railway, which is an important part of the East African railway network. Currently, CRBC has branches in nearly 60 countries around the world, of which 28 are in the BRI countries, and more than 150 overseas projects under construction.[1]

### 10.3.1   The Internationalization Process of CRBC

The internationalization of CRBC illustrates the path followed by other state-owned Chinese enterprises in their "go global" process. It may be divided in three consecutive stages: "stepping out", "planting in", and "going out".

"Stepping out" means that the company relies on intergovernmental diplomacy and foreign economic relations to undertake foreign aid projects. It is a way to access global markets at a low risk. Through this process, the company can fully understand political, economic, cultural, and other factors in the host country; get to know the local market operation model; and accumulate talent with overseas business and managerial experience. "Planting in" means actively participating in the market competition with local and multinational enterprises after learning the local market and gaining a firm foothold. Through high-quality and high-efficiency engineering projects, CRBC can establish its own brand reputation and expand its influence to win recognition and praise from the government and people of the host country. "Going out" refers to making use of the host country as a platform to radiate over neighboring countries with similar cultural and political backgrounds with the purpose of deeply rooting in the country's market and having a localized operating foundation.

Chinese multinational enterprises (CMNEs) did not choose the same internationalization path as their Western counterparts. Instead, they opted for their own Chinese uniqueness. For example, they tend to choose international markets with a low degree of legal construction and enter through mergers and acquisitions to gain technology and knowledge and achieve leapfrog internationalization. In some industries, CMNEs have also presented unique models, such as the "overseas aid construction" in the construction industry and the "rural encirclement of cities" in the communications industry (Du, Shi and Chen, 2018).

Due to their special institutional background and latecomer identity (Ramamurti and Hillemann, 2018), the liability of "emergingness" of CRBC and other CMNEs makes them generally fall short of strong international resources or capabilities to establish their advantages so as to participate in international competition. The BRI provides a springboard for internationalization and for CMNEs to catch up with strong competitors in a relatively rapid manner through active asset- and opportunity-seeking activities and the use of network advantages and preferential policies in overseas countries.

The BRI offers a unique and fertile ground for such a path. It had a profound impact on CRBC's transformation and internationalization upgrading by bringing new opportunities for large-scale infrastructure interconnection and communication projects which otherwise might not have existed. Propelled by the higher-order motivation of "country mission", state entrepreneurs at CRBC and other state-owned enterprises eagerly seized and pursued these opportunities. As early as in 2014, projects such as the Mombasa Special Economic Zone (SEZ) in Kenya, Bitong Port SEZ in Indonesia, Pointe Noire New Port in Congo, and Serbia Industrial Park have been signed successively. In 2015 alone, major projects such as the Mombasa–Nairobi Railway in Kenya, Karakoram Highway Phase II in Pakistan, Karnaphuli Road Tunnel under the River Karnaphuli in Bangladesh, and the E763 (Surčin–Obrenovac) highway project in Serbia (see below) were also contracted (Chen, 2019).

### 10.3.2    State Entrepreneurs

Serbia is a major link in the BRI due to its geographic location as a hub for both the maritime and land corridors and a gateway to Europe (Figure 10.1). The connections between Serbia and China started years before the establishment of the BRI, but it was this mega project that conferred the vision and the roadmap to follow. When in August 2009 Serbian president Boris Tadić visited China, it was only the prelude for many projects to come. In the following year, CRBC established an office in Belgrade and won the bid for the construction of the 21.26-kilometer Zemun–Borca Bridge. Looking back, Mr. Liu, the office's financial manager, recalled:

> If we undertake this kind of EPC project, the most important is to meet the needs of the owners. You see, our main competitor was the famous Austrian constructor Strabag. CRBC defeated it with its higher cost performance, shorter construction period, and significant advantages in solving financing channels. Strabag would have taken a longer period than us. We, industrious Chinese, are good at conducting

labor-intensive projects, and Strabag cannot do this kind of thing. They can only work 8 hours per day; we can work overtime for a united goal.

In 2011, at its inauguration, Chinese Premier Wen Jiabao would refer to the bridge as "the first business card for Chinese enterprises to enter the Central and Eastern European market".[2]

Although the Zemun–Borca Bridge project made the CRBC brand famous in the Serbian market, the country's budget for infrastructure development was limited. Mr. Liu said: "At that time, we submitted many kinds of bids, but Serbia's GDP [gross domestic product] per capita was only 6,000 US dollars and the population is just 7 million people. Many projects were not implemented because of budget problems." Therefore, the state entrepreneurs at the CRBC Serbia Office began to explore diversified business operations and proposed the construction of the Serbia–China Industrial Park as the first industry park in Serbia's history to be invested in by Chinese enterprises. In November 2015, during the 4th Summit of Central and Eastern European Countries and China, CRBC accompanied the Serbian government delegation to visit the Suzhou Industrial Park in Eastern China. The visitors believed that this was exactly what Serbia's economic development needed. After lengthy negotiations, at the Second Belt and Road International Cooperation Summit Forum in April 2019, CRBC and the Serbian government signed an investment agreement. The Park is located on the north bank of the Danube River in Belgrade, with a total area of 3.2 square kilometers. It is divided into three sub-parks: a processing and manufacturing park, a business logistics park, and a high-tech park.

### 10.3.3 Diversification

Continuing to intensify its reach, the CRBC Serbia Office also expanded into the local railway construction market. As the Mombasa–Nairobi Railway constructed by CRBC in Kenya had attracted worldwide attention, the global railway construction market increasingly accepted CRBC, a latecomer in the field of railway construction. At the same time, China, Serbia, and Hungary put forward the idea of jointly building the Hungary–Serbia Railway (Belgrade to Budapest), upgrading the original railway to a modern and fast one meeting European standards.

The Chinese government hoped to leverage Chinese funds to promote Chinese technology, Chinese equipment, and the Chinese high-speed rail brand to go global. Therefore, it recommended China Railway International Group to participate in the project, but the Serbian government expressed the wish that CRBC should also participate. In November 2015, during the 4th Summit of Central and Eastern European Countries and China, the contract for the modernization and reconstruction of the Serbian Section of the Hungary–Serbia Railway was signed and financed by the Export-Import Bank of China. It officially started in November 2017. In the joint venture, CRBC holds 42 percent of the shares, and China Railway International 58 percent.

In 2016, President Xi Jinping visited Serbia and both countries announced the establishment of a comprehensive strategic partnership. Then CRBC was awarded the business contract for the E763 Expressway's Surčin–Obrenovac section, financed by the Export-Import Bank of China. This is the Serbian section of the pan-European Corridor 11, with a total length of 258 kilometers. Mr. Liu said:

> Section 4 of Project E763 was supposed to be completed on January 5, 2020. After considering the progress of our project, including the intention of the local government to improve their credibility, as well as the wish of the Chinese Embassy to improve the image of Chinese enterprises in Europe, the completion was on December 19, 2019. Due to the efforts of our team this was the first project to be completed ahead of schedule in Serbia.

The early completion and quality have provided the CRBC Serbia Office with an advantage in tracking follow-up projects. Using Serbia as a springboard market, under the BRI roadmap the office started to enter surrounding countries with similar economic, trade, and cultural backgrounds, like Montenegro and Croatia.

In December 2014, CRBC signed the North–South Expressway Project in Montenegro with a contract value of 809 million euros. It was the largest project with the largest contract amount among the special funds for cooperation between China and Central and Eastern European countries at that time. Then the CRBC Montenegro Office was established. In January 2018, the CRBC Serbia Office successfully signed the Pelješac Bridge Project in Croatia in the form of a joint venture. This was the first time that CRBC entered the European Union market, and the first time that a Chinese enterprise won a bid for a European Union-funded project. In the same year, the CRBC Croatia Office was established. Mr. Liu remembered with emotion:

> In the Pelješac Bridge, 85 percent of the funds were provided by the European Union, and 15 percent by the Croatian government. It was a real victory for a Chinese enterprise to enter the European market. Before we had always used funds from the Export-Import Bank of China and the China Development Bank. But for this project, we were using funds from the EU. That's completely different in nature.

### 10.3.4 Local Embeddedness

The Serbia–China Industrial Park Project expanded the business scope of CRBC in Serbia, transforming it from a traditional engineering contractor into an investor and operator. The Serbian section of the Hungary–Serbia Railway not only contributed to the diversification, but also added a joint venture to the business model which improved the competitiveness of CRBC in key projects and laid a foundation for the company to further penetrate the European market. Backed up by diplomacy and dialogue between China and Serbia under the scope of the BRI, objectives started to converge. The CRBC Serbia Office not only maintained its traditional advantages of road construction, but also successfully expanded to industrial parks and the railway business through diversified and innovative business models and the Serbian government's trust in CRBC.

Taking the Serbian market as a springboard, the office quickly responded and grasped market trends in Central and Eastern Europe, leveraging key projects in neighboring countries. Mr. Liu said:

> It is possible that one of [your] colleagues is having lunch in Serbia, but you may not see him at night. He may fly to Croatia or Poland for business, to bid. It is possible that the government may send you a letter on the second day to inform you that you are selected as a candidate and are going to have an interview. You need to fly there right away. If we have a base camp, a springboard here, we can rush forward better, take fast decisions, and seize opportunities. It is precisely because we have a solid foundation here that we have the energy to develop the surrounding markets.

Figure 10.2 shows the network embeddedness of the CRBC Serbia Office along two main development stages. At the entry stage, the main participants were the governments of the two countries, Chinese financial institutions, local suppliers, and local subcontractors. In the current development stage, the office diversified to different businesses, expanded to neighboring countries, and included different sources of funds, and, besides local suppliers, it integrated Chinese suppliers. In both stages the concern was to keep strong links (durable bonds) between the office and all the participants.

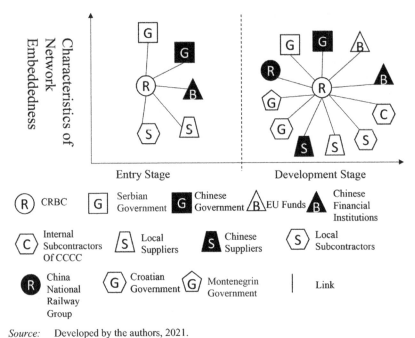

*Source:*   Developed by the authors, 2021.

*Figure 10.2     Evolution of the CRBC Serbia Office*

The steady progress of the BRI has accelerated and promoted the internationalization level of Chinese companies, but it is officials like Mr. Liu, acting on the spot, who develop local embeddedness by nurturing economic and social connections.

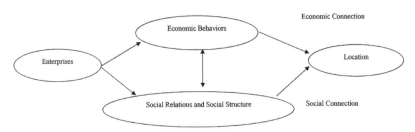

*Source:*   Developed by the authors, 2021.

*Figure 10.3     Concept relations of local embeddedness*

In Figure 10.3, enterprises are the main embedded subjects, and the location (referring to the local market of the host country) is the object. The economic connection is a way of linking subjects and the object, but social connection is the enabler that allows embeddedness in the more abstract construct of social relations and social structure. Mr. Yuan, Deputy Chief Economist of the CRBC Kenya Office from 2016 to 2019, commented: "You need time to be familiar with the market and project management. It's a process you must go through. It's important to maintain an army for a thousand days to use it for an hour. You can't make money as soon as you come into a market."

Mr. Wang, Deputy General Manager of the CRBC Pakistan Office, concurred: "We have two main resources. One is performance, the other is interpersonal network[s]. There is performance history and performance stories. Performance history is what we need to build, but it cannot be achieved overnight; it needs the accumulation of time."

International opportunities are unexpected discoveries in the market that arise from international perception and creativity in the process of globalization. They are more abstract and not so easy to recognize and pursue; they are gaps in unbalanced market supply and demand in different geographies (Berglund and Korsgaard, 2017). The changing political, economic, and social environments of the countries along the routes, as well as the different languages, cultures, business rules, legal systems, and industry standards, make it more difficult for Chinese enterprises to adapt to and manage the process of internationalization. In the context of the BRI, they rely on cooperation policy stimuli, resource commitment, resource endowment, and network location between China and the host countries to gain insight into the needs of customers and provide solutions that are highly compatible with those needs, thus overcoming the liability of latecomers and emergingness (Luo and Tung, 2007). But, as in the case we have examined, at the end of the day it is the entrepreneur, the government official who, at a given moment of place and time, is at the helm of a particular office who determines success. Like any other entrepreneur he takes risks, identifies opportunities, pursues resources, and then acts flexibly and swiftly. This state entrepreneur is not only risking his job but his "face" and, as he deeply feels it, the reputation of his country. Whether he is doing so for the benefit of a state-owned enterprise or for that of his own private company is not relevant, because the behavior is the same, except that failure may not be an option.

## 10.4 SHENZHEN: ORGANIC, BOTTOM-UP INNOVATION

In contrast, both in geography and in mindset, lies the case of Shenzhen. In recent years, China has successfully built some city-centric economic circles and development areas. For example, Beijing–Tianjin–Hebei is the capital economic circle of China and the largest and most dynamic region in the north, including Beijing, Tianjin, Baoding, and Tangshan. The Yangtze River Delta Economic Circle has Shanghai at its center and comprises 30 cities, including Nanjing, Hangzhou, Suzhou, Wuxi, and Xuzhou. The Guangdong–Hong Kong–Macau Greater Bay Area is a city agglomeration composed of two special administrative regions, Hong Kong and Macau, and nine cities, including Guangzhou, Shenzhen, and Zhuhai, where Shenzhen is arguably the shining star. In each one of these economic circles there is one leading private company that deserves being part of the acronym BAT, standing for *B*aidu (or ByteDance, as some argue), *A*libaba in Hangzhou, and *T*encent in Shenzhen.

Cities (as Engel et al., 2018 noted), with their ability to attract talent, retain investment, and draw infrastructures, have been epicenters of innovation in the first two decades of the 21st century. Indeed, urbanization spurs productivity and triggers firms' innovation through the spatial agglomeration of economic activities. For some time, researchers have been focusing attention on Chinese cities as COI (Zhang, 2014), and many of those in the above economic circles would fit the designation in terms of new product intensity. But none does so better than Shenzhen. Shenzhen is a city where people walk in the bright streets with their heads lifted up, as if they were enchanted.

So, what kind of "innovation attraction" does Shenzhen have? Why is innovation in Shenzhen greater than elsewhere? Throughout the development of China's 40 years of reform and opening up, Shenzhen has created a miracle of human urban development. It has become a beacon of innovation in terms of policy systems, economic aggregates, talent advantages, market mechanisms, urban construction, technological innovation, business environment, and cultural construction. In 2020, Shenzhen's GDP was 2767,02 billion yuan (427.6 million US dollars), ranking third in China's major cities and surpassing Guangzhou, the fourth-largest city, by more than 250 billion yuan, and growing at a faster pace than Beijing or Shanghai. In 2020, Shenzhen's per capita GDP reached 205,898 yuan (31,820 US dollars), 25.9 percent higher than that of Guangzhou's, and 37.9 percent and 42.2 percent higher than Beijing and Shanghai respectively (China National Bureau of Statistics, 2021). Shenzhen's innovation and development capabilities are not only leading the country but have become a banner for the development of China's high-tech industries with a growing global influence. Shenzhen is now recognized worldwide as a digital technology powerhouse and, in any classification of cities' business environment, consistently ranks among the first three in China, along with Beijing and Shanghai. The wonder is that, unlike Beijing or Shanghai, which are hundreds or thousands of years old, Shenzhen is a new city, built out of a small fishing village and swamp land in the glimpse of one generation.

### 10.4.1 Becoming Shenzhen

In 1979, as part of China's open-up policy, Shenzhen, alongside Zhuhai, Shantou, and Xiamen, was declared an SEZ to experiment with market-oriented economic policies. Located in the southern coastal area of Guangdong Province, with Dapeng Bay in the east, the Pearl River Estuary in the west, Hong Kong's New Territories in the south, and Dongguan and Huizhou in the north, the city covers an area of 2,020 square kilometers and has a growing population of over 12.5 million. It is a core city in the Pearl River Delta region, a gateway and bridgehead for the mainland. Close to Hong Kong, it was quick to absorb the essence of foreign culture and utilize it to its own advantage. A strong export center by the sea whose volume has already surpassed Hong Kong's own port, with a modern airport and other infrastructures, its unique geographical location, natural conditions, and human resources made Shenzhen an ideal place to develop an open economy and carry out international economic and technological cooperation.

In the first decade of its SEZ status, Shenzhen developed as the electronic factory of the world, replicating others' designs and eventually supplying most of the global production. In so doing, Shenzhen acquired knowledge in reverse engineering and international markets. It is not clear when exactly the city changed its strategy, but by 2010 it was already known for quality and homegrown innovation. Based on private initiative and adaptive government design, Shenzhen is the result of a masterplan fueled by fearless experimentation from the local government and entrepreneurs alike.

### 10.4.2 The Government Component

According to the entrepreneurs who live and thrive in it, Shenzhen's governance is characterized by a "small government and a big society". This governance model has given room for a looser development and for a number of leading companies to emerge, of which Huawei, Tencent, DJI, Rouyu, Mindray, BYD, Vanke, Ping An Group, Foxconn, and China Star Optoelectronics are only a few examples. In recent years, Shenzhen has offered cash bonuses to Nobel laureates to attract them to relocate to the city, and successively promulgated regulations and policy measures, such as the Shenzhen SEZ Talent Work Regulations and Measures to Promote the Priority of Talent Development, to encourage the systematic optimization of innovative talent policies so as to become a global-talent-attraction field.

On August 18, 2019, the *Opinions of the Central Committee of the Communist Party of China and the State Council on Supporting Shenzhen to Build a Pilot Demonstration Zone for Socialism with Chinese Characteristics* were officially released, reasserting the commitment to building a modern, international, and innovative city by 2025, and reiterating Shenzhen's strategic positioning as a high-quality development highland, a model of urban civilization, a benchmark for people's livelihoods and happiness, and a pioneer in sustainable development. The *Opinions* pledged that, by the middle of this century, Shenzhen will be a global benchmark city with outstanding competitiveness, innovation, and influence.

In 1993, Shenzhen voluntarily gave up the national Companies' Law that limited investment in intangible assets to 35 percent, thus forcing technology startups to uselessly acquire tangible assets such as real estate and reduce the value of knowledge, their most important asset. In 1996, as part of the city's 9th Five-Year Plan (1996–2000), Shenzhen clarified its strategic thinking to become a "world class city" based on high-tech industries, and guided enterprises to establish research and development (R&D) institutions to enhance independent innovation capabilities, a decision made 10 years prior to any other city in China. In terms of support to innovation, Shenzhen has established a special funding system that combines direct funding, risk compensation, and other diversified methods, as well as a combination of pre-process, in-process, and post-event funding. On average, more than 200 projects are supported annually.

In recent years, Shenzhen has aimed at innovation at the source, arranging no less than 30 percent of dedicated funds to invest in basic and applied research every year, establishing a batch of high-standard colleges and universities through cooperative education, and striving to further enhance its innovation capabilities through the combination of production, education, and research. In 2019, the Shenzhen Municipal Government issued the Shenzhen Science and Technology Management Reform Plan, which included "22 scientific reforms", the implementation of a "reward system" for project recommendation, an "invitation system" for review experts, and a "lead review system" for project review and funding. After the COVID-19 outbreak, a specific "reward system" was launched for scientific research on the prevention and control of new coronavirus pneumonia, which maximized the effectiveness of scientific research funding for epidemic prevention and unleashed innovative vitality to suit Shenzhen's motto: "Let those who can do it."

Shenzhen not only encourages but also protects innovation. On June 30, 2019, an amendment to the Regulations on the Protection of Intellectual Property Rights in the Shenzhen Special Economic Zone was passed, and a special chapter, "Judicial Protection", was added to clarify that punitive measures are applicable for serious infringements of intellectual property rights. A set of data proves the achievements of Shenzhen's efforts: in 2019, Shenzhen had 106.3 invention patents per 10,000 population, eight times the national average. Li Yi, chairman of Shenzhen Guangfeng Technology and elected Innovative and Entrepreneurial Model Figure for the 40th Anniversary of Shenzhen Special Economic Zone, emphasized that patents are an organic and important part of R&D: "Successful companies are similar, but unsuccessful companies are different. Entrepreneurs should pay attention to the protection of intellectual property rights and the construction of intellectual property teams at the beginning of their business and use intellectual property rights to build their own competitiveness" (DayDayNews, 2019).

### 10.4.3 Talent Advantage

Talent attraction is indispensable to entice and root Entrepreneurs, Management, and Professionals, which are three main components of a COI. At the beginning of the city's establishment, Shenzhen had only two engineers; by the end of 2019, it had 1.835 million professional and technical personnel; by June 2020, there were already more than 2 million, and over 10,000 high-level domestic talents were contributing to science and technology in the city. In addition, more than 140,000 overseas students have been introduced, and an "international talent highland" is being formed in Shenzhen.[3]

In April 2011, Shenzhen began to implement the "Peacock Plan" for attracting high-level overseas talents, focusing on promoting the development of pillar industries such as high-tech, finance, logistics, and culture, and aiming at cultivating strategic emerging industries through gathering a large number of overseas high-level innovative and entrepreneurial talents and their teams. The peacock allegory is aimed at inspiring would-be entrepreneurs to "fan their feathers" in the city that gives them the right environment. Actually, the gathering of "peacocks" brought new changes to Shenzhen's industrial landscape. Companies like BGI Genomics, Guangqi Automobile, and DJ Innovations are just a few of the many grown from these industry leaders. At the end of 2015, the "Peacock Project" had introduced a total of 63 innovative teams and 60,000 returnees working in the fields of electronic information, biomedicine, new materials, medical equipment, advanced manufacturing, and new energy.[4]

With the accelerated flow and integration of innovative elements such as industry, academics, capital, and talents, Shenzhen is gathering more powerful innovation energy and is accelerating towards building an international technological innovation center with global influence.

### 10.4.4 Market Mechanisms and Mobility of Resources

Enterprises are the mainstay of the market, and only when enterprises are strong can the economy be strong. Nowhere in China are private enterprises more prevalent than in Shenzhen. With 90 percent of businesses in private hands, they can consciously innovate by converting the pressure of the market into investment in innovation to form a driving force for progress.

Yue Xin, Deputy Director of the Shenzhen Municipal Market and Quality Supervision Commission, recently reminded reporters that Shenzhen has 45 industry-university-research-funded alliances, 150 incubators, more than 500 scientific and technological service institutions and 46,000 venture capital/private equity institutions, which is one-third of those existing in the country.[5] This agglomeration of resources, including large pools of capital, has formed a complete ecological chain from product development to financing and commissioning.

The development of Shenzhen's "City of Innovation" brand benefited from the relatively open market mechanism formed during the reform and opening up that transformed the city into one of the most market-oriented regions in China. Wang Shaofeng,[6] a local entrepreneur, commented that the main strength of enterprises in Shenzhen is that

> they can sensitively capture the results of technological innovation, quickly transform the technology into products to form an enterprise, and then create an industrial chain. Before an enterprise becomes an innovation entity, it must become a market entity. If you are not a market entity and have no sense of competition, you will definitely not have the motivation to innovate.

At Shenzhen's inception, entrepreneurs came to the forefront and became leaders, organizers, and risk-takers of technological innovation.

The open-market mechanism is concentrated in six 90 percent statistics: 90 percent of innovative enterprises are local, 90 percent of R&D personnel work in enterprises, 90 percent of scientific research investment sources enterprises, 90 percent of patents are generated in enterprises, 90 percent of R&D machines are built in enterprises, and over 90 percent of invention patents for major scientific and technological projects come from leading enterprises. The biggest advantage of this technological innovation ecosystem is the effective connection among R&D, production, and market. There are more than 30,000 high-tech companies in Shenzhen[7] and a large number of industry leaders with strong innovation capabilities. Huawei became the first Chinese company to rank among the top 50 global R&D expenditure companies. BGI and Tencent were selected as part of the top 50 most innovative technology companies in the world by *MIT Technology Review*.[8] A large number of young scientific and technological innovation talents stand out, including Wang Jun, founder and CEO of iCarbonX, and Zheng Hairong, researcher at the Shenzhen Institute of Advanced Technology, Chinese Academy of Sciences.

### 10.4.5 An Innovative Society: Key Behaviors

The urban culture of Shenzhen is unique in China as an all-immigrant culture, so that Mandarin is used as the common language instead of Cantonese, the local dialect. Tolerance, rationality, pragmatism, openness, and enterprising attitudes are the spiritual core of the city. Shenzhen's immigration culture has injected endless momentum into urban innovation and brought a high level of heterogeneity. A metropolis with a population of 17.56 million people of which less than 320,000 are native means that about 98.3 percent of Shenzhen's population is composed by new immigrants.[9] They come from all over the country and arrive with various motives and dreams, with one thing in common: they are "dissatisfied" with their original place of residence and go there to achieve and realize their own satisfaction.

Wu Linqi[10] is one of such immigrants. Born in Inner Mongolia and with a major in biochemistry, Wu worked for 12 years in his hometown of Hohhot until 2003, when he decided to travel south and try his luck in Shenzhen. After some failed attempts, in 2016 he founded Shenzhen Target Gene Technology, a company engaged in genetic testing and in research and development of genetic intervention technology in fields such as tumors, immunity, chronic diseases, myopia, and anti-aging. He received a first round of 10 million yuan (1.55 million US dollars) from angel investment followed by other rounds and is now planning an initial public offering. The company has developed 30 products and applied for 13 patents, of which four have already been obtained. Wu said:

> Because I had little entrepreneurial experience, no clear business direction, and no team, I ended up in failure. In my hometown I would not have dared a restart, but in Shenzhen failure is accepted and understood. People are willing to accept all kinds of new ideas and do not feel depressed. Since I arrived here, I have a broader vision and a strong learning atmosphere. Affected by this environment, I successively completed a master's and a doctoral degree and found internal motivation to complete a number of inventions and turn them into products to realize a greater value in life. If you climb the mountain, you are the summit.

For every immigrant who goes to Shenzhen, "breaking into Shenzhen" means saying goodbye to tradition and losing some of his or her original cultural habits. This characteristic has enabled the city to form an innovative culture and atmosphere with the core principles of daring to take risks, advocate innovation, pursue success, and tolerate failure. Another feature of immigrant culture is that it can accommodate different cultures, which allows newcomers to maintain their own personalities and tolerate and learn from each other to align their interests, a key behavior of an innovative society (Engel et al., 2018).

Shenzhen residents are also relatively young, and open to experimentation and new technologies. The city often serves as a test bed for new high-tech services; for example, self-driving buses or fully automated convenience stores. Residents can hardly remember the last time they saw a bill or a coin. At the same time, the "octopus" model formed by the immigration network can use its many arms to quickly and efficiently access domestic and foreign resources, establishing global linkages to obtain and integrate the latest information and improve the efficiency and success rate of innovation.

The "entrepreneurial city" theory pioneered by Romer (1990) notes that the key to its success lies in the accumulation of human resources, capital, knowledge and concepts, and the secret to attracting the agglomeration of these urban development elements is institutional innovation. Shenzhen undoubtedly has such "quality". Having been the first market-oriented experiment in China, Shenzhen has filled to perfection the roles of "window", "experimental field", and "vanguard", and created an unusual atmosphere in the country of "looking for the market, not for the mayor".

Miao Xiang,[11] an angel investor in Shenzhen, agrees:

> If the residents of a city are not acceptant of new things, no new projects or industries can be developed. Secondly, they must be willing to share information. Other aspects, such as the support of the local government or the capital market, are relatively minor; they are the icing on the cake, not the decisive factors.

Miao explains that, since the Internet is a soft asset, the core resources are talents. Where do these talents come from?

> Initially they were mainly students returning from overseas who got to work for the big BAT companies and then left to set up their own ventures, in diverse industries sharing the same basic technology. They did not want to change cities and, steadily, clusters of innovation started to grow and mature in these cities.

However, Miao made a different move. Born and raised in Hangzhou, in 2011 – having worked for Alibaba for two years – he decided to transfer to Shenzhen, where he thought there would be more job opportunities. Recently he started to invest in artificial intelligence, health, and entertainment: "As long as I invest in projects that are small enough and profitable enough, I am interested." Results have been mixed: "There are not many suitable projects; especially there are not many suitable leaders."

For years, the technological sector in China has flourished thanks to both the huge size of the home market and also a lack of regulation, or of its enforcement. In a meeting of the Central Committee of the Communist Party of China held on August 30, 2021, President Xi Jinping restated the will to fight the "irrational growth of the capital" and the "disorderly expansion of the technological sector" through a vast ongoing regulatory campaign to promote "orderly competition".[12] Budding entrepreneurs welcome many of these anti-monopoly measures, but one may sense the potential for tension between highly aggressive entrepreneurs testing boundaries while seeking speed and scale, and the tendency and need for regulators to seek control. In an emerging COI environment, the "rules of the road" are not clear, and the boundaries not well identified, or even known. A natural back-and-forth oscillation may occur.

### 10.4.6   Industry Chain Advantages

Innovation is not just a new idea; it needs the support of a complete industrial chain to achieve industrialization. From creativity to products, manufacturing is needed; from products to markets, financing is needed. The biggest advantage of Shenzhen is that it can quickly industrialize innovation. After 40 years of development, the city has a relatively complete upstream and downstream industrial chain, forming a gathering of technology, capital, information, and talents in both the soft and hardware fields. In Shenzhen, within one kilometer of Huaqiangbei (one of the largest electronic markets in the world), one can find all the raw materials that makers need. In less than a week, the entire process of "product prototype–product–small batch production" can be completed at a cost equivalent to 5 percent of Silicon Valley's.[13] For example, there are many processing factories in Shenzhen and surrounding areas that can produce a printed circuit board of good quality and for a good price. Shenzhen's manufacturing base plus the industrial chain advantages accumulated by a highly developed market economy with strong global linkages make innovation in Shenzhen more convenient and a "maker's paradise"; an ideal place for product launching.

Shenzhen's active innovation activities also benefit from its developed financial industry. Shenzhen is the center of China's venture capital, aggregating one-third of the country's venture capital institutions. They offer programs with rich opportunities, such as the Chaihuo Makerspace or HAXLR8R, an entrepreneurial incubator for makers based in Shenzhen and San Francisco that selects potential entrepreneurial teams from around the world and incubates them in its office in Huaqiangbei. It is precisely because of these comprehensive services led by venture capital that makers in Shenzhen can enjoy the benefits of Silicon Valley at a fraction of the cost, in the most vibrant startup scene. Shenzhen's ability to innovate, which the world is increasingly wary of, not only stems from policies from the top, but mainly from the creative energy of many budding tech entrepreneurs at the bottom.

In the past, Shenzhen has laid a good foundation for the development of high-tech industries. Now it is developing towards basic science and technological innovation. In this way, scientific research funds are invested at the earliest stage, and then returned to scientific research and innovation so that a new round of higher-tech and higher-level innovation may be carried out, forming a positive and self-sustained cycle. "Where do you live?" one may ask Shenzhen residents. It is not unusual that they will respond with pride in their smiling faces, "in Shenzhen". They surely know that there are very long days ahead, but each day is like a staircase that one must climb step by step.

## 10.5   CONCLUSIONS

China has been a major source of disruption in the established world order for the past 40 years and has questioned many of the established assumptions. From a Western perspective, how can a country develop without following the Western-defined concept of democracy? More importantly, how can it become a technological hub and challenge the established technological dominance?

In this chapter we examined two contrasting models towards the development of "China made" COI: one, the BRI, with two major corridors circling by land and by sea the Eurasian continent, responds to the needs and motivations of Chinese state-owned companies. It is designed and promoted by the Chinese government through the development of global networks with mutual dependency continuously nurtured by government diplomacy. Engel and del Palacio (2009) define a COI as "an environment", albeit a particular one. By building transport and communication infrastructures, the BRI paves the way for this environment and is an engine of economic growth not only for China but for those other countries entangled in the extensive network designed by China and developed upon the establishment of covalent and durable bonds that characterize a Super-COI (Engel and del Palacio, 2009). This network approach to success is aimed at deploying and accessing complementary resources in a virtuous cycle, as it occurs in the world super-clusters.

In contrast, Shenzhen portrays a bottom-up approach, organic and not by design. Attracted by the success of large homegrown giants like Tencent and Huawei, many talents congregate in the city, coming from all parts of China and abroad. Business-friendly policies and a strong local industrial chain make Shenzhen a place for new sources of innovation and business growth.

In both cases, however, the way is paved with many pitfalls. The BRI opens a demand for new growth drivers, since China needs to transfer its surplus and high-quality production to the globe, but in so doing CMNEs must overcome political, cultural, economic, and other types of uncertainties that characterize most of the countries along the routes. In addition, multinational enterprises from developed countries still hold the dominant position in the global business network system. Their capabilities of integrating global resources and the ability to control the global network system continue to affect the overall pattern of business. For Shenzhen, some new trends in national policies, such as antitrust restrictions directed at Internet platforms and restrictions on cross-border listing, may be a reason for concern. While many ponder what the original words "preventing disorderly expansion of capital" proffered in December 2020 by top policy makers exactly mean, some may sense considerable risks for the investment industry.

Several years after the 2014 article, we still ponder what the balance between state and private enterprises will be in the Chinese economy, but we are perhaps missing China's cultural tendency to consider everything holistically and not by mutually exclusive parts: "All flowers in full blossom make a beautiful spring", the Chinese saying goes. In any case, the distant observer should not doubt China's willingness to experiment.

## NOTES

1.  www.crbc.com/site/crbcEN/Introduction/index.html?id=d6cc50be-6584-4bd7
    -9beb-bd9327080751.
2.  http://news.sohu.com/20141218/n407071213.shtml.
3.  Hongbing Zhong, *Shenzhen Business Daily*, August 14, 2020, https://wxd
    .sznews.com/BaiDuBaiJia/20200814/content_406820.html; Statistical Bulletin
    on National Economic and Social Development in 2019, www.sz.gov.cn/cn/
    xxgk/zfxxgj/tjsj/tjgb/content/post_7801447.html.
4.  Xiaowen Lei, *Guangming Daily*, www.xinhuanet.com/politics/2016-05/10/c
    _128972504.htm.
5.  Xiaowen Lei, *Guangming Daily*, www.xinhuanet.com/politics/2016-05/10/c
    _128972504.htm.
6.  Wang Shaofeng was personally interviewed in November 2020.
7.  Yu Zhang, *Shenzhen Special Zone Daily*, "SZ firms among world's 50 smartest companies", www.eyeshenzhen.com/content/2019-07/03/content_22229830
    .htm.
8.  "Huawei and Huaqiangbei and Foxconn in Shenzhen China are leveraging global technological innovation!", www.sohu.com/a/205515818_464025.
9.  www.sznews.com/content/mb/2021-05/17/content_24219483.htm.
10. Wu Linqi was personally interviewed in November and December 2020.
11. Miao Xiang answered questions by email in three instances in April 2021.
12. www.gov.cn/xinwen/2018-05/11/content_5290309.htm.
13. "How the 'City of Innovation' Shenzhen was made", www.chinadaily.com.cn/
    dfpd/sz/2015-04/15/content_20441532.htm.

## REFERENCES

Berglund, H., and S. Korsgaard (2017) Opportunities, Time, and Mechanisms in Entrepreneurship: On the Practical Irrelevance of Propensities. *Academy of Management Review*, *42*(4): 731–734.

Cao, M., and Q. Liu (2016) The International Tax Planning Methods for Three Cross-border Incomes of "Go Global" Enterprises: Based on Observations from Countries (Regions) along the "Belt and Road". *Economic System Reform*, 17.

Chen, P. (2019) Prospect on Human Resource Management of International Engineering. *International Engineering and Labor*, 27.

China International Contractors Association (2018) *The Belt and Road Infrastructure Development Index Report 2018*. Macao: China International Contractors Association.

China National Bureau of Statistics (2021) https://new.qq.com/rain/a/20210225A04M3C00.

China's State Council Information Office (2019) *China and the World in the New Era* (in Chinese). Beijing: People's Publishing House.

DayDayNews (2019) Li Yi founder of Guangfeng Technology: Put the Stock Price Aside and Engage in the Main Business Firmly. https://daydaynews.cc/en/technology/105303.html.

Du, Y., X. Shi, and Q. Chen (2018) Research on the New Model of "Embeddedness-Connection" of CMNEs Internationalization under Network Relations. *Journal of University of Electronic Science and Technology of China* (Social Science Edition), *20*, 54–57.

Engel, J.S. (2015) Global Clusters of Innovation: Lessons from Silicon Valley. *California Management Review*, *57*(2), 33–65.

Engel, J.S., J. Berbegal-Mirabent, and J.M. Piqué (2018) The Renaissance of the City as a Cluster of Innovation, *Cogent Business & Management*, *5*(1). https://doi.org/10.1080/23311975.2018.1532777.

Engel, J.S., and I. del Palacio (2009) Global Networks of Clusters of Innovation: Accelerating the Innovation Process. *Business Horizons*, *52*(5), 493–503. https://doi.org/10.1016/j.bushor.2009.06.001.

Luo, Y., and Tung, R. (2007) International Expansion of Emerging Market Enterprises: A Springboard Perspective. *Journal of International Business Studies*, *38*(4), 481–498.

Ministry of Commerce of China (2018) *Report on China's Outward Investment Development 2018*. Beijing: Ministry of Commerce of China.

Ramamurti, R., and J. Hillemann (2018) What Is "Chinese" about Chinese Multinationals? *Journal of International Business Studies*, *49*, 34–48.

Romer, P. (1990) Endogenous Technological Change. *Journal of Political Economy*, *98*, S71–S102.

SWUFE (Southwestern University of Finance and Economics) (2018) *Report on the Globalization of Chinese Enterprises*. Beijing: Social Sciences Literature Press.

Tai, P., and J. Li (2019) China's Foreign Direct Investment: Experience Summary, Problem Examination and Promotion Path. *International Trade*.

Trigo, V., and L. Qin (2014) China: Emergence of an Entrepreneurial Economy in an Uncertain Environment in J. Engel (ed.) *Global Clusters of Innovation: Entrepreneurial Engines of Economic Growth around the World*, Cheltenham, UK and Northampton, MA, USA: Edward Elgar Publishing, 247–268.

Wang, J., Z. Chen, and S. Long (2016) An Empirical Analysis of the Impact of Infrastructure Investment along the "Belt and Road" on China's Economic Growth – Based on a Multi-sector Input–Output Perspective. *Journal of Jiangxi University of Finance and Economics*, *2*(104), 11–19.

Zhang, H. (2014) *How Does Agglomeration Promote the Product Innovation of Chinese Firms?* RIETI Discussion Paper Series 14-E-022, Research Institute of Economy, Trade and Industry, www.rieti.go.jp/en/.

# 11. Strategy for economic recovery from the COVID-19 disaster: Japan aims to become a startup nation again

**Shigeo Kagami**

## 11.1 INTRODUCTION

The International Institute for Management Development, a business school in Switzerland known as IMD, started publishing the IMD World Competitiveness Ranking in 1989. Japan was boldly placed first in the first issue, and for several years afterward maintained that position. However, Japan was ranked in 30th place in 2019.

After reaching a historical all-time high at the end of 1989, the Nikkei Stock Average plunged to roughly half that amount in 1997, when Hokkaido Takushoku Bank went bankrupt and Yamaichi Securities, celebrating its 100th year in business in the same year, ceased its operations.

What has been happening to Japan during the past 30 years?

As President of the Japan Academic Society for Ventures and Entrepreneurs (JASVE), the author proposed to JASVE board members that, when Japan's government was about to announce a state of emergency due to the coronavirus on April 7, 2020, JASVE should put together an urgent proposal for Japan's innovation ecosystem. This proposal consists of seven specific recommendations: (1) a mindset change for policymakers: It is not big enterprises but startup companies that will revive Japan; (2) breaking down regulations and rules that block startup companies seeking to overcome social issues; (3) startups being a driving force for government-led social change projects; (4) an increase of the mobility of human resources in large companies; (5) continuous government support for private venture capital; (6) continuous support for securing a system for university startups; and (7) continuous reform of entrepreneurship education. The details of these seven recommendations will be discussed in Section 6.

The proposal was issued and disseminated to the public on April 8, 2020, a day after the government's declaration. I thought that this proposal, in connection with COVID-19, would be a trigger by which we should reconsider the measures for economic recovery by recognizing the importance of entrepreneurship and ecosystem for startups as a driving force for "New Japan" in "with- and post-COVID-19" environments.

It is important to understand how the new coronavirus disaster could accelerate the progress of the startup ecosystem in Japan; in other words, turning a pinch due to COVID-19 into a great opportunity. While the pandemic has forced all management teams to be responsive to the new challenges, it can be expected that entrepreneurial ventures, due to their intrinsic agility and opportunism, will play an important role again as they did during and after the Second World War.

It is certain that various bedrock regulations, rules, and customs that have served as obstacles for startups are being altered or destroyed due to the immediately compelling circumstances. The collapse of hospitals and medical institutions due to COVID-19 has forcefully expedited the growth of startup companies involving online medical treatment and online medication guidance. Prior to the new coronavirus pandemic, the Japan Medical Association did not allow online medical care, and thus did not allow technology startups to enter medical service. As a general rule, online medical care was based on the premise that the first visit would be done face to face. However, due to the spread of coronavirus infections in 2020, online medical treatment at the first visit was also permitted as a special measure.

Medical services are not the only sector that has experienced deregulation as a business opportunity for entrepreneurs. With the progress of teleworking, the improvement of employee productivity has become an obvious and visible agenda for most of the big Japanese companies, leading to possibly dramatic increases in mobility within Japanese corporate society. As a result, it would be realistic to relocate human resources from large companies to startup companies.

Entrepreneurship education, which is an important component of the startup ecosystem, has also experienced great changes through the transition to online education during the COVID-19 pandemic. Education in entrepreneurship may also have a greater chance of expanding its base within educational institutions, such as universities, through the introduction of compulsory online education. In fact, in 2020 Entrepreneur Dojo, the University of Tokyo's flagship entrepreneurship education program that the author started in 2005, dramatically expanded the number of students enrolled to reach over 700, simply because we offered education online instead of offline in a classroom with a capacity limitation. This type of university reform could also be an opportunity to reduce the disparities between cities and local regions that have existed in entrepreneurship education.

This chapter, therefore, examines the challenges facing Japan in trying to recover from three decades of economic depression; the correlation of this economic malaise to the evolution of an innovation ecosystem; the roles of the key actors, including academia, industry, big businesses, and the government in addressing the entrepreneurial gap and in fostering technology commercialization and innovation; and Japan's challenges and opportunities brought about by the COVID-19 pandemic.

## 11.2　BACKGROUND: 30 YEARS OF DETERIORATION OF JAPAN'S COMPETITIVENESS

Many of the companies that drove Japan's postwar innovation were founded in the late 1930s and 1940s. Toyota Motor Co. was established in 1937, Sony in 1946, and Honda Motor Co. in 1948. Japan's postwar economic miracle (a miracle of economic development) was supported by a set of many companies with entrepreneurial mindsets that stood up in the burnt fields of the defeat in the Second World War. Japan at that time was undoubtedly a startup nation, and it can also be said that it was full of entrepreneurship, everywhere in the land. That environment revived Japan into a brilliant and innovative country.

The Japanese economy continued to grow quickly into the 1980s, to the point where it was threatening to overtake the US economy. Japan's high savings rate made Japanese banks flush with funds, and the trade surpluses produced by boom export sectors caused the value of the yen to rise. Money readily available for investment, combined with financial deregulation and overconfidence, resulted in waves of aggressive speculation. Interest rates were raised during the 1990–1991 period to prevent out-of-control inflation, which effectively burst the bubble, causing a decade-long drop in stock prices, which declined even further in the global crisis of 2008. Since the late 1990s Japan has been struggling with an ongoing economic depression and malaise. (Kagami, 2014).

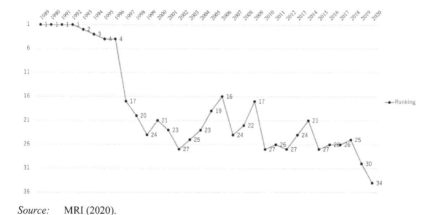

*Source:*　MRI (2020).

*Figure 11.1*　　*IMD World Competitiveness Ranking: Japan*

Looking at the changes in Japan's overall ranking in the IMD World Competitive analyses, it maintained its number one position from 1989 to 1992, after the end of the bubble era, and until 1996 it remained high, within the top five places. However, in 1997, when financial-system instability surfaced, it plummeted to 17th place, then closer to mid-20th place for the next two decades, and finally to 34th in the latest version, in 2020 (Figure 11.1).

As the indicators that determine competitiveness change from time to time, it is not appropriate to simply compare the overall rankings of the past and present. Especially in recent years, there has been a tendency to emphasize the three factors of "globalization," "information and communications technology (ICT)," and "human resources or 'talents'." In all of these factors, Japan lags far behind the global competition.

Another aspect of showing Japan's competitive position in the world is the ranking of corporations in terms of market capitalization. Table 11.1 shows the top 20 companies in the world by market capitalization in 1989 and 2019. Thirteen Japanese companies were among the top 20 companies in 1989. The top four companies were Japanese banks, followed by ExxonMobil and GE. In 2019, Apple, Microsoft, Amazon, Alphabet (Google), and Facebook were the top five market cap companies in the world, but no Japanese companies were found in the top 20 (Table 11.1).

*Table 11.1a*    *Top 20 market capitalization companies in the world, 1989*

| 1989 ranking | Company | Country | Market cap (USD billions) |
|---|---|---|---|
| 1 | Industrial Bank of Japan | Japan | 104.29 |
| 2 | Sumitomo Bank | Japan | 73.30 |
| 3 | Fuji Bank | Japan | 69.40 |
| 4 | Dai-Ichi Kangyo Bank | Japan | 64.04 |
| 5 | Exxon Corp. | United States | 63.84 |
| 6 | General Electric USA | United States | 58 |
| 7 | Tokyo Electric Power | Japan | 56.50 |
| 8 | IBM Corp. | United States | 55.66 |
| 9 | Toyota Motor Corp. | Japan | 53.25 |
| 10 | AT&T | United States | 48.95 |
| 11 | Nomura Securities | Japan | 46.81 |
| 12 | Royal Dutch Petroleum | Netherlands | 41.00 |
| 13 | Philip Morris Cos | United States | 38.58 |
| 14 | Nippon Steel | Japan | 36.59 |
| 15 | Tokai Bank | Japan | 35.35 |
| 16 | Mitsui Bank | Japan | 34.99 |
| 17 | Matsushita Elect Ind'l | Japan | 33.36 |
| 18 | Kansai Electric Power | Japan | 33.13 |
| 19 | Hitachi | Japan | 32.21 |
| 20 | Merck & Co | United States | 30.75 |

*Source:*    CNBC (2014).

*Table 11.1b*　　*Top 20 market capitalization companies in the world, 2019*

| 2019 ranking | Company | Country | Market cap (USD billions) |
|---|---|---|---|
| 1 | Apple | United States | 1068.38 |
| 2 | Microsoft Corp. | United States | 1057.42 |
| 3 | Amazon | United States | 869.36 |
| 4 | Alphabet | United States | 862.97 |
| 5 | Facebook | United States | 530.22 |
| 6 | Berkshire Hathaway | United States | 511.65 |
| 7 | Alibaba Group | China | 440.34 |
| 8 | Tencent | China | 403.16 |
| 9 | J.P. Morgan Chase & Co. | United States | 385.49 |
| 10 | Visa | United States | 381.79 |
| 11 | Walmart | United States | 338.87 |
| 12 | Johnson & Johnson | United States | 337.02 |
| 13 | Nestle AG | Switzerland | 301.75 |
| 14 | Procter & Gamble | United States | 293.98 |
| 15 | Exxon Mobil Corp. | United States | 286.07 |
| 16 | AT&T | United States | 281.1 |
| 17 | Samsung Electronics | South Korea | 280.9 |
| 18 | ICBC | China | 275.71 |
| 19 | Bank of America Corp. | United States | 275.56 |
| 20 | Mastercard | United States | 271.47 |

*Source:*　　VALUE (2019).

In 1979, Professor Ezra Vogel of Harvard University wrote *Japan as Number One* (Vogel, 1979). A bestseller, with over 700,000 copies sold, in it Professor Vogel analyzed the factors behind the high growth of the Japanese economy after the war and the highly rated Japanese-style management. It became one of the triggers to re-evaluate Japan's unique economic and social systems, which were influencing business organizations around the world. As a student myself at that time, I remember imagining a bright future for Japan.

In 1984, two years after I graduated from university, a shocking book was published. It is *The Essence of Failure* (*Shippai no Honshitsu*) by Ryoichi Tobe, Ikujiro Nonaka, and others who were young researchers at the National Defense Academy of Japan at that time. They discussed the six cases of the battles of Khalkhin Gol, Midway, Guadalcanal, Invar, Leyte Gulf, and Okinawa, and they asked why Japan lost. The authors concluded that over-adapting to the environment; relying on lessons learned from previous successful experiences, such as the Battle of Tsushima, in which Japan defeated the Baltic Fleet during the Russo-Japanese War; and acting on bureaucratic organizational principles and via personal networks, were key factors that made Japan unable to pursue innovation and military rationality. The key is to relearn (called "rejection of learning" or "unlearning") without being caught up in past successes.

The authors of the book also turned to postwar corporate management in Japan. Since almost 40 years had passed since the last war (at the time of publication in 1984), many of the once-innovative business leaders had become old. Compared to the top management in the United States, the age of Japanese top executives was unusually high, and their past successful experiences were embedded in the business framework. The authors said that Japanese corporate organizations had become more and more stubborn and resistant to rejecting past learning. The authors' foresight can be seen in the fact that in 1984, the eve of the bubble economy, Japanese corporate organizations needed to ask whether they could create their own innovation capabilities in order to respond to increasingly changing environments. Interestingly, until about five years ago, large mature Japanese companies thought that startups were the target of CSR support, but now they are thinking that their innovation cannot be realized without partnerships or mergers and acquisitions (M&As) with startups.

What has happened to Japan's innovation ecosystem during the past few decades? Many people argue that the lack of entrepreneurship after the burst of Japan's bubble economy could be an answer to the question. As detailed in previous work (Kagami, 2014), factors other than change-resistant management, such as risk-aversion in the Japanese culture, group ethics promoted in Japanese education, the low status of entrepreneurial career paths, bankruptcy law constraints, and scarcity of risk capital from angel and venture investors, have also contributed to the decline of entrepreneurship and innovation in Japan. Since entrepreneurship is the wellspring of growth in the modern market economy, the relative dearth of entrepreneurship in Japan has contributed to the nation's economic malaise over the past three decades. To revitalize its sluggish economy, Japan saw the need to create incentives to promote startups and rapidly commercialize patented, cutting-edge technologies, and looked to the national universities to lead this effort.

## 11.3    ENTERING THE 21ST CENTURY: INCORPORATION OF NATIONAL UNIVERSITIES BECOMES A DRIVING FORCE FOR ENTREPRENEURSHIP AND INNOVATION

The national universities, such as the University of Tokyo and Kyoto University, have been leading scientific research in Japan and contributing to new knowledge creation in the international academic communities. Japan has been one of the greatest producers of Nobel Prizes in the world during the last couple of decades, second only to the United States in the 21st century. Japan is the first and most highly awarded Nobel Laureate country in Asia.

As of 2020, there have been 28 Japanese winners of the Nobel Prize: eleven physicists, eight chemists, three for literature, five for physiology or medicine, and one for efforts towards peace.

As detailed in previous work (Kagami, 2014), the national universities were formerly part of the government with university staff recognized as civil servants. This made the universities bureaucratic, unresponsive to changing demands, and unable to effectively engage with other actors in society, including the private industry sector.

Soon after the new century started, Japan's policy makers began to develop ideas for granting the national universities greater independence from government. A government announcement in June 2001 suggested that the universities should be granted independence. Following the passage of the National University Corporation Law in the summer of 2003, the national universities were granted independence from the government on April 1, 2004.

In terms of the driving force for innovation, "independence" basically means three things:

1.  The National University Corporation Law clearly says that national universities should disseminate and utilize their research results to society and contribute to its development, including innovation.
2.  Soon after the incorporation of national universities, the government began to decrease the budget allocated to each national university by 1 percent per annum. This meant, for example, the deduction of USD 10 million a year from the annual revenue of the University of Tokyo. In 2004, the University of Tokyo depended on tax money or "operational grants" from the Ministry of Education, Culture, Sports, Science & Technology (MEXT) for approximately 50 percent of its budget; in 2019 these government financial supports comprised only 33 percent of the university's budget. It has become very important for national universities to gain more and more external funding to maintain the level of quality and quantity of their research and education.
3.  After the incorporation of national universities in 2004, intellectual properties such as patents derived from the research activities of university professors have become a university asset. Before April 2004, although researchers needed to report their inventions to their university, intellectual property rights and ownership belonged to the individual researchers. The rules of intellectual property management have also changed accordingly. The royalties for technology licensing by national universities are distributed among the inventors (researchers), the departments the inventors belong to, and the university headquarters in the ratios of 40 percent, 30 percent, and 30 percent respectively. The new rule of intellectual property rights implemented in this way is almost equivalent to that

of the leading US universities, including Stanford and the Massachusetts Institute of Technology. The researchers no longer have to pay patent fees themselves, and the situation where intellectual property rights including patents are owned by an institution rather than an individual is usually much more effective and efficient in terms of licensing practices, both for a licenser and a licensee. In this way, Japanese universities, recognized by policy makers as a major contributor to Japan's innovation, have needed to be creative and motivated enough to contribute to the commercialization of their technologies for innovation through university startups.

## 11.4    THE UNIVERSITY OF TOKYO AS A MODEL FOR UNIVERSITY ENTREPRENEURSHIP AND INNOVATION IN JAPAN

The University of Tokyo's Office of Innovation and Entrepreneurship (formerly the Office of Science Entrepreneurship and Enterprise Development, or SEED; the office name has just changed to Office of Startup Promotion), a part of the Division of University Corporate Relations (DUCR), was founded in 2004 at the time of incorporation of the national universities, with a mission to promote university entrepreneurship at the University of Tokyo. The office has been evolving its functions during the past 16 years.

During the first several years of this period, SEED was devoted to two major responsibilities. They might be considered as a foundation for promoting university entrepreneurship.

The first responsibility was to establish a tripartite system for effective support of university entrepreneurship, comprised of three main actors: (1) SEED or the Office of Innovation and Entrepreneurship, a central office for entrepreneurship education, consulting and mentoring, and startup incubation; (2) TODAI TLO (Technology Licensing Organization), a technology-transfer office dedicated to the University of Tokyo; and (3) the University of Tokyo Edge Capital Co. (UTEC, currently UTEC Partners), a venture capital arm dedicated to the university.

The second actor of this system, TODAI TLO (*TODAI* means "the University of Tokyo" in Japanese), is the 100-percent-owned tech-transfer subsidiary of the university. It acts as a bridge to pass technologies developed at the University of Tokyo to industry, offering a one-stop service providing access to intellectual property belonging to the university. Founded in August 1998 (six years before the incorporation of national universities) by several faculty members of the university, TODAI TLO became the university's wholly owned company after the university became a national university corporation, and now employs 45 professional staff.

The third actor of the system, UTEC, is a seed- and early-stage technology-focused venture capital firm associated with the University of Tokyo. UTEC was founded in 2004, when the Japanese national university reform took place. It has managed four funds since 2004. Its first fund is USD 75 million (at approximately JPY 110 to one US dollar), its second fund USD 65 million, the third USD 135 million, and the fourth USD 225 million; altogether, USD 500 million. These funds have been devoted to investing in seed- and early-stage startups based on technologies and talents primarily from the University of Tokyo. Having exclusive access to the university's inventions, UTEC works closely with its researchers to "co-found" startup companies for innovation. As of March 2021, UTEC has invested in more than 110 companies, with 12 initial public offerings (IPOs) and 17 M&As or other exits to date. Most successfully, PeptiDream, a profitable biotech venture founded in June 2006 and based upon the research from the University of Tokyo, which went public on the Mothers Market of the Tokyo Stock Exchange on June 11, 2013, is an example of a university startup co-founded by a scientist, an entrepreneur, and UTEC. PeptiDream became a company of the first section of Tokyo Stock Exchange in 2015. The market capitalization of the company is approximately USD 6 billion as of March 2021.[1] The details of this company will be discussed later in this chapter.

In 2016, another investment/venture capital firm, UTokyo Innovation Platform Co. (UTokyo IPC), 100 percent owned by the University of Tokyo, was founded, made possible by the government initiative often called the "Specific Research Utilization Support Project" under the Industrial Competitiveness Enhancement Act. Under this government support scheme, approximately USD 1 billion was distributed to the four leading national Japanese universities: the University of Tokyo, Kyoto University, Osaka University, and Tohoku University. This financial support for the four universities was dedicated to founding a university subsidiary venture capital company like UTEC at each of these universities. Since the University of Tokyo, which received approximately USD 400 million out of the USD 1 billion, already had UTEC and did not need another venture capital company, the university decided to create an investment company with slightly different characteristics from UTEC. That is UTokyo IPC.

UTokyo IPC has two funds: IPC Fund 1 (period: 15 years; size: USD 230 million) was formed in December 2016. This is a fund-of-funds, with limited partner (LP) participation in six venture capital companies (VCs), including UTEC Partners for seed- and early-stage investment, and it makes direct co-investments in middle- to late-stage entrepreneurial ventures. The second fund, AOI Fund 1 (period: 15 years; size: USD 28 million) was established in 2020. This is devoted to investing in joint ventures and carve-outs, partnering primarily with big companies. For example, UTokyo IPC and a business partner will form a joint-venture startup company to pursue commercializing joint inventorship between the University of Tokyo and this partner company. This fund is now expected to expand to USD 200 million or more. During the last three years, UTokyo IPC has played a critical actor role in the startup and innovation ecosystem at the Universty of Tokyo, now a quadripartite system (Figure 11.2).

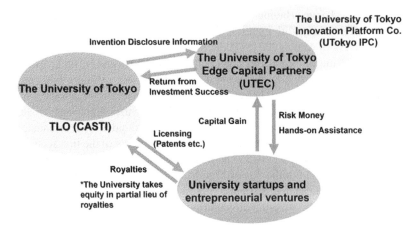

*Source:* DUCR, University of Tokyo.

*Figure 11.2*    *University entrepreneurship ecosystem in the University of Tokyo*

The second responsibility during SEED's early period was to establish the university's policy to promote university entrepreneurship. Under the National University Corporation Law (Article 22, Clause 5) and according to the preface of the Charter of the University of Tokyo, an important mission of the university is to return the fruits of its research to society. One way to accomplish this mission is to ensure that our intellectual property, including our patents, is put to practical use. With regard to this, the University of Tokyo Intellectual Properties Policy clearly asserts the importance of promoting the practical application of inventions and other intellectual property through university startups. The policy states: "As one measure to return the fruit of intellectual creativity to society, the university should proactively be involved in using startup businesses to commercialize inventions." Thus, maintaining a positive environment for supporting startups became one of the tasks assigned to the University of Tokyo.

The key activities of SEED or the Office of Innovation and Entrepreneurship include (1) entrepreneurship education, (2) incubation, and (3) gap funding.

The first entrepreneurship education program, created in 2005 – one year after the incorporation of national universities – is the University of Tokyo Entrepreneur Dojo (a training school, like judo practice), where both undergraduate and graduate students can learn how to commercialize their ideas and inventions. The program provides a couple of hundred students with entrepreneurship education and a business plan competition every year. During the past 16 years, more than 4,000 students have completed the program. More than 100 "graduates" are, as founding members, involved with newly created entrepreneurial ventures (Figure 11.3).

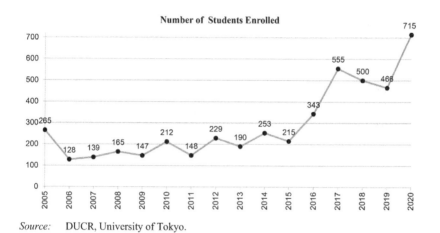

*Source:* DUCR, University of Tokyo.

*Figure 11.3*     *Number of University of Tokyo Entrepreneur Dojo students*

The author has been in charge of several new entrepreneurship education initiatives. For the last decade he has taught a course called Innovation & Entrepreneurship at the Graduate School of Engineering, which provides students with an opportunity to formulate business plans, based upon technologies available in research labs of the University of Tokyo. Many students from abroad participate in this program. In the Graduate School of Engineering, the author has also co-taught a bioengineering training course, where graduate school student teams formulate new business proposals by commercializing their patentable ideas and research outcomes in the areas of life science and biotechnology. In addition, since 2019 the author has led a new entrepreneurship education program, Entrepreneurship Seminar, for the first-year students of the Komaba Campus. This allows students access to the experience of the Entrepreneur Dojo without having to commute to the Hongo Campus from the Komaba Campus. In 2020, due to COVID-19, both the dojo and the seminar were offered online.

In August 2016, a new program, Hongo Tech Garage, started. During more than a dozen years of experience at the Entrepreneur Dojo, it has been observed that some of the best students initially react negatively to words such as "venture" and "business plan." We recognized the need to develop a new program for students who could not be scooped up by the Entrepreneur Dojo. We also knew that many of these students had a strong desire to develop something (hardware and software) that they could not freely make in their laboratory. Hongo Tech Garage aims to create a makerspace that supports those students. Fortunately, we were able to get donations from a large company, so we prepared a workshop equipped with machine tools, created a "secret base" like a student hangout, and created an intensive Spring/Summer Founders Program.

Furthermore, in the new "Todai to Texas" program, the University of Tokyo-related startups and student projects are dispatched to and exhibited at the South by Southwest (SXSW) exhibition held every March in Austin, Texas, in the United States. The student team that participated in this program and exhibited the robot prosthesis Suknee at SXSW in March 2017 received the Student Innovation Award. Past winners include Twitter (2007) and Airbnb (2011).

From 2014 to 2016 we conducted another exciting program, EDGE (Enhancing Development of Global Entrepreneur), an entrepreneurship education initiative for young researchers, including postdoctoral researchers and doctoral program and other graduate school students. The EDGE program was sponsored by MEXT. The objective was to develop innovation-driven researchers to promote entrepreneurship in the academic institutions and to establish an innovation ecosystem in Japan. Young researchers who were familiar with research but were not comfortable in converting their research into a business were the main targets for the program, which required all the participating teams to make a business pitch in English in front of VCs in Silicon Valley.

MEXT prepared the Next Generation Entrepreneur Development Project (EDGE-NEXT) as a successor program of EDGE in 2017, and the University of Tokyo was selected again for financial support by MEXT, funding entrepreneurship education for young researchers until the end of March 2022.

EDGE-NEXT is a challenging project that has never existed before, incorporating self-propelled driving in five years into key performance indicators (KPIs), and collaborating with about 30 domestic universities, overseas universities, and cooperation support organizations under five consortia groups led by five leading academic institutions, including the University of Tokyo. Under EDGE-NEXT, each university needs to demonstrate its own advantage regarding characteristics such as experiences outside classroom lectures centered on teaching materials, and new education techniques for undergraduate students, young researchers, and adult students, including problem-solving workshops, presentations of business plans, and pitches in front of VCs in Silicon Valley.

The second key activity of SEED or the Office of Innovation and Entrepreneurship is to build incubation functions together with incubation facilities. The University of Tokyo Entrepreneur Plaza opened in summer 2007 to provide support for university technology startups. The facility is equipped with wet laboratories to meet the increasing demands of life-science-related technology venture businesses originating from the university. The construction of the plaza was made possible by a charitable contributor. In addition to this facility, because of the increasingly strong demand from the University of Tokyo-related startups for incubation, the University of Tokyo Entrepreneur Lab, another startup incubation facility, started operation in October 2018. We also have other smaller facilities on the Komaba and Kashiwa campuses. Altogether we have 100,000 square feet of capacity for startup companies.

More than 70 university startups have so far been incubated at those incubation facilities by SEED or the Office of Innovation and Entrepreneurship, and, as of March 2021, four of those companies – PeptiDream, PKSHA Technology, Euglena, and Morpho – have gone public.

Another key activity for which SEED or the Office of Innovation and Entrepreneurship has been responsible is a gap fund to promote the university startup ecosystem in the University of Tokyo. The major universities in the United States have gap funds, and the University of Tokyo was finally able to set up its own fund in 2018. It aims to bridge the gap between research and commercialization, by funding activities such as creating prototypes to verify and improve the practicality of research results and test runs to acquire additional data for commercialization. Projects from University of Tokyo researchers, when selected by the dedicated committee, are given approximately USD 60,000 each. Approximately 100 projects so far have been selected and granted.

The University of Tokyo has been making progress little by little, year by year, since 2004, when it became incorporated, and now the university is the greatest producer of university startups in Japan (Table 11.2). The National University Corporation Act has allowed the university to (1) become an owner of patents or intellectual property rights as a licenser of technologies based on university research through the university's TLO, (2) set up a venture capital "arm" dedicated to the university (UTEC and UTokyo IPC), (3) build incubation facilities in the campuses, and (4) offer various entrepreneurship education programs to both students and researchers to promote academic entrepreneurship.

In 2019 the Ministry of Economy, Trade and Industry (METI) conducted a survey on 1,092 schools, corporations, and organizations such as universities, colleges of technology, TLOs, incubation facilities, and prefectures. According to the survey, the number of Japanese university-launched venture companies increased by 288 from 2018 to 2,566 by September 2019.

*Table 11.2     Number of university startups founded: making history*

| Ranking | University | 2019 | 2017 | 2016 | 2015 | 2008 |
|---------|------------|------|------|------|------|------|
| 1 | University of Tokyo | 271 | 245 | 216 | 189 | 125 |
| 2 | Kyoto | 164 | 140 | 97 | 86 | 64 |
| 3 | Tsukuba | 111 | 98 | 76 | 73 | 76 |
| 4 | Osaka | 106 | 93 | 74 | 79 | 75 |
| 5 | Tohoku | 104 | 56 | 53 | 50 | 57 |
| 6 | Kyushu | 90 | 81 | 70 | 63 | 55 |
| 7 | Waseda | 82 | 74 | 62 | 65 | 74 |
| 8 | Keio | 81 | 51 | 42 | 40 | 51 |
| 9 | Nagoya | 76 | 69 | 38 | 33 | 28 |
| 10 | Tokyo Institute of Technology | 66 | 53 | 50 | 53 | 57 |
| 11 | Digital Hollywood | 51 | 52 | 43 | 42 | 19 |
| 12 | Hokkaido | 50 | 49 | 48 | 48 | 43 |
| 13 | Hiroshima | 45 | 43 | 38 | 39 | 38 |
| 14 | Ryukoku | 43 | 43 | 36 | 33 | 27 |
| 15 | Kyushu Institute of Technology | 42 | 39 | 39 | 43 | 45 |
| 16 | Aizu | 33 | 29 | 29 | 28 | 23 |
| 17 | Okayama | 30 | 31 | 28 | 29 | 28 |
| 18 | Ritsumeikan | 29 | 26 | 32 | 29 | 35 |
| 19 | Kobe | 28 | 31 | 26 | 24 | 33 |
| 20 | Nagoya Institute of Technology | 28 | 27 | 21 | 21 | 14 |

*Source:*     METI (n.d.).

Before 1989, there were only 54 university-launched startups, but in 1995 the number exceeded 100 companies, and in 2004 it increased to 1,207. Although the growth of university-launched ventures was temporarily sluggish in 2008 due to the economic slowdown caused by the Lehman Brothers crisis, the total exceeded 2,000 companies in 2017. The establishment of university-launched startups continued to accelerate, with an increase of 288 companies in 2019 that was the highest ever.

By university, the University of Tokyo was the top with 271 companies, followed by Kyoto University with 164, the University of Tsukuba with 111, Osaka University with 106, and Tohoku University with 104. These top five schools are famous national research universities affiliated with the former Imperial University.

## 11.5  CASE STUDIES

### 11.5.1  PeptiDream

PeptiDream is a biopharmaceutical company founded on July 3, 2006, and based on novel peptide expression and platform-selection technologies developed by the company cofounder Dr. Hiroaki Suga, Professor at the Graduate School of Science of the University of Tokyo.

As detailed in previous work (Kagami, 2014), several years after PeptiDream was founded the company's intellectual properties management was strongly supported by TODAI TLO, and the company was financially supported by UTEC as a lead investor. Both TODAI TLO and UTEC were fully involved with the company's business growth even before it was incorporated. The University of Tokyo's Office of Innovation and Entrepreneurship also helped the company as an incubator by offering lab and office spaces, including the University of Tokyo Entrepreneur Plaza.

PeptiDream went public in June 2013 and became listed on the first section of the Tokyo Stock Exchange in December 2015. In July 2016, the company signed a strategic alliance agreement to give a nonexclusive license of PeptiDream's Peptide Discovery Platform System (PDPS) technology to Genentech. In April 2017, the company signed a multi-year multi-target discovery deal with Janssen. In August 2017, it relocated corporate headquarters to Tonomachi, Kawasaki City, Kanagawa Prefecture, one of the largest newly founded biotech clusters in Japan. In June 2018, PeptiDream signed a strategic alliance agreement to provide a nonexclusive license of PDPS technology to Merck & Co., and in June 2019 the company signed a New Peptide Drug Conjugate discovery deal with Novartis AG.

PeptiDream, with over 150 employees, has expanded its business dramatically. In the 2020 financial year, it reached JPY 11.7 billion, or approximately USD 106 million, in net sales; JPY 7 billion, or USD 63 million, in operating profit; and JPY 44.5 billion, or USD 40 million, in net profit.[2]

PeptiDream is one of the role models of a typical and ideal university technology startup. The tripartite system of SEED, TODAI TLO, and UTEC worked together very effectively to foster the growth of the company. The market capitalization of PeptiDream once reached approximately USD 8 billion.

### 11.5.2   PKSHA Technology

In October 2012, PKSHA Technology was established for the purpose of the data analysis business using machine learning technology.

After engaging in business intelligence work at Boston Consulting Group's Tokyo and Seoul offices, Dr. Katsuya Uenoyama participated in the establishment of the Silicon Valley office of a major internet company and engaged in large-scale log analysis work for web products. After obtaining a doctorate (in machine learning) from Dr. Yutaka Matsuo Laboratory of the Graduate School of Engineering of the University of Tokyo, Dr. Uenoyama became an Assistant Professor at Matsuo Laboratory and founded PKSHA Technology. He is currently the representative director (President) of the company. In 2020, he was selected as one of the Young Global Leaders 2020 of the World Economic Forum. In September 2017, PKSHA Technology went public and was listed on the Mothers Market of the Tokyo Stock Exchange.

PKSHA Technology once used the university's incubation facility Entrepreneur Plaza, and Dr. Uenoyama is a frequent speaker of the university's entrepreneurship education programs.

The latest annual sales of PKSHA Technology were approximately USD 70 million for the period of 2019–2020, and its net annual profit reached approximately USD 17 million.[3]

PKSHA Technology once reached over USD 2 billion in market capitalization. A dozen other promising startups related to artificial intelligence (AI)/deep learning and founded around the University of Tokyo's Hongo Campus are following PKSHA Technology's success. Many people say that these companies have created the notion of "Hongo Valley," a new cluster of AI-related startups around the campus of the University of Tokyo.

## 11.6   CHALLENGES FACING UNIVERSITY ENTREPRENEURSHIP FOR THE STARTUP INNOVATION ECOSYSTEM IN JAPAN

United Nations Secretary-General Antonio Guterres warned on March 31, 2020 that the outbreak of the new coronavirus was the "greatest test" for the world since the Second World War.[4] There is no doubt that the new coronavirus disease is a major test for Japan. Japan's economic strength has been questioned, and quite a few people question whether Japan will survive and come back as a powerful country again or continue to lose its competitiveness in the global competition.

Should we not now be aware that we are in the midst of a historic turning point? It is an era when the old paradigm is no longer fully functional. At the same time, it can be said that this is creating a foundation for people and society to actively accept new possibilities. However, as history has shown, the paradigm that has dominated until now is not so easy to get rid of. When a new paradigm emerges, no matter how clear its rational basis, it will encounter the worldview of the past and meet strong resistance from those who have significant investments in maintaining the status quo. Opening up a new era requires creative thinking and bold action to seize exciting opportunities. Some of the steps forward are becoming clear.

### 11.6.1 It Is Startup Companies That Will Revive Japan

As was the case in Japan after the defeat in World War II, creative entrepreneurial ventures that boldly challenge risks are essential in order to survive this unprecedented national crisis caused by the new coronavirus. Having a commonly shared understanding of the importance of entrepreneurship will be the starting point for Japan's transformation in the future.

Japan is gradually changing to a society that highly values entrepreneurs and entrepreneurship. It is important to continue the great momentum of the current startup ecosystem. This includes minimizing the risks of business development and financing that startup companies currently face. We must take the risk of seeing drastic environmental changes as an opportunity for startups and passing on the compulsory social changes caused by COVID-19 to business opportunities. If we can implement these actions, Japan can take a firm step on the road to becoming an entrepreneurial nation again.

### 11.6.2 Breaking Down Regulations and Rules That Block Startup Companies Seeking to Overcome Social Issues

In order to overcome challenging social issues, it is essential to thoroughly break down the regulations and rules that block the path of startups that try to solve problems based on the logic of customers and markets. There are still many "bedrock regulations" in Japan. A bedrock regulation is a regulation that prevents "relaxation" of barriers to startups by forming a "trinity scrum" of government agencies (government offices), long-established politicians driven by their special interests, and industry groups in charge of regulation. It is said that there are many bedrock regulations in fields such as medical care, agriculture, education, and employment, but if the bans are lifted and liberalized, the roles of each ministry and government office will disappear and jobs will be lost. Politicians will also lose their "rights." In addition to online medical care discussed earlier in this chapter, clarification of employment rules for "limited regular employees" who only work in limited places and work contexts, lifting of the ban on ride-sharing in private cars, and free disclosure of real estate registration information online are examples of breaking down the regulations.

Japan, a high-cost country with a declining birthrate, an aging population, and a high number of natural disasters, could be considered to be one of the advanced countries that has the most social issues in the world. However, because of this, Japan should also have a great number of business opportunities. Japan's potential to become one of the most effective problem-solving advanced nations in the world would be very high, thanks to the serious social problems that Japan has been forced to encounter.

Through regulatory reforms that can allow full use of the new technologies and knowledge accumulated in the Fourth Industrial Revolution, Japan is sure to come back as an effective country again for innovation. When introducing ICT as a new communication and work tool, the speed of entrepreneurial ventures that are developing cross-industry technologies could be a strong power and competitive advantage that makes the world much better. It is important to break through the bedrock of regulations in order for startups to become a change agent to solve serious social problems.

### 11.6.3  Startups as a Driving Force for Government-Led Social Change Projects

It is necessary to create an environment in which the government can take the lead in projects for solving major social issues, and startup companies rather than big companies can take the lead in implementing such moonshot projects. Traditionally, large companies have been nominated for large government-led projects, under which startups may contribute, but startups are not the main players. It is important to change the way government procurement is executed so that startup companies can easily enter into the country-led challenging projects.

Even if it is a state-led project, the government should make a direct contract with a startup company with state-of-the-art technologies and utilize its sense of speed to move the cross-sectional project with multi-stakeholders. If there is concern about the continuity of project execution, it is essential to have a professional intermediary (venture capital, and so on) mediation function that fosters startups and promotes a business/financial alliance with mature large companies.

### 11.6.4  Increase the Mobility of Human Resources in Large Companies

In Japan, nobody can deny that under the lifetime employment system, talented people at large companies may stay with their employers for the rest of their lives and pursue their higher corporate positions by leading corporate reforms. On the other hand, many startups have a challenge in recruiting great human resources, hoping that talented people available in big companies will join a newly founded startup as a management team member or a C-level executive for a particular operating function, like chief financial officer.

It seems that, partially because of COVID-19, there is now a change in the labor market, with high liquidity or mobility that enables the executives and employees of big companies to play an active role in key positions at startup companies.

Until several years ago, it had not been possible to drastically change people's sense of job security and stability, where excellent young people were still oriented towards large companies. However, after they saw many large companies go bankrupt in this century, young people who want to challenge their own potential are changing their mindset in such a way where they do not depend on large organizations for their fate. Instead, they are relying on independent working conditions where they can capitalize their own abilities. The percentage of people who are thinking about starting a business or changing jobs to improve their abilities has increased sharply.

When the life span is extended to 100 years, it is not realistic to continue working for one company for one's entire life. If universities can provide education that supports the mobilization of human resources who want to take on new challenges, including recurrent education, the mobilization of human resources from existing companies to startups will inevitably accelerate.

### 11.6.5   Continuous Government Support for Private Venture Capital

There is concern that the source of the supply of risk money that should be provided to startup companies will be narrowed due to COVID-19. The government and related fund agencies should continue and expand support through LP investment in private VCs.

Deep-tech startups that want to expand their business globally will especially play a leading role in contributing to the next generation of innovation in Japan. These entrepreneurial ventures are currently expanding into the United States, Europe, China, and Asian countries, and have been developing bases for market development, but due to the new coronavirus, they are faced with both domestic and overseas problems at the same time. In addition, R&D-intensive startups have been raising funds for future possibilities without sales, and although the supply of risk money has been secured to some extent, it is easily imagined that the financing plan will go wrong due to the postponement of IPOs, for example.

By 2019, many venture capital firms succeeded in large-scale fundraising, and corporate venture capital centered on large corporations has been actively established. In addition, the establishment of a new fund in collaboration with overseas private equity funds is being considered. It is indispensable to continue the financial support of Japanese startup companies to avoid the situation where many potential tech startups need to stop their operations due to the deterioration of their cash positions.

### 11.6.6 Continuous Support for Securing a System for University Startups

University technologies in most cases need gap funds to build a rapport between science and business to actualize innovation. Gap funds are used for prototypes, data acquisition for patenting, and formulating commercialization plans. R&D-intensive startup supports are often offered by the government or the government's funding agencies, including STS (seed-stage technology-based startups) and NEP (the NEDO Entrepreneurs Program) offered by the National Research and Development Corporation New Energy and Industrial Technology Development Organization (NEDO), and the university-initiated new-industry-creation program (START) of the Japan Science and Technology Agency. Funding efforts such as these need to be continued.

### 11.6.7 Continuous Reform of Entrepreneurship Education

As previously indicated, MEXT has been putting emphasis on the importance of Japan's startup and innovation ecosystem. The government-led programs, such as EDGE-NEXT, would be a typical initiative that needs to be maintained sustainably. New educational contents and programs are being developed and online education is being carried out as a norm under COVID-19. Since one of the main purposes of EDGE-NEXT is to run its own entrepreneurship education, the amount of subsidy is rather small, but it is required to gradually achieve the KPIs on a self-propelled basis by gaining external cooperation such as corporate donations and tuition of corporate participants. Academia, industry and government need to somehow cooperate to further expand entrepreneurship education together given that Japan's universities are faced with financial difficulties in maintaining newly created entrepreneurship education programs.

## 11.7 CONCLUSION

In an era of turbulence that occurs once in 100 years, it will probably be the entrepreneurs who jump into the storm of change and lead the change. Needless to say, large companies are still important players for innovation, but I am convinced that the immediate protagonists will be startup companies and entrepreneurs. As was the case with Toyota Motor Corporation 80 years ago, the corporate founders emerged from the tumultuous times before, during, and shortly after the Second World War to become the protagonists of a major transformation of the postwar Japan as startup entrepreneurs.

Table 11.3 shows the number of unicorn companies by country in 2021. A unicorn company is a privately owned startup that has a current valuation of USD 1 billion or more. Once a company has gone public (through an IPO) or has been acquired, it is no longer termed a unicorn. All figures are estimated as of March 2021 based upon the latest publications of sources.

The number of unicorn companies in China was bigger than those of the United Kingdom, India, Germany, Israel, Brazil, South Korea, France, Japan, Indonesia and Switzerland combined. Japan has only five unicorn startups. Compared to the United States or China and given the fact that Japan is one of the leading national economies globally, Japan's startup ecosystem looks still nascent.

*Table 11.3*     *Number of unicorn startups: country ranking (as of March 2021)*

| 1 | United States | 317 | | 13 | Singapore | 4 |
|---|---|---|---|---|---|---|
| 2 | China | 137 | | 13 | Hong Kong | 4 |
| 3 | United Kingdom | 29 | | 13 | Canada | 4 |
| 3 | India | 29 | | 13 | Sweden | 4 |
| 5 | Germany | 16 | | 17 | Australia | 3 |
| 6 | Israel | 12 | | 17 | Netherlands | 3 |
| 6 | Brazil | 12 | | 19 | South Africa | 2 |
| 8 | Korea | 10 | | 19 | Colombia | 2 |
| 9 | France | 9 | | 19 | Spain | 2 |
| 10 | Japan | 5 | | 19 | UAE | 2 |
| 10 | Indonesia | 5 | | | Others | 13 |
| 10 | Switzerland | 5 | | | | |
| | | | | | Total | 629 |

*Source:*     CB Insights (2021).

It is important to recognize that COVID-19 would possibly be able to accelerate the progress of the startup ecosystem in Japan, turning a pinch into a great opportunity. While the traditional paradigm of Japanese-style management has been forced to change significantly at an accelerating rate due to the pandemic, it could be expected that the entrepreneurial ventures play an important role again, as they did during and after the Second World War.

The last concluding message: Resurrection from the new coronavirus disaster – Japan aims to become a startup nation again!

## NOTES

1.  Valuation from Yahoo Finance.
2.  www.peptidream.com/ir/index.html.
3.  https://unsdg.un.org/sites/default/files/2020-03/SG-Report-Socio-Economic
    -Impact-of-Covid19.pdf.
4.  https://unsdg.un.org/resources/shared-responsibility-global-solidarity
    -responding-socio-economic-impacts-covid-19.

## REFERENCES

CB Insights (2021), "Total number of unicorn companies," www.cbinsights.com/research-unicorn-companies.

CNBC (2014), "What a difference 25 years makes" (April 29), www.cnbc.com/2014/04/29/what-a-difference-25-years-makes.html.

Japan Academic Society for Ventures and Entrepreneurs (JASVE) (2020), *An Urgent Proposal Resurrection from the New Coronavirus Disaster: Japan Aims to Become a Startup Nation Again*. www.venture-ac.ne.jp/wp-content/uploads/2022/02/%E7%B7%8A%E6%80%A5%E6%8F%90%E8%A8%80%E6%9B%B8%E3%80%8C%E6%96%B0%E5%9E%8B%E3%82%B3%E3%83%AD%E3%83%8A%E3%82%A6%E3%82%A4%E3%83%AB%E3%82%B9%E7%A6%8D%E3%81%8B%E3%82%89%E3%81%AE%E5%BE%A9%E6%B4%BB%E3%80%8D.

Kagami, S. (2014), "Japan: The University as a Driver for Innovation in Japan in Response to Two Decades of Economic Depression," in Engel, J. (ed.), *Global Clusters of Innovation: Entrepreneurial Engines of Economic Growth around the World*, Cheltenham, UK and Northampton, MA, USA: Edward Elgar Publishing.

METI (Minister of Economy, Trade and Industry) (n.d.), University Startup Surveys (*Daigakuhatsu Venture Jittaitou Chousa* in Japanese), www.meti.go.jp/policy/innovation_corp/start-ups/start-ups.html.

MRI (Mitsubishi Research Institute) (2020), "Japan's competitiveness as seen from the IMD 'World Competitiveness Yearbook 2020' Part 1: Japan's overall ranking fell from 30th to 34th" (October 8), www.mri.co.jp/knowledge/insight/20201008.html.

Tobe, R., Nonaka, I., et al. (1984), *The Essence of Failure* (*Shippai no Honshitsu* in Japanese), Tokyo: Diamond.

VALUE (2019), "World top 100 companies by market cap as on Oct 20, 2019," www.value.today/world-stock-news/world-top-100-companies-market-cap-oct -20-2019.
Vogel, E. (1979), *Japan as Number One*, Tokyo: TBS-Britannica.

# 12. Supporting innovation in India through a special Service Organization

**Manav Subodh**

## 12.1  INTRODUCTION

To be effective in my mission, I learned early on that it is always helpful for multi-national corporations (MNCs) to collaborate closely with local and national governments. This coordination can amplify resources and remove or avoid bureaucratic minefields. It has, however, always been a challenge to make government machinery work in tandem with corporate and business agendas. The two institutions exist in separate yet overlapping realms. How can you align such divergent agendas to create a win–win solution for all parties involved? How can you make this process more engaging to ensure that it develops a thirst to innovate in your populace? Can you use this thirst to create meaningful and lasting social change? This chapter presents the approach of using special-purpose social service resources to address these challenges. These resources can be part of the MNC or independent Service Organizations. We will investigate case studies involving both approaches, understand their respective benefits and challenges, and finally look forward to understanding the challenges and opportunities for this Cluster of Innovation (COI) development activity as new, robust technology platforms such as artificial intelligence (AI) come to the fore.

As someone who has spent more than 20 years working at the crucial intersection of business and government, I understand that getting these two entities to work with, and more importantly *for*, each other is no easy task. My Corporate Affairs stint at Intel Corporation allowed me to explore first-hand the surprising intricacies and complexities of aligning corporate agendas to that of the government while working from within an MNC. My mandate at Intel was profoundly simple: to help the company build a favourable relationship with the government and be seen as a trusted partner in the space of technology.

This seemed easy enough. Intel was already working towards computerizing government schools and pushing the curriculum in engineering colleges to focus on building innovative and creative thinking in young minds. I remember thinking to myself, "Surely, this would suffice in gaining some traction and visibility with the state or even national government?" I thought it was the perfect intersection of agendas, a win–win for both parties involved. Intel gets to be the face of India's technology wave and the government gets computers in schools. But is the government's agenda ever so simple?

A company is a streamlined organization with clearly articulated goals and a singular driving force in the form of a business model. A government, on the other hand, is structured very differently. The scope of its mandate is far more ambitious, its goals are innumerable and its driving force is the (anything but singular) demands of the people who have elected it. Populist demands drive government agendas – and despite education being a priority for all, it simply was not the populist demand of the hour.

It is through this insight and my subsequent years of experience of working both within and outside an MNC in a special Service Organization that I was able to formulate a framework to help comprehend the Indian government's populist agendas that have been cemented over the years. There are four dimensions to this framework: jobs, agriculture, healthcare and social inclusion. Education was, if anything, a sub-dimension within social inclusion. It was only after this realization that I was able to push Intel to work within this framework to service and address one of these dimensions by identifying and capitalizing on what I like to call the "shift". What exactly do I mean by a shift? A "shift", as I will continue to refer to it, is a global or national reaction or response to a change or stimulus in the environment (be it economic, ecological or even a change in technology cycles). Every economy experiences these "shifts", whether it was 9/11 triggering a shift towards innovating with cyber-security, or Covid-19 resulting in the shift towards accelerating the digital revolution. It is only by anchoring their business models to respond to these global and national shifts that MNCs can hope to build this favourable relationship with government agendas and to sustain their business.

Through this chapter, I intend to take you along my journey of experimenting with and formulating this framework, as I set out to build a regional COI, connecting MNCs with governments and education systems.

The first section will discuss my initial time at Intel, where I worked within the MNC structure to drive initiatives, while the second will explore three experiences across my time of working in a special Service Organization outside the MNC, starting with the failure of my "smart village" initiative, and then the subsequent successes of working with other large technology corporations to drive their government engagement on AI. I will then conclude the chapter by sharing some insights that can be used to create a strategy that aligns to the government's populist agenda.

Having served as a bridge between these two different yet ubiquitous worlds, I can only tell you this: the scope of a country to innovate can only be fully realized when these worlds are working with and for each other. Aligning business goals to concurrently serve government agendas is the "secret sauce" that will take any developing economy to the next level. I detail the so-called recipe for this secret sauce in the pages to come.

## 12.2   THE BIRTH OF A NEW BUSINESS MODEL BASED ON THE "SHIFT" (2004–2014)

### 12.2.1   Making Sense of a Challenging Mandate

During the start of my career at Intel, I was a part of the Corporate Affairs team. Our job was simple: to build and maintain Intel's relationship with the government and its institutions in the pursuit of future collaboration and expansion. I was assigned to the sphere of India's engineering universities, with the goal of influencing the curriculum to inspire and fuel a research and innovation mindset in students. What did this entail?

My role was to work closely with India's top tier of engineering colleges, the Indian institutes of technology (IITs) and National Institute of Technology, to develop an in-house research agenda that was aligned to the global technological landscape and its ever-changing needs and demands. If parallel processing was the wave of the future, I would push for a module on it to be included as a part of the curriculum. When multi-core processing was slowly being introduced, I worked to create a project that focused on building this competency in students.

What was in it for Intel, one might wonder? Why did we invest all this energy towards ensuring that the IIT curriculum was updated to reflect the latest happenings? Was it all a selfless act of philanthropy? Not quite. Intel accrued two benefits from this mutual effort. The first was that this served to develop a keen and eager pipeline for a future workforce that saw Intel as the face of technology in India. The second was that this helped build a relationship with the universities to facilitate collaborative research in the tech space.

While it certainly was successful in both these regards, how did this effort fare in building a relationship with the government? As it turned out, the government did not immediately care much about this program. While the scope of our project was certainly ambitious and admirable, the scale was dwarfed in comparison to the government's agenda. Servicing a mere handful of elite engineering colleges to build a research mindset was definitely not the need of the hour in a developing country like India, where more than one-third of the population was illiterate and suffering from systemic poverty. As our effort did not engage with the immediate demands of the populace, we were unable to truly gain any traction with the government on this initiative.

### 12.2.2   Learnings from My Counterparts and Peers at Intel

One of my counterparts at Intel had better luck while working with the K–12 school education system. The scale of this project was large enough to catch the attention of the government. As mentioned in the introduction, the agenda here was to enable the computerization of schools and use this as a means to develop a creative mindset in young students. While the scale of this project was appreciated by the government, the scope was far too ambitious to see any near-term results. In fact, Microsoft beat us to this computerizing wave with a simpler strategy. It developed software tools like Excel, PowerPoint and Word that were ready to use for administrative purposes, and it offered to teach them to government school teachers. What good is a computer if you do not know how to work it? In other words, and in the context of our approach, how can you develop a creative mindset in students when teachers themselves do not know how to use the tools intended to fuel creativity? I took note of this difference and tucked it away in my mind for future reference.

It was when I looked at my Intel counterparts in the developed ecosystem of the United States that I realized something else. The team there had built a curriculum that focused on creating a spirit of entrepreneurship. In partnership with the Haas School of Business at University of California, Berkeley, they created a program, Technology Entrepreneurship Education: Theory to Practice, that incorporated lessons learned from Silicon Valley veterans to build a comprehensive curriculum on scaling up an operation. The idea here was that once you have developed first-class research facilities and agendas, how can you commercialize this space so that these innovations can be adequately scaled and operationalized?

This was the first "shift" that I observed – the shift towards entrepreneurship as a means to empower individuals and break them out of the poverty cycle through innovation. I understood this shift as being a direct product of the success of the Silicon Valley model – the answer to monopolistic and corporate culture, the era of the disrupter. Within a decade or two of opening up its economy, India began to take this cultural and economic shift very seriously. I was fascinated by this and saw a lot of potential in aligning Intel's work in India to speak to this shift.

### 12.2.3   The Power of the "Shift"

The Congress government of that time was driving a nascent agenda of entrepreneurship in 2008, an agenda that has now been fully realized by the current

Bharatiya Janata Party government through various initiatives like Make in India and Atma Nirbhar Bharat (Hindi for "self-reliant India"). The national shift was, of course, responding to a global one. It was only after looking at the fruits of Silicon Valley's success that the Indian government sought to mimic and import a similar ecosystem here.

I ran Intel's Entrepreneurship program in India during this nascent and crucial stage and was able to strike up an important partnership with the Ministry of Science and Technology. Intel's agenda at the time was simple: to develop a problem-solving and innovative mindset amongst students in academia. Instead of focusing on enabling individual entrepreneurs through a *Shark Tank*-like approach of providing funding, they wanted to build a culture of innovation in the collective mindset of our future engineers. We partnered with business incubators in technology and engineering colleges across the country to implement this program, and we strove to supplement India's technical proficiency with a culture of business management and innovative thinking. The underlying thinking behind this was as simple as the agenda: if India's tech industry were to grow from within, Intel's share of this market would increase in proportion. The rising tide of technology would lift us all.

As a result, Intel became the first government partner in the sphere of technology entrepreneurship, and enjoyed many of the first-mover advantages, much like Microsoft did with school education. Everybody was talking about how Intel was going to help the country leapfrog from a dependent position to a self-sustained one. By helping draft the initial policy, we laid the early foundation for this wave of entrepreneurship, an agenda that also suitably addressed the populist demands of jobs. As a consequence, Intel became a friendly and trusted face in the eyes of the Indian government.

It was through this experience that I began to appreciate the power of observing and capitalizing on these "shifts". Only by identifying this shift towards entrepreneurship and by helping the government move from 0 to 1 were we able to get our foot in the door.

### 12.2.4 Taking the "Shift" to Other Countries (2010–2014)

My success with getting traction for Intel in India was followed up by another exciting opportunity: to help Intel build its relations with other emerging and developing economies in the Middle East and Africa by leveraging entrepreneurship. This was an extremely important market for Intel, not just from a diplomatic perspective (supporting the peacebuilding efforts of President Obama's US Government in the Arab world) but, more importantly, because the next billion computer users would be from emerging economies. Imagine getting in at the ground floor.

My pitch at that time was straightforward: change course from the status quo modus operandi of setting up research labs and providing bare-bone internships to Arab youth. Instead, focus on identifying the "shift" taking place in the Middle East and tailor your agenda to meet the populist demands arising from that context. The reason my model worked in India was because it addressed specific demands that arose from the economic context. Importing the model to other countries means importing that analysis to suitably tailor the strategy, not simply duplicating it.

The next step for me was clear. I travelled across countries in the Middle East and Africa from Jordan, Egypt, Tunisia and Kenya to Lebanon, Saudi Arabia and Turkey. Through these visits, I learned about the many challenges faced by MNCs while entering a politically turbulent zone. Mimicking Silicon Valley was not a near-term reality, since these countries simply did not possess the technical competencies required to set up this kind of infrastructure. With low literacy rates, even their education systems were yet to develop a curriculum that focused on innovation. These were all time-consuming and resource-draining activities and served as a barrier to MNCs (much like Intel) who hoped to engage with this region. These efforts to engage also failed mostly because they were unable to address the immediate demands of the government.

It was after many visits and brainstorming sessions that I formulated the Intel Youth Enterprise. This initiative focused on training young minds on how to open and run small businesses through the innovative use of technology. We taught them how to take simple ideas and operationalize them to ensure a steady income. Some of the businesses were quite novel. For example, one student started an online cloud service to send flowers; another opened an online bakery store. This program, we hoped, would direct a lot of the anger and violence that we saw erupt during the Arab Spring towards productive and sustainable outcomes.

How did Intel benefit from this? Again, it was straightforward. By encouraging the adoption of technology and computers for the purposes of business, Intel was laying the groundwork in its future market and getting its foot in the door at the right time. It was through this mutual benefit, this alignment of interests which is one of the characteristics of a COI, that the initiative was able to take off and, in the process, help many people empower themselves and gain economic mobility. It was also a much leaner and resource-efficient strategy for Intel for entering developing economies.

To complete the picture, my next project was focused on identifying the shift in mature and developed economies like the United Kingdom, Germany, France, Israel, China and even the United States. Intel had already lost the first-mover advantage in mobile phones, and wearable technology was looking like the next disruptor. After working closely with the Intel CEO's office, we developed the Make it Wearable initiative. Within a year, we launched a start-up at the Consumer Electronics Show in Las Vegas that focused on innovating with this technology. The driving philosophy again was to provide tech leadership to an emerging shift in innovation and facilitate a smooth market entry for this technology spearheaded by Intel.

### 12.2.5   Lessons Learned

These initial years at Intel provided the seeds for many future ideas and initiatives. It was here that I learned how to take a traditional MNC and work from within to become a social service provider in the entrepreneurship ecosystem and augment existing government initiatives. These are a few of the lessons from this experience:

- While identifying the "shift", place the initiative in the larger context of the country and populist demands to which the government is accountable: You need to keep a keen eye out to observe a shift taking place – this can be a shift in government or policy direction, a shift in innovation, a shift in technology cycles, and so on. Strike fast, because there is no better place to be than the first one through the door. Make sure that your business agenda is aligned towards this shift in a way that is addressing the populist demands and the need of the hour. Long-term goals have their place in strategy, but only when packaged together with quick wins and immediate, tangible results that the government can appreciate.
- Identify an agenda that helps the government take a big shift from 0 to 1: As any big shift takes place, getting from 0 to 1 is always the biggest challenge for the government. There are more questions than it can handle and no concrete answers in sight. It is in this space that experimental pilots and scaled-down interventions make sense. Governments are eager to find thought-partners who can help them co-create an agenda from a simple idea borne out of the shift. This approach is exactly how Intel was able to accomplish an agenda of driving entrepreneurship for 15 years in partnership with the government of India.
- As an MNC, make your philanthropy and corporate social responsibility (CSR) strategy robust: While philanthropy certainly has its place, MNCs are definitely not its primary drivers. There is no dearth of innovative business models that can be employed to augment existing government initiatives and make positive, lasting social change as part of your CSR strategy. You need to engage with the cultural and economic context and build your model around the existing coordinates set forth by this map. If the approach is right and the plan is solid, there is benefit to be shared on both sides.

With these insights, Jobs and Tech Leadership became my two go-to pillars for any corporate strategy when working with the government. For the most part, this strategy worked to deliver some of Intel's successes that I have outlined above. Building on this accomplishment, I began to think about leaving my corporate job and helping other companies do business with the "bottom of the pyramid" and align to the government's agenda. This led to the birth of my smart village initiative.

## 12.3 TAKING MY MODEL TO THE VILLAGES: REORIENTATION THROUGH FAILURE (2015–2016)

### 12.3.1 Sensing Opportunity at the "Bottom of the Pyramid"

After getting the initial taste of success at Intel, I started thinking of new ways to test and further solidify my working model. I decided to take my experience and migrate to what most economists called the "bottom of the pyramid" by embedding myself in local and rural economic networks instead of traditional MNCs.

It was at this moment that I ended up establishing a special Service Organization by the name of 1 Million for 1 Billion (1M 1B). This was to fill an absence that I had sensed in the ecosystem – an absence of what you might call a Hybrid Organization. There was a need to bring a culture of innovation and creativity to traditional civil society organizations and non-profit organizations. This was the mindset missing in the development ecosystem. In a hybrid organization, I could help drive corporate agendas and partner with the government to assist with the execution. Taking the intentions and capabilities of a corporation and marrying it with a government mandate seemed like the only way to adequately address certain populist demands.

We first established 1M 1B as a 501(c)(3) non-profit organization in 2014 in the United States. The idea at the time was to initially work and generate funding/partnerships there and eventually shift our work across the world, with a big focus on India. I founded the organization with my sister, who had a background in healthcare, which allowed us to focus on both entrepreneurship and health as a two-pronged agenda. The vision was simple: to activate a million people and help them impact a billion people and create a world with balanced prosperity. The offering was even simpler: we will work with organizations and provide them with a framework and some funding to execute our joint vision. As the umbrella organization, we also planned to showcase great work done by these non-profits. Our partnership and accreditation with the United Nations (UN) allowed us to host our first annual summit in the UN Headquarters in New York within six months of starting up.

The early strategy was to keep the non-profit status in the United States and work with like-minded non-profits from other developing countries in the Middle East, Africa, Caribbean and Vietnam. We would subcontract the program to these organizations and provide funding and advisory support to run experiments in the field of student innovation. This strategy did not work as well as we thought for the first two years – outsourcing experiments proved to be a challenge as a lot of the work required iteration since it was all quite new (digital innovations and AI for good, as examples, were still extremely nascent ideas from 2014 to 2016). Organizations that mostly specialized in execution and implementation did not possess the necessary skill sets to engage with ideas that were at an experimental stage.

As if a sign from God, a policy shift came in 2016 in India in the form of a law mandating all business entities in India to allocate 2 per cent of their profit stream towards development work by way of CSR. This made us rethink our strategy and consider establishing a team there to conduct the experiments ourselves. We subsequently put together a team and established a non-profit in India around that time to tap into this CSR funding and leverage it to develop a regional innovation cluster that focused on AI. From being at the top of the pyramid, we decided to migrate to the bottom and get our hands a little dirty. The agenda we started with was that of smart villages.

There was an interesting discursive shift taking place in the realm of rural development at the time. The emergence of the concept of smart cities had prompted policy-makers and economists to think about utilizing the power of digitizing a region to transform the bulk of rural India through a smart village initiative. This policy discourse was inspired by the vision of Mahatma Gandhi's philosophy of an *Adarsh Gram* (an ideal village), and thus quickly picked up traction in political circles. Could this be India's solution towards addressing the growing rural/urban divide and strengthening India's village economy?

It is important to understand why India's villages were such an important area of focus. Although the population of India is becoming younger and more urban (the urban population increased from 20 per cent in 1960 to 35 per cent in 2011), more than 65 per cent of the country's population is in the rural hinterlands (2011 Census data). With a total of over 680,000 villages, it is difficult to imagine our country developing without including our rural villages. While "smart cities" were trending across the globe, India was using this as an opportunity to leverage this development model to champion an initiative that was truly inclusive by fixing its own backyards first.

Everybody had their own idea of what this *Adarsh Gram* could look like. IT experts said it should be an internet-enabled village with smart classrooms, tele-medicine and smartphones. Infrastructure companies, on the other hand, thought that a smart village should have better roads, better access to hospitals and more public facilities. Others said that we should improve the agricultural set-up in the villages. It was difficult to arrive at any kind of consensus and there were more questions than answers. This was the coveted 0-to-1 space that I spoke of in the earlier section, the sweet spot to enable the government to take a big action.

On top of this, there was a history of most corporations struggling with their rural initiatives. MNCs had tried to do work in rural villages in the past but had difficulty in seeing any kind of success. Scaling up operations always posed a resource challenge and most operations had to be outsourced to local non-governmental organizations. Most corporations struggled to work in villages because they had no channel through which to gain an audience with the local populace. This absence rendered most of their initiatives as top-down with no representation of the target audience.

What if I could establish and embed a high-quality workforce within the villages to work with the population? What if we could make this a research facility that helps the locals express what they need and co-create it with other companies? In other words, what if I built this missing channel as a bridge between the corporates and villages? This could be a game-changer, especially given the current traction around digitizing smart villages. I got my team at 1M 1B to work on this immediately.

### 12.3.2   Building a Bridge is Harder than It Looks

While different stakeholders struggled to agree on what this smart village could be, there was no "wrong" direction or agenda per se. What we needed to do was narrow down the gamut of solutions by involving the local populace and co-creating the last-mile delivery with the companies. The villagers best knew what they needed. We made a small village in the East Godavari region of Andhra Pradesh in Southern India our lab to test this model.

The first thing I decided to focus on was sourcing a high-quality workforce to work as an intermediary between the companies and the villages. I looked for Teach for India[1] alumni, graduates from the best universities and corporate stalwarts who wanted to give back to society to create a high-quality team who could work to operationalize the vision.

After building this team, we did two things. The first was to build a representation of the people in the villages. We went door-to-door informing them of our work and asking them questions to assess their needs and economic demands. In parallel, we decided to take a page out of University of California, Berkeley's pioneering work on open innovation by setting up an open innovation lab and inviting many companies to join. The lab would also be open to everybody to access and give their feedback on the products being innovated.

While speaking with the villagers, we learned of many problems they faced. We then took such issues – the lack of functional electricity in the house, clunky water-purification technology or an absence of education technology in schools – to large corporations in Silicon Valley in the hope of developing novel technological solutions to address these contextual problems.

We managed to get close to 50 large companies to participate in these open innovation labs and submit their technology for consideration. There were two aspects to this participation: technological innovation and business model innovation. While most companies were able to handle the technology applications, many struggled with applying their fixed business model to the ever-changing local context of each of these villages. It was here that we provided some value. By promising to facilitate and co-create the last-mile delivery, we helped make products business-ready by working on the finer aspects of price points, potential avenues to finance the production and even small changes to the user interface to make it more user-friendly.

The villagers were able to express their problems, the companies were developing technology that directly addressed their needs and my team was working as an intermediary to make these products a reality. Everything seemed like it was in place. I even gave a TEDx talk on the underlying philosophy of this business model, which was received at the time as a pathbreaking and visionary solution. This is probably why it took us all by surprise when the idea completely tanked.

### 12.3.3   Hindsight Is Not Foresight

Was I naive to think that the barrier to meaningful engagement between the village and corporates was the absence of a bridge? Perhaps. It is only after reflecting with the gift of hindsight that I was able to understand that the larger underlying issues embedded within the political environment and local workforce development were responsible for obstructing rural and corporate engagement.

As I mentioned earlier, getting corporations to engage in rural agendas was never an easy task. The government charter was a populist one and the only thing it wanted from companies was to drive investment in the region by addressing either agriculture, jobs or education. Companies possessed neither the expertise nor the resources to adequately address these spheres at scale, and it became very challenging for most to cultivate a working relationship with the government under these conditions.

The smart village initiative came in as low-hanging fruit for corporates eager to build relations with the government. It did not require intensive resources or an extensive agenda and provided easy access to good public relations. The fact that it was merely a marketing exercise and a feature in a case study for these companies meant that they sent no actual brain power or researchers. They stopped at providing the technology and did not provide inputs during the last-mile delivery. Without their complete buy-in, the initiative was bound to peter out and become nothing more than a consumer electronics show for corporates in the villages.

We realized that this project was heading towards failure 20 days before our presentation to the chief minister of the state. In that small timeframe, we realized that what we actually should have done was to outsource this last-mile creation to rural entrepreneurs who were far better placed to execute this model in local contexts. To salvage what we could, we spent those 20 days mobilizing these entrepreneurs to create and pitch their own start-up or product ideas to the chief minister. Maybe we could still create some positive impact in their lives.

It was unfortunate that on the day of the presentation, the corporates ended up maximizing their face-time with the political leaders until the chief minister had to leave because of bad weather. The rural entrepreneurs never got to pitch their ideas, and to this day I remember seeing their faces fall in disappoint- ment. At the end of the day, it was the villagers who gained the least from and worked the most for this initiative. The question that was burnt into my mind was still the same: how can we help empower these people?

### 12.3.4 Lessons Learned

While the smart village initiative definitely proved to be a compelling story, it failed to make any real impact. What are some of the lessons to be learned from this failure?

- No equal counterpart at the "top of the pyramid": Something I did not realize while migrating to the bottom of the pyramid was that, without a counterpart at the top, there would be nobody to drive this agenda and push the corporations to sense the larger opportunity at hand. There was nobody who could mobilize these tech companies to send their best people and develop their agenda in tandem with the government. This severely impacted the coherence of the strategy. In setting up my hybrid organiza- tion, I realized that I had embedded it too deep into the grassroots, whereas the center of gravity should have been closer to the corporates.
- We failed to embed this initiative within the education system: The team that we set up was not in partnership with any of the local education bodies, and our strategy did not address teachers and students. As I look back at my time with Intel, the one key take-away from its overall approach was its determination to influence and shape the curriculum of education insti- tutions to align with the broader agenda being driven. Building capacity at

the local level and investing in this educational development was crucial to gain trust and embed yourself within the system.

- Utilize your strengths, and do not go backpacking in muddy waters: I realize now that my time and effort would have been better spent driving the corporations to align their agendas to the government and giving them a recipe on how to work with people in the villages. The education system should have been driving the research and innovation, instead of the corporations. While my temporary migration certainly taught me a lot, the biggest lesson it gave me was to go back to doing what I was best at.

## 12.4    HOMECOMING (2018 ONWARDS)

### 12.4.1    Embracing the Wave of AI

As one door closes, another opens. My work with the smart village initiative caught the attention of IBM, which was looking for somebody to shape its skilling and education initiatives under CSR with the aim of growing India's digital workforce and getting young people future-ready. As with Intel, the agenda was similar: to strengthen India's technology culture and industry in the hopes of increasing IBM's size of the pie. As with Intel, IBM had to focus on ensuring that it was able to align itself to the government populist mandate. I was more than eager to jump back into the familiar waters of aligning corporate agendas with "shifts" in the economy and government demands.

After spending three years of experimenting with 1M 1B, we were ready to scale. In this time, we were able to figure out a structure for the team, which we brought to IBM in 2019 to help us scale and implement our strategy for its skill development program. We concurrently established ourselves as a full-fledged non-profit with an ability to attract and secure CSR funding after adhering to the necessary compliances. The program worked towards skilling unemployed individuals and creating linkages to secure them with jobs. We further partnered with IBM to help it develop its AI for Good strategy for schools. The pilot is currently being scaled in 300 schools, covering 15,000 students and 10,000 teachers. It was through this corporate partnership and the CSR funds that we were able to execute our vision.

This move also worked to remedy some of the mistakes of the smart village initiative. I realized that in the initial years of 1M 1B, I had situated my program too closely to the grassroots and, in doing so, lost my vantage point and my strengths. This initiative with IBM brought me back to working with corporate agendas and helping them devise implementation strategies. If 1M 1B were to be successful, our functions would need to bridge across the three stakeholders of corporations, governments and education systems.

The big shift taking place during this time was the emerging wave of AI or machine learning. People were talking about how we could use AI to impact climate change, improve economic development and, when deployed responsibly, create positive social impact. I sensed an opportunity to marry my own personal agenda of developing the villages with the AI agenda. Maybe I could finally bring a smile to those disappointed faces using the power of AI. This could be a homecoming in more ways than one.

However, as in the early phases of any shift, AI was greeted with suspicion and reluctance: "Will it take away our jobs?" "Will it make half of our work redundant?" "What kind of new jobs will it create?" The challenge was to help people understand that AI was ultimately a language to articulate and express solutions, a tool that empowers.

Melinda Gates spoke at an International Monetary Fund (IMF) event in Bali, Indonesia, around this time. She recounted that these were exactly the kind of questions being asked when Excel first launched. Accountants were scared that they would lose their jobs and become redundant. As we now know, quite the opposite happened. Excel birthed a new kind of accountant with a specialized expertise and provided them with the tools to efficiently and easily carry out their jobs. Ms Gates predicted that this would happen with AI as well. It might take away a few jobs, but in the long run AI is going to create new and *better* jobs. I took these words seriously and worked with IBM to help the government ride this wave instead of working against it, working in the 0 to 1 space once again.

Learning from past mistakes, I did not execute this agenda immediately, but rather spent a year investigating the problems and the role that AI could play. I worked closely with teachers, held focus group meetings to co-develop the strategy and involved the local system of education in the project's development stage. Through the smart village initiative, I realized that involving stakeholders in the execution stage was too little too late. They needed to be included from the very start.

## 12.4.2   Working with India's Industrial Training Institutes

According to India's latest census data (see Figure 12.1), formal educational training is a privilege enjoyed by a small percentage of the population. Most girls end up dropping out from school and do not even make it beyond 10th grade. It is under this backdrop that India's industrial training institutes (ITIs) become important, since these institutions provide hope in the form of vocational training allowing the local workforce to stay in the villages and get better jobs.

If we wanted to ease the adoption of AI by the masses, there was no better place than to start with India's 15,000 ITIs, whose target demographic was the low- to medium-skilled workforce. The Eleventh Five-Year Plan of India also launched a National Skill Development Mission in 2007 that sought to restructure and expand India's vocational training to empower individuals to seek better jobs in their hometowns instead of migrating to the city. This would foster a spirit of rural development and localized economic growth.

I suggested that IBM partner with the Ministry of Skills and Development to include AI as a part of the ITI curriculum. We built this curriculum in collaboration with the ministry, including suggestions for how AI could be utilized to improve one's skills and get better jobs.

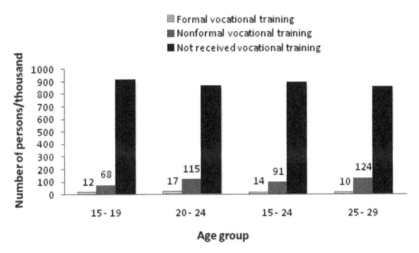

*Source:*    Report No. 517 by the National Sample Survey Office, India.

*Figure 12.1    Vocational training in India*

### 12.4.3    How Can We Forget the School Education System?

This was, of course, a Band-Aid to tide over the longer process of using AI to drive systemic reform. ITIs were simply treating an existing problem. How could we prevent this problem from even arising? In parallel, I convinced IBM to work with schools earlier in the education system. We pushed the Ministry of Education and the Central Board of Secondary Education to include AI as early as in the high schools. We advocated to not include AI simply under the Computer Science curriculum. AI is a language and thus should be integrated in the classroom across many subjects, as useful to the biology teacher as to the language instructor.

As a further step, I worked to pilot an AI module for students as a part of their project-based learning. Students who opted for this project had to learn how to use AI in order to create a solution that would serve farmers in the villages. This was nothing but old wine in a new bottle – a new version of the smart village initiative. Students came up with some brilliant ideas, including a chatbot for girls to give tips on sanitary health and an AI bot that helped tally accounts and gave financial tips. Over 10,000 students participated in this project and worked towards a vision of creating and deploying AI responsibly. The pilot proved to be a big success and is now being scaled across 300 schools. We are setting up a global academy of teachers where over 10,000 teachers will get trained on this module so that they can implement it in their schools and engage 150,000 students in AI.

These two initiatives demonstrated the potential power of including the education system in aligning corporate and government agendas. This was actually a leaner and smarter version of the smart village initiative. Crowdsourcing innovative solutions and ideas from bright minds to drive systemic reform in the villages worked this time because we chose to situate 1M 1B with the apex regulatory body, while working with schools and devising implementation strategies for curriculum roll-outs. This allowed us to create and be the bridge between IBM and other ministries to align their interests through a joint agenda.

### 12.4.4   Lessons Learned

Now that the model of bridging corporate and government agendas had been successfully tested, I wanted to apply it to other organizational agendas. Currently we are working with Adobe, Facebook and Amazon on how to use AI, augmented reality (AR) and virtual reality (VR) to enhance creativity. This aligns with the most recent shift towards integrating problem-solving and creativity in classrooms in India, ushered in by the 2020 National Education Policy. What better way to respond to this shift than to leverage the power of AI and other digital technologies?

Another shift taking place all over the world is towards digital learning, caused by the widespread crisis brought about by Covid-19. As schools continued to remain closed for over a year, discussions around how to make classrooms more engaging carried on with little progress. To address this problem, we are working with Adobe to leverage its creative cloud and AI tools to infuse a virtual classroom experience with some flavour. Can we enable teachers to create videos and lessons using these tools and help them over time build their own capacity to teach?

AI is primed to propel us into the 21st century and expedite our digital revolution, starting from our classrooms. However, with this revolution also comes digital fatigue – all of us can relate to excessive screen-time and mental exhaustion. Digital wellness and digital citizenship is an agenda waiting to be picked up as a priority area by the government. Cyber-security is another 0-to-1 space that we are yet to act on. As we embrace technology, we must also be cognizant of the electronic waste that will be produced. It becomes imperative to think about how companies can work with the government to green our digital future and recycle this waste.

Indeed, the future has many new challenges in store for us. The only thing that I can say with confidence about the years to come is that I will continue working with companies to help them pick the right agenda to align with government and other players to embrace the shifts of our times.

## 12.5   CONCLUDING REMARKS

In addition to the lessons learned at each juncture through my 20-plus years of experimenting with different strategies and roles, there are a few broader lessons that I would like to highlight. I hope this encourages others to work towards strengthening and connecting the various moving parts in their own COI to drive meaningful change.

- There is a place for everything.

    There is an underlying organizational context within which I operated in each phase of my experience. I started my journey by working within the corporate structure at Intel and driving an agenda of entrepreneurship that was able to align itself to fulfil a government mandate of jobs. Upon shifting out of Intel and occupying the role of a hybrid special Service Organization as 1M 1B, I was able to realize different roles and experiments that could be run while working independently – things I could not do from within Intel. And it was only after moving closer to the corporates as 1M 1B that I was able to successfully carry out my vision.

    Each context and space requires a different solution and strategy. Whether you are working as an independent organization or as the government, you need to curate your strategy by fully acknowledging where you are situated and what strengths that position provides. Appreciate that regardless of how ambitious your vision might be, you are still functioning within a COI where each stakeholder has a stake and role to play.
- More importantly, there is a time for everything.

    I have used the term "shift" very often throughout this chapter. It is important to further explain this phenomenon and why it is so important to time your agenda.

    There are hundreds of ideas and agendas out there that are trying to take off. They are in what I call the 0-to-1 phase (seeding and piloting). For example, the agenda of digital wellness and digital citizenship exists within this phase. A few corporates might be seeding this idea and a few others might be running small-scale pilots and experiments, but there is not yet any discernible traction at the systemic level for this idea.

Then comes a change in the external environment – be it an economic crisis, an ecological one or even a worldwide health crisis. This change acts as a trigger to elevate a certain agenda from the 0-to-1 phase to the 1-to-2 phase (scaling and implementation). Some of the "shifts" of the last two decades are summarized in Table 12.1.

*Table 12.1     List of a few of the agendas in India that "shifted"*

| Agenda | When did it "shift" from 0-to-1 to 1-to-2? | Triggered by |
|---|---|---|
| Entrepreneurship | 2008 | Loss of jobs and livelihoods |
| Digital adoption of smartphones in villages | 2016 | Launch of the Jio 4G network by Reliance Telecom |
| The "gig" economy | 2016 | Loss of jobs and livelihoods |
| Digital skills revolution (Fourth Industrial Revolution) | 2020 | Covid-19 lockdown |
| AI | Yet to fully transition | Future jobs and automation |
| AR and VR | Yet to fully transition | 2020 National Education Policy |
| Digital wellness and citizenship | Yet to fully transition | Online schooling: children spending more time at home due to the closure of schools |
| Environmental, social and governance (ESG) | Yet to fully transition | Dow Jones Sustainability Index |

The first shift I mentioned was towards an agenda of entrepreneurship in 2008. Its success can be explained by the fact that it was triggered by the increasing loss of jobs and a populist desire for economic mobility. The other "shifts" that I worked on (those of wearable technology and smart villages) are ideas that continue to remain in the 0-to-1 phase to this date, which perhaps explains their relative failure. They are yet to be scaled and implemented at a systemic level because there was no trigger to highlight their urgency. They did not meet any populist or market demand. A trigger can be anything: changes in the economy, ecological disasters, techno-logical innovations, cultural processes or even terrorist attacks. However, regardless of its source, the shift is triggered in four important spheres that dictate policy direction and populist support: jobs, food, healthcare and social inclusion. This leads to the 2-to-3 phase (policy integration and adoption), where systematic changes are formalized as part of the surrounding context.

The key task necessary to leverage the opportunity of "shifts" is to look for the different ways that certain global or national events can serve as triggers to elevate agendas. At present, we have seen the Covid-19-induced lockdown (a health crisis) trigger and elevate the agenda of digital inclusion, what many are calling the Fourth Industrial Revolution. The interactions between these shifts and their manifestations are complex and specific to each context.

To ride the waves of emerging "shifts", it is important to understand the underlying agendas of major COI players as well as the forces driving the trigger events. Successful initiatives and strategies arise through the recognition and alignment of the agendas of COI components – such as Major Corporations and Government – leading to win–win solutions and to satisfying the populist or market demands. Sometimes bridging these different agendas and moving ideas into piloting and experimentation (the 0-to-1 phase) and then on into scaling and implementation (the 1-to-2 phase) can be accomplished within existing corporate or government organizations. Sometimes it is necessary to work outside existing structures in order to take the necessary steps. Special Service Organizations, such as 1M 1B, can play a significant role in bridging these agendas. In any case, the two questions that must always be asked are: am I currently occupying the most optimal role in my COI? And how can I tailor my agenda to meet the ever-changing needs of the present time? Being innovative means being at the right place in the right time – where preparation meets opportunity.

## NOTE

1.    Teach For India (TFI) is a non-profit organization and a movement of leaders that was founded by Shaheen Mistri in 2009, and is a part of the Teach For All network. It runs a two-year Fellowship program that recruits promising college graduates and working professionals to serve as full-time teachers in low-income schools for two years.

## REFERENCES

Berkeley's pioneering work on open innovation: https://corporateinnovation.berkeley .edu/.

IMF and World Bank Group 2018 Annual Meetings schedule: https://meetings.imf.org/ en/2018/Annual/Schedule.

Intel Youth Enterprise: https://blogs.intel.com/csr/2011/09/power_of_dreams_and _imaginatio/#gs.dbbs71.

Make it Wearable Initiative: https://newsroom.intel.com/news-releases/intel-make-it -wearable-challenge-shines-spotlight-on-judges-who-will-help-set-the-stage-for -future-wearable-technology/#gs.dbbkym.

Manav Subodh's Amazon page: www.amazon.com/Manav-Subodh/e/B018BCPEKE %3Fref=dbs_a_mng_rwt_scns_share.

Melinda Gates speaking at an IMF event: https://edition.cnn.com/videos/tv/2018/10/ 12/news-stream-intv-melinda-gates-imf-world-bank-bali.cnn.

Rural and urban population distribution in India, 1960–2011, sourced from 2011 Census Data from the Office of the Registrar General, India: https://censusindia.gov .in/.

Technology entrepreneurship education: www.berkeley.edu/news/media/releases/ 2005/08/01_ih.shtml.

# 13. Australian Sports Technologies Network: adding value through creating synergies

## James Demetriou, Martin Schlegel and Danny Samson[1]

### 13.1 INTRODUCTION: WHAT IS SPORTS TECHNOLOGY?

This chapter documents the development of Australia's sports cluster, centered and coordinated around the Australian Sports Technologies Network (ASTN). We begin with a detailed description of sports technology and its quite recent development as an industry, then trace the development of the ASTN-centered ecosystem and its components. Finally, we consider how, having developed as a domestic cluster, this ecosystem based in Australia has been incrementally developing regional and global networks and bonds.

### 13.2 BACKGROUND

'No money, no medals', the Australian prime minister was told by athletes full of what the Australian media entitled 'Aussie anger' in a 'day of tension'. What had happened?

As Australian Olympic gymnast Phil Cheetham recounted, it had been a very informal and non-confrontational conversation between athletes returning from the 1976 Olympic Games in Montreal and the prime minister. Australian Olympic team members were attending a welcome reception and outlined to the prime minister how other countries' approach to sport and athlete support 'easily outstripped Australia'.[2] As a country, Australia 'failed to win a gold medal at the Montreal Olympics, which was regarded as a national embarrassment'[3] to the country.

According to the archived timeline of the Australian Institute of Sport (AIS),[4] the AIS was established in early 1980 as a high-performance sports training institution located in the Australian Capital Territory of Canberra.

Since the early days, the AIS had been encouraging and enabling 'the best research in the country to pursue new technologies, practices, ways of teaching and learning, and systems specifically designed to boost high performance outcomes'.[5] Based on his interest in electronics, Phil Cheetham commenced studies in electrical engineering in Sydney, Australia, before continuing his pursuit to qualify for a second Olympics by moving to the US at the end of the 1970s. Whilst training at Arizona State University he enrolled in a master's degree in biomechanics. 'Combining science and his sport'[6] as his master's thesis, Phil created motion analysis software to digitize and annotate, frame by frame, body joint movement for gymnasts. From these early beginnings, Phil ended up taking a position working for the US Olympic and Paralympic Committee at the Olympic Training Center in Chula Vista, California, where his position as a sport technologist working with track and field athletes evolved into being director of sport technology and innovation.

Whilst Phil might not be the only or first former athlete who combined a passion for sport with an interest in science and technology, his story highlights that at the intersection of human performance and science, technology, engineering and math (STEM), a discipline evolved which we, as of today, refer to as 'sports technology' or 'sportstech'. However, it is important to note that sportstech entails more than sports equipment, apparel, protective supplies or materials. Indeed today, besides on-the-field technologies used in monitoring health and improving performance of athletes of all abilities, off-the-field technologies involving sports business applications, fan engagement, broadcasting, sports infrastructure and communication are also considered part of sportstech. As such, the taxonomy of sportstech has become a widely discussed topic by defining the application verticals within the sports sector and combining these with the technologies impacting sports on and off the playing field. When defining sportstech, it is important to not only look at the underlying technologies but also define their application or uses in sport. On the one side, a matrix can help define how different technologies, like materials, sensors, data and others, assist in providing solutions to users ranging from athletes and consumers to managers.[7] On the other side, from an application point of view, a sportstech framework distinguishing technologies between activity and performance, fans and content, management and organization as well as eSports has been introduced to assist in creating a common understanding of the sportstech industry and its structure.[8]

Nevertheless, a technology stack combining machinery, equipment, infrastructure, materials, hardware, software and services which find utilization in sport seems to be better suited to describe and categorize the technologies used in sports and aggregated as sportstech. The sportstech stack groups more than 30 different technologies into four main categories, from advanced materials, sensors and devices, medical, health and biotech to communication technologies (see Figure 13.1). In particular, the ever-growing segment of communication technologies used in sports now spans from artificial intelligence (AI) and machine learning (ML) algorithms to big data analytics, broadcasting, media content and social media. As data analytics of cloud-based, personalized and identifiable athlete data become more prevalent, questions in relation to privacy and cyber-security have been elevated as part of the sportstech discussion. This also includes the ever more important compliance question as data services provided on a global basis must comply with the specific requirements in the respective local or regional jurisdiction where they are made accessible. Specifically, examples like the European Union's General Data Protection Regulation and the California Consumer Privacy Act illustrate some of the complexity in this regard. However, the notion that governmental regulation can spur innovation and competitive adoption in sportstech can be likened to the history of environmental policy and regulation in California stimulating and incentivizing innovation as described by Vogel.[9]

Furthermore, as events, venues and stadiums must accommodate patron safety and provide incident-contract-tracing, paperless and remote ticketing solutions, for example, built on blockchain technology or using advanced biometric recognition technologies, like facial recognition, have been deployed in sportstech as part of event and facility management.

| Communication Technology | | | | Advanced Materials | |
|---|---|---|---|---|---|
| AI/ML | Analytics | AR/VR | Big Data | Fibers & Textiles | Composites |
| Blockchain | Broadcasting | Cloud | eSports & Fantasy | | |
| Media & Content | Mobile | Privacy | Remote Cellular - Broadbent | Coatings, Adhesive & Elastomers | Nano Materials |
| Security & Cyber | Social Media | Streaming OTT | Wagering | | |
| Biomechanics | | Cognition & Psychology | | IoT | Wearables |
| Nutrition | | Strength & Conditioning | | Video | Robotics |
| Medical, Health & Biotech | | | | Sensors & Devices | |

*Source:* Schlegel (2020)[10].

*Figure 13.1    The Sportstech Stack*

Interestingly, in the late 1990s an Australian-developed wearable sensor technology was advanced through a partnership between the AIS and the federal government's Cooperative Research Centre. It was originally developed to maximize the performance of Australian athletes at the 2000 Sydney

Olympics, and an elite-athlete wearable company using a global navigation satellite system was later founded in Melbourne in 2006.[11]

The example highlights how a wearable sensor technology is used to collect athletes' training and competition sports performance data. However, such activity data is not only used to monitor and improve athletes' performance. In addition to the on-field application, data is, for example, analyzed and provided in the form of statistics to broadcasters and in the form of analytics to the wagering markets. Furthermore, the example highlights how the company's business model has evolved from sensor and device hardware sales to a software-as-a-service offering. Since its early days, the sports technology company has been listed on the Australian stock exchange and is globally working with professional sports teams in all major professional leagues – all the different codes of football, basketball and stick-and-ball games across almost 3,000 teams and 40 sports.

In addition, the example underlines how a political focus on the importance of high-performance sport has assisted in disseminating key information, promoting innovation and contributing to research agendas. Using targeted government funding combined with creating partnerships and assisting commercialization of research can be seen as a prime example of the 'entrepreneurial state', as introduced by Mazzucato.[12]

Given the origins and history of the AIS, Australian-born sports technologies have traditionally focused on on-the-field human performance technologies. However, when looking beyond elite sports to fitness, wellness and health, the 'business of sport' extends beyond sports performance to a number of off-the-field technologies. Based on the idea that sport is an application rather than a sector, technology applications including software and apps, ML, AI, blockchain, advanced manufacturing, robotics, the Internet of Things, big data analytics, augmented/virtual reality, 3D printing, advanced materials, genomics and life sciences including biotech and medtech, as well as autonomous systems, can nowadays find use in sport. The State Government of Victoria, through its startup agency LaunchVic, commissioned professional services firm KPMG to analyze the state of the ecosystem, identify stakeholders and assess some of the opportunities sportstech is providing.[13] Looking at uses of sportstech, the analysis identified five application verticals, ranging from social media, marketing and fan engagement to stadiums and facilities, wearables and performance technologies, sports analytics and event management technology. Furthermore, the report recognized with eSports and media, broadcasting and sponsorship two additional segments that expanded the application use of sportstech (see Figure 13.2).

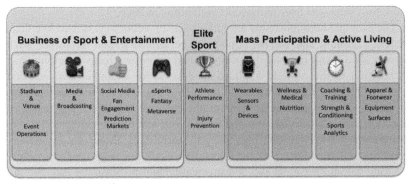

*Source:*     ASTN (2020)[14].

*Figure 13.2     Expanded application uses of sportstech and adjacent industry sectors*

The report affirmed ASTN's perspective that sportstech intersects with other key industries: 'With one of the objectives of sportstech being to enhance human performance, there is an unsurprisingly significant crossover with other sectors, in particular health.'[15] The analysis, therefore, confirmed a concept that the ASTN had observed from very early stages: sportstech provided opportunities for cross-market knowledge-transfer and collaboration opportunities. As such, human resources, retail, tourism, security, health and wellbeing, medtech, big data analytics, business management, gaming and media/entertainment were identified as some of the other sectors to benefit from a collaboration with sportstech. The analysis also confirmed the notion of sportstech as a testing and validation ground for these cross-market segments. Furthermore, the report acknowledged how government leadership and support has acted as a catalyst to drive sector establishment and equated government activities to other sectors; for example, the Victorian biotech sector in the early 2000s or the fintech sector in the Australian state of New South Wales (NSW). Finally, the analysis concluded that, first, globally and locally sportstech is a fast-growing sector, and second, the ASTN's home in the state of Victoria 'holds the undisputed position as the sporting capital of Australia' in what the report concluded to be a 'strong and credible sportstech sector'.[16]

13.3 THE AUSTRALIAN SPORTS TECHNOLOGIES
NETWORK: THE FORMATIVE YEARS (2010–2017)
– A PIONEER IN DEVELOPING A SPORTS
TECHNOLOGY CLUSTER OF INNOVATION

In 2010, sports technology as an industry was only considered to be in its
infancy. Fast-forward 10 years, sportstech is synonymous with the development and evolution of the US$800 billion global sports industry. Today, we
think of wearable technologies; sports data and video analytics; and stadium,
event and broadcast technologies, as well as advances in performance wear
and sports equipment, as examples of sportstech innovations. Sportstech is
nowadays considered as important as other technology fields like healthtech,
medtech or fintech, to name just a few.

The emergence of world-class sports innovations from Australia in the early
2000s (coinciding with the Sydney Olympics in 2000), complemented by the
country's highly regarded track record in sports performance, events management and sports science and coaching expertise, provided the platform to
establish a coordinated approach to developing and promoting the sportstech.
This rise in importance along with increasing awareness provided the primary
impetus for developing the ASTN and its mandate and mission to educate and
build the structure of the sportstech ecosystem in Australia and beyond.

Today, there are almost 50 sportstech clusters, networks and accelerator
programs globally, mainly located in the key sports markets of the US, Europe
and the UK. Many of the world's largest sports clubs, federations, leagues and
brands are now either leading or participating in these initiatives to either/both
accelerate technology development and/or uptake of technologies within their
organizations. These initiatives have taken many forms with various mandates
– some industry- or government-led, some league- or club-led, whilst others
have had corporate and venture capital seeds.

As a pioneer in leading a coordinated approach to developing a regional
sportstech ecosystem, the ASTN has become a highly respected member of
the international sports technology community. Its initiatives and programs
were the first of their kind in the world for the industry and have helped to
promote Australia's industry and connect it to the world. It has provided
the basis for developing long-term relationships with many leading leagues,
federations, clubs and other sportstech initiatives in key markets, and provided
a coordinated platform for Australia's leading sports innovators to take their
technologies to the world.

### 13.3.1    The Grassroots: From Building Early 'Weak Ties' to 'Durable Bonds'

The seeds for establishment of the ASTN began in 2010 when a group of Australian sports technologies companies discussed how working together could improve their businesses. The potential for coordinated global marketing of technologies and expertise was a focus of these discussions and remains a key objective of the ASTN to this day.

Around the same time ICT Geelong – a regional IT cluster based just outside Melbourne's metro area in the state of Victoria – was exploring opportunities to build national and international recognition of the region's IT industry. The concept of 'IT and sports' was identified as a potential niche opportunity. The region was home to one of the only globally recognized surfing clusters. It produced the likes of Rip Curl and Quiksilver that were global leaders in surfboard and wetsuit innovation and surf fashion. Leading research institutions were also based in the region, including Australia's national science research agency, the Commonwealth Scientific and Industrial Research Organisation (CSIRO), and Deakin University, who both worked with sports federations and firms to develop technology-based innovations in sports.

Between 2010 and 2011, the concept of a sports technology network developed through consultations with stakeholders including numerous firms, research institutions, sports federations, commercialization experts and investors with capabilities vested in developing the industry. Reflecting this interest and building on these casual networking exchanges ('weak ties'[17]), ICT Geelong, supported by a partnership with CSIRO and the AIS, elevated an 'IT and sports' stream into its annual investment pitching competition. More than 30 innovations were submitted to the competition, with the stream being won by Griffith University's QSports Technologies arm, for its wireless swimming device.

In October 2011, the federal government's Department of Innovation, Industry, Science and Research (via the Enterprise Connect[18] Innovative Regions Centre in Geelong) organized a workshop with 30 delegates which was facilitated by Prof. Jerry Engel from the University of California, Berkeley (UC Berkeley). Prof. Engel, as a global expert in Clusters of Innovation (COI) and venture capital education, shared his insights and experience as founder of the Lester Center for Entrepreneurship and Innovation at UC Berkeley. The workshop explored the viability of formalizing a network or cluster to pursue industry growth opportunities, which resulted in developing a business case to establish the ASTN with those in attendance identified as founding members.

In Prof. Engel's opinion the initiative opened up 'a genuine opportunity to develop the Australian sports technologies industry with the involvement of the quality and diverse range of expert stakeholders present at today's workshop'.

Led by an industry advisor at the federal government's Department of Innovation, Industry, Science and Research, the business case to establish the ASTN along with written support extended by more than 20 stakeholders was presented to Kate Lundy, Federal Minister for Sport and Assisting Minister for Industry and Innovation. In her role as Federal Minister and Senator at the time, Ms Lundy announced a two-year funding grant in April 2012 to establish the ASTN in the regional city of Geelong. Funding provided under the grant extended to supported initiatives including an annual sportstech conference, innovation masterclasses and bootcamps, pitching competitions and the development of membership and digital marketing collateral. In addition, the grant allocated funding to conduct an industry market study as well as the development of an industry export plan. As such, the government funding laid the foundation for the ASTN mandate to establish the first 'durable bonds' in the form of contractual and recurring relationships on both a domestic and, for the first time, an international level.[19]

### 13.3.2  The ASTN Mandate to Help Commercialize and Promote Australian-Inspired Sportstech Worldwide

In August 2012, the ASTN was formally established as a not-for-profit member-based organization compromising leaders from Australian sportstech firms, sports federations, sports retailers and manufacturers, researchers and investors. It was formed as a national collaborative network of organizations with a physical base in Geelong. Governed by an industry board[20] led by a chairperson, the ASTN appointed an executive director[21] to build the membership organization, facilitate programmatic access to commercialization expertise, foster introductions to investment capital and promote networking and collaboration amongst stakeholders. To this day, the ASTN mandate as the recognized national body to coordinate and represent sportstech industry stakeholders centers around the idea of improving Australia's domestic and international commercial opportunities by capitalizing on the country's world-class sports research, major sporting event and sports business expertise, and reputation globally. However, rather than a business or industry cluster as introduced by Porter,[22] the ASTN endeavored to build a 'Cluster of Innovation' with a view to 'adapt new technologies, create new markets and address large, global markets'.[23] Given the relatively small size of the domestic market in Australia as well as the niche of technology in sports, access to global markets had to be at the core of these ambitions. It was understood that, based on world-class sports science and sports business universities and research institutes, entrepreneurs could start and grow businesses locally which they had to take global eventually. Besides universities, research centers, entrepreneurs and service providers, government played a pivotal role in seeding the Cluster of Innovation in Australia. The other components of the COI, namely venture capital and mature corporations with a focus on sportstech, initially, were not fully developed or present in-country. As a result, apart from seed funding of its activities through government, the ASTN's behavior relied significantly on the mobility of its people in building relationships on a global level as well as understanding best practices from other COI and introducing these into its own programs. Equipped with these experiences, the ASTN board started sharing its know-how and educating stakeholders on how to adapt new technologies to applications and business models in sports.

### 13.3.3   Launching Programs to Support the Sector

Following years of fostering casual networking exchanges ('weak ties') amongst stakeholders domestically and internationally, in October 2012, the ASTN held the first-ever Australian Sports Technology Conference at its home base, which included the inaugural Sports Technology Innovation Bootcamp.[24] The event was attended by over 300 delegates and 30 industry expert speakers, with a special Australian edition of the international, peer-reviewed journal *Sports Technology*[25] showcasing work of some of Australia's leading sports technology researchers. At the same time, the ASTN published an industry study into the state of development, sciences and engineering of sportstech.[26] The 2014 study profiled Australia's small proportions of less than 1 percent of the US$250 billion global sports market at the time, whilst assessing the opportunity available to take advantage of the global market, including a recommended course of action. Specifically, the study outlined how improvements in industry collaboration and innovation processes, and access to markets and supply chains, as well as access to commercialization expertise and investment capital, were required.

Domestically, the ASTN secured its durable bond with the Australian Sports Commission (ASC), which supported ASTN members to exhibit and showcase at its biannual Our Sporting Future conference in Melbourne. This partnership was formalized in June 2013 through a two-year agreement with the ASC and AIS by centrally funding ASTN membership for more than 70 sports federations, including free access to ASTN activities and initiatives. The agreement provided a formal entry point for the ASTN to engage with sports federations to better understand their technology needs and priorities whilst connecting them to the emerging sports technology ecosystem. Furthermore, the ASTN and its members also delivered several digital innovation masterclasses for the sports federations, highlighting ways to manage digital transformation within their organizations. It also provided sponsorship of the ASTN Sports

Technology Conference and pitching competition series over the partnership period. At the same time, ASTN board members started to establish the organization's profile on the eastern seaboard of Australia by hosting a series of events in Sydney, Brisbane, Canberra and Melbourne to showcase members' sports technology expertise and capabilities.

### 13.3.4 Domestic Rollercoaster Ride: Big Win Followed by a Big Setback!

In 2013, the federal government's Department of Innovation, Industry, Science and Research announced an innovation support program called the Industry Innovation Precinct (IIP) Program. This program was designed to support the development of priority high-potential industry ecosystems to create jobs, investment, exports and research commercialization. The ASTN board agreed to pursue a submission to this competitive program, recognizing the need for government funding to support the infant but high-potential industry. The ASTN secured bid support from 30 of Australia's leading sportstech firms, sports federations, and research organizations in the form of a four-year grant matched to cash and in-kind contributions by the supporting third parties. Bid partners at the time included the ASC; the AIS; the Australian Football League (AFL); Tennis Australia; leading sports technology firms such as Catapult Sport, Fusion Sport, Champion Data, Belgravia Group, POD Active and Interact Sport; and a number of leading sports-focused universities and research institutions.

The ASTN-led initiatives focused on knowledge-building, commercialization, business growth and international expansion with the aim to produce AU$600m in new revenues, AU$250m in new exports and 1,500 new jobs over a 10-year period. In August 2013, the ASTN's bid was announced as one of only eight successful submissions.[27] The funding, with the bid partners' support, would provide the platform to establish a truly national and coordinated approach to developing the sportstech industry and connecting it to international markets. However, with a change of federal government in October 2013, the IIP Program was subsequently abolished in mid-2014 by the incoming government, resulting in the ASTN bid being formally scrapped. This was a huge disappointment and setback for the ASTN given the time, resources and investment that had been put into the bid by the ASTN itself and its partners. This severely impacted the ability to potentially fast-track the development of the Australian sportstech industry and place it at the forefront of the global industry. Post the abolition of the IIP Program, the incoming federal government later launched a new industry innovation program in the form of the Industry Growth Centre Initiatives.[28] During a transition period, the Manufacturing Excellence Taskforce Australia (META) continued to back industry partnerships, with the ASTN Sports Technology Conference and various proof-of-concept projects between universities, sports and startups being supported before META was officially wound up in June 2015.

### 13.3.5  Building the 'Born Global or Die Local' Playbook by Drawing on 'Durable Bonds'

From an international perspective, the ASTN started to convert several frequent networking connections ('weak ties') into 'recurring business relationships with individuals in geographically distant communities'[29] ('durable bonds'). For example, at the 2013 ASTN Conference and Innovation Bootcamp, which was attended by over 350 delegates and hosted in Melbourne, the ASTN had engaged the former Head of Innovation at Nike headquarters in Oregon in the US, Erez Morag. Dr Morag, after leaving Nike and relocating from the US in the meantime, had become active in the sportstech cluster in Tel Aviv, Israel. Drawing on his experience from his time at Nike as well as his involvement in another innovation cluster, Dr Morag facilitated the Innovation Bootcamp sessions focused on improving the sports innovation processes within both sportstech firms and sports federations. Interestingly, whilst the facilitated knowledge exchange informed local founders, CxOs and administrators, the event also highlighted again the world-class quality of the local sportstech industry.

In late 2013, the ASTN pioneered the first sportstech accelerator in the world by commencing plans to start one of the first industry-focused accelerator programs. A funding grant extended by the City of Greater Geelong was used to establish a physical base and support the HeadStart program focused on advising and mentoring 10 high-potential sports technology startups over a 12-month period.[30] Several startups that participated in the inaugural program in mid-2014 have since then gone on to become world-class players within their own categories. A sports business student project turned into a cloud-based volunteer workforce engagement and management platform[31] which to date has been used by the organizers of the Super Bowl in the US.[32] A second participating company grew protective action sports gear[33] into a partnership with one of the world's largest sports medicine brands,[34,35] whilst a digital health form provider expanded into a fully integrated digital forms, approval workflows and online payments platform connecting schools and parents.[36]

Due to funding extended by META during the transition period, the ASTN was able to co-host the 2014 edition of the Australian Sports Technology Conference together with the Australian Sporting Goods Association (ASGA). With the help of ASGA, the conference now extended beyond researchers, startups and sports federations to also include for the first time sports manufacturers, retailers and wholesalers in Australia. Furthermore, the funding provided the ASTN with the opportunity to continue to engage with Prof. Engel and also attract Prof. Steve Blank of Stanford University to support the ASTN program delivery. As such, the ASTN was able to draw on the two individuals and their world-leading knowledge of technology, innovation and entrepreneurship education.[37] Engel and Blank's expertise and guidance provided a pivotal foundation for the ASTN in developing methodologies for future programs and initiatives. Much was learnt from the overseas engagement as well as the first accelerator program. Continued engagement and knowledge exchange both on the ground in Australia as well as in Silicon Valley provided the foundation for the methodologies developed for future accelerator programs over the years.

Prof. Blank's observation on what Australian sportstech entrepreneurs needed became an action point for the ASTN, its future programs and initiatives:

> What's been missing from regions outside of Silicon Valley is a "Playbook". A Playbook contains a team's strategies and plays … every region needs its own industry Playbook on how to compete globally. Entrepreneurs can jumpstart their efforts by sharing experience instead of re-inventing the wheel each time a new startup is launched. As the ecosystem become collectively smarter, the Playbook will change over time.

Developing an industry 'playbook' which outlines a roadmap and helps sportstech entrepreneurs fast-track their plans in testing, validating and building traction in the domestic market, then quickly accessing key global markets so that they can prepare for size and scale became a priority. This ASTN Playbook is specific to the nuances of the Australian regional market and the needs of Australian sports technology entrepreneurs in developing a 'Born Global or Die Local' mentality.

Finally, Prof. Blank's 'Lean Launchpad' methodology, now commonly used globally by startups as a pragmatic approach to develop and test their concepts, early on provided the framework for the ASTN's startup programs. This framework is complemented by the industry-specific knowledge and connections that the ASTN has built over 10 years to help entrepreneurs fast-track their plans and growth to be market-, investor- and export-ready.

### 13.3.6 Connecting the 'Sporting Capital of the World' to the Sportstech World by Building 'Covalent Bonds'[38]

The city of Melbourne has often been ranked the sporting capital of the world based on the quality of its year-round sports events calendar and the world-class sporting precinct located on the edge of the city center. Observing the work of the ASTN, the State Government of Victoria started to appreciate the strength of sportstech as a niche industry and how it complemented the state's major sports events portfolio, which included the Australian Open tennis event, a Formula 1 Grand Prix and the Melbourne Cup horse race. In November 2014, the state government extended support to the ASTN via the Manufacturing Productivity Networks (MPN) program, which provided the ASTN with the opportunity to deliver a suite of programs to support Victorian sportstech companies. The MPN program marked the start of an important and ongoing partnership between the State Government of Victoria and the ASTN. On the back of MPN assistance, the ASTN extended program offerings to develop export strategies and facilitate business-matching and trade missions to Europe, India and the US. For the first time, the ASTN was able to elevate its existing durable bonds with overseas partners into covalent bonds. For example, high-potential sportstech firms could gain access to the Global Access Program (GAP)[39] delivered at the University of California, Los Angeles (UCLA) in the US. The ASTN was able to plan and organize trade missions to Europe, India and the US as well as facilitating business matching, in-market research and entrepreneurship education. Besides 10 ASTN members having completed the six-month GAP, around 200 sports technology firms participated in these various programs over a three-year period, with the ASTN further developing and updating key elements of the playbook.

Under the MPN program, the ASTN formed a contractual agreement with leading global services firm PwC to deliver content to members on business structuring, research and development grants, as well as export-funding initiatives. ASTN and PwC's work highlighted that there is generally a lack of market research and business planning undertaken by Australian sportstech companies prior to exploring and pursuing new international market opportunities. Accordingly, delivery programs included everything from awareness of cultural nuances and understanding local market conditions to the structure of supply chains, and, for that reason were adopted into the continuously evolving ASTN Playbook, future programs and activities.

In 2016, the ASTN was relocated from Geelong to the city center of Melbourne and co-located with the office of a professional services law firm, which also entered into a contractual service partnership with the ASTN. This move reflected the concentration of sportstech firms based within the city of Melbourne, which today represents more than 60 percent of the national sportstech industry. At the same time, the ASTN successfully led a proposal to recommence its accelerator program in Melbourne in partnership with the State Government of Victoria's newly formed startup agency, LaunchVic.[40] Continuing development of the ASTN sportstech playbook was also part of the deliverables, as was the development and facilitation of a sports data hackathon in partnership with a Melbourne-based conference and event management firm. The partnership was also strengthened by the ASTN merging its original conference into the global sportstech conference series.[41] The newly formed partnership was a result of the ASTN board analyzing its strategy and continuing to update the playbook: By categorizing ASTN initiatives into advocacy, content and programs, the board determined that the partnership with Sports Tech World Series (STWS) would free up ASTN capacity to concentrate on content and program delivery. As such, appointing one of the STWS founders to the ASTN board[42] and relinquishing the original conference enabled the ASTN to expand its offerings to startups and export-ready and export-accelerator companies.

Throughout late 2016 and into 2017, the ASTN's connection with international markets continued to expand significantly. A delegation of 10 ASTN members attended the first-ever Australian sports technology trade mission to India in May 2016. The one-week market-intelligence and business-matching program had been developed for each participating firm with the support of the State Government of Victoria's Global Victoria trade team based in India. This provided a strong foundation for a future mission in October 2018 attended by over 30 Australian delegates. Coinciding with the Indian mission, the ASTN, together with a handful of leading sportstech firms, attended and presented at a three-day pre-Rio Olympic Games sport innovation event hosted by the Australian Trade and Investment Commission (Austrade), which was attended by more than 150 sports executives from South America. Although anticipated, a later showcase as part of the 'Australia' exhibition in the Olympic Games precinct during the Rio Games did not eventuate.

Back at home, a trade delegation from the Netherlands, which included 30 sports organizations, visited Canberra, Melbourne and Sydney as part of a business-matching and market-intelligence-sharing program. During the visit, a knowledge-sharing memorandum of understanding (MoU) was signed between the ASTN and its Netherlands equivalent, Sports + Technology,[43] based in the Dutch region of Eindhoven.[44]

On the back of the continued partnership with the State Government of Victoria, ASTN activities continued to grow, extending now from support for its accelerator programs funded by the startup agency LaunchVic[45] to trade mission programs supported by the export, trade and investment agency GlobalVic,[46] as well as Austrade. In early 2017, the ASTN led its first 10-day sportstech trade mission of 15 participating CEOs to the US, incorporating the MIT Sloan Sports Analytics Conference in Boston plus business-matching in San Francisco and Los Angeles with the likes of the San Francisco 49ers, the Golden State Warriors, Red Bull and the US Olympic Committee, as well as visits to Stanford University and UC Berkeley.

Particularly throughout 2018 and 2019, the ASTN further enhanced its export and trade offers for its members. The year 2018 saw the trade destinations expanded yet again to include Europe, with a trade mission to the Netherlands and Germany. On the back of its MoU, the ASTN returned the visit by its Dutch equivalent, Sports + Technology, from 18 months earlier with a study and business-matching tour to the Brainport region of Eindhoven. In addition, the partnership with STWS provided the opportunity for trade delegates to exhibit and present as part of the delegate program at the Amsterdam conference to connect with local sports federations and customers directly. Made possible through the personal relationships of the ASTN directors and connections with the German embassy in Australia, as well as the German-Australian Chamber of Industry and Commerce, the trade delegation program also included participation in the 2018 invitation-only Sports Innovation Summit facilitated by the organizers of the professional football (soccer) leagues in Germany, the Bundesliga.[47] Delegates also engaged with the Berlin-based accelerator and venture capital fund[48] created by the grandchildren of the founder of Germany-headquartered, global sports apparel company Adidas, in addition to visiting the organizers of the largest sports apparel and equipment trade show, ISPO,[49] hosted twice annually in both Germany and China.

In addition to Europe, 2019 saw a second trade mission to the US, including stops in Boston, Massachusetts; Atlanta, Georgia; San Antonio, Texas; and San Francisco, California. As well as conference attendance, the program offered multiple opportunities for in-market research, customer discovery and business-to-business-matching.[50] In the same year, the ASTN also added China to the list of export destinations. On the back of the expansion of the AFL into China, ASTN delegates visited Shanghai in May 2019 before returning for a sportstech mission to Beijing, including attendance of the invite-only annual Internet conference in Wuzhen.

Back on home soil, 2018 and 2019 saw the rollout of Australian Sportstech Week.[51] On the back of the STWS conference series, both partners combined the sportstech conference with an investor and pitching day, a hackathon event, ASTN innovation masterclasses and workshops, and integrated sportstech-related elements of the Victorian Invitation Program.[52] The addition of these inbound-driven initiatives was seen as key in building significant relationships with selected business leaders from around the globe, and laid the foundation for a number of 'covalent bonds' formed later as a result.[53] The event week showcased Australian sportstech expertise to the world and cemented the ASTN's position as one of the leading clusters in sportstech. The years 2018 and 2019 also saw for the first time the industry celebrate its best in establishing the Australia and New Zealand Sports Technology Awards.[54,55]

Following the successful trade mission model, the ASTN also investigated a first trade mission to South America at the end of 2019. A visit to Chile in September of that year explored opportunities under the federal government's free trade agreement (FTA). Similar to other destinations where Australia has a bilateral FTA, Austrade at the time maintained so-called Free Trade Agreement – Market Entry (FTA-ME) support programs for which organizations like the ASTN were eligible. At the time, Chile was of particular interest due to the FTA with the country which had been in force since 2015, as well as the prospects of Chile hosting the Pan-American Games in 2023. In-country connections to potential local partners and facilitators were made possible by again working with both federal and state government trade agencies as well as personal relationships the ASTN had built through its networks in Silicon Valley.[56] Unfortunately, all plans for a trade mission to South America as well as a second trade visit to Europe and the UK had to be abandoned and canceled due to the COVID-19 pandemic spreading, and resultant international travel restrictions being imposed. Instead, the ASTN and GlobalVic developed and rolled out a series of virtual trade missions and business-matching events involving the US[57,58] and UK.[59]

As the world hunkered down at home throughout the pandemic and 'remote' became the 'new normal' in 2020, the ASTN formalized an ongoing content and program delivery partnership with the Global Sports Innovation Center (GSIC), located in Madrid.[60] Both like-minded membership-based networks with similar organizational structures had an already existing relationship through knowledge-sharing and collaborating on the judging panel for the digital innovation pitching competition ISPO BrandNew, hosted in Munich in 2019.[61] As the ASTN had provided its one-on-one mentoring service throughout 2019 on occasions via online video conferencing means, such infrastructure became the only delivery option throughout the pandemic, like it did for obviously everyone. A previous MoU between GSIC and the ASTN was transferred into a delivery partnership agreement executed by both organizations to deliver the first live-online global pre-accelerator in sportstech.[62] The program connected researchers, practitioners and founders in the early startup stage to customer discovery, and market and competitor analysis as well as business model reviews. In addition, so called 'Learn from the best' sessions provided access to interactive question-and-answer sessions with founders and leaders of leading international and Australian sports businesses who have 'been there, done that'. During the pandemic, the program was delivered in a live-online format, which attracted founders from almost every metropolitan region of Australia in addition to a strong regional and even international audience. Due to the success of the pre-accelerator, both the ASTN and GSIC are now looking to continue the live-online delivery format even as restrictions on gatherings are being relaxed. Furthermore, the ASTN is now seeking formal support by the other states to extend the reach of its programs to NSW and Queensland. Based on previous experience of leaning on building personal relationships and representation, the expansion activities into the other Australian states have been underpinned by appointing a former Olympic athlete and sportstech sales and marketing executive to the ASTN board.[63] In addition, a partnership with the Varcis Group is also preparing the extension of activities into Asia.[64]

## 13.4 THE IMPORTANCE OF SPORT IN THE AUSTRALIAN QUEST FOR A SUPER-CLUSTER OF INNOVATION

### 13.4.1 Why Sport?

A lot has been said about the importance of sport for Australia as a country. The debacle in the 1976 Olympic Games, classified as a national embarrassment, the origins of the AIS and the government leadership role as the 'entrepreneurial state' have already been highlighted. The love of Australians for all kinds of sports, their sporting enthusiasm and engagement with all forms of sports, ranging from grassroots to the elite level, has been documented.[65] When the Futures Research Team at the CSIRO and the ASC documented some of the megatrends shaping sports in the coming decades starting from 2013, the team identified a trend they coined 'more than sports', recognizing benefits beyond competition.[66] The power of sports to unite communities and drive social inclusion for athletes of all abilities has been on display, particularly in Australia's multicultural environment.[67] Furthermore, the federal government defines 'Sport Diplomacy' as one of the Department of Foreign Affairs and Trade's key elements in engaging with the country's Asian and Pacific neighbors and beyond in 'bringing people, communities, nations and regions together […] through a shared love of sport'.[68]

The embedment of sport into the fabric of Australia's society creates a unique position for the industry to test and validate ideas and commercialize innovation. Founded in a strong history of sports science and sports business conducted at world-class universities and research institutions, the federated Australian sporting structure is both sophisticated in terms of structure and significantly diversified in terms of sporting activity covering all aspects from recreational to club level and elite and professional sports. In addition, the country's multicultural makeup provides for elements that can resemble aspects of the larger Asian, European and North American sports markets. Finally, at the same time the domestic market, with a population of 25.7 million as of mid-2020,[69] is small enough to test and validate quickly. The role of Australia as an ideal testbed for validating new concepts, products or services has been likened to a role for Australia as the 'global Peoria'.[70] Peoria, the oldest settlement in the US state of Illinois, has often been referred to by the advertising industry as a benchmark for mainstream taste due to its history, demographics and infrastructure.[71] Accordingly, the argument has been made that modern Australia can serve a similar role in a global context due to its multiculturalism and high level of urbanization, combined with vast distances between centers and the continent's environmental challenges.

Furthermore, the global competitive advantage in terms of on-the-field sporting success, a strong higher-education sport science and sports business background, and the previously outlined crossover of sportstech with other key industries, can be a growth opportunity en par with healthtech, fintech, foodtech and even resources when it comes to the products, services and jobs of the future knowledge economy. For example, services exports from Australia grew strongly from AU$13.3 billion in 1990 to AU$56.5 billion in 2010 and AU$100.3 billion in 2019.[72] During the COVID-19 pandemic, services exports declined to AU$72.6 billion in 2020.[73] Whilst services exports include international travel, both education-related and personal, the category also contains business services exports comprised of legal, engineering, financial, telco and computer information technology services, which have been growing significantly since 1990.[74] As a result, given the relative competitive advantage of Australia in sport, sportstech is seen as one of the future growth and export sectors.

### 13.4.2    The Value of Sport in Australia

As a country, Australia is known for a thriving sports economy,[75] and, as already mentioned, sport plays an integral part in people's lives in Australia. Overall, Australia spends AU$12.5 billion on high-performance sports, grassroot participation and infrastructure, funded through the ASC, all levels of government, the private sector and sports participants (see Table 13.1).

*Table 13.1    Who is funding sport in Australia and how money is spent*

| Investment domain | Funding body | | | | | | |
|---|---|---|---|---|---|---|---|
| | ASC | Federal gov't | State gov't | Local gov't | Private sector | Users paying | Total |
| High performance | 126 | 26 | 45 | | 1,835 | 797 | 2,829 |
| Participation | 50 | 19 | 156 | 14 | 624 | 7,287 | 8,150 |
| Infrastructure | | 140 | 449 | 890 | | | 1,479 |
| Total $ value (in AU$m) | 176 | 185 | 650 | 904 | 2,459 | 8,084 | 12,458 |

*Source:*    The Boston Consulting Group and Australian Sports Commission, *Intergenerational Review of Australian Sport*, p. 41 (2017).

According to industry reports, the economic activity of the Australian sports market is valued at AU$23.4 billion (see Table 13.2), including volunteer contributions. Recent estimates by the Productivity Commission of the Australian

Federal Government conclude that sport can contribute about a 15 percent or AU\$24.3 billion reduction in overall health care spending (see Table 13.3). Furthermore, a recent study estimates that sport provides a AU\$5 billion benefit to the education sector (see Table 13.4).

*Table 13.2　　Where economic activity occurs in sport in Australia*

|  |  | \$ value (in AU\$m) |
|---|---|---|
| Economic activity[a] | Social club facilities | 6,198 |
|  | Sports administration | 3,859 |
|  | Sports clubs | 3,254 |
|  | Sports facilities | 1,815 |
|  | Sports instructions | 638 |
|  | Sports betting | 589 |
|  | Subtotal | 16,353 |
| Health impact on work[b] | Increased productivity | 4,170 |
| Value of volunteer contribution[c] | 158 million hours at \$18.29 per hour | 2,890 |
|  | Total economic activity | 23,413 |

Note:　　[a] IBISworld Industry Report: Sports in Australia 2013 (information extrapolated to 2017).
[b] Commonwealth of Australia, Productivity Commission, *Shifting the Dial: Impacts of Health Recommendations – Supporting Paper No. 6*, p. 5 (2017).
[c] Boston Consulting Group and Australian Sports Commission. *Intergenerational Review*, p. 43.

*Table 13.3　　Expected reduction in health care costs*

|  | \$ value (in AU\$m) |
|---|---|
| Health care spending in Australia[a] | 162,000 |
| Reduction in health care costs due to prevention (avoided costs),[b] including:<br><br>• Taxpayer-funded income support for people in ill health<br>• Sickness payments<br>• Support payments for acquired disabilities<br>• Reduction in welfare expenses for people without health issues | 24,000 |
| Secondary effects of reduction in health care costs through lower taxes[c] | 300 |
| Total benefit to health care | 24,300 |

*Note:*　　[a] Commonwealth of Australia, Productivity Commission, *Shifting the Dial: Impacts of Health Recommendations – Supporting Paper No. 4*, p. 16 (2017).
[b] Commonwealth of Australia, Productivity Commission, *Report on Government Service 2016*.
[c] Commonwealth of Australia, Productivity Commission, *Shifting the Dial: Impacts of Health Recommendations – Supporting Paper No. 4*, p. 16 (2017).

*Table 13.4    Expected benefit to education*

| | $ value (in AU$m) |
|---|---|
| Improvements in education,[a] including: | |
| • Increased attendance rates (less absenteeism)<br>• Performance improvements of active students<br>• Tendency of more active students to extend<br>  education | 5,000 |

Note:      [a] Boston Consulting Group and Australian Sports Commission, *Intergenerational Review*, p. 44.

*Table 13.5    Return on investment in sport*

| | $ value (in AU$m) |
|---|---|
| Sports spending in Australia (subtotal Table 13.1) | 12,458 |
| Contribution to economic activity (subtotal Table 13.2) | 23,413 |
| Benefit to health care (reduction in health care costs) (subtotal Table 13.3) | 24,300 |
| Benefit to education (subtotal Table 13.4) | 5,000 |
| Total benefit | 52,713 |
| Return on investment | 1:4 |

Altogether, sport creates significant value for Australia. Approximately AU$4 is returned from every dollar spent in the sports sector. This rate of return is the result of the direct and indirect impact of sports spending, increased productivity of active workers, net health benefits of sports participation, and education benefits of childhood sports participation.

The approximately AU$4 of value created for each dollar spent in sport is calculated by dividing the more than AU$50 billion of benefits created from sport by the AU$12.5 billion spent on sport in 2016. The total return is estimated to be at least AU$4 for each dollar spent, as this number does not include the more intangible benefits of personal wellbeing, community cohesion and international reputation (see Table 13.5). The value of sport in a country like Australia highlights the economic benefits associated with adopting sports as part of an active lifestyle and its role in health prevention to reduce lifestyle diseases.

### 13.4.3    Formation of a Super-Cluster of Innovation through a Physical Sportstech Hub

Based on the understanding of having assembled the necessary components and having developed the required characteristics of a global COI, the ASTN is continuing to update its playbook and as one of the initiatives going forward strives to merge local partners and programs into a physical sportstech hub, which sector stakeholders have indicated as additional support required.[76] Such a hub is envisioned to co-locate startups, entrepreneurs and corporates as well as representatives from sports and universities to link these with other nodes of value and other COI.[77] Linking founders and entrepreneurs to financial centers and governmental regulatory centers had been identified as one of the key priorities in enabling access to investment and overcoming barriers to funding. Access to venture capital, but also at times the difficulty of navigating through grant monies, has been repeatedly reported as one of the underdeveloped pieces of the Australian sportstech ecosystem.[78]

A second aspect of the ASTN's quest to evolve into a 'Super-Cluster of Innovation'[79] is to translate existing networking ('weak ties') and contractual collaborations ('durable bonds') into coordinated, permanent and interdependent association ('covalent bonds'). For example, as of 2021, the ASTN has further formalized its existing relationship with the experts at UC Berkeley. Collaborative 'Open Innovation' activities are currently under review and scheduled to commence in 2022. The overall seeding of the project plan is again supported and underwritten by the State Government of Victoria's startup agency LaunchVic.[80] The delivery of new 'Open Innovation' activities and collaborative projects throughout 2021 and beyond is part of the overall operational sustainability plan that has been developed for the ASTN. At the core of these collaborative activities linking startups and corporates is the understanding that 'a combination of entrepreneurial activity with corporate ability seems like a perfect match – when it comes to agility, startups have an edge over large corporations, whereas large corporations sit on resources which startups can only dream of'.[81] On the one hand, corporates will be invited to provide technologies from their portfolio to startups who can utilize corporate resources to develop a solution, an activity typically referred to as 'Inside-Out Innovation' if seen from the corporate's point of view. On the other hand, corporates and startups can collaborate, where the startup brings forward its solution in the form of a product, service or new business model and the corporate provides much-needed market access. Such activity is typically contrasted as 'Outside-In Innovation' if again viewed from a corporate perspective.[82]

As a next step towards growing the COI domestically in Australia, the ASTN is looking to expand its state node operations. Based on existing weak ties of professional networks across the eastern seaboard of Australia, the ASTN has conceptualized a duplication of activities to the states of Queensland and NSW. Based on specific expertise across the sportstech spectrum, the NSW node in Sydney will look to place a particular focus on the media, broadcasting and over-the-top streaming sportstech verticals, including adjacencies in fintech and cyber-security. Following the announcement by the International Olympic Committee declaring Brisbane as the host of the Olympic and Paralympic Games in 2032,[83] the Queensland node in Brisbane is expected to center around major events, sporting infrastructure, community and fan engagement as well as the Olympic legacy, wearables and sports data analytics, smart apparel and footwear of Australian athletes and the role sportstech can play. Concentrating the attention of the respective node on a specific expertise across the sportstech spectrum will encourage node members to act in a complementary rather than a competitive manner with each other.

Following the notion of 'Australia as the global Peoria', the remoteness of the Australian market and resulting farness of an Australian subsidiary of a multinational to its regional or global headquarters in this scenario provides another advantage to the developing Australian sportstech Super-COI. The physical separation and distance between a subsidiary and its headquarters reduces the potential for the so-called 'corporate antidotes' of brand protection, sales execution and quality control to work against and eliminate the new 'incomplete' idea. In the truest sense of 'the new has to be organized separately from the old and existing',[84] the ASTN hub will help both startups and corporates to collaborate in a somewhat formalized and organized manner, but sheltered from burdens of existing policies, rules and measurements. An example from another industry sector, namely agtech, demonstrates how a hardware supply relationship[85] led from providing technology to an equity investment.[86] In this example, activities were driven by the local subsidiary without direct involvement from the overseas headquarters located in Germany. Once the project, using sensor technology to analyze the microclimate in a farming context, had matured and emerged from its infancy stage, which had been protected by the distance between the two locations of subsidiary and headquarters, the startup's growth was supported by entering export markets.[87] In addition, corporate marketing support by the main technology provider was extended to the agtech startup through the respective networks of the partners.[88,89]

Another aspect of building connections and relationships amongst geographically dispersed networks is the collaboration with other ecosystems to form a network of clusters. This includes the content- and program-delivery partnership with the GSIC located in Madrid, Spain as well as a formal referral and contractual support arrangement with the sport event-tech accelerator organized by Startup Bootcamp.[90] Based on its success running programs domestically, the ASTN is also starting to export its accelerator programs to overseas markets.

The Asian partnership between the ASTN and the Varcis Group,[91] based in Hong Kong with market entry to the burgeoning market in North East Asia (with China as a main focus), presents enormous opportunity for the ASTN and its members. In fact, in 2020 the Varcis Group transacted some 16 deals in Hong Kong by way of investments, joint ventures or licensed distribution deals.[92,93] Hong Kong is now the key entrepôt for Australian sportstech as it has common law, intellectual property and finance protections. With Hong Kong being the world's fifth largest stock market,[94] it also provides access to the enormous increase of Chinese private and state-owned enterprises now listed in Hong Kong. Compared to Shanghai (fourth largest stock exchange) or Shenzhen (seventh), the benefit of a wholly-owned foreign entity (WOFE) which is only based in Hong Kong means that WOFEs will enable these companies to repatriate profits and dividends back to Hong Kong without Chinese government controls. This partnership now provides sportstech companies with access to many of the world's largest sports apparel, distributors, manufacturers and suppliers to China. On the back of the Chinese government's commitment to grow sports from 2.5 percent of its GDP (gross domestic product) in 2015 to 3.3 percent by 2025, according to Bloomberg's calculations,[95] such market access can be a 'game changer' to sportstech.

To catalyze this, many of the ASTN/Varcis Group programs were announced[96] for mid- to late 2021 and 2022 via online technology and in-person delivery once international travel could resume safely; for example, through acquisition of the Asia rights,[97] the STWS conference, possibly to be hosted in late 2022.

Finally, various partners plan for more international collaboration with other sportstech networks beyond Asia, such as in India, which will then extend the ASTN's reach with existing links to other organizations in Europe[98] and the US[99] and ultimately morph into a Super-Cluster of Sports Innovation.

## APPENDIX: CASE STUDIES

The following is a series of short ASTN member case studies. Over the life of the ASTN we have seen each of these firms grow and evolve to become a global leader within its sports technology category. The CEOs have been active participants in ASTN programs, activities and events over the last eight years, and now willingly share their industry insights and business knowledge with the next generation of ASTN sports technology innovators.

## POD ACTIVE

POD Active is a product development firm specializing in joint protection for elite athletes and action sport enthusiasts based in Geelong. POD's mission is to reduce the risk and severity of ligament injuries in sport without restricting performance or compromising comfort. Its knee brace is considered one of the leading protective devices in the action sports sector. Its ankle brace was launched in 2016 and is distributed through the likes of major medical supply company DJO Global. Recently it has partnered with Ossur, another major medical supplier company.

POD Active was an inaugural member of the ASTN and has consistently participated in many of its programs, including innovation masterclasses, exhibition opportunities and advisory programs over nearly eight years. POD has been a delegate on numerous ASTN trade missions to the US and China and has completed the UCLA GAP to assist with its international market strategy on two occasions.

## ROSTERFY

Rosterfy is a scalable workforce engagement platform for volunteers and paid staff, generally used by large-scale events, sports federations, charities, local governments and universities. The solution reduces manual processes for workforce managers whilst increasing retention, engagement and attendance rates of volunteer databases. Clients include the NFL Superbowl, the Gold Coast Commonwealth Games, the ICC Cricket World Cup, Ironman, Expo 2020 Dubai and the AFL.

Launched in 2014, Rosterfy was a runner-up in the ASTN's 2015 Investment Pitching Competition. Rosterfy has formed a strong relationship with the ASTN since this time and has participated in ASTN's Accelerator program and been a delegate on ASTN-led trade missions to India and the US. Rosterfy has consistently attended ASTN innovation masterclasses and has actively presented at ASTN events and on panels to emerging sports tech innovators. The ASTN has been a regular sounding board for the co-founders on strategy as well as exploring growth and investor opportunities.

## SPONSERVE

Sponserve is a sponsorship management platform launched in 2015 in Canberra. The solution streamlines and enhances sponsorship servicing and inventory management through cloud-based software. It allows commercial managers of clubs and federations as well as brand sponsors to easily plan and track completion of required tasks, manage sponsorship inventory, and provide ongoing reporting and sponsorship acquittal. Within three years, Sponserve had secured more than 100 sports rights holders and brands around the world as clients, including Williams F1, Scarlets Pro14 Rugby, AS Roma, seven Premier League teams, the Australian National Rugby League, Cricket Australia and the Brisbane Broncos, amongst many others. In November 2018, Sponserve was acquired by Kore Software, a global leader in sponsorship asset management and reporting.

Sponserve was a runner-up in the ASTN's 2015 Investment Pitching Competition with Rosterfy. As a cash-strapped startup, it used the cash prize from the competition to visit potential international clients. Many new, high-profile clients were secured off this inaugural business development mission. The CEO at the time was grateful for the opportunity the pitching competition presented to his company, and still acts as an advocate to the ASTN by participating in program activities.[100] As part of the prize, Sponserve was also accepted into the ASTN's Accelerator program, and the ASTN remained an important sounding board for the CEO for business development as well as assessing other growth and investor opportunities. More recently, the CEO of Sponserve has become an important sounding board for emerging ASTN sports technology innovators through ASTN startup programs.

## GTG NETWORK (GENIUS TECH GROUP)

GTG Network's products are focused on generating large-scale consumer engagement through data analytics and gamification for sports and eSports by producing unprecedented data insights for fans. Founded in 2012, GTG Network has built sports data platforms for some of the biggest brands in sport, including Ladbrokes, Paddy Power, Sportsbet, DraftKings, Caesars Entertainment, the LA Lakers, Barstool Sportsbook and Cisco, to name a few. With a head office located in Melbourne, it has around 100 staff across the world, including in London, Jaipur, Warsaw, Manila and Tel Aviv.

The GTG Network and its co-founders have been active ASTN members since mid-2016. They have regularly attended ASTN innovation masterclasses and network events and contributed their insights on sports data to the broader sportstech community in Australia. The ASTN has been a regular business development sounding board for the GTG Network co-founders as the business spread its client base into new markets off-shore. A number of these introductions resulted in GTG securing important client partnerships.

## IDA SPORTS

Laura Youngson and Ben Sandhu founded Ida sports in early 2018. The idea stemmed from trying to solve a problem Laura faced as an avid amateur footballer, forced to buy men's or children's boots that were not anatomically correct for women and often of lower quality materials. After researching the market and speaking with other female athletes, Laura soon realized that this was a systematic problem – that everything was designed for men! In 2018, Ida developed a prototype of the boot – the Frankenshoe – and tested this with both amateur and professional athletes.

Ben and Laura cite the strength and density of Victoria's sports sector and culture of sport in Victoria as a key factor to their decision to base Ida sports in Melbourne.

A key part of this has also been the amazing network of women's sport – this has made Victoria a strong testing ground to trial their products and do market validation. Ida also acknowledges the strength of Victoria's university ecosystem and has utilized a number of supports. This was also a key factor for Laura, who is originally from the UK, to move to Melbourne to study entrepreneurship at the University of Melbourne.[101]

Ida previously participated in the ASTN accelerator program followed by a stint at the RMIT (Royal Melbourne Institute of Technology) Activator Accelerator.

Ida has worked with a number of Victorian universities to access a range of supports, including: student talent, internships and research capabilities (such as 3D printing). Ben and Laura also give back to the community – mentoring other startups and students.

Ida has finalized developing a prototype of each size of their boot. Ida gained valuable customer insight through a pop-up retail space where women can try the boot before they order. They are now looking to expand their presence into the US and the European market supported through a federal grant.

## NOTES

1.  We wish to acknowledge the significant contribution to the development of the ASTN and this chapter by our colleagues Craig Hill and John Persico.
2.  *Daily Telegraph* (1976). Retrieved on 10 February 2021 from https://philcheetham .com/wp-content/uploads/2012/09/Interview-with-PM-1976-Olympics.jpg.
3.  History of the Australian Institute of Sport. Retrieved on 10 February 2021 from https://en.wikipedia.org/wiki/Australian_Institute_of_Sport.
4.  Australian Institute of Sport, Timeline 1980–2011. Retrieved on 10 February 2021 from https://web.archive.org/web/20121019201559/http://www.ausport .gov.au/ais/history/timeline.
5.  Commonwealth of Australia, *Sport 2030: Achieving Sporting Excellence* (2018); see www.dfat.gov.au/people-to-people/sports-diplomacy#diplomacy and www .dfat.gov.au/sites/default/files/sports-diplomacy-2030.pdf.
6.  Ashley, K., *Applied Machine Learning for Health and Fitness*, Foreword by Phil Cheetham, Apress Media, distributed by Springer Nature (2020).
7.  Frevel, N., Schmidt, S.L., Beiderbeck, D., Pernkert, B., Subirana, B., Taxonomy of Sportstech, in Schmidt, S.L. (ed.), *21st Century Sports: How Technologies Will Change Sports in the Digital Age*, Springer Nature (2020).
8.  Penkert, B., Sportstech Framework 2019. Retrieved on 21 January 2021 from https://medium.com/sportstechx/sportstech-framework-2019-2b4b6fbe3216.
9.  Vogel, D., *California Greenin': How the Golden State Became an Environmental Leader*, Princeton University Press (2018).
10. Schlegel, M., Sports Technology Stack. Retrieved on 21 January 2021 from www.chemneera.com/about.
11. Catapult Sports, Our Story (2020). Retrieved on 21 January 2021 from www .catapultsports.com/about.

12.  Mazzucato, M., *The Entrepreneurial State: Debunking Public vs. Private Sector Myths*, Anthem Press (2014).
13.  https://launchvic.org/files/LaunchVic_SportsTech_Report_23Aug2019.pdf.
14.  Australian Sports Technologies Network (ASTN), What Is Sports Technology? Retrieved on 8 September 2021 from https://astn.com.au/who-we-are/.
15.  LaunchVic and KPMG, *The Sportstech Report: Advancing Victoria's Startup Ecosystem* (2019), p. 6.
16.  LaunchVic and KPMG, *Sportstech Report*, p. 5.
17.  Engel, J.S., *Global Clusters of Innovation: Entrepreneurial Engines of Economic Growth around the World*, Edward Elgar Publishing (2014), p. 21.
18.  www.bulletpoint.com.au/enterprise-connect/.
19.  Engel, *Global Clusters of Innovation*, Figure 1.2, p. 26.
20.  https://astn.com.au/board-members/.
21.  Appointment of Craig Hill as Inaugural Executive Director of the ASTN. History of the ASTN. Retrieved from https://astn.com.au/who-we-are/.
22.  Porter, M.E., *The Competitive Advantage of Nations*, Free Press (1990).
23.  Engel, *Global Clusters of Innovation*, p. 11.
24.  www.ausleisure.com.au/news/australian-sports-technologies-network-to-host -inaugural-national-conferenc.
25.  www.tandfonline.com/action/journalInformation?show=aimsScope& journalCode=rtec20.
26.  Samson, D., *Lifting Our Game: Developing Sports Technologies to Create Value*, Australian Sports Technologies Network (2014).
27.  www.sbs.com.au/news/rudd-to-launch-sporting-hub-in-geelong.
28.  www.industry.gov.au/policies-and-initiatives/industry-growth-centres.
29.  Engel, *Global Clusters of Innovation*, p. 21.
30.  www.ausleisure.com.au/news/sports-tech-businesses-get-a-headstart-into-300 -billion-market/.
31.  https://rosterfy.com.
32.  https://rosterfy.com/blog/rosterfy-to-power-its-sixth-consecutive-super-bowl/.
33.  www.podactive.com.
34.  www.donjoyperformance.com/pod-ankle-brace.
35.  www.donjoyperformance.com/donjoy-legacy.
36.  www.operoo.com/company/.
37.  www.smartcompany.com.au/startupsmart/advice/leadership-advice/aussie -sports-tech-startups-in-the-running-to-get-lean-with-steve-blank/.
38.  Engel, *Global Clusters of Innovation*, p. 22.
39.  www.anderson.ucla.edu/programs-and-outreach/global-access-program.
40.  https://launchvic.org/rounds/round-1.
41.  https://sportstechworldseries.com/events/#conference.
42.  Appointment of John Persico to the ASTN Board. Retrieved in February 2021 from https://astn.com.au/board-members/.
43.  https://sportsandtechnology.com.
44.  https://brainporteindhoven.com/int/.
45.  https://launchvic.org/about-launchvic.
46.  https://global.vic.gov.au/about-us/about-us.
47.  www.sportsinnovation.de/en/Home_1.
48.  www.leadsports.com/about.
49.  www.ispo.com.
50.  https://astn.com.au/wp-content/uploads/2019/03/usatrademission.jpeg.

51. https://sportstechweek.com.
52. www.bulletpoint.com.au/victorian-invitation-program/.
53. https://varcis.com/wp-content/uploads/2020/05/post1.pdf.
54. https://astn.com.au/pr-anzsta/.
55. https://anzsta.com.au/ceremony/.
56. https://executive.berkeley.edu/thought-leadership/blog/global-sports-technology-expert-shares-his-cobe-experience.
57. https://astn.com.au/usa-business-matching/.
58. https://global.vic.gov.au/for-exporters/trade-missions/sportstech-mission-to-the-usa-march-2021.
59. https://global.vic.gov.au/for-exporters/trade-missions/sportstech-mission-to-the-united-kingdom-april-2021.
60. https://astn.com.au/press-release-pre-accelerator/.
61. www.ispo.com/en/awards/ispo-brandnew/digital.
62. https://astn.com.au/pre-accelerator/.
63. Appointment of Natalie Cook OLY and Cameron O'Riordan to the ASTN Board for QLD and NSW Nodes. Retrieved in February 2021 from https://astn.com.au/board-members/.
64. Varcis–GSIC–ASTN press release. Retrieved in February 2021 from https://sport-gsic.com/varcis-group-and-global-sports-innovation-center-gsic-powered-by-microsoft-and-astn-launch-first-ever-sports-tech-pre-accelerator-in-asia-based-in-hong-kong/.
65. Schlegel, M.U., and Hill, C., The Reach of Sports Technologies, in Schmidt, *21st Century Sports*.
66. Hajkowicz, S.A., Cook, H., Wilhelmseder, L., and Boughen N., *The Future of Australian Sport: Megatrends Shaping the Sports Sector over Coming Decades – A Consultancy Report for the Australian Sports Commission*, CSIRO (2013).
67. www.sportswithoutborders.org.
68. Commonwealth of Australia, Australian Government, Department of Foreign Affairs and Trade (2019), *Sports Diplomacy 2030*. Retrieved in October 2019 from www.dfat.gov.au/sites/default/files/sports-diplomacy-2030.pdf.
69. www.abs.gov.au/statistics/people/population/national-state-and-territory-population/jun-2020.
70. Schlegel, M.U., *Australia: The Global Peoria?* Retrieved in February 2021 from www.researchgate.net/publication/325943267_Australia_-_The_Global_Peoria_The_Fourth_Industrial_Revolution_and_its_Relevance_to_Australia (2017).
71. https://en.wikipedia.org/wiki/Will_it_play_in_Peoria%3F.
72. www.abs.gov.au/statistics/economy/international-trade/international-trade-goods-and-services-australia.
73. www.abs.gov.au/statistics/economy/international-trade/international-trade-goods-and-services-australia/dec-2020.
74. Australian Government and Andrew, J.A., *Australia's Trade Performance 1990–2011*, Department of Foreign Affairs and Trade, Trade Competitiveness and Advocacy Branch (2015).
75. LaunchVic and KPMG, *Sportstech Report*, p. 11.
76. LaunchVic and KPMG, *Sportstech Report*, pp. 25–31.
77. Engel, *Global Clusters of Innovation*, p. 25.
78. https://launchvic.org/victorias-ecosystem.
79. Engel, *Global Clusters of Innovation*, p. 23.
80. https://launchvic.org/programs/astn-accelerator.

81.  Weiblen, T., and Chesbrough, H., Engaging with Startups to Enhance Corporate Innovation, *California Management Review*, Vol. 57, No. 2 (2015), pp. 66–90.
82.  Chesbrough, H., *Open Innovation Results: Going Beyond the Hype and Getting Down to Business*, Oxford University Press (2020).
83.  www.olympic.org/news/brisbane-and-aoc-invited-to-targeted-dialogue-for-the -olympic-games-2032.
84.  Drucker, P., *The Essential Drucker*, Harper Collins (2001), p. 138.
85.  www.iothub.com.au/news/bosch-invests-in-the-yield-to-fuel-iot-development -418729.
86.  www.bosch.com.au/news-and-stories/bosch-boosts-investment-in-agtech -leader/.
87.  www.austrade.gov.au/agriculture40/news/future-proofing-farm-management.
88.  https://news.microsoft.com/transform/videos/yield-feed-world-without -wrecking-planet/.
89.  https://australien.ahk.de/en/media/news-details/david-meets-goliath-with-robert -bosch-australia-and-the-yield/.
90.  www.startupbootcamp.org/accelerator/sport-eventtech-melbourne/.
91.  https://varcis.com/wp-content/uploads/2020/05/post1.pdf.
92.  https://varcis.com/wp-content/uploads/2020/05/VARCIS-PMY-Press-Release-v .2.pdf.
93.  https://varcis.com/wp-content/uploads/2020/05/tgsports.pdf.
94.  www.visualcapitalist.com/the-worlds-10-largest-stock-markets/.
95.  www.bloomberg.com/news/articles/2021-08-06/china-sees-sports-as-growth -driver-after-its-olympics-success.
96.  https://varcis.com/wp-content/uploads/2020/11/20201126-PRESS-RELEASE -ENG-FINAL.pdf.
97.  https://varcis.com/wp-content/uploads/2019/11/Media-Release-VARCIS -acquires-Asia-rights-to-Sports-Tech-World-Series-1.pdf.
98.  www.isportconnect.com.
99.  www.istassociation.com/sports-technology-partners.
100. www.astn.com.au/history.
101. LaunchVic and KPMG, *Sportstech Report*, p. 14.

# 14. Conditions for the implementation of a biotechnology Cluster of Innovation in Colombia: a benchmark of best practices with German clusters

**Christian Bruszies and Carlos Scheel**

## 14.1 INTRODUCTION

The global business environment presents an increasing demand for sustainable natural products, a market in which Colombia has had an interesting position, given the diversity of biological and genetic resources that it possesses and that offers special comparative advantages to global players. Colombian companies that apply biotechnology are in a constantly growing global business environment that demands more and more natural products that ensure the sustainable use of biodiversity. This demand is evident in industrial sectors such as cosmetics, pharmaceuticals, agri-food and natural ingredients. In the business sphere, Colombia has developed projects in green biotechnology in particular: biofertilizers and biopesticides for different crops, microorganisms for biofertilizers and bioremediation, production of algae for biofuels, genetically modified (GM) fish with optimized growth and waste composting. However, despite the efforts that the industry has made, the biotechnology clusters have not managed to achieve a consolidated position in the country, and they are still in the initiative phase.

This chapter will describe the results of a comparison study of two regional innovation clusters to identify the success factors and describe the roadmap the Colombian region must scale and replicate to have a successful clustering strategy for the development of the biotechnological industry of the Colombian region. The two regions are the Valle del Cauca department in Colombia, and another in Gatersleben, in Saxony-Anhalt, Germany. Both have similarities and differences that allow us to understand their degree of progress in the formation of network structures, such as innovation clusters.

The department of Valle del Cauca, with its capital city Cali, and the western Colombian region in general, is characterized by its great diversity of biological resources, which has favoured the construction of technological and institutional capacities around biotechnology and bioindustry. Since 2000, efforts have been made to consolidate capacities around biotechnology applied to agribusiness and bioindustry in an organized network structure compounded by big companies like Cartón de Colombia S.A./Smurfit Kappa Cali, Sucromiles S.A., Levapan S.A. and Recamier S.A.; private associations like the Biotec Corporation (a non-profit organization), the Cali Chamber of Commerce, ANDI-Valle (an industry organization of the region) and Asocaña (an association of the sugar industry); research institutes like Cenicaña, CIAT (Centro Internacional de Agricultura Tropical) and public/private universities like Universidad del Valle, the Javeriana Cali University, the Palmira National University, and ICESI; and the regional government (Gobernación del Valle), with public institutions like Procolombia (formerly Proexport). All these actors (Cluster of Innovation, or COI, components) were grouped with the purpose of forming the Bioindustrial Cluster of the Colombian West (CBOC), an industrial network of the region with the objective to generate positive economic, social and environmental impacts, using biotechnology as a catalyst and a transversal axis of innovation in the agricultural sector.

Gatersleben is a municipality of Seeland, located 10 km from the city of Quedlinburg and almost in the centre of the federal state of Saxony-Anhalt. It is recognized for its research and development regarding seeds. The natural wealth of this federal state involves its natural parks and biosphere reserves, which are home to a great variety of plants and animals (Sachsen-Anhalt, 2011). Gatersleben is located in one of the most fertile areas of Germany, in a historical and current centre of plant breeding, and is now the centre of excellence for plant biotechnology in Germany (IMG, 2019). Gatersleben's importance in plant biotechnology is largely due to the Leibniz Institute for Plant Genetics and Crop Research (IPK), which is home to Germany's largest crop gene bank and has over 60 years of research experience (GGG, 2018). In 1999, the first companies located in Gatersleben were IPK spin-offs. In 2000 a biotechnology centre was built, and in 2006 the Gatersleben Biotechnology Park was consolidated. Today, there is an extensive network that connects industry and business players with research entities and political agents.

To compare the situation of the two regions, the authors developed a Conceptual Model of Success Factors for implementing an innovation cluster system in biotechnology, taking into account the conceptual framework of "Systemic Competitiveness" of the German Development Institute (Esser, Hillebrand, Messner, and Meyer-Stamer, 1996) applying four dimensions of the enabling conditions: Meta, focus on the ability of social actors to jointly formulate visions and strategies and to implement policies; Macro, which refers to a stable and predictable macroeconomic framework; Meso, with the emphasis of specific policies and institutions to shape industries and their environment; and a Micro dimension, to identify conditions for enabling and continuously improving firms and networks of firms. According to these four dimensions, success factors for competitiveness could be determined, which are used to analyse the two cases as a benchmark study.

## 14.2   SITUATION OF BIOTECHNOLOGY IN COLOMBIA

The government of Colombia developed a public policy in the areas of education, science, technology and innovation (Misión Internacional de Sabios; Minciencias, 2019). The policy offers long-term strategies for the country to respond to productive and social challenges, complying with criteria of scale, replication and sustainability. The mission focus on eight areas: convergent technologies (nanotechnology, biotechnology, information technology and cognitive science; NBIC) – Industries 4.0; cultural and creative industries; sustainable energy; biotechnology, the environment and bioeconomy; oceans and hydrobiological resources; social sciences and human development with equity; life and health sciences; the basic sciences and space science. One of the development sectors that deserves special attention is biotechnology, because of its high impact on the competitive development of industries such as agriculture and the food industry, medical treatments, and the pharmaceutical and cosmetic industries. In these industries Colombia has comparative advantages because of its natural resources that provide opportunities to create a broad portfolio of research, sustainable development and innovation in a sector based on knowledge, such as biotechnology.

Currently, the country has five regional development zones in biotechnology: Bogotá-Cundinamarca; Bucaramanga, Santander; Caldas, Risaralda and Quindío; Cali, Valle del Cauca; and Medellín-Antioquia (Procolombia, 2013), and there have been some improvements in the organizational environment through governmental policy (CONPES, 2011) to further promote biotechnology in the country.

Colombian companies in the biotechnology sector, such as Ecoflora Agro Formulaciones SAS, Sucroal S.A. and Levapan S.A., are in a constantly growing global business environment that demands more and more natural products that also ensure the sustainable use of biodiversity. This demand is evident in industrial sectors such as cosmetics, pharmaceuticals, agri-food and natural ingredients (CONPES, 2011).

Currently agricultural biotechnology in the world is characterized for being more precise and rapid in improving the characteristics of plants as input for the food industry or to facilitate their processing. In addition, it contributes to ensuring the availability of food and its safety for consumers, due to the increase in the variety of foods available and greater production efficiency. The use of modern technologies, such as CRISPR, for the transfer of desirable characteristics, offers possibilities to increase the safety of GM plants and food products more than those generated by conventional breeding techniques (Bonciu and Sarac, 2017). Thus, modern agricultural biotechnology emerges as a possible tool for hunger reduction and to achieve food security and better nutrition, while promoting sustainable agriculture practices.

In Colombia, efforts in this direction have already been developed, such as GM crops of cotton, corn and blue carnations (Fedearroz, 2008). According to the Agricultural Plant Biotechnology Association (Agro-Bio, 2018), in 2002 Colombia began to participate in the use of GM crops with the sowing of blue carnations. The following year, GM cotton was approved under a controlled planting scheme; likewise, the same happened with GM corn in 2007, and in 2009 the planting of GM blue roses was approved (Figure 14.1).

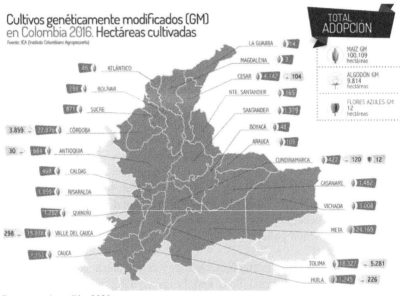

*Source:*    Agro-Bio, 2020.

*Figure 14.1     Map of genetically modified crops in Colombia*

Among the main benefits identified in the application of biotechnology in crops are the increase in productivity due to improvements in yield, a greater nutritional value of foods and the reduction of their costs. The study *Use of Genetically Modified (GM) Crops in Colombia: Economic and Environmental Benefits in the Field* confirms that from the arrival of the farming of cotton

(2003) and transgenic corn (2007) in Colombia, the impact on the environment that GM crops have made is favourable (Agro-Bio, 2018).

According to a measurement by the Environmental Impact Coefficient (EIQ), which is responsible for measuring the impact of phytosanitary products such as herbicides, insecticides and fungicides on the environment and on human health, over these past 15 years the adoption of transgenic crops in Colombia has resulted in a 26 per cent reduction in environmental impact. In Table 14.1 are the most relevant data on the impact of transgenic crops on the environment.

*Table 14.1     The impact of transgenic crops on the environment in Colombia*

| Transgenic crops: benefits for the environment | |
| --- | --- |
| Lower environmental impact | -26% |
| Use of insecticides on cotton | -27% |
| Use of insecticides in corn | -65% |
| Use of herbicides on cotton | -5% |
| Herbicide use in corn | -22% |
| Pesticide use | -19% |

*Source:*     Created by the authors based on Agro-Bio, 2020.

Colombia planted a total of 101,188 hectares of GM crops in 2019, distributed among 88,268 hectares of corn, 12,907 of cotton and 12 of blue flowers, according to figures presented by the Colombian Agricultural Institute, or ICA (Agro-Bio, 2020).

Actually, there are concerns about the increase in GM crops and the possible impact on the biodiversity of Colombia. In 2020, a draft legislative act that seeks to modify Article 81 of the Colombian Political Constitution was presented for the second time in the House of Representatives to prohibit the entry, production, commercialization and export of GM seeds. This proposal is not opposed to technological development, but rather proposes a sustainable development strategy that is coherent with the biodiversity of the country, as explained by Corporación Grupo Semillas Colombia (Slow Food, 2020).

The previous advances have been the result of the execution of multiple processes in which different research and development actors intervene. In 1997 Colciencias (the Administrative Department of Science, Technology and Innovation of the Colombian Government) began the National Biotechnology Program (NBP), which promotes biotechnology research through encouraging cooperation between academia, research centres, companies and the state.

The main areas of action of the NBP consist of:

- The consolidation of the biotechnology industry in Colombia
- The development and production of renewable and environmentally sustainable biofuels
- The promotion of knowledge and the protection and sustainable use of biodiversity

The characteristics of biotechnology-based companies and their products pose additional challenges for entrepreneurship and management, some of them related to innovative capacity. Hernández (2008) recognizes the importance of working in cooperation networks in which it is possible to access resources, knowledge and experience, and where the flexibility to react to changes is greater and the risk is shared. In this sense, the need for companies to cooperate with research centres and universities (research groups), under the control of and with special support from the state, is evident.

Taking into account the challenging objectives of the NBP, the Colombian policy document CONPES 3697 of 2011 recognizes that "there are still important gaps that prevent the commercial development of biotechnology from the sustainable use of biological and genetic resources from becoming a source of innovations that facilitate progress in the value chain, in more detail" (pp. 9–15):

- "Low national capacity for the development of modern bioprospecting activities" (p. 9), having as aggravating factors the lack of a clear institutional framework to guide bioprospecting activity, the dispersion or non-existence of information and the limited use of actual technologies
- "Incipient development of technology-based companies that make sustainable use of the biodiversity, especially biological, genetic and derivative resources" (p. 12)
- "Limitations for investments due to the difficulty of implementing regulations for access and use of genetic resources, as well as on the commercialization of biotechnological and phytotherapeutic products" (p. 14)
- "Low coordination and institutional capacity for the development of all those actions related to the commercial promotion of biotechnology based on the sustainable use of the biodiversity, particularly of biological, genetic and derivative resources along the value-added chain" (p. 15)

A strategic diagnosis of the environment (Innpulsa, 2013) reaffirms the existence of the previous problems and identifies additional weaknesses that are circumscribed in the political-regulatory, social, science-and-its-transfer, economic-financial and business-investment spheres. Table 14.2 presents a summary of them.

*Table 14.2*     *Weaknesses of the conditions for the development of biotechnology in Colombia*

| Political-regulatory: | Science-and-its-transfer: |
|---|---|
| • Institutional inefficiency and poor coordination<br>• Great difficulties and delays in accessing the genetic resources<br>• Regulatory gaps | • Research and development (R&D) requires a higher development level<br>• Fragmentation of R&D groups and dispersion of knowledge centres<br>• Lack of experience and knowledge in bio-technology-transfer processes |
| Business: | Economic-financial: |
| • Need to communicate the benefits of biotechnology applications in traditional sectors<br>• There are areas of technological demand not covered by academic institutions (need to search for international partners) | • Difficulties in mobilizing private venture capital<br>• Few specialized private investors interested in investing in the sector |
| Social: | |
| • The biotech sector has a bad image due to its excessive association with "genetic manipulation" | |

*Source:*     Created by the authors based on Innpulsa (2013).

The results of the analysis of weaknesses show different trajectories of biotechnological development that are explained by the historical, cultural and economic contexts of the countries and regions involved. Clusters in developing countries are characterized by: the predominance of small and medium-sized enterprises (SMEs), the lack of a critical mass of companies (especially in high-tech sectors), an informal organizational structure and the links between the cluster components being weaker compared with clusters of industrialized countries. In developing countries, the agricultural sector has begun to move towards high-value products and services, and to create more connections with the global market (Galvez-Nogales, 2010), and it has traditionally focused more on production rather than research.

After examining the situation of agrobiotechnology in Colombia, we proceed to consider world trends in biotechnology and the opportunities that Colombia has in this context.

## 14.3     TRENDS IN BIOTECHNOLOGY WHICH OFFER FURTHER OPPORTUNITIES FOR COLOMBIA

Although there is no universal concept of bioeconomy, it is defined by the Organization for Economic Co-operation and Development (OECD) "as a world in which biotechnology contributes to a significant part of economic production ... a bioeconomy involves three elements: biotechnological knowledge, renewable biomass, and integration of different applications" (2009, p. 22). Biotechnological knowledge allows the development of new processes for the development of a wide portfolio of products, involving intensive R&D and innovation. In turn, the use of efficient bioprocesses contributes to the optimal use of renewable biomass for the generation of such products as biofuels, paper and industrial chemicals.

The integration of knowledge within value chains opens the space for the development of three fields of application for biotechnology: primary production, health applications and industry applications. Primary production involves all sectors that make use of living natural resources such as forests, plants for cultivation, livestock animals and insects. Applications in the health sector include diagnostic techniques, drugs, nutraceuticals and some medical devices. Industrial applications cover plastics, chemicals, enzymes and environmental uses.

The bioeconomy, together with solutions that take advantage of the benefits of the combination of technologies and the Industry 4.0 model (Berger, 2016), offer important opportunities to reverse the negative effects of the dominant economic model. In this context, it is appropriate to consider some related technology trends.

- Green chemistry: This is an emerging field that focuses on work at the molecular level with the purpose of achieving sustainability. In the last decade this field of science has aroused wide interest due to its ability to harness chemical innovation to meet ecological and economical objectives simultaneously.

   Green chemistry is characterized by careful planning of chemical synthesis and molecular design to reduce adverse consequences. Through proper design, synergies can be achieved, not just trade-offs ... Because Green Chemistry focuses on achieving sustainability at the molecular level, important applications have been developed in sectors such as aerospace, automotive, cosmetics, electronics, energy, household products, pharmaceuticals and agriculture. (Anastas and Eghbali, 2010, p. 302)

- Green nanotechnology: The presence of toxic chemicals on the surface of metallic nanoparticles and nonpolar solvents limits their use in clinical applications. "Therefore, the biosynthesis of clean, biocompatible, non-toxic and environmentally friendly nanoparticles produced both extracellular and intracellular deserves merit." Green nanotechnology is based on the field of green chemistry for the design of nanotechnological solutions that meet economic, social and health and environmental objectives together (Nath and Banerjee, 2013, p. 4).

In nature, there are examples of processes for the synthesis of inorganic materials on a nano and micro scale that have contributed to the development of a research area based on the biosynthesis of nanomaterials. Nanoparticle biosynthesis has a bottom-up approach where the main reaction is reduction/oxidation. "Microbial enzymes or plant phytochemicals with antioxidant or reducing properties are generally responsible for the reduction of metallic compounds in their respective nanoparticles" (Nath and Banerjee, 2013, p. 12).

Based on these trends, the Colombian government is aware that biodiversity is a comparative advantage for the socioeconomic, environmental and sustainable development of the country and is promoting the commercial development of biotechnology through the use of biological, genetic resources and their derivatives (CONPES, 2011). The Colombian biodiversity program aims to promote the bioeconomy and the creative economy, which implies a change in dependence on the exploitation of non-renewable resources and primary agricultural products towards the development of a knowledge-based economy of high added value and environmentally and socially sustainable. The productive and sustainable challenge is a transformation of the productive structure towards industries and services with high technological content and the promotion of circular economy companies (Minciencias, 2019).

One of the promising fields for the use of green chemistry in Colombia is in the creation of value from the by-products derived from the production of bio-fuels (in Barrancabermeja, Santander). The National University of Colombia and the company Ecodiesel Colombia S.A. are working together to transform the glycerine derived from biodiesel production into a useful compound for industry and the environment (Fedebiocombustibles, 2021). This would contribute to the environmentally sustainable transition of the energy sector, the development of new productive capacities, the generation of technology-based ventures or companies, and the strengthening of the regional economy. The responsible use of Colombian biodiversity would promote the sustainable production of raw materials, taking advantage of technological convergence (Noriega, 2019) – concepts that are aligned to the Green Premium approach (Gates Notes, 2020), mainly involving the energy industry.

The wealth of Colombia's natural resources offers countless sources for research in green nanomaterials with opportunities for the development of solutions, with low energy use and low environmental impact, based on biosynthesis processes through the use of bacteria, actinomycetes, fungi and plants. The advantage of using plants for the synthesis of nanoparticles is that they are readily available and safe to handle and have a wide variability of metabolites that can aid in reduction. Some applications for these green nano-particles are labelling, sensors, drug dispensing, cancer therapies and cleaning up the environment (Nath and Banerjee, 2013, pp. 18, 20).

According to Noriega (2019), advances in biotechnology and green chemistry require:

- Development of human resources and their retention: Human resources trained in basic and applied sciences (for example, engineering) are needed for the development of new knowledge, capacities and skills for technology transfer (for example, oleochemistry, biochemistry) in the agro-industrial and industrial sectors of the country. Modernization of some existing undergraduate careers or the creation of new postgraduate programs are needed (for example, "Chemical engineering and biology" or "Chemical engineering and biotechnology", existing in some universities in the United States, United Kingdom and Switzerland).

- Public–private partnerships (PPPs) and internationalization: The green chemistry sector opens possibilities for the generation of personalized products (cosmetics, cosmeceuticals and organic products for personal care and hygiene), as well as materials used in large-scale production (for example, glycerine used in different detergents, plasticizers, paints). In this context, precompetitive PPP consortia with academia, industry and national and international allies (for example, investors) are an important option. Investment opportunities and the attraction of national and international capital require stable long-term science, technology and innovation (STI) policies.

- Associativity and innovation in public policies: It is very important to identify the technological gaps and strengthen relationships between the university, institutes and STI actors and companies, in order to achieve significant R&D in green chemistry, clean technologies and innovation, which will be a differentiating advantage in international markets. The unification and instrumentalization of the policies of the new Ministry of Science, Technology and Innovation; the Ministry of Information Technologies and Communications; the Ministry of Commerce, Industry and Tourism; Innpulsa (the Innovation Program of the development bank Bancoldex); SENA (the National Learning Service); PTP (the Productive Transformation Program) and other institutions is needed to achieve an interconnected, effective and efficient institutional framework.

- Mechanisms to guarantee market access: It is necessary to create mechanisms that allow these products to be competitive against fossil-fuel products. These mechanisms and/or incentives should promote national consumption and export to markets that recognize their added value.

These four factors correlate with behaviours in the COI Framework, such as the alignment of interests among the COI components of Government, Universities, Entrepreneurs and Major Corporations, which allows innovation in education as well as in technology, and the global perspective and linkages, which encourage access to international resources and markets (Engel, 2015).

## 14.4   BUILDING CLUSTERS OF INNOVATION FOR THE DEVELOPMENT OF THE BIOTECHNOLOGY SECTOR IN COLOMBIA

According to Ablaev (2018) and Engel (2014), the creation of innovation clusters is one of the best propositions for the development of a regional economy, taking into account the characteristics of the current competitive environment. Innovation clusters provide advantages by generating economic and scientific-technological impacts by promoting technological advance. In this context, COI have been defined as "global economic hot spots where new technologies germinate at an astounding rate and where pools of capital, expertise, and talent foster the development of new industries and new ways of doing business" (Engel, 2015, pp. 37).

Under the concept of innovation and the need to establish links between components of the cluster, it is necessary to observe both the relationships that are generated between companies and research centres (universities, technological development centres, science institutes, and so on) and the role they play in the cluster in promoting business innovation. According to Engel (2015), "in these ecosystems, resources of people, capital, and knowhow are fluidly mobile, and the pace of transactions is driven by a relentless pursuit of opportunity, staged financing, and short business model cycles" (pp. 37).

From the above concepts and practices, we have identified that for the case of the biotechnology cluster in Colombia the following characteristics must be present:

### Technological Accumulation, Knowledge Transfer and Absorption Capacity

Innovation clusters are catalysts for the development of new technologies; they incentivize innovation and promote the implementation of new technologies. They are characterized by having a sufficient "critical mass" of companies, researchers and support entities that are spatially agglomerated and globally connected in a network of COI (and sometimes Super-COI) or are components building a virtual network (non-geographic COI) in value chains without a physical flow of products (for example, software in animation films). Qian (2018) argues that entrepreneurship can serve as a mechanism for knowledge spillovers and, consequently, contribute to regional innovation and cluster-formation and drive economic development. Especially in biotechnology COI, universities and research institutes function as centres of technological diffusion where new knowledge can be put into practice to the extent that biotechnology companies and human resources are able to absorb it.

## Development of Special Value Chains and Catalysts for Business Innovation

COI contribute to a greater specialization of the production system by developing around a particular field of knowledge and technologies. Wixted (2009) points out that knowledge-accumulation processes influence the joint evolution of scientific specialization and industry. In this context, the clusters contribute to achieving the "smart specialization" objectives of the regions, such as the establishment of priorities for interregional interaction, in accordance with the directions of transformation of the sectoral structure of the region; involve different actors in the process; and create special structures for the implementation of interaction (Kostygova, 2019). Clusters offer the opportunity to exploit their inherent synergistic potential and the strategic exchange of knowledge between actors; in other words, the availability of knowledge, other resources and cooperation partners within the clusters favours the performance of business innovation. Similarly, companies benefit from social and institutional proximity within clusters, since group values such as trust and reciprocity are manifested.

## Access to International Markets and Businesses

Based on the conditions, capabilities and opportunities of the biotechnology industry in Colombia, focusing attention on the key characteristics of a COI identified by Engel (2014, p. 11) – adaptation of new technologies, creation of new markets and focusing on large global markets – will be a key issue for the success of the cluster in international arenas. The demand for products and services supplied by the cluster, combined with the competitive position of the cluster, outlines its growth potential. The demand for products and services supplied by the cluster, combined with the competitive position of the cluster, outlines the growth potential of the cluster. The competitive position of a cluster must be classified in relation to that of international competitors (benchmarking) and includes the ability of the cluster to obtain the necessary resources for growth. Managers at the cluster level have to be excellent at creating new business models that add value to companies.

## Generation of Social Capital and Networks

The generation of inter-organizational networks within clusters is especially important for the dissemination of information, exchange of resources, access to specialized assets (infrastructure and qualified personnel) and opportunities for inter-organizational learning through the development of new ideas and skills. In the COI Framework, this characteristic is described as "mobility of resources: money, people and technology" (Engel, 2014). According to Cohen and Fields (1999), social capital acts as a facilitator of collaborations and solid interactions between regional actors, contributing to the construction of innovation networks. Cooperation and rivalry, trust and responsibility (legal contracts) can coexist in the same space. The universities oriented to research and entrepreneurship that exist in innovation clusters fulfil a double function in high-tech sectors; on the one hand, they act as an anchor for resources, and on the other, they are an agent for the construction and configuration of social structures. Universities are means for companies and the region to develop and boost technology-based entrepreneurship throught technology transfer (Barra, Maietta, and Zotti, 2020; Cooke, 2001; Zucker, Darby, and Armstrong, 2002).

## The Capacity for Associativity

The success of the associativity strategy depends on the integration of economic regions, traditional production sectors and new high-tech productive activities that may have potential for regional economic development. Associativity models such as innovation clusters are an effective tool for small and medium-sized productive sectors such as biotechnology to be able to insert and maintain themselves in markets that are increasingly regional, open and competitive. In Scheel's (2014) study on prosperous regional value creation poles ("innovacities"), significant results have been generated that can be replicated with planned strategic policies, the provision of specific regional innovation and facilitating conditions. From this study it was identified that the associativity capacity (valuable interconnection of resources, influencers and interest groups) was one of the most important factors to achieve a certain disposition for the establishment of industrial clusters, knowledge clusters, networks of social entrepreneurship and/or regional COI. What is more interesting is that each region has shown different types of associativity, as well as different levels of learning through each association, which adds an additional component to the value system of each innovacity. In conclusion, given that each region has its own conditions, each one must be diagnosed individually, developing specific capacities and conditions for each sector, since not all sectors or industrial clusters have the same characteristics, capabilities and conditions.

## 14.5 CONCEPTUAL MODEL OF SUCCESS FACTORS FOR IMPLEMENTING A REGIONAL CLUSTER OF INNOVATION IN BIOTECHNOLOGY

According to Porter (1990), the competitiveness of nations is directly related to the capacity for innovation and updating of their industry. Porter recognizes the existence of significant differences in the competition patterns of countries, which lead them to be successful in certain sectors which the nation has encouraged through a dynamic and challenging environment. As Porter's framework was expanded by Engel (2014), the competitive environment results from coordinated and articulated actions of different components (Entrepreneurs, Government, Universities and Research Centres, Major Corporations, Investors, business associations, and Service Organizations) at the political, administrative, institutional, economic and social levels. Therefore, to be permanent, competitiveness requires the presence of a set of environmental factors in its different dimensions, acting in an interrelated and dynamic way, as a system, which favours increased productivity through innovation and improvement of the living conditions of the population. In this sense, in a globalized world not only companies but systems compete. For this reason, it is insisted that companies cannot be competitive if they are not inserted in networks, made up of multiple agents and institutions, which collaborate in creating the conditions to compete (Esser et al., 1996, 2013).

In this context, the concept of Systemic Competitiveness arises, which serves as a frame of reference for the analysis of the competitiveness of industrialized and developing countries and has been found to be a key competitive factor for the most innovative cities (Scheel and Pineda, 2017).

As mentioned above, the Systemic Competitiveness model proposed by Esser et al. (1996) is made up of four analytical levels: Meta, Macro, Meso and Micro; and it is characterized by linking elements belonging to industrial economics, innovation theory and industrial sociology (Figure 14.2).

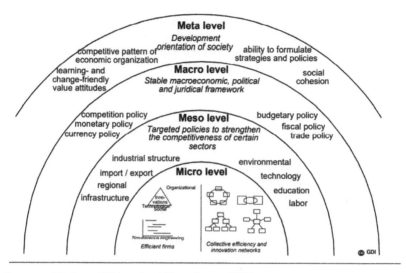

*Source:*     Altenburg, Hillebrand, and Meyer-Stamer (1998).

*Figure 14.2*     *Determinants of Systemic Competitiveness*

The model makes it possible to identify the most far-reaching success factors that enable or hinder the establishment of biotechnology clusters. Additionally, the model based on Systemic Competitiveness introduces regional (territorial) success factors. The characteristics of each level are described below.

**The Meta Level**

The Meta level expresses industrial governance and competitiveness. In the COI Framework, this is primarily in the realm of the Government component. Success factors are determined for the construction of a vision of biotechnology that focuses its attention on the particularities of the territory in which the cluster initiative is developed. Therefore, its constructs cover political and social issues:

- Public politics: Development policy based on innovation systems, a shared development vision (biotechnology), innovation policy, and the clarity and articulation of public policies.
- Creation of legitimacy and rule of law: Adherence to existing norms, values, expectations and definitions. Aligning the innovation in biotechnology to established modes or standards and the regulatory framework.

Applying the rule of law, the mechanism, process, institution, practice or norm that supports the equality of all citizens before the law.

- Social context: The most relevant social aspects are the perception of the development of biotechnology and the willingness to change and learn, social cohesion and the creation of awareness about clusters.

## The Macro Level

The Macro level includes the link between economic stabilization and liberalization, with the capacity for transformation. The macroeconomic success factors are determined for the promotion of innovation in biotechnology and deal with the economic-business components, endowment of resources and infrastructure:

- Macroeconomic context: Budgetary and internal and foreign trade policies. In addition, economic performance, production rates, exports and the business environment.
- Business environment: The territorial conditions that affect the clusters are policies to improve the quality of life, the presence of related sectors/industries or other clusters, and pre-existing knowledge represented in academic research or basic competencies of companies.

## The Meso Level

The Meso level provides support to the efforts of companies, formed by specific policies for the creation of competitive advantages, by the environment and by the institutions. In the COI Framework, this level incorporates the primary components (Government, Entrepreneurs and Major Corporations, Universities, Investors) and their actions. The success factors for the innovation cluster of the biotechnology sector are determined; among them are the territorial issues, the actors and their interactions, the infrastructure and the framework conditions that govern the conduct of the sector:

- Characteristics of the territory (region): Pre-existing agroecological and biotechnology knowledge and capabilities, physical infrastructure, culture of innovation, culture of entrepreneurship, territorial attractions, the existence of industries/sectors related to biotechnology, the labour market and the attraction of personnel, and the recognition of the region (branding).
- Competences of the actors and their interactions: The main actors of the cluster are the COI components of the political system (Government), the value-creation system (Entrepreneurs and Major Corporations), and the education and research institutions (Universities and Research Centres).

The success factors that promote the interaction between actors are sufficient social capital or critical mass, proximity, mutual cohesion, trust, cooperation, outsourcing and rivalry.

- Infrastructure and framework conditions: Key components are financing (Venture Capital, Government), a scientific-technological platform and service infrastructure (specialized Service Organizations). The success factors related to the framework conditions refer to such issues as the intellectual property protection system and the conditions and requirements for access to financing for innovation projects.

**The Micro Level**

The Micro level refers to technological and institutional requirements. The success factors for innovation in biotechnology companies and the functions that must be carried out during the entire life cycle of the innovations are determined, from the development of knowledge to the formation of markets and the creation of legitimacy of the innovations:

- Orientation of research and entrepreneurship: This includes the ability to strategically select the technological options to be developed; and the search for markets (market formation), business models and organizational structures.
- Development and dissemination of knowledge: Within the knowledge-development cycle, knowledge-creation and knowledge-adoption processes are generated (Adler, 1989), creating mechanisms for learning and modifying acquired knowledge for specific organizational circumstances and knowledge-distribution processes.
- Mobilization of resources: This includes the attraction of capital, the presence of venture capitalists, staff turnover within the cluster (mobilization and recycling, especially in start-ups), the diversity of skills and experience of staff and Open Innovation processes.

These descriptions of the success factors of each level of the Systemic Competitiveness model offer complementary views for the comparison of the two cases. The Meta and Macro levels focus their attention on the particularities of the territory in which the clusters are developed; therefore, their constructs cover political, social, economic-business, resource endowment and infrastructure issues. The Meso level deals with the components of the sector, including the actors and their interactions, the infrastructure and the framework conditions that govern the behaviour of the sector. And the Micro level determines the functions that must be performed throughout the life cycle of innovations, from knowledge development to market formation and creation of legitimacy of innovations.

The next section presents the results and the analysis of the two benchmarking cases, taking into account the success factors described in the Systemic Competitiveness model.

## 14.6    RESULTS OF A BENCHMARKING STUDY BETWEEN A COLOMBIAN AND A GERMAN BIOTECHNOLOGY CLUSTER

### Case: Valle del Cauca, Colombia

The biotechnology activities of the Valle del Cauca are embedded in a regional innovation system (Sistema Regional de Innovación de Biotecnología; SRIB) that according to its mission promotes an associative technological, ecological and socio-political platform for the region.

Based on the achieved results, there is still a need to consolidate the appropriate conditions for the development and use of biotechnology and life sciences as tools for development and prosperity in the region. In this context, in 2009 the Biotec Corporation presented to Colciencias the proposal "Regional system of biotechnology innovation for the agricultural, agro-industrial and bio-industrial reconversion of western Colombia: Contribution to its consolidation". It had a double objective: on the one hand, the institutional strengthening of the Biotec Corporation in harmony with the framework of the law and the policy of the National System of Science, Technology and Innovation of Colombia (SNCTI), and on the other, the "promotion of an associative technological platform for the region, support of [an] SRIB, that links, enhances and optimizes existing and future resources, convening academia and research centres, government, companies and national and international cooperation" (Sánchez-Mejía and Gutiérrez-Terán, 2013, p. 261).

In 2011, a roundtable was held, in which the University Network for Innovation of Valle del Cauca, the Regional Competitiveness Commission and the main actors and regional leaders in biotechnology participated with the purpose of structuring the Agroindustrial Park of the Pacific (Bio Pacífico), a geographical space in the Valle del Cauca unifying components like institutes of investigation and the National University as a COI initiative. As a result of the meeting, major projects were structured and defined in these three areas: (1) a network of innovation, development and commercial application of biotechnology and the use of biological resources in the cosmetic and pharmaceutical sectors of Valle del Cauca; (2) an agrobiotechnology platform to strengthen the competitiveness of agribusiness in Valle del Cauca and the

Pacific region, integrated into the Agroindustrial Park of the Pacific; and (3) the use of biomass as energy and a sustainable resource for the Valle del Cauca.

In the Valle del Cauca under the SRIB, the orientation of research and development in sectors with competitive potential in the territory has been defined. Knowledge has been developed in different areas, from the design of agricultural machinery through to more efficient agricultural business models, to the use of biotechnology as a tool for the improvement of agricultural, agro-industrial and bioindustrial chains. The SRIB initiative contemplates the generation of high-added-value agro-industrial ventures, awareness workshops have been held for technology-based entrepreneurship and initiatives for the creation of spin-offs have begun to emerge. In conclusion, the components in Valle del Cauca work in informally coordinated networks; a developed cluster structure for biotechnology innovation has not yet been generated.

Although the two territories have both decided to transform their history by focusing on this sector, Gatersleben in Germany, as an international reference point, has gained an advantage with important scientific and technological strengths (for example, Genebank and its Bioinformatics Center[1]), accompanied by a specialized support infrastructure for each stage of the business development (for example, financing, management), the core and supporting components of a COI.

## Case: Gatersleben, Germany

In 2012, Bayer CropScience AG opened its European Wheat Improvement Center in Gatersleben, from which it coordinates all the company's European research activities for wheat improvement (GGG, 2018). Importantly, the Green Gate Gatersleben (GGG) is an initiative of companies and research institutions in plants and biotechnology, as well as regional public authorities based in Gatersleben. GGG's aim is to jointly market and present Gatersleben and the skills and services of its partners to the outside world. "Under the umbrella brand 'Green Gate Gatersleben – The Plant Biotech Center', the GGG partners define the activities that they will carry out jointly, such as symposia, seminars and joint participation in trade shows" (Eise and Stuber, 2016, p. 106).

In 2014, the government of Saxony-Anhalt adopted the Regional Innovation Strategy (RIS), which establishes a series of measures for the development of the bioeconomy and identifies the sector as one of the main markets in the region. A partner advisory council (WISO[2]), which deals with European Union funds and comprises scientific associations, non-governmental organizations, civil society organizations and other associations, participated in the RIS development process. In addition, the BioEconomy group brings together partners from industry and science who are key players within the regional bioeconomy; they are strongly involved in the development and implementation of the RIS. The BioEconomy group covers the states of Saxony-Anhalt and Saxony (Leipzig, Dresden) and is concentrated around the Leuna chemical-industrial complex in this region. The aim of the RIS is to develop the Central German region and transform it into an international model for the bioeconomy. Specifically, the Saxony-Anhalt strategy focuses on improving the competitiveness of SMEs in the region and generating smart, sustainable and socially inclusive growth and promoting innovation, through developing this COI.

## Conclusions of the Benchmarking Study

After a benchmarking analysis of the two regions, we arrived at the results of the matching success factors, shown in Figure 14.3. The strengths of the cluster in Germany are in the factors of public policy, financing and technology infrastructure, labour, services and cluster management. Germany has more experience in the formation of networks and clusters and gets decisive support from the regional government (financing for six years). Furthermore, Saxony-Anhalt regional policy prioritizes networking rather than strengthening science and technology infrastructure because that was the focus of previous policies. Saxony-Anhalt is financially supported by the European Structural Funds and significant foreign investments. The business environment of Saxony-Anhalt is more favourable than that of the Valle del Cauca in Colombia because it offers high levels of security and protection of intellectual property, a reliable legal system, easy and fast procedures and free consulting services from governmental agencies.

The strengths in both regions lie in the capacity factors of the actors and their interregional and international links. Innovation policies pay attention to similar issues, especially to strengthening the innovation capacities of SMEs. In Valle del Cauca, knowledge has been developed in different areas, from the design of agricultural machinery through to more efficient agricultural models, to the use of biotechnology as a method for the improvement of agricultural, agribusiness and bioindustry chains. At Gatersleben, partners have developed knowledge to provide customer-oriented products and services on topics such as marker-assisted breeding, crop transformation, technology enablement, plant genetics and phenotypic analysis, among others.[3] The exports of the two regions are concentrated in countries with which they have trade agreements, America and Europe, respectively.

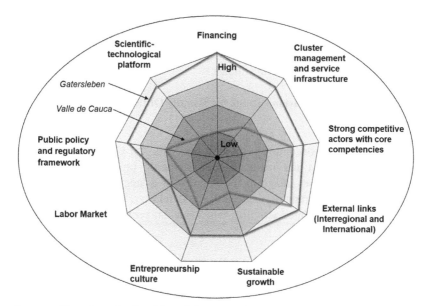

*Source:* The authors, developed from their own unpublished research data (2020).

*Figure 14.3 Benchmarking results on matching success factors*

The weaknesses in both regions are in the labour market factor. The two regions suffer from a labour market that is large enough for administrative positions but insufficient for growth in the biotechnology area. In the case of Valle del Cauca, most of the personnel are employed in the commercial and service sectors, while in Saxony-Anhalt the problem is the emigration of students and graduates.

The greatest weakness in the Valle de Cauca region is in the factors of sustainable growth. The inadequate physical infrastructure (Internet, transport, information and communication technologies, and so on) in the region is an obstacle for the development of clusters, and the insufficient sources of financing and government support are a barrier for the development of innovation projects. And as usual, the lack of the rule of law for most regulations and policies in the region is a very significant barrier.

## Benchmarking Conclusions about the Results Obtained at the Meta Level

The two regions have a strategic direction for regional development with prioritization of sectors with the application of advanced technologies. The development of an economy based on natural resources (agriculture-agribusiness) is important for both regions; however, in the regional planning documents of Saxony-Anhalt it is evident that biotechnology has a more decisive role in territorial development than in Valle del Cauca. The two regions have made efforts to articulate their public policies.

### Benchmarking Conclusions about the Results Obtained at the Macro Level

Regarding the macroeconomic environment, Valle del Cauca has an important participation in the national gross domestic product (GDP), while Saxony-Anhalt has an image in the country as a lagging region. The two regions have an important presence in the food industry, the chemical industry, and agriculture and related activities, which encourages the development of the territories.

### Benchmarking Conclusions about the Results Obtained at the Meso Level

The two regions have fertile soils suitable for agricultural activities, and research institutes concentrate knowledge and skills in agricultural and biotechnology issues. Although there are large business players in both regions, the majority of companies are SMEs. Saxony-Anhalt promotes innovation in SMEs through the Competence Network for Applied and Transfer-Oriented Research (KAT).

### Benchmarking Conclusions about the Results Obtained at the Micro Level

The two regions have an orientation towards research and development in sectors with competitive potential in their territory. In Valle del Cauca, under the SRIB, four macro-projects related to bioprospecting, technological innovation in agriculture and health, the development of the fruit industry, and the building of capacities for agriculture, agribusiness and bioindustry are prioritized. On the other hand, in Gatersleben the orientation of biotechnology research has a higher level of scientific research, in such areas as mutagenesis, cereal transformation, plant phenotyping, proteomics and metabolomics.

*Table 14.3*     *Benchmarking results: Meta, Macro, Meso and Micro analysis*

| Construct | Valle del Cauca | Gatersleben (Saxony-Anhalt) |
|---|---|---|
| Meta – public policy<br>• Shared development vision<br>• Science-based development policy<br>• Innovation policy<br>• Clarity in the articulation of policies | Importance of the agro-industrial sector (biotechnology is not a fundamental factor in policies of the sector). | Biotechnology plays a decisive role in productive transformation. Financial support from the government is significant. |
| Meta – social context of biotechnology<br>• Perception of the development of biotechnology<br>• Willingness to change | Low level of acceptance. | Low level of acceptance. |
| Macro – macroeconomic context<br>• Economic performance<br>• Production<br>• Exports<br>• Business environment | Important participation in the national GDP. | Image in the country of a lagging region. Favourable business environment for investments. |
| Meso – characteristics of the territory<br>• Pre-existing biotechnology and agroecological knowledge and capabilities<br>• Physical infrastructure<br>• Culture of innovation<br>• Entrepreneurship culture<br>• Industries/sectors related to biotechnology<br>• Labour market and employee-attraction | Strong in agroecological resources. Most personnel are employed in the commerce and services sectors. | Strong knowledge base in agrobiotechnology. A determined drive for innovation in SMEs. Emigration of students and graduates. |
| Meso – actors' competencies<br>• Facilitator or director<br>• Political system<br>• Research and education<br>• Value-creation system | There is no appointed facilitator or director. Centralized political system. | BMD GmbH (a service company that works as an agency to support the transfer of research findings into business) manages the regional biotechnology cluster. The federal system allows more regional autonomy. Excellent infrastructure for technology transfer. |

| Construct | Valle del Cauca | Gatersleben (Saxony-Anhalt) |
| --- | --- | --- |
| Meso – interaction between the actors<br><br>• Collaborative philosophy and collective ownership<br>• Attraction of competitive actors<br>• External links<br>• Networking | The SRIB initiative contemplates the interregional integration of the Pacific departments. | All the actors in the cluster are equal and have a strong participation. Plant biotechnology network (100 partners). The successful cluster attracts new players. |
| Meso – infrastructure<br><br>• Financing<br>• Scientific-technological (ST) platform<br>• Infrastructure of services | It is not entirely clear how the SRIB will be financed. It is planned to deploy the ST platform in different regions. | Tailor-made financing for innovation and specialized in R&D for plant breeding.<br>Complete ST platform (basic research to business incubation, all in one region). |
| Meso – macro conditions<br><br>• Intellectual property rights system<br>• Regulatory framework (clear and unified frameworks for action)<br>• Conditions and requirements for access to financing for innovation projects | Difficulties in accessing genetic resources. Regulatory gaps. Financing of STI projects through royalties is complex. | Clear and efficient intellectual property rights system with a regional patent office.<br>The SRIB awards 120 grants a year for innovation projects. |
| Micro – orientation of research | Five large thematic groups (energy, food, health, environment, industry). | High level of specialization (for example, mutagenesis, cereal transformation, plant phenotyping, proteomics). |
| Micro – development of knowledge | Knowledge development in different areas: agricultural machinery, agricultural models, *in vitro* plant production. | Development of specialized knowledge in plant biotechnology. |
| Micro – diffusion of knowledge | Diffusion of laboratories of research institutions through seminars, workshops, advice to farmers, and so on. | Through a technology-transfer infrastructure, access to databases, newsletters, consultancies. |

| Construct | Valle del Cauca | Gatersleben (Saxony-Anhalt) |
|---|---|---|
| Micro – entrepreneurship activities | The SRIB initiative gives momentum to high-added-value agro-industrial entrepreneurship. There are some spin-off initiatives. | Technology-transfer centres act as business incubators. The ego.-INCUBATOR program supports the activities of university incubators. |
| Micro – mobilizing of resources | The most mobile resources are human and technological resources. | Access to sufficient financial resources, human talents, knowledge and experience. |
| Micro – market-generation | Companies form markets and legitimize their products through the adoption of standards. | Companies follow the regulations and apply strategies to build trust with customers and society in general. |
| Micro – creation of legitimacy | | |

*Source:* The authors, developed from their own unpublished research data (2020).

## 14.7 ROADMAP FOR THE DEVELOPMENT OF THE BIOTECHNOLOGICAL INDUSTRY IN COLOMBIA

According to the 2019 Misión Internacional de Sabios (Minciencias, 2019, p. 25), "for Colombia [the goal is] to achieve benchmark positions in some specific segments of Science Technology and Innovation (STI) based on the country's biodiversity, convergent technologies and industry 4.0." To achieve this goal, Colombia must overcome challenges at the different levels posed by Systemic Competitiveness to develop the components and behaviours of a COI more fully.

For the Meta level, it is necessary to consolidate an ethical culture for the development, commercialization and sustainable use of technology, which implies "understanding the local dynamics of social trends and preferences and the social acceptance of biotechnologies and their representative products of biological origin" (Bezama, Ingrao, O'Keeffe, and Thrän, 2019, p. 1). Furthermore, it is necessary to establish mechanisms for inter-institutional coordination between the entities that formulate public policies and the entities that exercise regulation and control functions.

At the Macro level, it is necessary to generate favourable macroeconomic conditions for investment in biotechnology and related sectors and the definition of mechanisms that guarantee the access of new technologies to the market.

At the Meso level, the transformation of the educational system is decisive for the development of suitable personnel for the biotechnology sector; also, the articulation between the universities and the national STI system is required to generate synergies and promote technological development under a shared approach, coupled with the establishment of a regional "critical mass" through the promotion of clusters and networks (Bezama et al., 2019).

Finally, it will be essential for companies to optimize their capacities for innovation and technology management, which is the responsibility of the Micro level.

For companies to benefit from the advantages offered by being part of an innovation cluster, they must develop a set of particular skills and competencies (see Figure 14.3). Although these advances are encouraging for the sector, they are not enough, because it requires the consolidation of the necessary conditions that favour its development and the identification of the success factors of the COI that promote the sustainable use of biotechnology and life sciences as mechanisms for the development and the prosperity of the region. As a conclusion of the benchmarking study, the success factors in which the experts on each case agreed are: public policies, a regulatory framework, financing, service infrastructure, the labour market, ST platforms, an entrepreneurship culture, strong actors with competitiveness and core competencies, external links, sustainable growth and cluster management and services (Table 14.4).

In conclusion, according to a study by Scheel (2014, p. 278), it is clear that in developing countries there is a two-stage approach to the implementation of an RIS:

> the basic activity to implement RIS strategies must be focused on creating the right conditions to support innovation ecosystems. Regions with hostile local conditions, insufficient resources and poor connectivity, must build effective innovation ecosystems, overcoming the barriers present in those regions to achieve a transparent rule of law, allowing infrastructure, provision of business environments of innovation, effective associativity of all members of the innovation chain and an inclusive government, in which everyone is linked to support visionaries and provocateurs of sustainable wealth creation, before starting any associative strategy.

Once the regions are ready with most of the structural conditions obtained, the next critical success factor is the way in which the stakeholders (entrepreneurs, administrators, financiers, academics, and social and political institutions) effectively capture the systemic interconnection of social, economic, geopolitical and environmental factors. This requires a strong link between individuals, innovation chains, business structures, social needs, and harmonious governance towards a common goal: the creation and exchange of sustainable wealth for the entire region. This is a key factor that this and any COI must pursue. It is a common practice in Latin American countries that these purposes change

*Table 14.4    Results: coincident success factors*

| Success factor | Proposition |
|---|---|
| Public policies | Clarity and coherence of policies in biotechnological and agricultural innovation are essential in the development of cluster initiatives. |
| Regulatory framework | A coherent and complete regulatory framework (access to genetic resources and commercialization) is essential for the development of a successful biotechnological network. |
| Financing | Insufficient sources of funding and government support are a barrier to the development of innovation projects. |
| Service infrastructure | The services of marketing agencies, patent attorneys and consultancies for entrepreneurs significantly impact the development of the cluster. |
| Labour market | The deployment of qualified workers has an important effect on the successful development of SMEs in the cluster. |
| ST platform | Successful technology transfer requires an ST platform that drives research and entrepreneurial activities. |
| Entrepreneurship culture | A weak entrepreneurship culture (lacking start-ups, spin-offs, installation of foreign companies) prevents clusters from growing. |
| Strong competitive actors with core competencies | The sustainability of the cluster depends on its ability to attract, link and retain strong players. |
| External links (interregional and international) | Cluster companies need to link into and interact with global markets and value chains to develop "spillovers". |
| Sustainable growth | The cluster promotes the entry of new companies, the strengthening of existing ones and cooperation with related clusters. |
| Cluster management | The cohesion and development of the cluster need a facilitator who acts as director, administrator and moderator between different entities. |

*Source:*    The authors, developed from their own unpublished research data (2020).

with the electoral times, which bring discontinuity to all long-term plans, mainly for intense capital- and technology-based industries (Scheel, 2014).

Transferring these concepts (Scheel, 2011) to the development of an innovation cluster in biotechnology in Colombia, three development stages are identified: the Constant Performance Stage, Growth Stage and Maturity Stage (Figure 14.4).

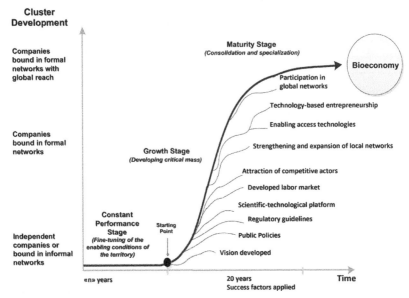

*Note:*    Adaptation based on Scheel (2011). In Gatersleben the first companies arrived in 1999, which is why we consider 20 years a reasonable time to measure the growth.

*Figure 14.4    Towards the construction of a biotechnology cluster in Colombia*

## Constant Performance Stage

There are some companies that have developed capacities around biotechnology; some act independently and others participate in informal networks within the territory. R&D levels are scarce due to the low involvement in common projects of the key actors of the innovation system and the availability of resources. Therefore, it is necessary to start a period of preparation, to fine-tune the enabling conditions of the territory, implying a greater participation of public financial funds.

## Growth Stage

This stage begins when enabling conditions are reached. There are clear, articulated and simplified political, strategic and regulatory guidelines. The conditions and opportunities for development of the biotechnology sector are attractive and mark the migration of competitive actors to the region, which leads to the accumulation of sufficient critical mass and the creation and strengthening of local and extraterritorial formal sectoral and research networks, which give impetus to the formation of the cluster. The labour market has adequate levels of specialists in biotechnology to respond to the needs of companies in the territory. In addition, a greater availability of resources from public, private and international cooperation sources contribute to the consolidation of an ST platform with the capacity to respond to the challenges of research and technological development of the actors in the region. R&D efforts are centralized in prioritized areas.

### Maturity Stage

The strengthening of the ST platform leads to the development of new technologies and the birth of new biotechnology-based companies. In this stage, a high level of specialization has been reached in the prioritized research areas that has become the foundation for the development of various technological applications, facilitating migration to the establishment of a bioeconomy. The cluster is consolidated and is an active participant in global networks for the development of the bioeconomy. At this stage new local and international markets must be identified and confronted.

## 14.8   CONCLUSIONS

The purpose of this study was to diagnose and analyse the situation of the biotechnology industry in Colombia and to explore the capabilities, conditions, practices and alliances the industry must have in order to achieve world-class performance. Faced with this perspective, the Colombian government is aware that biodiversity is a comparative advantage for the country's socioeconomic, environmental and sustainable development, and envisions the commercial development of biotechnology using biological, genetic resources and their derivatives. To achieve the levels of the success factors of the cluster in Germany, it is essential to establish policies and instruments oriented to the creation and development of technology-based companies and institutions that promote this type of activity. At the same time, it is necessary to effectively coordinate the three stages and their respective success factors for the development of a competitive bioeconomy in Colombia.

From the perspective of the COI Framework, the comparison of Valle del Cauca and Gatersleben highlights the importance of the supporting COI components (Government, Universities, Professions, Management) in creating the enabling conditions for the major COI components (Entrepreneurs, Venture Capital, Major Corporations) to operate efficiently and collaboratively in the essential behaviours for creating and growing a COI.

Government plays a critical and ongoing role in the development of a COI. The most critical enabling condition is, of course, the rule of law, which is severely challenged in Colombia (Salama, 2022). As demonstrated in Gatersleben, the provision of high security and protection of intellectual property, a reliable legal system, favourable policies and regulations and fast procedures provide the secure foundation for the development of business activities and relationships. Direct government investment in infrastructure and in aspects of other components, such as research, technological and entrepreneurial education in universities, seed funding for new ventures or operational funds for hybrid organizations like business incubators and accelerators, is also a key aspect of a successful COI.

Universities are also early players in the development of innovation clusters. Though their motivation to gain benefits from research conducted at their institutions, they are often the magnets that attract entrepreneurs, venture capitalists and major corporations who recognize the potential business opportunities offered by the research. Universities also foster the informal relationships or weak ties that are first steps in the formation of global interconnections and networks. Other supporting components, such as professional and industry organizations, can play significant roles in developing global markets and networks. Together, these supporting components create the fertile soil in which a COI can grow.

Finding the most effective ways to establish and maintain the enabling conditions and supportive factors is often the largest challenge for developing economies. There is no single roadmap or solution, since each local context is unique. However, identifying the presence and absence of key components and systemic competitive success factors can provide guidance for investment of time and resources.

## NOTES

1.   The Leibniz Institute of Plant Genetics and Crop Plant Research in Gatersleben (IPK) is a research centre that deals with issues of modern biology, mainly by studying cultivated plant species. The institute is structured into four scientific departments: Gene Bank, Cytogenetics and Genome Analysis, Molecular Genetics and Molecular Cell Biology.

2.   Wirtschafts- und Sozialpartner (Economic and Social Partners) has the task for Saxony-Anhalt of accompanying and controlling the promotion of various projects within the framework of the European structural and investment funds.

3.   The Leibniz Institute heads an international consortium to physically map and sequence the barley genome. At the Plant Genome Resources Centre (PGRC), biological resources and enabling technologies are developed, such as molecular markers and cereal transformation.

# REFERENCES

Ablaev, I. (2018). Innovation clusters and regional development. *Academy of Strategic Management Journal*, 17(3), 1–10.

Adler, P. (1989). Technology Strategy: Guide to the Literature, in R. S. Rosenbloom and R. A. Burgelman (eds), *Research on Technological Innovation, Management and Policy*. Greenwich, CT: JAI Press.

Agro-Bio (2018). Cultivos genéticamente modificados: Colombia 2018. www.agrobio .org/transgenicos-en-colombia/.

Agro-Bio (2020). Cultivos genéticamente modificados: Colombia 2020. https://agrobio .org/actualidad/los-cultivos-transgenicos-siguen-marcando-terreno-en-colombia.

Allen, T. J. (1977). *Managing the Flow of Technology: Technology Transfer and the Dissemination of Technological Information within the R&D Organization*. Cambridge, MA: MIT Press.

Altenburg, T., Hillebrand, P., and Meyer-Stamer, J. (1998). *Building Systemic Competitiveness: Concept and Case Studies from Mexico, Brazil, Paraguay, Korea and Thailand*. Berlin: German Development Institute.

Anastas, P., and Eghbali, N. (2010). Green chemistry: principles and practice. *Chemical Society Reviews*, 39(1), 301–312.

Barra, C., Maietta, O. W., and Zotti, R. (2020). The effects of university academic research on firms' propensity to innovate at local level: evidence from Europe. *Journal of Technology Transfer*, 46(2), 483–530.

Beluhova-Uzunova, R., Shishkova, M., and Ivanova, B. (2019). Concepts and key sectors of the bioeconomy. *Trakia Journal of Sciences*, 17(1), 227–233.

Berger, R. (2016). *The Industrie 4.0 Transition Quantified: How the Fourth Industrial Revolution Is Reshuffling the Economic, Social and Industrial Model*. www .rolandberger.com/en/Media/New-study-Industrie-4.0.html.

Betancur Giraldo, C. M. (2017). *Bioeconomía y sectores potenciales en Colombia*. N.p.: BIOinTropic. www.dnp.gov.co/Crecimiento-Verde/Documents/comite/sesion %206/BIOECONOM%C3%8DA%20Y%20SECTORES%20POTENCIALES %20EN%20COLOMBIA%2005122017.pdf.

Bezama, A., Ingrao, C., O'Keeffe, S., and Thrän, D. (2019). Resources, collaborators, and neighbors: the three-pronged challenge in the implementation of bioeconomy regions. *Sustainability*, 11(24), 7235.

Bonciu, E., and Sarac, I. (2017). Implications of modern biotechnology in the food security and food safety. *Annals of the University of Craiova – Agriculture, Montanology, Cadastre Series*, 46(1), 36–41.

Cohen, S. S., and Fields, G. (1999). Social capital and capital gains in Silicon Valley. *California Management Review*, 41(2), 108–130.

CONPES (2011). *Documento CONPES 3697 – Política para el desarrollo comercial de la biotecnología a partir del uso sostenible de la biodiversidad*. Bogotá: Departamento Nacional de Planeación.

Cooke, P. (2001). Regional innovation systems, clusters, and the knowledge economy. *Industrial and Corporate Change*, 10(4), 945–974.

Eise, B., and Stuber, W. (2016). *Green Gate Gatersleben: The Green Gateway to the World*. Magdeburg: Saxony-Anhalt.

Engel, J. S. (2014). *Global Clusters of Innovation: Entrepreneurial Engines of Economic Growth around the World*. Cheltenham, UK and Northampton, MA, USA: Edward Elgar Publishing.

Engel, J. S. (2015). Global Clusters of Innovation: lessons from Silicon Valley. *California Management Review*, 57(2), 36–65.

Esser, K., Hillebrand, W., Messner, D., and Meyer-Stamer, J. (1996). Competitividad sistémica: nuevo desafío para las empresas y la política. *Revista de la CEPAL*, 59.

Esser, K., Hillebrand, W., Messner, D., and Meyer-Stamer, J. (2013). *Systemic Competitiveness: New Governance Patterns for Industrial Development*. London: Routledge.

Fedearroz (2008). Colombia y el reto biotecnológico, hacia un sector agrícola competitivo. www.fedearroz.com.co/noticias/noticiasd2.php?id=73.

Fedebiocombustibles (2021). En nueva planta piloto se producirá glicerina útil. www.fedebiocombustibles.com/nota-web-id-2835.htm.

Ferras-Hernández, X., and Nylund, P. A. (2019). Clusters as innovation engines: The accelerating strengths of proximity. *European Management Review*, 16(1), 37–53.

Galvez-Nogales, E. (2010). *Agro-Based Clusters in Developing Countries: Staying Competitive in a Globalized Economy*. Rome: United Nations Food and Agricultural Organization.

Gates Notes (2020). Introducing the Green Premiums. www.gatesnotes.com/Energy/Introducing-the-Green-Premiums.

GGG (Green Gate Gatersleben) (2018). What is Green Gate Gatersleben? http://green-gate-gatersleben.com/.

Hernández, M. C. (2008). Propuesta de apoyo para una gestión eficiente de la biotecnología. *Revista EAN*, 62, 5–26.

IMG (2019). Invest in Saxony-Anhalt. www.invest-in-saxony-anhalt.com/location-analysis-saxony-anhalt.

Innpulsa (2013). *Estudio sobre el potencial de la industria de la biotecnología en el país*. Bogotá, D.C.: Bancoldex.

Kostygova, L. (2019). Prospects of development of resources recycling on the basis of interregional interaction with the use of "smart specialization" of regions. *International Multidisciplinary Scientific GeoConference: SGEM*, 19(4.1), 757–762.

Laperche, B., Sommers, P., and Uzunidis, D. (2010). *Innovation Networks and Clusters: The Knowledge Backbone*. Brussels: Peter Lang.

Minciencias (2019). *Propuestas de la Misión Internacional de Sabios 2019*. N.p.: Gobierno del Colombia.

Nath, D., and Banerjee, P. (2013). Green nanotechnology: a new hope for medical biology. *Environmental Toxicology and Pharmacology*, 36(3), 997–1014.

Noriega, M. d. P. (2019). *Colombia – Líder en química verde: creando valor agregado a partir de la Biodiversidad, Biocombustibles y Biotecnología*. N.p.: Gobierno del Colombia.

OECD (Organization for Economic Co-operation and Development) (2009). *The Bioeconomy to 2030: Designing a Policy Agenda*. Paris: OECD.

Porter, M. (1990). The competitive advantage of nations. *Harvard Business Review*, 1(1), 73–90.

Procolombia (2013). Inversión en el sector Biotecnología. www.inviertaencolombia.com.co/sectores/servicios/biotecnologia.html.

Qian, H. (2018). Knowledge-based regional economic development: A synthetic review of knowledge spillovers, entrepreneurship, and entrepreneurial ecosystems. *Economic Development Quarterly*, 32(2), 163–176.

Sachsen-Anhalt (2011). Facts and figures. www.sachsen-anhalt.de/fileadmin/Bibliothek/Politik_und_Verwaltung/StK/STK/Publikationsliste/Alle/2011_Kurz_und_Knapp_engl.pdf.

Salama, J. (2022). Defending their land, paying with their lives. *National Geographic*, 214(3), 100–119.

Sánchez-Mejía, M., and Gutiérrez-Terán, A.-M. (2013). Proceso de Construcción del Sistema Regional de Innovación de la Biotecnología para la Agricultura, la Agroindustria y la Bioindustria-SRIB en el Valle del Cauca-Colombia. *Journal of Technology Management & Innovation*, 8, 52–52.

Scheel, C. (2011). Innovacities: in search of breakthrough innovations producing world class performance. *International Journal of Knowledge-Based Development*, 2(4), 372–388.

Scheel, C. (2014). Colombia and Mexico: innovation and entrepreneurship as a new paradigm for regional development in Latin America, in J. S. Engel (ed.), *Global Clusters of Innovation: Entrepreneurial Engines of Economic Growth around the World*. Cheltenham, UK and Northampton, MA, USA: Edward Elgar Publishing.

Scheel, C., and Pineda L. (2017). *Innovacities: Impact of Regional Innovation Systems on the Competitive Strategies of Cities*. Bogotá: Universidad Jorge Tadeo Lozano.

Slow Food (2020). Colombia's fight to reduce GMO cultivation and save biodiversity. www.slowfood.com/colombias-fight-to-reduce-gmo-cultivation-and-save-biodiversity/.

United Nations (2009). *Asia-Pacific Trade and Investment Review 2008*. New York, NY: UN.

Von Braun, J. (2018). Bioeconomy: the global trend and its implications for sustainability and food security. *Global Food Security*, 19, 81–83.

Wixted, B. (2009). *Innovation System Frontiers: Cluster Networks and Global Value*. Vancouver: Springer.

Zucker, L. G., Darby, M. R., and Armstrong, J. S. (2002). Commercializing knowledge: university science, knowledge capture, and firm performance in biotechnology. *Management Science*, 48(1), 138–153.

# 15. The Brazilian innovation ecosystem takes off

**Flavio Feferman**

## 15.1 INTRODUCTION

### 15.1.1 Chapter Overview

The Brazil chapter in *Global Clusters of Innovation* (Engel 2014), explored the rise of the Porto Digital urban technology park and Cluster of Innovation (COI) in Northeast Brazil, a case that illustrated the importance of institutional collaboration involving the private sector, academia, and government, as well as the role of local leadership for cluster development. The Porto Digital chapter also provided a historical perspective, including Brazil's long history of economic booms and busts, as well as the diminishing economic role of the state in the 1990s, which led to greater interest in innovation ecosystems and cluster-based economic development as alternative models (Feferman 2014).

Since that chapter was written, Brazil endured another of its notorious boom–bust cycles: the economic growth, social progress, and optimism of the 2000–2012 period gave way to nearly a decade of economic, political, and health crises.

But from the mid-2010s to 2021, something unexpected happened: the Brazilian innovation ecosystem took off, reaching an entirely new scale and level of professionalism. The present chapter addresses the recent innovation boom in Brazil, focusing primarily on São Paulo, which serves as the core of a regional network of innovation hubs in Southeast and South Brazil, with further connections to smaller innovation centers in other parts of the country, such as Porto Digital. The chapter will refer to this network as the "Brazilian innovation ecosystem," and will address the main institutions (COI "components") and changing behaviors that characterize the ecosystem, following the COI Framework presented in Chapter 2 of this book. With São Paulo at the center, this ecosystem operates as a national "network of COI (NCOI)," with flows of capital, talent, and knowledge across the network.[1]

To further define the Brazilian innovation ecosystem – and employing the COI lens of "entrepreneurial innovation" – the ecosystem primarily encompasses information technology (IT) and digital services, though digital technology is applied across many sectors such as financial services, e-commerce, education, health, real estate, and logistics, among others. As explained in *Global Clusters of Innovation* (Engel 2014), a COI is characterized by innovation processes, behaviors, and institutions, rather than by a specific sectoral focus. Innovation also happens in more traditional Brazilian economic sectors – including industry, agriculture, energy, mining, and conventional services – but in these settings it tends to follow a more traditional "corporate innovation" model, with support from government research institutions (Freeman and Engel 2007). This pattern is evolving, and large corporations, even in more traditional sectors, are becoming more involved in the Brazilian innovation ecosystem through Open Innovation programs or by creating hybrid institutional components such as corporate Accelerators or Corporate Venture Capital (CVC) units.[2]

In 2020, the Brazilian innovation ecosystem accounted for nearly 60 percent of all venture capital (VC) investments in Latin America, which underscores its importance. Investments reached a record US$2.5 billion in 2019, declining slightly to US$2.4 billion in 2020 during the Covid-19 pandemic (LAVCA 2014–2021). But 2020 still saw a record number of venture deals (282) and a record amount invested in local currency terms, following a sharp appreciation of the dollar. Preliminary analysis of announced deals through August 2021 indicates another banner year, with projected annual funding of US$7–9 billion – three times the previous record – and around 400 deals expected for the full year.[3]

But the path to scale took decades. A previous surge in startup investment during the dot-com years (1995–2000) eventually fizzled and did not lead to sustained growth of the innovation ecosystem. Furthermore, despite favorable macroeconomic and political conditions over the following decade, Brazil endured a long "nuclear winter of tech" between 2001 and 2009. After a gradual restart, the innovation ecosystem took off between 2015 and 2021, when Brazil experienced exceptional growth in VC funding, successful startups, and institutions that support entrepreneurship. This recent boom – much larger and more sustainable – happened amid political turmoil, two recessions, and the Covid-19 pandemic. What factors contributed to this remarkable take-off? And, in turn, how is the Brazilian innovation ecosystem helping to address the pandemic and other health, social, and environmental challenges?

This chapter analyzes the three main factors that contributed to the current innovation boom: secular trends related to technology, institutional (COI "component") development, and cultural and behavioral change. It also contrasts the Porto Digital case with the evolution of the São Paulo innovation hub, which has followed a much more private-sector-driven model. This emphasizes one of the key lessons about COI: different regions can follow diverse innovation strategies and there is no single "blueprint" for COI development (Engel 2014). Next, the chapter describes the spatial and "virtual" configuration of the Brazilian innovation ecosystem, characterized by connections between the São Paulo and other regional innovation hubs, as well as by an extraordinary concentration of COI components in the southwest zone of the São Paulo metropolitan region.

Finally, the chapter illustrates how the latest generation of Brazilian startups has focused on using technology to solve uniquely Brazilian problems: the institutional challenges collectively known as the "Brazil Cost"[4] and myriad other frictions and inefficiencies that characterize the Brazilian economy and daily life in the country. As technology takes center stage in many sectors, this new generation of tech companies and founders is also uniquely positioned to address resilience related to social, health, and environmental challenges. In the words of Brazilian VC pioneer and Monashees founder Eric Acher, "Our startups see problems as opportunities, and Brazil has many opportunities."[5]

The chapter is informed by meetings and collaborations over the past decade with leading participants in the Brazilian innovation ecosystem, through my Business in Brazil class at the University of California, Berkeley (UC Berkeley) (2012–2020), as well as through my experience as director of the UC Berkeley Lean Startup program in Brazil (2016–2017). During my academic trips to Brazil, I had the opportunity to observe first-hand the transformation of the ecosystem. I met with several VCs, accelerators, startups, mature corporations, universities, government institutions, and non-governmental organizations working to promote entrepreneurship and innovation. I am grateful to the people and institutions that hosted my class and to our partners in the Lean Startup program for their collaboration and generosity, and for sharing their experience and wisdom.

### 15.1.2   The Cubo Story

During August 2015 I traveled to São Paulo with a group of 70 MBA students as part of my Business in Brazil course, one of the classes I teach at the UC Berkeley Haas School of Business. Among other company meetings and discussion forums, we met with the founders of Cubo, an innovation hub under construction in Vila Olímpia, a modern neighborhood in the southwest part of the city. The scale of the project seemed almost too ambitious: plans for the cube-shaped, remodeled building included 54,000 square feet of space over six floors, designed to host startups, corporate partners, investors, students, and events related to entrepreneurship and innovation. Cubo represented a unique institutional collaboration between Itaú-Unibanco, the largest Latin

American bank, and Redpoint eVentures (RPeV), a pioneering Brazilian VC firm with ties to Silicon Valley. Significantly, Cubo was conceived as an Open Innovation space that would connect the various participants of the Brazilian innovation ecosystem in São Paulo, rather than as an internal corporate innovation center for Itaú-Unibanco.

Cubo was launched a month later in September 2015, and the opening event was hosted by its Managing Director Flavio Pripas, RPeV Managing Partner Anderson Thees, and representatives from Itaú-Unibanco. Among the attendees was Sergio Furio, the CEO of a 40-person fintech startup called Bankfácil, who subsequently wrote that Cubo would become "the envy of Silicon Valley … a space that would create synergies among the actors of the technology ecosystem in Brazil."[6]

When I returned to São Paulo with another MBA class in March 2016, Cubo was already a runaway success, buzzing with activity. We had to improvise a meeting space in the sixth-floor lounge. "Don't feed the unicorn" was inscribed on one of the glass walls, somewhat optimistically. Cubo had clearly struck a chord, addressing huge pent-up demand and interest in innovation and entrepreneurship in São Paulo, a trend observed in many other Brazilian cities.

Within three years, Cubo had already outgrown its space and moved to a new building – *Cubão*, or "big cube" – with 12 stories, five times the space, and the capacity to host 250 startups in residence. By the end of 2020, Cubo had 25 corporate and institutional sponsors and hosted numerous programs and events, broadening its reach beyond São Paulo with digital programs. As is turns out, the project that seemed too ambitious in 2015 underestimated its own potential.

The opening of Cubo in 2015 was a watershed event for the Brazilian innovation ecosystem, signaling the beginning of the remarkable recent transformation. Several other successful innovation hubs, accelerators, VC funds, and corporate innovation programs were launched from the mid 2010s through 2021. Cubo also exemplified the important institutional synergies and collaborations that characterize COI and that contributed to the ecosystem take-off in Brazil, bringing together VCs, corporate partners, and startups in a common physical and virtual space. Similar synergies and collaborations were also central to the Porto Digital case.

Meanwhile, Bankfácil, the fintech startup in attendance at Cubo's inauguration, is now called Creditas and has grown to 3,000 employees. In December 2020, Creditas received a Series E investment round valuing the company at US$1.75 billion and making it Brazil's newest tech "unicorn" (a privately held startup with a valuation above US$1 billion) at the time. Most Brazilian unicorns reached this status since 2018, and during 2019 only the United States and China created unicorns at a faster pace (Crunchbase 2020).

How did the Brazilian innovation ecosystem reach this point? We begin with a brief historical perspective on the evolution of the innovation ecosystem, focusing on the Internet and IT.

## 15.2    BRAZIL'S INNOVATION ECOSYSTEM TIMELINE

### 15.2.1    The Dot-Com Years and the First Generation of Brazilian Tech Companies (1995–2000)

The Internet in Brazil began in the late 1980s as a collaboration between government, academia, and the social sector. Starting in the mid 1990s, numerous regional Internet service providers drove the expansion of the Internet in the country (Knight 2014). As the Internet grew, Brazil experienced a short-lived surge of startup activity and investment during the dot-com years of 1995–2000. The first wave of Brazilian tech startups focused on Internet access and navigation, including portals (UOL, BOL, ZAZ), search sites (Cadê, Apontador), web hosting companies (Locaweb, IG), and early e-commerce firms (Submarino, Netshoes, and comparison shopping site Buscapé).

In parallel, Brazil had several important software and IT services companies from an earlier vintage, including Totvs (founded in 1983), Módulo (1985), Linx (1985), Stefanini (1987), and MV Sistemas (1987). Totvs, an enterprise software firm based in São Paulo, acquired numerous tech startups during the 2000s and 2010s, supporting the growth of the innovation ecosystem. The most successful Latin American tech company originating in the dot-com period was Mercado Libre (Mercado Livre in Brazil), an e-commerce marketplace founded in Argentina in 1999 by a group of Stanford MBAs, with Brazil as its primary market.

During the dot-com years, there were few specialized VC firms in Brazil – Intel Ventures was perhaps the first. Capital for startup investments most often came from foreign funds, opportunistic investors, or from Brazilian private equity firms, which were already well established in the country. But many early investors had limited experience with the Silicon Valley VC model, which involves longer investment horizons, mentoring, and networking with potential partners and customers. As a consequence, startups were often placed under immediate pressure to generate positive cash flow.

Similarly, during the dot-com years Brazil had few other COI institutional components devoted to startup formation and growth. The main innovation institutions at the time were research centers, technology parks, and university-based incubators, organized under the national association Anprotec, as well as government innovation agencies such as FINEP and its state-level counterparts, which provided research funding and startup grants. The Porto Digital technology park, established in 2000, was an early innovation hub, along with other tech parks. Important incubators included Cietec (São Paulo), Gênesis and COPPE/UFRJ (Rio de Janeiro), Inova (Belo Horizonte), and Celta/Alfa (Florianópolis).

### 15.2.2  The Long Nuclear Winter of Tech (2001–2009)

Brazil entered a prolonged period of macroeconomic stability and economic growth during the Lula presidency (2003–2010), epitomized by the famous "Brazil takes off" cover story in *The Economist* issue of November 2009. Despite the favorable economic scenario, the bursting of the dot-com bubble in 2001 dampened the enthusiasm for tech investing globally, and Brazil entered a protracted "nuclear winter of tech."

Paradoxically, the economic boom created further headwinds for the innovation ecosystem. Inflation-adjusted interest rates remained high for an extended period, making fixed-income investments much more attractive relative to alternative investments such as VC, and therefore discouraging potential limited partner (LP) investors in Brazil. Furthermore, continuing high interest rates, coupled with a commodity boom during the latter half of the 2000s, led to significant appreciation of the Brazilian real, making Brazilian assets more expensive to foreign investors.

Despite these headwinds and the dampened enthusiasm for tech investing following the dot-com era, a few Brazilian VCs believed in the long-term potential of the innovation ecosystem and began operating during the "nuclear winter." These included (in chronological order) VC firms Ideasnet (founded in 2000), DGF (2001), Monashees (2005), Antera (2005), SP Ventures (2007), Astella (2008), Confrapar (2008), CVentures (2008), Inseed (2008), Iporanga (2009), and Brazil's first dedicated impact investor, Vox Capital (2009), among others.[7] A few private equity companies also started to focus more on early-stage investments.

The federal innovation agency FINEP was the first Brazilian government institution to support seed and VC funds, through its Inovar program, established in 2000. In 2007, the Brazilian National Economic and Social Development Bank (BNDES) launched the Criatec program, which provided further support for the emergence of the VC industry in the country.[8]

During the nuclear winter there were still few other institutions devoted to startup formation and growth. Exceptions included university-based incubators and tech parks, mentioned earlier, as well as a few early entrepreneurial hubs. Endeavor began operating in Brazil in 2000 and continues to serve as an important nexus for mentoring, capital, and networking in the innovation ecosystem. Some of the earliest accelerators came from the social sector: Artemisia (founded in 2004) and Quintessa (2009). The Porto Digital technology park continued to evolve during the 2000s, becoming a center for entrepreneurship in Northeast Brazil, while the CERTI Foundation, ACATE/Miditec, and Tecnopuc park (2003) served as innovation hubs in southern Brazil. Other technology parks appeared, including Sapiens (2002), UFRJ (2005), and BH-Tec (2005). And in 2000, Robert Binder organized the Brazilian Private Equity and Venture Capital Association (ABVCAP), which grew to become an important forum for VC and the tech industry.

Yet, by the end of 2009, the innovation ecosystem remained underdeveloped for a country of Brazil's size – the seventh largest global economy at the time. Few notable startups gained prominence during the nuclear winter. Most success stories during this period pertained to exits for companies that were founded in the dot-com years or earlier: the acquisition of Akwan by Google in 2006 and initial public offerings (IPOs) for portal UOL (in 2005), software firm Totvs (2006), and e-commerce companies B2W (2007) and Mercado Libre (2007). But over a period of nearly ten years during the tech winter, these represented a small number of notable exits.

Towards the end of the nuclear winter, a landmark deal signaled a possible changing of seasons. In late 2009 global tech investor Naspers acquired Buscapé, the comparison shopping company born during the dot-com era, for US$342 million, a staggering sum for Brazil at the time. The deal provided an early indication that the Brazilian innovation ecosystem could produce scalable startups with high pre-IPO valuations and with big potential returns for investors and founding teams.

### 15.2.3   The Tech Spring: New Beginnings, Ongoing Challenges, and the Second Generation of Brazilian Tech Startups (2010–2014)

The period of 2010–2014 saw a gradual rebirth of the Brazilian innovation ecosystem, with encouraging new developments mixed with ongoing challenges. This period set the stage for the entrepreneurial boom during the latter half of the 2010s.

During this "tech spring" period of 2010–2014, a second generation of Brazilian tech startups emerged and grew, including some companies that were founded earlier during the tech winter. Dubbed "copycats" or "clones," these companies sought to emulate established consumer Internet business models, mostly from US tech companies. Some notable examples included Peixe Urbano (which followed the Groupon model), ride-hailing companies Easy Taxi and 99 Taxis, real estate portals Viva Real and Zap, and e-commerce retailers Dafiti, BrandsClub, and Beleza na Web (Beaurline and Gomes 2014). Investor Rocket Internet, which followed the clone model on a global scale, entered Brazil in 2011 and invested in Easy Taxi and Dafiti, among other companies.[9]

The "copycat" label was somewhat misleading and unfair because many second-generation startups were already adapting business models to the Brazilian market context. For example, Peixe Urbano innovated by using a hybrid strategy that included street sales, and when Groupon entered Brazil it copied tactics from its local competitor, which it eventually acquired.[10]

With the Brazilian innovation ecosystem showing signs of emerging from its nuclear winter, along with improving global economic conditions following the "Great Recession" of 2007–2009, international investors and VC firms flocked to Brazil and Latin America between 2010 and 2012, leading to a short-lived expansion. Prominent US venture capital firms established a local presence, while other international VCs traveled to Brazil on a regular basis. Concurrently, a new generation of Brazil-focused VC firms emerged, including local Brazilian firms and international VCs with a sustained local presence and a long-term commitment to Brazil and Latin America: RPeV (2011), Valor (2011), Kaszek (2011), Qualcomm Ventures (circa 2011), Bossa Nova (2011), Triaxis (2012), e.bricks/Igah (2013), Crescera (2013), and Endeavor Catalyst (2013), among others.

But the influx of new international and local investors eventually resulted in an imbalance during 2012–2013, with too much capital chasing a limited number of deals, leading to high valuations. At the time, Brazil still had too few scalable startups and experienced founders, and the market for tech products and digital services was still evolving. Many startups were not growing at expected rates, while others were struggling to become profitable after rapid initial revenue growth. During 2013–2014, many opportunistic investors left the market, and some prominent international VCs closed their Brazilian offices (*New York Times* 2013).

About a year later, in March 2014, I traveled to São Paulo and met with Anderson Thees and the RPeV team. The general sense was that the recent hype had diminished, and valuations were starting to look more reasonable. Thees believed that the remaining Brazil-focused investors, which had replaced some of the international VCs and opportunistic investors that left the market, were committed and planned to remain involved for the long haul. These specialized investors had a better understanding of the Brazilian market and the idiosyncrasies of the business environment, strong local connections, and a sense for the business models most likely to succeed in Brazil and in other similar emerging markets.

But local knowledge alone was not sufficient. Thees also noted the importance of bringing the Silicon Valley "model" to the Brazilian ecosystem, meaning not just providing capital, but also being patient about profitability and exits, and offering mentoring, management expertise, and connections to help startups succeed. In subsequent visits to Brazil, Eric Acher from Monashees echoed this sentiment, describing Monashees' collaborative approach to working with startups, which combined the Silicon Valley method with his experience as a former McKinsey consultant. This Silicon Valley VC style had been lacking during the earlier dot-com surge in Brazil, when many investors followed a private equity approach that emphasized control and early profitability.[11]

Even so, while the number of VC firms grew and the Silicon Valley approach became more prevalent during the tech spring, the Brazilian innovation ecosystem still lacked a critical mass of institutional components for startup formation and growth. University-based tech parks and incubators remained important, but Brazil had few accelerators, private sector innovation hubs, and corporate innovation programs involving startups. This was another important reason for the lack of scalable startups at the time, which led to too much capital chasing too few deals during 2012–2013.

But during the tech spring the first well-known, for-profit Brazilian accelerators began to emerge, such as 21212 and Papaya in Rio de Janeiro (2011, 2012), WOW and Ventiur in Porto Alegre (2013), and a group of accelerators and startup hubs in the São Paulo region that remain important to this day, such as Startup Farm (2011), ACE/Aceleratech (2012), Wayra (2012), Baita (2013), Distrito (2014), and Worth a Million (2014), as well as Plug (2012), one of the first co-working spaces dedicated to startups. New social-impact accelerators and hubs also appeared.

Government also played a role in the emergence of accelerators. Much like the FINEP Inovar and BNDES Criatec programs, which previously sought to quicken the development of VC in Brazil, the federal government launched the Startup Brasil program in 2013, which promoted entrepreneurship through partnerships and funding for accelerators.[12] Several Startup Brasil accelerators have since thrived. Similarly, the Inovativa program, also launched in 2013, promoted entrepreneurship through an ecosystem approach, partnering with accelerators, startup hubs, associations, mentors, and investors.

Corporate participation in the innovation ecosystem remained negligible during the tech spring. Isolated examples included accelerators Wayra (owned by Telefónica of Spain) and ACE (which had initial support from Microsoft), as well as corporate investors such as Qualcomm Ventures, Intel Ventures, Totvs Ventures, and broadcasting group RBS.

Despite the rise in VC investments during the tech spring, there were relatively few landmark deals or exits during the period. Yet there were several early-stage investments during this time, and some of the second-generation "copycat" companies received follow-on funding. Furthermore, many of the future Brazilian unicorns were founded and began growing during the tech spring. Equally important, the institutional components that underpinned the ecosystem take-off – such as specialized VCs and Accelerators – began to evolve during the period.

## 15.2.4 The Deteriorating Economic and Political Scenario Starting in 2013

The Lula presidency (2003–2010) saw a period of sustained economic growth and social progress, building on a legacy of macroeconomic stability established by his predecessor Fernando Henrique Cardoso. The economic expansion was driven by a commodity export boom, increased consumer spending, and higher government expenditures supported by growing tax revenues. Again, the period was epitomized by the famous "Brazil takes off" cover of *The Economist* in 2009.

The tech spring unfolded under a deteriorating economic and political scenario during the first term of President Dilma Rousseff (2011–2014), Lula's successor. Declining commodity prices, coupled with controversial economic policies, led to slowing growth during 2012–2014 and concerns about the direction of the economy. Political tensions also rose during Rousseff's presidency, beginning in 2013 with street protests against poor public services, the high cost of living, and corruption. In September 2013, *The Economist* again featured Brazil on its cover, but this time with the tagline "Has Brazil blown it?" The following year, the *Lava Jato* ("Car Wash") investigation began to expose widespread corruption involving several political parties, including the ruling Workers' Party (PT).

The tech boom period (2015–2021), to be discussed further below, began and evolved during one of the most turbulent times in Brazilian history. As Rousseff's second term started in 2015, commodity prices continued to spiral downwards, hammering export revenues, economic growth, and confidence in the economy. Brazil entered a deep, protracted recession with negative growth rates recorded during 2015–2016. The economic crisis and ongoing *Lava Jato* investigations severely weakened Rousseff's popular and political support, leading to her impeachment for a technicality related to government financial accounting.

Dissatisfaction with the economy, with corruption, and with traditional political parties eventually led to the election of an outsider, right-wing populist Jair Bolsonaro, who took office in January 2019. During its first two years in office, the Bolsonaro administration was criticized for its management of education, environment, and social programs. As the Covid-19 crisis began in 2020, Bolsonaro frequently downplayed its severity and clashed with state governors and members of his own administration over the response to the pandemic. This led to a chaotic response to the crisis. Cases and deaths soared, making Brazil the second largest global hotspot for the disease during much of 2020. The Covid-19 pandemic resulted in another severe recession in 2020, with an economic contraction of 4.1 percent, the largest in 24 years.

This extraordinary sequence of events underscores that macroeconomic cycles and political winds did not correlate with the development of the ecosystem. Lula's presidency and the economic boom during the 2000s coincided with the Brazilian nuclear winter of tech. Rousseff's first term in office, from 2011–2014, under a deteriorating scenario, provided the backdrop for the tech spring. And finally, the technology ecosystem took off during the most severe period of economic, political, and health crises between 2015 and 2021.

In an interview with *Forbes* in 2019, during the innovation boom years, Buscapé co-founder and RPeV Managing Partner Romero Rodrigues remarked that "Over the recent years we have seen a total decoupling of macroeconomic conditions from the development of the national innovation environment" (*Forbes* 2019). Monashees founder Eric Acher, meeting with my Berkeley class in the same year, was incisive: "There is no correlation between GDP [gross domestic product] and VC returns. Tech is not about the pie getting larger, it's about shifting the pie. And during a crisis people need to be more ingenious and use technology." Other factors were far more influential for the development of the innovation ecosystem.

### 15.2.5    The Innovation Ecosystem Takes Off and the Third Generation of Brazilian Tech Firms (2015–2021)

The inauguration of Cubo in September 2015 was an important marker for the Brazilian innovation ecosystem. During the following years, Brazil experienced exceptional growth in VC funding, new deals, and successful startups, as well as a significant expansion of institutional components that support entrepreneurship and innovation. This section reviews some key metrics and highlights from the boom years, and the subsequent section will discuss the factors underlying the take-off.

The timeline in Figure 15.1 illustrates the development of the innovation ecosystem, comparing annual Brazilian GDP growth with one of the key indicators of ecosystem development, VC investments in US$ millions.

After initially rising during the tech spring, VC investments temporarily declined in 2016 during the depths of the recession and the impeachment crisis. But investments then took off to new levels starting in 2017, with each year bringing a fresh record in amounts invested. The Covid-19 crisis temporarily slowed deal-making between March and May of 2020, but investments subsequently resumed their rapid climb despite the ongoing pandemic and the second severe recession in five years. By the end of 2020, annual VC investments had reached US$2.4 billion − a seven-fold increase compared to 2014, at the end of the tech spring. With the depreciation of the Brazilian real between 2018 and 2020, a trend that accelerated at the start of the pandemic, investments in local currency reached a record of R$13 billion in 2020.

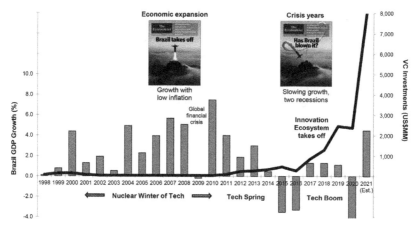

*Note:* VC investment data from the Association for Private Capital in Latin America (LAVCA) is available starting in 2011. An illustrative trend line is provided for prior years. Estimated funding for 2021 is US$7–9 billion, and the average of this range is used.
*Source:* Developed by the author with data from IBGE (Brazilian Institute of Geography and Statistics), International Monetary Fund, and LAVCA, based on a concept by Monashees. Images: Copyright © 2009, 2013, The Economist Group Limited, London 2008.

*Figure 15.1    Brazilian innovation ecosystem and economic timeline*

Preliminary analysis of announced deals from January through August of 2021 indicates another breakthrough year, with an estimated US$7–9 billion in funding projected for the full year, likely tripling the previous record.[13] Most of this capital continues to be invested in the São Paulo COI.

While investments only took off starting in 2017, the year 2015 is identified as the beginning of the boom years because of other important factors: the rapid institutional development that began in the mid 2010s, with new accelerators, innovation hubs such as Cubo, and corporate involvement in the ecosystem; the emergence of Brazil's third generation of tech startups around 2015, when many of these companies received early funding rounds; and technological and cultural trends that reached a tipping point in the mid 2010s, also helping to transform the innovation ecosystem. Further, some of the capital deployed starting in 2017 was raised by VC firms at the beginning of the tech boom period.

The number of annual venture deals rose from very low levels in 2010 to more than 100 deals per year by the end of the tech spring in 2014, and then to a record 282 deals in 2020. Preliminary data for 2021 indicate about 400 deals for the full year, another record.

The average deal size rose from around US$2.8 million at the end of the tech spring to a record US$11.5 million in 2019, reflecting the evolution of later-stage funding in the innovation ecosystem. While the average deal size declined to US$8.5 million in 2020 during the pandemic, it still reached a record level of R$46 million in local currency following the appreciation of the US dollar. Preliminary data through August 2021 indicated that the average deal size would more than double in 2021, reaching about US$20 million, as a result of continuing growth in later-stage funding and new "mega rounds." The median deal size was estimated at around US$2 million, including many early-stage deals.[14]

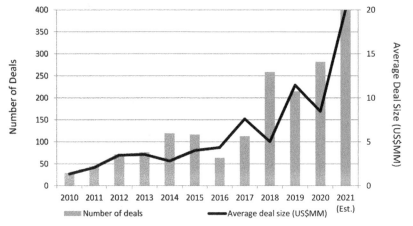

*Source:*    Developed by the author with data from LAVCA.

*Figure 15.2*    *Number of venture deals and average deal size, 2010–2021*

Venture funding deals, acquisitions, and IPOs accelerated between 2017 and 2021, creating around 40 Brazilian tech companies with private or public valuations above US$1 billion. Most of these firms had reached these valuations within the previous five years, and over 80 percent of these companies were based in the São Paulo metropolitan region.[15]

As noted above, between 2015 and 2021 a third generation of Brazilian startups appeared, including the first significant cohort of Brazilian unicorns. These startups had business models that were much more tailored to the Brazilian market, targeting specific frictions and inefficiencies across economic sectors, as will be discussed in more detail later in the chapter. As of mid 2021, the recent generation of tech unicorns included more than 20 companies, with more expected during the second half of 2021 (some of the unicorns became public companies, following IPOs).[16] Again, over 80 percent of these companies were headquartered in São Paulo. The Brazilian unicorns were extensively covered in the business media, raising the profile of the innovation ecosystem.

During the boom years, early-stage VC investments expanded as existing VCs raised new funds and a new cohort of Brazilian VC firms entered the market, including: Canary (2016), Domo (2016), Mindset (2016), OneVC (2017), Maya (2018), Alexia (2019), Atlantico (2019), Norte (2019), and Volpe (2020). New private sector accelerators and startup hubs appeared, such as: Cubo (2015), Darwin (2015), Google (2015), Liga Ventures (2015), Cotidiano (2016), Eretz Bio (2017), Fábrica de Startups (2017), and Inovabra (2018). Several accelerators/hubs also began investing in early-stage ventures.

Later-stage funding had been a major gap in the ecosystem during the tech spring of the early 2010s, and particularly challenging for Series B and Series C rounds. During the boom years, several major growth funds from the United States, Europe, and Asia became more active in Brazil, providing most of the growth capital for the third generation of Brazilian startups. In 2017, for the first time Brazilian startups began raising later-stage rounds above US$100 million. The entry of Softbank in 2019, with a US$4.6 billion fund devoted to Latin America (and mostly to Brazil) was a watershed event, with reverberations down the entire funding chain. The fund was more than twice the size of all venture investments in Latin America during the previous year. The continued growth in later-stage funding led to several mega-rounds of US$200–500 million for Brazilian tech unicorns between 2018 and 2021. Fintech Nubank raised a record US$750 million round in 2021, while becoming one of the largest global digital banks.[17]

Similarly, there were relatively few exits during the tech spring, which had constrained the development of the innovation ecosystem. Exits through mergers and acquisitions (M&As) and IPOs accelerated during the boom years, especially between 2018 and 2021, enhancing economic incentives for startups and earlier-stage investors across the ecosystem.

The acquisition of 99 by Chinese ride-sharing platform Didi Chuxing for US$1 billion in January 2018 was another watershed event, similar to Naspers' purchase of Buscapé almost a decade earlier. The deal generated buzz for the innovation ecosystem, as well as big returns for early investors. (Along with the entry of Softbank in 2019, the 99 deal reinforced the growing ties between the Brazilian ecosystem and Asia.) This was followed by the US$1.8 billion acquisition of Brazilian data center company and unicorn Ascenty in September 2018. Subsequent major deals during 2020 included the acquisition of VivaReal/Zap by OLX for $600 million and the acquisition of retail software company Linx by fintech Stone for US$1.1 billion. As 2021 began, Brazilian business software leader Totvs acquired leading market analytics startup Resultados Digitais for US$340 million. Numerous other M&A deals during the boom years − including acquisitions by well-funded startups and former unicorns that went public – underscored the growing dynamism and movement of capital in the ecosystem.[18]

There were also several notable tech IPOs during the boom years, beginning with e-commerce company Netshoes in 2017, the first major tech IPO since Linx software in 2013, during the tech spring. The following year edtech Arco Educação went public on the NASDAQ, along with digital bank Banco Inter on the Brazilian B3 stock exchange. The three largest IPOs during the late 2010s involved fintech companies – PagSeguro (2018), Stone (2018), and XP Investimentos (2019) – signaling the leading role of fintech in the Brazilian innovation ecosystem. By the end of 2020, each of these three companies had a market capitalization of around US$20 billion, making them the largest publicly traded Brazilian tech firms. Privately held Nubank reached a valuation of US$30 billion in mid 2021, placing it among the top five global fintech start-ups.[19] Exits through IPOs accelerated during 2020–2021, with seven public offerings in 2020, ten IPOs during January–May 2021, and several others scheduled for later in the year.

By mid 2021, the Brazilian innovation ecosystem had reached a new level, with record funding, and accelerating exits through M&A activity and IPOs, as well as a cohort of high-profile tech companies. As mentioned above, in 2019 only the United States and China created more unicorns; Brazil tied Germany with five, and was ahead of Israel, India, and the UK with four.[20] Numerous tech companies were making an impact in sectors such as financial services, e-commerce, business productivity, education, health, real estate, and logistics/mobility.

To be sure, this was an overdue development: Brazil had long been one of the world's largest economies, but its innovation ecosystem had lagged behind developed countries and emerging market peers such as China, India, and Israel. During the boom years, the ratio of VC funding to GDP in Brazil climbed from 0.02 percent in 2014 to around .43 percent in 2021 (estimated), rapidly bridging the gap to international references such as the United States (0.78 percent) China (0.51 percent), and India (0.38 percent), though still well behind "startup nation" and global leader Israel (2.56 percent).[21]

## 15.3   CRITICAL FACTORS FOR THE TAKE-OFF

Why did the Brazilian take-off happen only in the latter half of the 2010s? This section will address the role of technological trends, institutional development, and cultural and behavioral change.

### 15.3.1   Secular Trends Related to Technology

As previously noted, macroeconomic trends and political events did not fundamentally influence the growth of the Brazilian innovation ecosystem. Rather, *secular trends* related to technological changes had a greater impact on the recent development of the ecosystem. During the 2010s major technology shifts occurred across three related areas: telecommunications infrastructure, IT infrastructure, and application platforms.

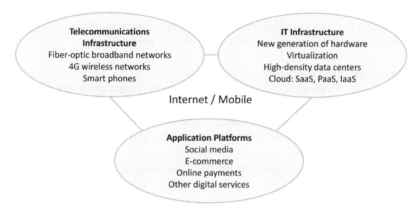

*Source:*   Developed by the author.

*Figure 15.3    Technological changes during the 2010s*

**Telecommunications infrastructure**
During the tech spring, investors were concerned about market size limits, as discussed in a 2013 *New York Times* article on tech investing in Brazil.[22] Despite having a consumer market of over 200 million people, only half of Brazilians accessed the Internet in 2013, and most with slow or expensive connections, requiring a laptop or desktop computer.

The expansion of fiber-optic broadband networks and the deployment of 4G wireless technology transformed telecommunications networks globally and in Brazil. Fixed-line broadband and Wi-Fi access expanded rapidly during the 2010s, particularly in urban areas, with better coverage, higher connection speeds, and declining costs, even though regional and socio-economic disparities persisted. Wireless 4G became widely available in Brazil around the mid 2010s, just as smart phones were becoming cheaper and ubiquitous. According to CETIC.br, by 2017, smart phone penetration reached 71 percent in Brazil. Our book *Broadband in Brazil* recounts the evolution of broadband Internet in the country (Knight, Feferman and Foditsch 2016).

## IT infrastructure

IT Infrastructure also evolved rapidly during the 2010s. The newest generation of hardware (blade servers, storage arrays, hyper-converged infrastructure, networking equipment), coupled with ongoing advances in virtualization, contributed to increasingly efficient, high-density data centers. Concurrently, the 2010s saw the rapid development of cloud computing, with Microsoft, Google, and IBM building large-scale data centers and launching new cloud-based services to compete with market leader Amazon Web Services. The cloud computing revolution introduced innovations such as software as a service (SaaS), platform as a service (PaaS), and infrastructure as a service (IaaS), allowing companies to rent virtualized infrastructure, applications, and tools, managing remote computing resources in public, private, or hybrid clouds.

## Impacts on consumer markets

The growth of broadband and smart phones accelerated consumer Internet penetration during the latter half of the 2010s, while advances in IT infrastructure enabled companies to deliver digital services at larger scale and lower cost. In economic terms, both the demand and supply curves shifted, significantly expanding markets for digital services. These technological trends led to growing tech markets for social media, e-commerce, online payments, and other digital services. Social media, in particular, was a driving force: Brazilians were avid users of Orkut, Google's early social network, and subsequently transitioned to Facebook and to a new generation of social media platforms. During the tech boom e-commerce and digital payments grew at double-digit annual rates, following global secular trends. By the late 2010s Brazil became a top-five global market for Google, YouTube, Facebook, WhatsApp, Instagram, Uber, LinkedIn, and Netflix.[23]

## Impacts on tech firms

These trends also allowed Brazilian tech companies to leapfrog previous technology cycles, adopting cloud-based, "mobile first," and social media-focused strategies, following a model established by Chinese tech companies. As mobile devices became cheaper, the mobile revolution also reduced some of the regional and socio-economic disparities in Internet access. This allowed Brazilian tech firms to offer new digital services to lower-income households, as well as to small and micro businesses.

The cloud revolution had important impacts on startup cost structures and business models. First, tech companies were able to reduce capital expenditures (CapEx) for software acquisition and for IT infrastructure such as servers, storage, and networking equipment. Further, tech companies no longer had to build or lease data center space (with expensive support infrastructure, such as power and cooling equipment). Flexible, on-demand cloud resources allowed tech companies to rent computing, storage, and software at a low initial cost and expand capacity as needed. Reducing CapEx was particularly important in a country like Brazil, with a historically high cost of capital. The pandemic further accelerated the pace of cloud adoption.[24]

Second, the pay-as-you go SaaS, PaaS and IaaS models allowed startups worldwide to quickly access and integrate digital tools into their internal systems and customer offerings, delivering these services through web browsers or mobile apps. As a result of these innovations, both cost-to-market and time-to-market declined. Data show that Brazilian unicorns are now reaching this status in fewer years.[25]

In short, the technological advances during the 2010s gave rise to important secular trends that facilitated the rapid growth of the Brazilian innovation ecosystem.

### 15.3.2 Institutional Component Development

Institutional (COI "component") development was the second major factor underlying the recent innovation boom. As noted in previous sections, the Brazilian innovation ecosystem remained underdeveloped during the dot-com years and the tech winter, and while it evolved significantly during the tech spring, important gaps remained at the beginning of the boom years in 2015. Institutional development accelerated in the latter half of the 2010s, with new sources of funding, expansion of accelerators and innovation hubs, and much greater corporate involvement in the ecosystem, among other developments.

*Table 15.1*   *Brazilian innovation ecosystem: institutional (COI component) development, 2000–2021*

| | | Dot-com 1995–2000 | Tech winter 2001–2009 | Tech spring 2010–2014 | Boom years 2015–2021 |
|---|---|---|---|---|---|
| Core Components and related Hybrid Components | Major Corporations and CVCs | | | 10s | 100s |
| | Entrepreneurs (tech startups) | 100s | 100s | 1,000s | 10,000s[1] |
| | Investors (VCs, angel groups) | | (few) | 10s | ~100 |
| Other Hybrid Components | Accelerators and private hubs | | | 10s | ~100 |
| | Incubators and tech parks | 10s | 100s | 100s | 100s |
| Government: regulatory framework | | | | | Evolving |
| Tech infrastructure: broadband, mobile, cloud | | | | Evolving | Evolving |

*Note:*     [1] As of mid 2021, startup hub Distrito tracked more than 12,000 startups at various stages of development[26].
*Source:*     Author estimates. Concept based on the COI Framework in Chapter 2 and ecosystem diagrams by RPeV.

Table 15.1 summarizes the evolution of selected institutional components of the Brazilian innovation ecosystem, and this section discusses some important institutional developments during the boom period.

**Investors**
During the boom years the funding chain became much more robust, with additional capital across all stages of investment: seed, early stage, later-stage growth, and strategic acquisitions and exits. The availability of equity capital was enhanced by several trends: the growth of local venture capital (including new firms and follow-on funds raised by existing VCs); the rapid development of CVCs in the country; the proliferation of angel investors, including startup founders; and the significant expansion of cross-border investments. Further, capital raised by larger tech firms in mega-rounds and IPOs was recycled in the ecosystem through strategic acquisitions and investments in smaller startups. By 2021, the innovation ecosystem included more diverse and deep-pocketed investors that filled prior gaps in the funding chain.

More broadly, there was renewed interest in equity investing in Brazil during the boom years. The country had a legacy of high interest rates, and their decline to historic lows between 2015 and 2020 (amid the ongoing economic malaise and low inflation) made equity investments more attractive compared to fixed-income assets, funneling capital to public and private equity markets. (Unfortunately, both inflation and interest rates began climbing in 2021.) As a reflection of this trend, new crowdfunding platforms gained traction, allowing individuals to invest directly in tech startups, and began having an impact on seed-stage investments.

The recycling of capital and expertise within the innovation ecosystem – much like in Silicon Valley, Israel, and other leading COI – was an important theme during the boom years. Several experienced founders formed new startups, became active angel investors, joined existing VCs, or started new VC firms. Investment deals in 2020 and 2021 included contributions from founders and executives of several Brazilian tech companies and unicorns. Similarly, VC companies such as Kaszek, RPeV, OneVC, Honey Island Capital, and Atlantico were started by former tech entrepreneurs, continuing to seed the ecosystem with experience, capital, and management expertise. Other tech entrepreneurs founded accelerators and startup hubs, such as Cubo. Hence, experienced entrepreneurs played a fundamental role in institutional development during the boom years.

**Accelerators, innovation hubs, and institutions for collaboration**
Crucially, during the current boom, Brazil also reached a critical mass of other institutional components involved in the formation and growth of startups: accelerators, innovation hubs, corporations that actively participate in the

ecosystem, universities, and specialized service providers. These components have complementary relationships within a COI, often working in tandem. The absence of key institutions ("institutional voids") therefore hinders the formation and growth of COI.

The timeline in Figure 15.4 compares the evolution of a selected group of major VC firms with other institutions devoted to startup formation and growth. The latter category primarily includes accelerators, but also innovation hubs, startup spaces, and a few other "institutions for collaboration" such as sectoral associations and entrepreneurship programs. This "judgment sample" encompasses most of the leading COI institutions in the São Paulo metropolitan region, as well as a few other important VCs, accelerators, and startup programs based in other regions of the country. The figure displays separate data series for profit-focused institutions and social-impact-focused institutions.[27]

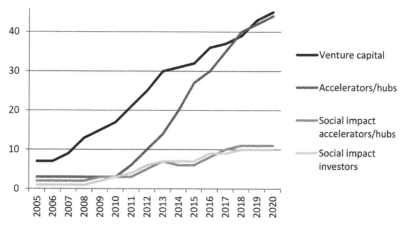

*Source:*    Developed by the author.

*Figure 15.4*    *Timeline: comparing the evolution of venture capital and accelerators/hubs (selected group of leading institutions in Brazil)*

As illustrated by the figure, the evolution of institutions for startup formation (accelerators, startup spaces, innovation hubs) lagged behind the development of VC in Brazil by several years. The gap was significant during the nuclear winter and the tech spring, but quickly narrowed starting in 2014 and into the boom years, as a significant new wave of accelerators and startup hubs joined the ecosystem, including hubs sponsored by major corporations (such as Cubo and Google Accelerator, both started in 2015), independent private accelerators, and a new generation of impact accelerators. Most of these accelerators and startup hubs were based in the São Paulo metropolitan region.

This lag in the development of Brazilian accelerators was not surprising: accelerators are a more recent institutional innovation worldwide. The first successful commercial accelerator in the United States, Y Combinator, was established in 2005, decades after the emergence of VC in Silicon Valley. As they developed, Brazilian accelerators began to improve the number and quality of scalable startups in the country, bringing better balance to the innovation ecosystem and specifically between the supply of capital (investors) and demand for capital (startup founders and management teams). Many accelerators play a hybrid role, also investing in early-stage companies.

Finally, it is important to highlight the role of other institutions for collaboration. Startup spaces and hubs – such as Endeavor, Cubo, and Inovabra – convene the various participants of the COI, promoting collaboration and knowledge-sharing as well as synergies and serendipity that lead to new business opportunities. Similarly, industry associations – such as ABVCAP, ABSTARTUPS, or Bay Brazil in Silicon Valley – play multiple roles, such as expanding business networks, coordination, policy advocacy, and knowledge-sharing.

**Corporate participation**
Corporations also play multiple roles in a COI: they provide capital through investments and strategic acquisitions, collaborate with startups through Open Innovation programs, create new startups via spin-offs, serve as a source of demand for products and services offered by tech firms, develop technical and managerial talent, create knowledge, and consolidate domain expertise.

Corporate participation in the Brazilian innovation ecosystem was another important institutional gap during the tech winter and tech spring. Even at the start of the boom years in 2015, there were few companies that actively participated in the ecosystem. The inauguration of Cubo – along with the growing interest in corporate innovation and Open Innovation globally – sparked a transformation in Brazil. By the end of 2020, there were literally hundreds of corporate innovation initiatives involving the ecosystem: CVC funds, corporate accelerators, collaborations with independent accelerators and startup hubs, startup-in-residence programs, hackathons, and startup challenges.

Table 15.2 displays a timeline for selected examples of well-known corporate innovation programs in the Brazilian ecosystem. Early pioneers included Intel Ventures, Qualcomm Ventures, Totvs Ventures, Embraer, Mercado Libre Ventures, and accelerator Wayra (affiliated with telecommunications company Telefónica). But as the timeline indicates, most corporate programs began during the boom period.

The earliest corporate programs tended to focus on CVC, following the global rise in CVC. An analysis of venture deals in 2020 indicates that corporate tech investments continue to grow in Brazil, with large tech companies and unicorns supporting the ecosystem through investments and acquisitions. According to innovation hub Distrito, CVC investments in Brazil rose from US$199 million in 2020 to US$622 million during January–August 2021, likely reaching close to US$1 billion for the full year.[28]

More recent corporate innovation programs increasingly involve accelerators, Open Innovation activities, or other close collaborations with startups. The number of corporate accelerators has been growing and these accelerators and startup hubs now span a variety of economic sectors: financial services (Itaú-Unibanco, Bradesco, Porto Seguro, BTG Pactual), telecommunications (Telefónica, Oi), Healthcare (Neo Química and Eretz Bio, affiliated with Einstein Hospital), technology (Google, Samsung), petrochemicals (Braskem), Logistics (Tegma, Randon), and agriculture (Raízen). Additionally, independent accelerators such as Distrito, Liga Ventures, and Fábrica de Startups ("Startup Factory") specialize in Open Innovation programs and work with multiple corporate clients. Both corporate investment and corporate accelerators have now become important institutional components of the innovation ecosystem.

And finally, the entry and expansion of multinational tech firms – initially Microsoft, Oracle, Cisco, and Yahoo, followed by Google, Facebook, Uber, and Amazon, among others – has supported the development of the ecosystem through multiple pathways, including talent development, startup programs, and investments, and by promoting cultural and behavioral change.

### Universities, entrepreneurial training, and the Berkeley Lean Startup program

In 2015, our team at the UC Berkeley Haas School of Business received a grant from the US State Department to pilot the Berkeley Lean Startup program in Brazil. The Lean Startup methodology, developed by Berkeley-Haas and Stanford professor Steve Blank, provides entrepreneurs with the tools to quickly test their business models by "getting out of the building" and learning directly from customers.

At the beginning of the boom years in 2015, there were few scalable entrepreneurship training programs in Brazil that utilized an in-depth, project-based learning approach. This was an important gap, because Brazil still lacked the deep entrepreneurial experience of Silicon Valley and other leading COI, with multiple generations of tech founders, serial entrepreneurs, and experienced mentors. Given this gap, initiating training programs for Brazilian entrepreneurs was particularly important.

*Table 15.2*    Timeline: selected examples of corporate participation in the ecosystem

**(1) Accelerators/hubs (selected examples)**

| | 2005 | 2006 | 2007 | 2008 | 2009 | 2010 | 2011 | 2012 | 2013 | 2014 | Innovation boom years 2015 | 2016 | 2017 | 2018 | 2019 | 2020 |
|---|---|---|---|---|---|---|---|---|---|---|---|---|---|---|---|---|
| Braskem Labs | | | | | | | | | | | | | | | | |
| boostLAB (BTG Pactual) | | | | | | | | | | | | | | | | |
| Cubo (Itaú-Unibanco) | | | | | | | | | | | | | | | | |
| Distrito (multiple partners) | | | | | | | | | | | | | | | | |
| Eretz Bio (Einstein) | | | | | | | | | | | | | | | | |
| Google Accelerator | | | | | | | | | | | | | | | | |
| Inovabra/Habitat (Bradesco) | | | | | | | | | | | | | | | | |
| L'Oreal/Fábrica de Startups | | | | | | | | | | | | | | | | |
| Neo Acelera | | | | | | | | | | | | | | | | |
| Oi Oito | | | | | | | | | | | | | | | | |
| Oxigênio (Porto Seguro) | | | | | | | | | | | | | | | | |
| Pulse (Raízen) | | | | | | | | | | | | | | | | |
| Samsung Ocean | | | | | | | | | | | | | | | | |
| TegUP Ventures | | | | | | | | | | | | | | | | |
| Wayra (Telefônica) | | | | | | | | | | | | | | | | |

**(2) Corporate Venture Capital (selected examples)**

| | 2005 | 2006 | 2007 | 2008 | 2009 | 2010 | 2011 | 2012 | 2013 | 2014 | Innovation boom years 2015 | 2016 | 2017 | 2018 | 2019 | 2020 |
|---|---|---|---|---|---|---|---|---|---|---|---|---|---|---|---|---|
| Algar Ventures | | | | | | | | | | | | | | | | |
| Axon Ventures | | | | | | | | | | | | | | | | |
| Bradesco Inovabra | | | | | | | | | | | | | | | | |

| (1) Accelerators/hubs (selected examples) | Innovation boom years |
| --- | --- |
| Construtech Ventures | |
| Embraer | |
| Globo Ventures | |
| Intel Ventures | |
| Marcado Libre Fund | |
| Positivo Corporate Ventures | |
| Qualcomm Ventures | |
| Randon Ventures | |
| Santander Innoventures | |
| Totvs Ventures | |
| Z-Tech (Ambev) | |

*Source:* Developed by the author.

We eventually partnered with VC firm Antera, local business schools (UDESC-ESAG and COPPEAD-UFRJ), incubators, IT firms, and other institutions to deliver two eight-week Lean Startup programs in Florianópolis and Rio de Janeiro during 2016–2017.[29] Florianópolis, a mid-sized city and innovation hub in southern Brazil, has the most tech startups per capita in the country.

Our objective was not just to train teams of entrepreneurs, but also to coach Brazilian instructors and mentors, and to build the capacity of local institutions. The Berkeley team trained nearly 50 startup teams, more than 200 entrepreneurs, 30 mentors, and 15 professors, as well as six corporate innovation teams that participated in the program. The "train the trainers" approach ensured the continuation and expansion of the Lean Startup program at the participating institutions. According to our partner Prof. Reinaldo Coelho, from UDESC-ESAG business school: "Our undergraduate business program was completely restructured, and now the last two years of the program are largely dedicated to the Lean Startup and forming new ventures, with the Berkeley methodology at the heart of the entire process."[30]

Berkeley's contribution was part of an ongoing cultural and behavioral transformation in entrepreneurial training at Brazilian universities. During the boom years, universities became much more active and launched numerous entrepreneurial initiatives: Lean Startup programs, startup competitions, new or revamped incubators and accelerators, maker-spaces, hackathons, and corporate partnerships. This represented a significant change because Brazilian universities (especially public universities) had traditionally been hesitant to engage in business-oriented programs. In addition to university-based programs, private entrepreneurial training and executive education programs also proliferated during the tech boom years. This strengthening of entrepreneurial training and universities contributed to the expansion of the Brazil innovation ecosystem.

### Government: support for research and ecosystem growth

The Brazilian government also played a role in the development of the innovation ecosystem, but not a central role in the case of the São Paulo innovation hub. Brazil has numerous centers of academic excellence and research institutions, primarily organized around federal and state universities, and produces leading-edge research in many fields. Public support for innovation also includes federal and state-level innovation agencies (FINEP and its state counterparts), as well as a network of tech parks and university-based incubators organized under Anprotec.

While many startups originated in Brazilian public universities and research institutions, the linkage between research and commercialization has traditionally been weak, as compared to developed countries. Most successful Brazilian startups focus on applying or adapting existing technologies to the Brazilian market ("applied innovation"), rather than building companies based on scientific and technological breakthroughs. However, as the ecosystem matures this is likely to change.

As noted earlier, the Brazilian government also supported the emergence of the innovation ecosystem by establishing or funding programs dedicated to the development of VC (FINEP's Inovar and BNDES' Criatec), accelerators (Startup Brasil and Inovativa), and entrepreneurial training (Inovativa, BNDES' Garagem, and programs by the small business agency SEBRAE, among others). Garagem, an incubation and acceleration program established in 2018, changed its focus in 2020 to support startups addressing social and environmental issues, which is seen as a gap and opportunity in the ecosystem. A growing number of government and university-based programs continue to promote the development of the Brazilian innovation ecosystem and are particularly important in areas outside the country's main innovation centers.

Yet, despite contributions from government programs and universities, the development of the São Paulo COI was driven primarily by the private sector, including VC firms, private accelerators, innovation hubs (such as Cubo) and corporations, as discussed earlier in this section. As the economic center of Brazil, São Paulo already had a critical mass of institutions and private sector agents and was therefore less dependent on public resources and government coordination to "jump start" the local innovation ecosystem.

### Government: support for coordination and governance

Public institutions (including public universities) often play an important role in COI planning, coordination, and governance, as discussed in other chapters of this book. The Brazil chapter of *Global Clusters of Innovation* (Feferman in Engel 2014) discussed the "Triple Helix" strategy central to the development of the Porto Digital COI, involving government, academia, and the private sector. Following this strategy, Porto Digital also established a centralized governance institution (NGPD) to enhance planning and coordination, with representation from the public sector, universities, and companies.

In contrast, the São Paulo COI exhibits different forms of coordination and governance, led by the private sector: formal and informal collaborations between firms, syndicated funding deals, professional networks, and private sector institutions that promote collaboration such as Cubo, Endeavor, and sectoral associations. The governance model in São Paulo is decentralized and relies on multiple hubs and networks. Again, these contrasting experiences reinforce one of the main findings of *Global Clusters of Innovation* (Engel 2014): that there is no single playbook for COI development, and that each region may follow a unique strategy based on its specific context.

### Government: legal and regulatory environment

A primary function of government is to provide a safe, stable society and a well-functioning business environment. This includes effective legal, regulatory, and tax systems; protection of property rights; and fair adjudication of disputes. Pervasive red tape, overly complex legal requirements, and tax complexity and burdens have always been an integral part of the "Brazil Cost," hampering the creation and growth of tech startups.

Another institutional development during the boom years has been the recent progress of the legal and regulatory environment, with laws and regulations impacting the Internet, investment funds, and startups:

- In 2014, Brazil enacted the Internet Civil Rights Framework (*Marco Civil da Internet*), which establishes a set of principles, rights, and responsibilities for Internet use in the country, including net neutrality and data privacy.[31]
- In 2016, the Brazilian Securities and Exchange Commission (CVM) issued new rules for VC and private equity funds, which previously operated under an inadequate framework.
- In 2019, the Brazilian Congress passed the Temporary Measure for Economic Liberty. Among many provisions, the measure instituted protections for LP investors in VC funds and reduced some of the administrative requirements commonly faced by startups. In March 2021, a temporary measure amended Brazilian corporate law to institute further protections for minority shareholders.
- In 2021, the Brazilian government approved the Startup Framework (*Marco Legal das Startups*), which includes measures to simplify the creation of new companies, regularize the status of angel investors, promote innovation, and facilitate startup access to government procurement contracts.
- Also in 2021, the National Monetary Council, which oversees the Brazilian financial system, approved the country's first set of open banking regulations, which were expected to boost the fast-growing fintech segment. A series of regulatory changes had previously opened opportunities for innovation in telemedicine.[32]

In addition to legal and regulatory hurdles, the onerous tax system continues to pose challenges for companies, which face multiple types of taxes, complex procedures, and sometimes puzzling incentives. For example, Anderson Thees from RPeV explained that "there is an unfortunate confusion between SMEs [small and medium-sized enterprises] and startups [by government]. Tax incentives apply only to companies with revenues under a [certain threshold], so there is no incentive for growth."[33]

As of 2020, Brazil still fared poorly in the World Bank's Doing Business report, ranking 124 out of 190 nations, with improvement in some indicators but with particularly low scores for items such as starting a business, obtaining permits/registrations, getting credit, and paying taxes (World Bank Group 2020). Similarly, the Global Entrepreneurship Monitor report for 2020–2021 highlighted weakness in government policy related to taxes and bureaucracy (Global Entrepreneurship Monitor 2021). While the Brazilian legal and regulatory environment is improving, the impact of the recent changes will depend on their detailed provisions and effective implementation.

**Specialized service providers**
The broad Faria Lima Avenue cuts through the center of the Jardim Europa, Itaim Bibi, and Vila Olímpia neighborhoods of São Paulo. This area is lined with modern office buildings, banks, and shopping centers. Within a few blocks, a promising startup team can meet with several potential VC investors, consult with multiple law and accounting firms, visit the gleaming Google and Cubo buildings, or hire office space at WeWork. Southwest São Paulo serves as the nexus of the Brazilian innovation ecosystem, with the highest density of VCs, private innovation hubs, and notable startups. Many specialized service providers have emerged in this area and more broadly in São Paulo: law firms and accountants experienced in early-stage ventures, industry associations, co-working spaces, recruiting firms, consultants, training institutions, data center and web hosting companies, and other business services.

Many Brazilian startups themselves specialize in business-to-business (B2B) services, helping other startups and SMEs with core business functions. For example, startups receiving funding in 2020 included B2B companies focused on sales and customer service, accounting, finance, payments, cash flow management, human resource management, energy bill management, and logistics, as well as compliance with legal and bureaucratic requirements. The development of these specialized services was greatly enhanced during the boom years and is another important aspect of institutional development.

### 15.3.3   Cultural and Behavioral Change

The previous sections discussed the first two pillars of the innovation boom – technological trends and institutional development. The third pillar, cultural and behavioral change, addresses behaviors outlined in the COI Framework: entrepreneurship, mobility of resources, alignment of interests, and international orientation.

## Entrepreneurship as a career

Over the past few years there has been an increased acceptance of entrepreneurship as a legitimate and even prestigious career path by a new generation of Brazilians, including entrepreneurship focused on social and environmental impact. Entrepreneurial success stories from abroad – including Brazilian co-founders of Facebook and Instagram – reinforced the entrepreneurial ethos in Brazil. And local success stories provided validation, from the earlier generation of tech firms to the new cohort of founders and unicorns. These entrepreneurial role models inspired a cultural and business transformation in the country.

These stories also helped to popularize the entrepreneurial aspiration and panache in a country that historically had mixed feelings about business and personal ambition, perhaps rooted in traditional values of modesty, conservatism, and risk aversion regarding career choices. The new entrepreneurial mindset has helped to funnel talent into the ecosystem. There is greater mobility and acceptance of risk, at a time when secure government or corporate jobs seem less attainable in the midst of the economic crisis that began around 2013 and continued as of mid 2021 with Covid-19. We have witnessed Berkeley-Haas Brazilian MBA graduates eschew high-paying corporate or consulting jobs to become entrepreneurs, with some recently receiving funding for their startup ventures, including Floki (a procurement platform for food retailers) and Flourish (a savings reward platform).

## Corporate culture and Open Innovation

Changes in business culture and strategy were also important for the emergence of the Brazilian innovation ecosystem. Between 2015 and 2021 a wave of cultural change swept over Brazilian corporations, with companies embracing innovation and Open Innovation as strategic imperatives. With the dissemination of the Open Innovation paradigm (Chesbrough 2003), local companies and multinational firms operating in Brazil increasingly reach outside corporate boundaries to interact with startups and with institutions in the innovation ecosystem. As discussed previously, during the boom years a growing number of companies established CVC teams, accelerators, or partnerships with innovation hubs, independent accelerators, or universities. These types of collaborations reflect a growing culture of cooperation, mobility of resources, and alignment of interests in the Brazilian innovation ecosystem.

## Cultural change related to international orientation

The COI Framework emphasizes the importance of an international orientation, including adopting a global strategic perspective (for markets, technology, talent, and financing) and establishing global ties and bonds (relationships with other COI, such as the close ties between Israel and Silicon Valley). This international dimension is particularly important for countries with small domestic markets, such as Israel, Taiwan, Chile, and Singapore, and was underdeveloped in the Brazilian innovation ecosystem, as discussed in the Porto Digital case, in part due to the large domestic market in Brazil (Feferman 2014).

During the tech boom years, the Brazilian ecosystem, and especially the São Paulo COI, developed a stronger outward orientation and connections with other clusters. Some of this is seen directly in the flows of capital, talent, knowledge, and tech deals, which also reflects a greater mobility of resources. Cross-border investments increased significantly with the participation of global funds from the United States, Asia and Europe in later-stage deals, and there are now a number of cross-border VCs and later-stage funds operating in São Paulo. Some of Silicon Valley's best-known incubators (500 Startups, Plug & Play, Y Combinator) have established a local presence or partnerships. As noted earlier, Didi's acquisition of 99 signaled China's growing influence, and Chinese tech business models (combining mobile, social, e-commerce, and artificial intelligence) increasingly serve as a reference for Brazilian investors and startups. Successful startups and technology firms based in São Paulo are developing a global mindset, with expansion plans encompassing other Latin American countries and the United States. Larger tech companies, such as Totvs and Movile, have already expanded internationally and established a presence in Silicon Valley.

The international movements of talent and global networks are also growing. Leading tech startups such as Nubank, Creditas, Loft, Loggi, and Guiabolso all include international "expats" in their founding or management teams, and some Startup Chile entrepreneurs have relocated to Brazil in search of larger markets. Going from south to north, Brazilian serial entrepreneurs moved to Silicon Valley and founded Brex, one of the Valley's leading fintech unicorns. Many Brazilian VCs and entrepreneurs studied abroad and established strong connections with Silicon Valley and other COI through alumni and professional networks. The cultural change and growing outward orientation are also reflected in the growth of formal and informal networks with other COI, including institutions such as Bay Brazil, dedicated to facilitating ties between Silicon Valley and the Brazilian innovation ecosystem.

Having reviewed the driving factors for the recent expansion of the innovation ecosystem – technological trends, institutional development, and cultural and behavioral change – the following section takes a more in-depth look at the geography of the ecosystem and the São Paulo hub.

## 15.4    THE SPATIAL CONFIGURATION OF THE BRAZILIAN INNOVATION ECOSYSTEM AND THE SÃO PAULO HUB

As described in the Introduction, São Paulo serves as the nexus of a regional network of innovation clusters in Southeast and South Brazil, with further connections to smaller innovation centers in other parts of the country. This chapter refers to this network as the "Brazilian innovation ecosystem," and it can be seen as a national NCOI, analogous to the Global NCOI described in *Global Clusters of Innovation* (Engel 2014). The São Paulo COI has the largest concentration of COI institutional components in the country, including the vast majority of VC firms, most of the marquee tech firms and unicorns, many of the leading accelerators, several universities and technology centers, and numerous specialized input providers. This section describes the spatial configuration of the Brazilian innovation ecosystem and analyzes the clustering of institutional components in the São Paulo region.

### 15.4.1   São Paulo as the Center of a Network of Innovation Clusters (NCOI) in Brazil

Through flows of finance, knowledge, and talent, the São Paulo hub (or São Paulo COI) is connected to other regional innovation clusters that surfaced around capital cities of Southeast and South Brazil: Rio de Janeiro, Belo Horizonte (including the "São Pedro Valley" tech ecosystem), Curitiba, Florianópolis, and Porto Alegre. These innovation hubs are home to important institutions and notable startups, and also grew significantly during the boom years. Figure 15.5 provides a visual depiction of São Paulo (*SP*, the largest COI) and other regional innovation hubs in Brazil. The solid lines indicate the stronger bonds between São Paulo and other innovation hubs in Southeast and South Brazil, which interact through the capital, talent, and product markets.

Smaller innovation hubs have evolved outside of the Southeast and South regions, the most notable being the Porto Digital COI in the city of Recife, in Northeast Brazil. Interest in tech-based entrepreneurship is growing across the Northeast, Center-West, and North regions, with tech hubs evolving in larger cities such as Brasília, Fortaleza, and Salvador. There are pioneering efforts in the Brazilian Amazon, in cities such as Manaus, Belém, and Macapá, where entrepreneurs are building local IT capabilities or addressing sustainable development in the Brazilian rainforest. The transition to a more digital world with online learning, virtual business relations, and the delivery of digital services – all accelerated by the Covid-19 pandemic – will open new opportunities for geographically remote innovation hubs and entrepreneurs.

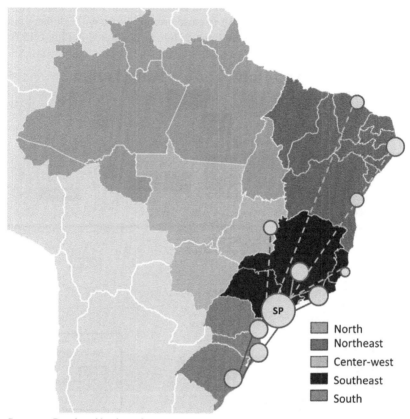

North
Northeast
Center-west
Southeast
South

*Source:* Developed by the author.

*Figure 15.5* *The network of Brazilian innovation hubs*

### 15.4.2 Overview of the São Paulo COI: The Three Urban Sub-Centers

While digital business interactions will shorten distances and perhaps render location less important, an analysis of the São Paulo cluster reveals a striking pattern of concentration. Many of the institutions that comprise the Brazilian innovation ecosystem are located not just within the São Paulo municipal boundary, but in a small area in the south-west part of the city. In the case of the São Paulo COI, the complementarities, synergies, and coordination inherent to a COI are enhanced by location and proximity.

Mapping the COI companies and institutions shows that the São Paulo COI is organized around three sub-centers in close proximity: we will call them the Core Hub, the Paulista Hub, and the Impact Hub, as illustrated in Figure 15.6.

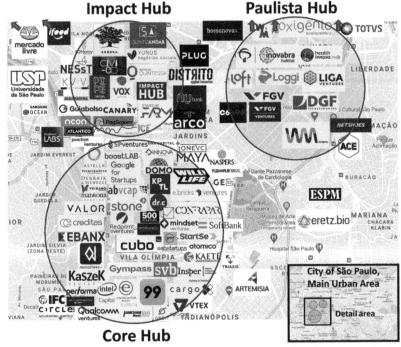

*Source:* The author, with data from Crunchbase, LinkedIn, Pitchbook, and company web sites.

*Figure 15.6    Map of the São Paulo COI*

- The Core Hub: Centered around the neighborhood of Vila Olímpia and adjacent areas, the Core Hub includes the majority of major VC companies operating in Brazil. The Core Hub also hosts many tech companies and unicorns, accelerators, innovation hubs (Cubo, Google, Endeavor), and sectoral associations such as ABVCAP. This area also congregates many specialized service providers, such as law firms, financial advisors, recruiting firms and training institutions, including INSPER business school.
- The Paulista Hub: The Paulista Hub is located about four miles away from the Core Hub, in a traditional finance and business center of São Paulo along Paulista Avenue. This hub includes several well-known accelerators

and startup hubs, a smaller number of investors and unicorns, and the FGV business school.

- The Impact Hub: A third hub of entrepreneurial activity is located about two miles north of the Core Hub. This hub congregates most of the leading institutions involved in impact entrepreneurship in Brazil, including impact investors, impact accelerators, and social innovation hubs. The Impact Hub area of town also encompasses institutions more closely aligned with the for-profit Core Hub, including VCs, for-profit accelerators, tech companies, and about half a dozen unicorns, led by fintech Nubank. The University of São Paulo, Brazil's largest and most prestigious public university, is located just to the east of the Impact Hub.

The São Paulo COI extends beyond these three urban hubs to adjacent metropolitan areas and nearby cities such as Campinas (a science and technology center anchored by Unicamp university) and São José dos Campos (a technological hub anchored by Brazilian aerospace giant Embraer and the Aeronautics Institute of Technology, or ITA). The cluster also extends to other cities in the state of São Paulo, with contributions from local universities, research centers, incubators, and accelerators.

### 15.4.3　Proximity in an Increasingly Digital World

Though some important regional institutions are located outside of the city of São Paulo, the São Paulo COI remains remarkably compact, centered around three urban hubs in close proximity, with competitors and collaborators often within walking distance, or a short ride away by Uber or the local 99 app. Again, this compact configuration facilitates synergies, serendipity, and collaboration within the cluster. This collaboration is enhanced by common spaces and innovation hubs such as Cubo, Inovabra, Endeavor, and Distrito, as well as by the numerous accelerators and universities in the area.

The proximity specifically facilitates COI behaviors such as mobility of resources (money, people, know-how), entrepreneurial processes, and alignment of interests, incentives, and goals (enhanced by frequent personal interactions) (Engel 2014). Further, São Paulo's international vantage point has increasingly promoted a global strategic perspective and global ties and bonds.

São Paulo's connections also reach beyond the state to other COI in Brazil, forming the network that comprises the Brazilian innovation ecosystem. The growth of digital business interactions should strengthen this national network, and perhaps promote COI behaviors through the digital medium, rendering location less important. And yet, prior to the pandemic, concentration seemed to be increasing as companies and talent continued to migrate from other regions of Brazil to São Paulo.

## 15.5   STARTUPS ADDRESSING BRAZILIAN CHALLENGES

Emerging markets are characterized by myriad inefficiencies across product, capital, and labor markets: missing or inefficient market intermediaries, high transaction costs, and information asymmetries; uneven access to financial services, education, and health; underdeveloped logistics and distribution networks; and imperfect legal and regulatory systems and weak property rights, among other frictions and "institutional voids" (Khanna, Palepu, and Bullock 2010). Readers familiar with Brazil will recognize many of these elements as part the infamous "Brazil Cost" – the inefficiencies and challenges that plague business and daily life in the country. But these frictions also offer business opportunities for tech startups. As Mercado Libre (Meli) founder and longtime CEO Marcos Galperin once remarked, "The more inefficient retail is, the more value we can provide to a society."[34]

### 15.5.1   The Mercado Libre Story

I first visited Meli's office in São Paulo around 2000, shortly after the company was founded as an online auctions site for Latin America, modeled after eBay (eBay acquired a 20 percent stake in Meli a year later). Stelleo Tolda, with whom I had gone to high school in Rio de Janeiro and to university in California, had recently left a career in investment banking to join Galperin (his fellow Stanford Graduate School of Business classmate), as General Manager for Brazil, Meli's main market. At the time, the Brazilian headquarters consisted of a modest, mid-sized office space near downtown São Paulo. As we met for coffee, Stelleo described Meli's recent growth and shift in marketing strategy from an expensive TV campaign (typical for rising dot-com companies at the time) to an approach that relied on lower cost media such as the nascent online advertising.

Over the next 20 years, Meli branched out from auctions and grew to become the largest e-commerce company in Latin America. Meli went public in 2007 on the NASDAQ and by the end of 2020 had achieved a market capitalization of US$80 billion, twice that of eBay.

As I returned to visit with different groups of Berkeley students, Stelleo (by then Meli's global Chief Operating Officer) generously took time to meet with us and described the company's strategy: focusing on the customer experience by addressing multiple inefficiencies (institutional voids) in Brazil's retail market. To create a seamless customer experience, Meli established an ecosystem of connected businesses, including e-commerce (Mercado Livre), seller marketplaces (Mercado Shops), payments (Mercado Pago), logistics (Mercado

Envios), advertising (Mercado Ads), and most recently credit (Mercado Crédito). Its new suburban campus in the city of Osasco rivals Silicon Valley's best corporate spaces – far removed in time and space from the modest office near downtown São Paulo. In March 2021, Tolda was named Meli's global President for Commerce.

Meli was part of the first generation of Latin American tech startups during the dot-com years. It was then unfairly branded by some as an eBay "copycat" or "clone." However, Meli's business model had evolved far beyond auctions, with many innovations and specific adaptations for Brazil and Latin American markets: in addition to the "ecosystem approach" to enhance the customer journey and fill institutional voids, Meli was the first auction site to adopt the "buy it now" option, effectively transitioning to a fixed-price seller marketplace.

Meli borrowed the online auction concept from eBay, but then innovated by modifying and adapting the business model to the Brazilian and Latin American markets. Perhaps more than any other company, Meli inspired the strategy for the third generation of Brazilian tech firms: borrowing ideas and then building (or adapting) digital business models to address specific inefficiencies, pain points, and opportunities across product, capital, and labor markets in Brazil. Meli was also instrumental in establishing a foundation for e-commerce in Latin America.

### 15.5.2 The Third Generation of Brazilian Tech Startups

The third generation of Brazilian tech firms encompasses a range of startups addressing frictions and inefficiencies in the country:

- Fintechs that are expanding financial services, lowering costs, and promoting financial inclusion within the highly concentrated Brazilian financial sector;
- B2B service providers addressing business efficiency and compliance with Brazilian laws and regulations (there is a large productivity gap across different types of firms in Brazil);
- Proptech companies bringing new services and more transparency to real estate markets, as well as more efficiency to construction;
- Logistics companies focused on urban mobility, deliveries, and cargo transport;
- Agtech companies offering technologies to the vast Brazilian agricultural sector, including solutions for small-scale producers;
- Healthtech startups improving access to medical services or increasing efficiency in the health sector;

- Edtech companies expanding access to education and to specialized training in labor markets; and
- Govtech startups focused on improving the efficiency of public services and promoting citizen-to-government collaboration.

According to Eric Acher from Monashees, "Brazil has an oligopolistic economy, flat productivity, and [limited] investment in education and infrastructure. Solutions are coming from the bottom up with entrepreneurs."[35]

Recent VC deals spanned a variety of sectors, led by fintech (20 percent of total deals), software (12 percent), and transportation and mobility (11 percent) (Table 15.3). Again, the vast majority of VC investments in the Brazilian innovation ecosystem focus on IT and digital services, but applied to different sectors. Fintech accounted for around 40 percent of the VC investment volume, reflecting larger deal sizes compared to other segments. Based on 2019 data, deal flow was heavily skewed to the Southeast region of Brazil and São Paulo (77 percent), followed by the South (17 percent), Northeast (4 percent), and Center-West (2 percent) (ABVCAP and KPMG 2020).

*Table 15.3      Sectoral distribution of VC deals, 2018–2019*

| Sector | % of deals |
| --- | --- |
| Fintech and insurancetech | 20 |
| Software | 12 |
| Transportation and mobility | 11 |
| Adtech and marketing | 10 |
| Healthtech | 7 |
| Edtech | 6 |
| Agtech and foodtech | 4 |
| Constructech and proptech | 4 |
| HR tech | 3 |
| Marketplaces | 3 |
| Retailtech | 3 |
| E-commerce | 2 |
| Energy and cleantech | 2 |
| Other | 15 |

*Source:*   The author, with data from ABVCAP and KPMG.

These more recent business models are tailored to the Brazilian market context, including customer preferences, the institutional environment, bottlenecks, and idiosyncrasies of the domestic market. For example, fintechs Conta Azul and Contabilizei provide specialized financial software for SMEs, addressing Brazil's complex tax and legal requirements. Arco Educação, founded in

Northeast Brazil and now based in São Paulo, tailors its online educational platform to Brazilian curriculum requirements and student preferences, while promoting innovation in learning. Fintech company Creditas, recognizing that Brazil has some of the highest consumer interest rates and banking fees in the world, reduces loan costs by accepting multiple types of collateral and developing proprietary credit scoring systems. And business software company Totvs initially prioritized local software installation, rather than cloud-based systems, recognizing infrastructure bottlenecks related to broadband speed and reliability, particularly for SMEs. Implementing these tailored business models also involves understanding and navigating Brazil's complex legal and regulatory requirement.

This knowledge of local markets and institutional environment, coupled with customized business models, provides a competitive advantage for Brazilian tech firms. International tech giants – despite other advantages such as scale, financial resources, and brand – often do not possess the same level of market experience or tailored offerings. Amazon's e-commerce business, a late entrant in Brazil, remains behind Mercado Libre. PayPal faces competition from local payment companies such as Stone, EBANX, and PagSeguro, and established a partnership with Meli's Mercado Pago to strengthen its position in Latin America. Totvs, which offers business software tailored to Brazilian SMEs, remains the market leader in enterprise resource planning software, ahead of global giants SAP, Oracle, and Microsoft.[36]

Leading Brazilian VC firms have long recognized the opportunities, competitive advantages, and social value involved in investing in startups that address frictions and institutional gaps in the Brazilian market. Monashees founder Eric Acher observed that the third generation of Brazilian startups typically innovate by applying existing technologies to local problems ("applied innovation"), rather than by commercializing scientific or technological innovations. Hence most investments involve execution risk rather than technology risk. Anderson Thees from RPeV noted that "patents are encouraged but are not a key defense here."[37]

There are exceptions and, as the ecosystem matures, leading-edge technology may play a greater role. A recent article by VentureBeat highlighted Brazil's burgeoning capabilities in artificial intelligence,[38] and Brazil produces world-class research in other fields. In the future, leading-edge innovation may yet spark a fourth generation of Brazilian startups, but the approach of addressing frictions, institutional voids, and unmet opportunities provided a solid foundation for the current innovation boom.

But does a domestic (or Latin American) market orientation limit the ability to scale? This was a legitimate discussion during the tech spring: despite the overall scale of the Brazilian economy, investors were concerned about the size of the domestic tech market. But the aforementioned secular trends related to technology have greatly expanded the market for digital services. E-commerce, an indicator for tech markets overall, experienced double-digit annual growth between 2015 and 2020, and grew by an astonishing 75 percent in 2020 during the pandemic.[39] Furthermore, the Covid-19 pandemic has accelerated the adoption of many types of digital services. Finally, recent exits involving tech companies operating primarily in Brazil have validated the market potential and investment thesis of addressing gaps, frictions, and the "Brazil Cost."

## 15.6 THE PANDEMIC, THE INNOVATION ECOSYSTEM, AND RESILIENCE

During March 2021, the Covid-19 pandemic continued to take a heavy toll in Brazil, with the rapid spread of dangerous new variants, slow pace of vaccination, and health care systems close to collapse in many areas. At the time, Brazil reported the highest global numbers of cases and deaths.[40] President Bolsonaro and his administration continued to face widespread criticism for their handling of the crisis, and a parliamentary inquiry on the pandemic response was initiated in April 2021. By early June 2021, cumulative cases climbed above 17 million and the total death toll approached 500,000, the second highest tally globally. (Daily cases subsequently declined as the vaccination campaign accelerated.)

Under this sobering scenario, it is difficult to write about the innovation ecosystem, the pandemic, and resilience. Nonetheless, there are a few uplifting stories on how the innovation ecosystem is contributing to resilience and, in turn, how the pandemic may influence the ecosystem.

### 15.6.1   How the Ecosystem Addressed the Pandemic

Since the third generation of Brazilian tech startups focuses on addressing specific frictions and challenges in the Brazilian market, and with IT becoming central to many sectors such as health care, financial services, and education, the Brazilian innovation ecosystem and technology-based startups are uniquely positioned to address resilience for the current pandemic, as well as other social and environmental challenges. The potential contribution of the ecosystem is augmented by tech-based enterprises in Brazil's social-impact sector.

As the Covid-19 pandemic accelerated in early 2020, the Brazilian innovation ecosystem quickly mobilized to address the crisis. For example, Eretz Bio, one of Brazil's leading health innovation hubs, launched a program that redirected the efforts of its startups to address the pandemic, including modifying existing solutions, launching new products and services, or adapting business models to tackle Covid-19. The initiative encompassed startups focusing on solutions for patients (telemedicine, digital support, and monitoring), health professionals (decision support, diagnostics, and education), and hospitals and clinics (equipment, case management, and hospital infrastructure).[41]

Also early in the pandemic, govtech startup Colab, a leading Brazilian citizen-to-government engagement platform, partnered with health analytics startup Epitrack to launch Brazil Without Corona (*BrasilSemCorona*), a crowd-sourcing platform dedicated to collecting data and building a national coronavirus-tracking map. Shortly afterwards, Cubo co-founder Itaú-Unibanco launched All for Health (*Todos pela Saúde*), a broad R$1 billion (around US$200 million) initiative for Covid-19 relief addressing information dissemination, protection (including the distribution of personal protective equipment, or PPE), medical care, and research.[42]

Over the next few months, LAVCA compiled information on several other initiatives by tech firms. Some examples shared by LAVCA included:

- Health startups quickly scaled telemedicine capacity.
- Numerous tech startups were involved in initiatives such as developing new diagnostic tests, information systems for health providers and patients, and tools to help governments and hospitals purchase and manage supplies and equipment.
- Logistics tech companies offered their infrastructure to distribute testing kits, PPE, meals to health workers, and other essential goods.
- Edtech companies provided free access to their online platforms and live-streaming capabilities to millions of public school students in Brazil, in partnership with local governments.
- Many tech companies instituted programs to help small businesses and impacted workers, including temporary relief, medical care, mental health, and job-placement services.

While the main heroes in Brazil, and elsewhere in the world, have been the healthcare workers on the front lines, the innovation ecosystem quickly mobilized and made significant contributions, including direct support for medical professionals and hospitals.

### 15.6.2   Entrepreneurship and Resilience in Other Areas

Tech startups, and IT more broadly, are starting to have an important impact on resilience related to other social and environmental challenges. Information is now central to almost every endeavor, be it financial services, education, monitoring deforestation in the Amazon, or trading carbon credits.

Fintech has experienced the fastest growth and will likely have significant near-term impacts on challenges such as financial inclusion and the high cost of credit for consumers and SMEs, which imposes a significant burden on indebted families and small businesses. Further, numerous academic studies have identified important linkages between financial services and economic development.

Fintech market leaders are expanding financial services in Brazil on a large scale, including to underserved segments. And several smaller fintech start-ups that received venture funding during 2020–2021 specifically address underserved segments such as the unbanked, the underbanked, SMEs, and microentrepreneurs, with services such as payments, microcredit, financial management, insurance, and banking. More will certainly follow, and the fintech sector is achieving the critical mass required to have a significant impact.

Investments in education and health startups have trailed fintech, but the pandemic has accelerated the adoption of distance learning, online educational platforms, telemedicine, and health information systems. Brazil had two edtech IPOs during the boom years, Arco Educação and Vasta Educação, and the number of edtech startups grew from 246 to 559 between 2014 and 2020. Similarly, between 2014 and 2019 the number of healthtech startups rose from 160 to 389, and a cohort of healthtech companies gained increasing visibility.[43]

A small number of companies in the innovation ecosystem are also tackling environmental challenges. During 2020, two tech startups with Brazilian connections, Moss and Pachama, received funding to focus on carbon credits to address deforestation.[44] In 2021, Quiron, a data analytics platform for forest threat management, received seed funding. Startups such as Fazenda Futuro focus on plant-based sources of protein – beef production releases methane and promotes deforestation in the Amazon, both of which contribute to global warming. And, more recently, a group of Brazilian investors, biodiversity researchers, and economists founded re.green, a social enterprise with R$389 million in initial capital (around US$80 million) and the ambitious goal of restoring one million hectares of rainforest by leveraging carbon credits and sustainable forestry activities.[45]

Another important and promising new area is the growth of programs and seed funds supporting women, LGBTQ+ people, Afro-descendants, and other under-represented entrepreneurs, including initiatives supported by Google, Microsoft (in partnership with WE Ventures), Nubank, and Paypal.[46]

### 15.6.3  Future Impacts of the Pandemic on the Innovation Ecosystem

The Covid-19 pandemic may have a lasting impact on the Brazilian entre-preneurial ecosystem by accelerating technology adoption and by bridging the geographical distance between startups, customers, innovation hubs, and investors in a country of continental proportions.

For consumers, the pandemic has accelerated the transition to digital services such as e-commerce, fintech, edtech, and healthtech, with the longer-term potential to improve standards of living. For businesses, the Covid-19 restrictions have accelerated digital transformation, including greater use of cloud computing, the digitalization of management functions, and the adoption tools that enable hybrid work, such as video conferencing and collaboration software. In December 2020, *The Economist* predicted that the pandemic will "give way to an era of rapid productivity growth" as companies invest in digital transformation (*The Economist* 2020). These trends will further expand markets for digital services, benefiting the entire innovation ecosystem.

The shift to virtual business will also shorten the distance between the participants and institutional components of the innovation ecosystem. For example, during 2020–2021, many Brazilian accelerators and startup hubs transitioned to virtual or hybrid delivery models, reaching entrepreneurs around the country and connecting them with the major innovation centers. In early 2021, Allen Taylor, Managing Director of investor Endeavor Catalyst, wrote the article "Redrawing the Map," which argued that the pandemic will decouple the historical relationship between capital and geography, leading to "more unicorns in more places" (Taylor 2021).

In Brazil, this potential decoupling could mean more investments outside of São Paulo, perhaps opening opportunities for startups in places like Northeast Brazil or the Amazon, and reducing the current regional disparities. Time will tell whether technology will reduce the importance of location and the benefits of agglomeration and physical proximity observed in the São Paulo hub.

## 15.7   CONCLUSION

This chapter argues that the remarkable transformation of the Brazilian innovation ecosystem, centered around the São Paulo COI, was due to a combination of secular trends related to technology, institutional development, and cultural change. Over the past few years, the innovation ecosystem reached an entirely new scale and level of professionalism and is now poised to make significant contributions to economic development, productivity growth, and standards of living in the country. The mobilization of the ecosystem during the pandemic provides a salient example of these potential contributions, and tech companies are addressing deep-seated challenges in areas such as business productivity, financial services, health care, education, logistics, and environmental management.

Behind these broad trends, the transformation of the innovation ecosystem has also been about individual stories and examples of collaboration: early founding teams that persevered despite the challenges of doing business in Brazil; people who left promising careers to dedicate themselves to a startup, to a new VC firm, or to join organizations that were helping the ecosystem grow and mature; Brazilian professors who promoted entrepreneurial education in their institutions; or public sector leaders who supported the growth of the innovation ecosystem. Over the past ten years, I had the good fortune to meet many of these protagonists and pioneers, and to hear their stories. They all shared a mix of idealism, hope, and conviction that entrepreneurship could be a force for good, that it could address some of Brazil's seemingly intractable challenges and boundless opportunities.

## NOTES

1. See Engel (2014), Chapter 1, for a description of cluster networks.
2. See Chapter 2 of this book for a definition of COI components and hybrid sub-components.
3. Author calculations with data from LAVCA.
4. The "Brazil Cost" (*Custo Brasil*) is a set of institutional challenges including high financing costs, a complex legal and regulatory environment, bureaucracy, high tax burdens, skills gaps, inefficient public services, corruption, poor infrastructure, and macroeconomic instability.
5. Personal communication.
6. www.linkedin.com/pulse/cubo-envy-silicon-valley-sergio-furió/.
7. Author research on Brazilian VCs and accelerators is based on information from Pitchbook, Crunchbase, LinkedIn, LAVCA, ABVCAP, Anprotec, and Contxto, as well as personal communication with various VCs and accelerators.
8. https://lavca.org/2010/11/11/finep-celebrates-10-years-of-inovar-nearly-r5b -committed-to-vc-in-brazil/ and www.bndes.gov.br/wps/portal/site/home/ mercado-de-capitais/fundos-de-investimentos/criatec.
9. https://exame.com/negocios/10-empresas-financiadas-pelo-rocket-internet-dono -da-dafiti/.
10. Interview with Anderson Thees, RPeV (2014).
11. Interviews with Anderson Thees, RPeV (2014), and Eric Acher, Monashees (2018, 2019).
12. Startup Brasil and Inovativa web sites.
13. Author calculations with data from LAVCA.
14. Author calculations with data from LAVCA.
15. Author analysis with data from Pitchbook.
16. The recent cohort of unicorns, through mid 2021, included: 99, Arco Educação, Ascenty, C6 Bank, Creditas, EBANX, Gympass, Hotmart, iFood, Loft, Loggi, MadeiraMadeira, Mercado Bitcoin, Movile, Neon, Nubank, Nuvemshop, PagSeguro, Quinto Andar, Stone, Unico, Vtex, and Wildlife Studios. Compiled based on information from Pitchbook, Crunchbase, LAVCA, and various media reports.
17. Data and reports from Pitchbook, Crunchbase, and LAVCA.
18. Pitchbook and media reports.

19. https://techcrunch.com/2021/06/08/fintech-all-star-nubank-raises-a-750m-mega-round/.
20. Crunchbase (2020).
21. Estimates based on data from Pitchbook, LAVCA, IVC-Israel, Statista, and World Bank; Brazil estimate is for 2021, all other countries for 2020.
22. *New York Times* (2013).
23. McKinsey (2019–2020).
24. www.forbes.com/sites/forbestechcouncil/2021/01/15/how-the-pandemic-has-accelerated-cloud-adoption/?sh=603979da6621.
25. McKinsey (2019–2020).
26. https://distrito.me/en/data-and-content/.
27. Author analysis based on data from Pitchbook, Crunchbase, LinkedIn, LAVCA, ABVCAP, Anprotec, and Contxto.
28. https://labsnews.com/en/news/business/corporate-venture-capital-in-brazil-skyrocketed-in-2021-to-622m-distrito-survey/.
29. Partners in Florianópolis included UDESC-ESAG business school (led by Prof. Reinaldo Coelho), CERTI Foundation and the Inovativa program, the ACATE technology association, and IT firms Softplan and Flex, among others. Partners in Rio de Janeiro included the COPPEAD business school at the Federal University of Rio de Janeiro (UFRJ) and the COPPE/UFRJ incubator. Other supporting institutions included FIRJAN and BNDES. The Berkeley team was composed of the author, Andre Marquis, Mark Searle, Elizabeth Saunders, Ayliffe Brown, and Pedro Moura. The Antera team included Robert Binder, Andre Massa, and Eduardo Marinho.
30. Personal communication.
31. See Knight, Feferman, and Foditsch (2016).
32. The legal and regulatory summary is based on newsletters by law firms Madrona and Veirano and articles by LAVCA and Endeavor. For open banking, see: www.zdnet.com/article/open-banking-kicks-off-in-brazil/.
33. Interview with Anderson Thees, RPeV (2014).
34. *Financial Times*, "Marcos Galperin: founder of Latin America's eBay," May 19, 2015.
35. Interview with Eric Acher, Monashees (2019).
36. www.zdnet.com/article/totvs-and-sap-lead-enterprise-software-market-in-brazil/.
37. Interview with Anderson Thees, RPeV (2014).
38. https://venturebeat.com/2020/01/12/brazil-is-emerging-as-a-world-class-ai-innovation-hub/.
39. Mastercard Recovery Insights survey, April 2021.
40. *O Globo* newspaper, March 25, 2021.
41. Eretz Bio, Covid-19 strategy brochure.
42. LAVCA bi-weekly newsletters, 2020–2021.
43. Data from Distrito, as reported in www.statista.com/statistics/1193133/brazil-edtech-startups/ and https://labsnews.com/en/articles/business/health-tech-boom-latin-america-brazil/.
44. LAVCA bi-weekly newsletters, 2020–2021.
45. *Valor Econômico*, "O Ambicioso Projeto Ambiental que Atraiu Arminio e João Moreira Salles," April 6, 2022.
46. LAVCA bi-weekly newsletters, 2020–2021.

# REFERENCES

ABVCAP, APEX, and inBrazil. *Impact Investing in Brazil*, 2020.

ABVCAP and KPMG. *Consolidação de Dados 2020, Indústria de Private Equity e Venture Capital no Brasil*, 2020.

Anprotec, CNPq, and Brazilian Ministry of Science, Technology and Innovation. *Mapeamento dos Mecanismos de Geração de Empreendimentos Inovadores no Brasil*, 2019.

Atlantico. "Latin American Digital Transformation Report." PowerPoint presentation, 2021.

Beaurline, D., and D. Gomes. "Brazil Startup Report." PowerPoint presentation, 2014.

Chesbrough, H. *Open Innovation*. Harvard Business Review Press, 2003.

Crunchbase. Online company database and *Crunchbase 2019 Annual Review*, 2020.

Engel, J.S. *Global Clusters of Innovation: Entrepreneurial Engines of Economic Growth around the World*. Edward Elgar Publishing, 2014.

Feferman, F. "Brazil: Good Governance in the Tropics – The Rise of the Porto Digital Cluster of Innovation." In *Global Clusters of Innovation: Entrepreneurial Engines of Economic Growth around the World*, edited by J. Engel. Edward Elgar Publishing, 2014.

*Forbes*. "2019: The Year of Tech Startup Exits in Brazil," January 23, 2019.

Freeman, J., and J. Engel. "Models of Innovation: Startups and Mature Corporations." *California Management Review* 50, no. 1, 2007.

Global Entrepreneurship Monitor. *2020/2021 Global Report*, 2021.

Khanna, T., K. Palepu, and R. Bullock. *Winning in Emerging Markets*. Harvard Business Press, 2010.

Knight, P. *The Internet in Brazil*. AuthorHouse, 2014.

Knight, P., F. Feferman, and N. Foditsch. *Banda Larga no Brasil (Broadband in Brazil)*. FGV Direito Rio & Figurati, 2016.

LAVCA (Association for Private Capital in Latin America). Various annual reports and bi-monthly newsletters, 2014–2021.

McKinsey. "Brazil Digital Report." PowerPoint presentation, Brazil at Silicon Valley Conference, 2019 and 2020.

*New York Times*. "Despite Stumbles, a Promising Path for Start-Ups in Brazil," May 21, 2013.

Pitchbook. Online database on venture capital, private equity and M&A, various dates. www.pitchbook.com.

Taylor, A. "Redrawing the Map." *Medium*, January 13, 2021.

*The Economist*. "The Pandemic Could Give Way to an Era of Rapid Productivity Growth," December 10, 2020.

World Bank Group. *Doing Business: Comparing Business Regulation in 190 Countries*. 2020.

# PART IV

# Conclusion

# 16. Clusters of Innovation: lessons learned and final thoughts

## Jerome S. Engel

Two years ago, when we started this project to revisit the concept of Clusters of Innovation (COI), our work was stimulated by the huge changes that were racking the globe, from the shock of the pandemic to the slower but pervasive impacts of the technology revolution and its rapid dissemination. My colleagues and I had, for the previous decade, been immersed in pursuing the deployment of our skills to build our local and global innovation capacities. Some of us worked from the passive perch of academic research, and others of us as practitioners and community builders. Even those of us who are situated in academia were for the most part engaged in the daily endeavor to build the innovative capacity of our communities. All of us brought to this work an a priori understanding of the COI Framework, and either explicitly or implicitly it influenced our work. So taking the opportunity to individually and collectively step back and reflect was undertaken with enthusiasm. What would we see when we looked back on our own endeavors through this lens? Had the lessons we had learned and documented in our 2014 volume stood the test of time?[1] Were there new observations and learnings to capture and share? Had we made any progress in answering the questions we had raised? Were there yet new questions to add to the list?

## LESSONS LEARNED

The investigations captured in this volume cover ten geographic business ecosystems and one non-geographic ecosystem. They are a diverse group, including highly mature, vigorous and industrialized settings, rural and undeveloped regions, reindustrializing older cities and new emerging regions. Some are looked at from a national or international network perspective and some are tightly circumscribed geographies. Some had strong government influence while others were dominated by emergent entrepreneurial energy. Some gained affinity and benefits from a common industry. Many were defined by their geography, while others considered geography irrelevant. Could robust learnings be derived from such an eclectic group? Moreover, would the COI

Framework apply and bring value to the investigation of the innovation ecosystem development across such diversity? Below are some of the more poignant lessons learned:

## 1    Silicon Valley Is Indeed a State of Mind: The Culture of 21st-Century Entrepreneurship Is Global

The most important lessons to be taken from the example of Silicon Valley are cultural, not physical. The optimistic, opportunity-seeking, value-creating culture of Silicon Valley is not based on its geographic characteristics. It is a process, not just a place. It is in fact a way of doing business, a manner of conduct (behaviors). Certainly, the region does benefit from a wealth of local resources – human, institutional and financial (components) – but the culture that exploits them is not captive to them. Across all the ecosystems investigated, we found the presence of entrepreneurial hunger and capability. Each ecosystem manifested its own uniqueness. Imitating Silicon Valley, or any other ecosystem for that matter, is not a recommended path. However, looking for best practices, learning from them rather than copying them, and localizing them to suit each community's individual attributes does reap benefits.

## 2    It Works, Is Useful and Is Evolving: The COI Framework Is an Effective Tool That Can Be Adapted to Divergent Circumstances

While there is tremendous variability and local adaptation in the COI around the world, the COI Framework proved itself to be a useful framework for analysis and investigation of both mature and emerging ecosystems. Despite this diversity, we learned again that COI share certain key characteristics: the main ingredients, the key components or actors that make up the ecosystem of the innovation community, and, more importantly, the characteristic behaviors or ways that these actors interact to create and support the culture of entrepreneurship and innovation which leads to new enterprises and rapid scaling of new businesses.

In looking deeply at the current cases, we learned it was useful to distinguish between those components that are most typically the initiators of innovation (that is, Entrepreneurs, Venture Capital Investors and Major Corporations) and those that support them (that is, Government, Universities, Management and the Professions). In addition, the ecosystem participants (Components) identified in the Framework were expanded to reflect the increasing importance of a new category of participants: Hybrid Organizations (for example, Accelerators, Incubators, Service Organizations) that operate at the interface of the components, increasing the mobility of resources (for example, ideas, technology, funding, people), thereby increasing the scope and speed of value-seeking behavior.

The COI Behaviors, especially the mobility and alignment of interests among the Core Components, have always been an essential and implicit element of the COI Framework. Some elements of this process have previously become an important innovation management process known as Open Innovation. Our research has shown that overlaying the COI lens on the Open Innovation approach can broaden and illuminate in a new way the Open Innovation interactions. Taking this one step further, we found it useful to create a new management tool, the COI Open Innovation Matrix, to organize, codify and structure how the identification, sourcing and integration of innovation can be built into the fabric of the enterprise.

### 3     How People Behave, and the Structure of Their Agreements, Is Critical: The Classic Emphasis on the Components of an Innovation Ecosystem Can Be Misleading

Past research has often focused on the components, participants and elements of an ecosystem, or the quantity of certain inputs (for example, venture investment) or outputs (for example, patents). After all, these can be counted, quantified and measured. There is historical data. Communities can be ranked, trends identified. Our work also includes articulating the critical components of the COI. But as we investigated the successes and challenges of both mature and emerging COI, the factor that made the most difference was the ability of the community to evolve a culture that embraced opportunity-seeking behavior, enabling entrepreneurship, mobility of resources and alignment of interests through shared risk-taking and a global perspective. Opportunity-seeking behavior was not just by Entrepreneurs but by all the key elements of the ecosystem, including Investors, Major Corporations and the supporting elements such as Universities, Government, professional Management talent and the Professions.

### 4     COI Behaviors Helped Provide a Rapid Response to the Covid-19 Pandemic: The Entrepreneurial Community was Ready to Engage and Deliver

The onslaught of the Covid-19 pandemic was a global disruption. Was technology innovation important in allowing the damage of the onslaught to be mitigated? Certainly. But it was not technology in isolation. It was technology in action. The actions were taken by people, institutions, governments and companies, big and small. And those actions often involved interactions that reflected the COI Behaviors illuminated so clearly in the COI Framework.

Most notable was the lightning-fast development of highly effective vaccines. These lifesaving breakthroughs were the result of several key COI Behaviors. For example, the rapid development of the Messenger RNA (mRNA) technology to create the Pfizer–BioNTech vaccine was the result of years of incremental progress, and its rapid testing and deployment relied on a win–win collaboration between a major corporation and an entrepreneurial venture. Likewise, the Oxford–Vaccitech–AstraZeneca vaccine exemplified a triangle of collaborators: the major corporation, an entrepreneurial startup and a leading research university. Moderna took another approach. It relied on eight rounds of venture investment over as many years to build its business. Importantly, these venture rounds, initially led by technology venture capitalists, in later rounds included participation by major drug companies, including Merck, AstraZeneca and others.

This, of course, is not the only example – just the most notable. We could point to many others, including the emergence of ubiquitous communication platforms (for example, Zoom), online retail, food delivery or many other foundational shifts that have occurred. The COI Framework has proven itself a useful lens to investigate, understand and deploy strategies to encourage the creation and sustaining of the cyclone of value creation that is a COI.

## 5 Geography Is Playing a Different Role: Once Dominant, Now Simply an Interesting Factor

Perhaps one of the most profound changes in the last ten years has been the evolving role of geography. Information technology is making the world ever smaller, and international commerce and collaboration are commonplace, with increasing international interdependence and opportunities. The criticality and innovative capacity of these global networks was clearly illuminated by the case of the Norway–Sri Lanka healthcare collaboration. It exemplified how a collaborative global COI network may act in very agile and adaptive ways to develop, standardize, distribute and scale solutions quickly in response to an immediate need. The Australia case provides an example of how the development of regional and global network bonds through the efforts of a nonprofit member-based organization has enabled an emergent local sportstech cluster to commercialize and promote Australia-inspired sportstech worldwide and to adapt nimbly during the COVID-19 pandemic.

Recently, the development of a new type of COI, bound together by business model rather than through geographic boundaries, has arisen. Exemplified by the Product Led Growth COI, this is a further example of the rapidly evolving role of geography. Geography's apparent irrelevance makes this perhaps the ultimate example of a global network of innovation. Its evolution is so extreme that to a very knowledgeable observer, the network appears in fact to operate seamlessly to such an extent it is not a network but rather a single COI – defined not by geography, but by a common business model. This is, in some ways, a totally new type of cluster, fully complemented with Entrepreneurs, Investors and Major Corporations, where geography is irrelevant. On the other hand, it is, in many ways, a very traditional industrial agglomeration! Either way, it is clear that we need to understand that the role of geography and location is undergoing rapid evolution.

As we look forward, we see on the horizon countervailing forces that may cause location to be an emerging factor. The shock of Covid-19 has disrupted international trade and supply chains. Governments are implementing national strategies to "bring back" what may be considered critical competencies (for example, returning battery manufacturing and chip fabrication to the US). Such moves may have profound impacts, especially damaging perhaps to emerging economies that either have small domestic markets or lack critical resources. It is too early to tell if such disruptions will be long-lasting.

## 6    Diversity in COI Development Is the Rule, Not the Exception: Leadership Can Emerge from Any Sector

There is no single blueprint for COI development or augmentation. In our 2014 volume we concluded by asking for further investigation into exactly how COI evolve. Who takes the first step? Who leads? Can we all follow the same roadmap? Our investigations in this volume demonstrate clearly that there is no one roadmap and that each community will evolve with leadership emerging from various participants, and in various ways. For example:

- Universities: In Munich, Japan and Singapore, universities have led the way in developing COI ecosystems, with varying degrees of government support.
- Venture Capital: In Brazil and Shenzhen, the driving force was private sector agents – venture capital firms, accelerators and hubs, fueled by in-migration of motivated, talented entrepreneurs.
- Service Organizations: In Australia and Norway, professional business associations have taken the lead in developing national and global COI networks. In India, specialized service organizations have been used successfully to bridge the gaps between government and major corporations to make COI more cohesive and effective in addressing needs of the population.
- Government: In Colombia, the importance of government in providing enabling conditions, such as the rule of law, highlights the challenges facing COI in some developing countries. In Barcelona, Singapore and China, government has played the key role in developing innovative eco-

systems and global networks. Public investment in research and support for technology transfer and commercialization are broadly and successfully deployed across most developed economies. This was broadly explored in our first volume. Novel approaches highlighted in this volume include in Barcelona and in Singapore the use of the public sector as a first customer, to diminish risk and to generate demand to promote solution-scaling. In Barcelona, the constructive engagement of city residents in helping shape the evolution of COI governance has proven to have fundamental advantages and demonstrates that government and the public sector at large can play important roles in COI development.

• Major Corporations: In Singapore, as part of an open economy framework promulgated by government, major multi-national corporations played a key role in the initial development of Singapore's rapid economic development. In India, corporate social responsibility programs linked to government agendas have fostered entrepreneurship and innovation, including support for broadening the reach of technical and business education.

## 7    Rules for Building a Cluster of Innovation: Old Lessons Are Still Valuable

At the conclusion of our first volume, in 2014, we laid out ten insights for building a COI. Our further work has validated these truths, so they bear repeating.

1.  Local adaptation is essential.
2.  Build on strengths, not concepts.
3.  Government has an essential role.
4.  Educational institutions (should) do more than (just) teach and research.
5.  Interpersonal networks are a driving force.
6.  Export-dependent clusters benefit from building strong COI.
7.  COI can be a basis for urban renewal.
8.  Major corporations, including multi-national corporations, (can) play an important role.
9.  COI Behaviors (can) help (build and) sustain regional competitive advantage.
10. COI can be a platform for diversification.

Brief but pithy, the list is a useful guide to prioritize actions that will create, enhance and sustain innovation ecosystems.[2]

# FINAL THOUGHTS

## Questions and Challenges

As we come to the end of our investigations, we can ponder the significance of what we have learned and how we can put it to work. Certainly, there are many important pragmatic tactical issues that will confront those who put to use the lessons learned and the tools of analysis provided. Below are some pragmatic questions that provide a starting point. Additionally, there are also overarching strategic issues that set the context for the entire endeavor. Both are critical to long-term success.

## Pragmatic Tactical Questions

Engaging in tactical, even granular, questions such as these can be a good place to start.

1.  What is the definition and what are the boundaries of the community?

    Who are the constituents of a community? What are its boundaries? Why are these boundaries meaningful? What is the definition of the community? Which of the members would self-identify with the other constituents as being part of their community? To what extent do they share convergent, competitive or disparate goals?

2.  How do we assemble and enhance the COI Components?

    Taking an inventory of a community's constituents, elements and institutions is a natural starting place for COI assessment, and many communities may well believe they have much of that information. It is unlikely that such pre-existing data will be sufficient. Worse, it may even be misleading. Starting with the questions of definition, boundaries, objectives, common interests and alignment raised above, one can then assess the competency, comprehensiveness and adequacy of the relevant components. Where there is strength, we may find the seeds of leadership. Where there is weakness, remedial action may be possible, but shorter-term success may be found in outreach to the global network for resources that may find benefits in collaboration and engagement.

3.  How do we encourage the COI Behaviors?

    The evolution of constructive COI Behaviors, those that enable personal and organizational wins by creating rather than extracting value, are subtle but crucial elements of the best COI. Society places constraints on the most damaging behaviors through law and regulation. These are not the mechanisms that can work to build a culture of COI behavior. Indeed, behavior is such a soft element that its very definition is problematic.

How can we encourage and support the mobility, entrepreneurial practice, alignment of interests and global perspective the best COI exemplify? As an example, the culture of a COI often encourages a gifting economy, where an individual's stature is elevated by how one facilitates networking and useful connections. How can this collective commons be nurtured to create a win–win culture that accelerates value creation? Tacit wisdom and cultural norms are often conveyed without explicit articulation. Cultural elements such as these are communicated by modeling successful individuals, entities and groups. Best practice can also be highlighted by those with the platform to do so, such as educators, media and government. This can be a slow generational transition. Enabling and enhancing this process is a challenge.

4. Who takes the first step? Who leads?

Different organizations and individuals have different motivations and payoffs. For some, success can yield a personal fortune. For others, success simply yields recognition, and perhaps a ton of more work to do. One's personal and organizational motivations for active engagement, passive support or even resistance and sabotage depend on one's context. Short-term exigencies can overwhelm the best of intentions. Finding champions who have the personal and organizational resources and alignment will be important over the short and longer terms. But sometimes that first step can be a small one. It is not always necessary to have a complete entourage of capabilities to make those key first steps. It is more important that they be successful, no matter their scale. How can we identify leadership as it emerges and evolves?

5. Who are the leaders?

"The leaders", in this sense, does not necessarily mean the leaders of organizations, governments, universities or businesses. The leaders may not even know they are leaders. They emerge and can be identified by their actions. They lead and influence by example rather than exposition. In the sincerest sense, leadership is not assigned; it is recognized. Can the Framework's analysis of COI Behaviors be a guide in identifying which of a community's emerging leaders should be highlighted and supported?

6. Can we all follow the same roadmap?

The recommendation of COI theory is that each cluster benefits from building on its own natural contours, its best attributes and strategic advantages. This just makes sense. But how then does one get alignment and agreement on action? How can communities learn from each other if they are all divergent? While not following the same roadmap, can the COI Framework provide a rubric for inter-cluster communication and cross-cluster learning?

7. How can you build on local strengths?

Having a clear understanding of a community's strengths depends of course on the goal being pursued. Depending on the goal, not all "strengths" may be equally relevant. How does one choose which to prioritize and support? What should be the criteria: for example, relevance to immediate local competitiveness or relevance to longer-term global opportunities? This is a very productive arena for inquiry. Divergent views may reflect divergent goals. This question is foundational.

8. How do you manage "the commons"?[3]

The tension between private objectives and the exploitation of common resources is a struggle as old as time immemorial. In building COI we encounter this issue in many places. Easily identifiable points of contention include the use of public funds to build infrastructure, support education, provide healthcare and social services, and fund research that is then exploited by private interests. It is natural for parties to lobby to secure resources and support for their own vested interests. How can the COI Framework help create collaborative cohesion and action?

9. What is the role of the public sector, including universities, and local and national government?

In our latest iteration of the COI Framework, we aggregated Government with other entities, such as Universities and the Professions, as "Supporting Components". When assessing the Supporting Components, it is important to recognize their individual distinctiveness. They are unique entities with different purposes, priorities and constituencies. What is the role of each relative to the COI? How are they distinct? While these are more passive elements, private sector actors will generally be motivated by self-interest with relatively short payback cycles. What works in the public sector? Governments require special consideration. At all levels, national, regional and local, they are critical stakeholders. Properly aligned, they can be enablers. Improperly educated or motivated, they can be disabling roadblocks. The case studies in this and our previous book included examples of both.

10. What role can and should leading multi-national firms play?

Forming global linkages is a core tactic for overcoming local COI deficiencies and accessing broader opportunities. It can help access venture capital, product partnerships and new markets. What role can foreign or multi-national firms play in this strategy? How can the COI Open Innovation Fit and Location Matrix be helpful in making these assessments?

11. Are we talking only about economic development or must we include social development as well?

As the experiences of Barcelona and Colombia have demonstrated, we should consider the impact of the social well-being of the broader society

and the real or perceived impact of the innovation economy on it. What kinds of social sector innovations are supportive of building a COI? Are there factors that will impose unintended or negative consequences? How does one prioritize between social needs and economic development?
12. How should we take into account technology and industry trends?

Many emerging innovation clusters concentrate on the benefits of agglomeration. This can be an excellent strategy. Governments often support such policies since they create clear pathways for investment and competency development. How do we balance these focused efforts with other objectives? How do we avoid the self-imposed constraints and risks of over-concentration? Many have seen the downside of the loss of mobility that can come from over-concentration. This is a particular risk in emerging economies.

This partial list is intended to provoke further thinking and provide a starting point for ongoing inquiry. These questions are often best pursued by direct discussions with stakeholders, not surveys or polls. There is not a single answer to any of these questions, nor is the list intended to be complete. It is a place to get started. Action does not require a thorough analysis. Incremental progress is progress, and the road is never straight, nor the answer simple.

## Overarching Strategic Challenges

At the time of this writing, it is clear that modern industrial society, and indeed the world as we know it, is facing challenges to its continued existence, let alone prosperity. Climate change and environmental degradation create existential physical threats. Social upheaval that spurred the desire for social inclusion, equality, human rights and opportunity challenges us to define and conduct ourselves in concert with our values. Political evolution, regional wars, massive refugee migration and the degradation of our public institutions bring into question the very viability of democracy and capitalism.

Every era has its challenges, and perhaps ours are no more extraordinary than most. No matter. It is clear that the challenge of our times is to recognize that our daily activities, no matter how worthy, have an impact on these higher-order strategic challenges and therefore must be conducted in such a way as to serve a broad societal benefit. As we go forward to build COI, let us do so with the furtherance of our collective mission in mind.

## NOTES

1. Of the 12 lead contributing authors, nine had been contributing authors to our 2014 volume, Engel, J. (ed.) (2014), *Global Clusters of Innovation:*

*Entrepreneurial Engines of Economic Growth around the World*, Cheltenham, UK and Northampton, MA, USA: Edward Elgar Publishing.

2.   For a fuller discussion of the items on this action list, as well as many of the fundamental elements of the COI Framework see our 2014 book, ibid.

3.   Peter Barnes describes "the commons" as a set of assets that have two characteristics: they are all gifts, and they are all shared. A shared gift is one we receive as members of a community, as opposed to individually. All have access, but no one party is responsible for its custody and care. Examples of such gifts include air, water, ecosystems, languages, music, holidays, money, law, mathematics, parks, open source software and the Internet. See Barnes, P., Rowe, J., and Bollier, D. (2003), *The State of the Commons: A Report to Owners*, Minneapolis, MN: Tomales Bay Institute.

# Index

Printed and bound by CPI Group (UK) Ltd, Croydon, CR0 4YY

16/04/2025

14658378-0002